THE EXPANSION OF ENGLAND

THE EXPANSION OF ENGLAND

Race, ethnicity and cultural history

Edited by
Bill Schwarz

London and New York

First published 1996
by Routledge
11 New Fetter Lane, London EC4P 4EE

Simultaneously published in the USA and Canada
by Routledge
29 West 35th Street, New York, NY 10001

© 1996 editorial matter Bill Schwarz; © individual
contributions to their authors

Typeset in Palatino by Keystroke, Jacaranda Lodge,
Wolverhampton
Printed and bound in Great Britain by
Clays Ltd, St Ives, PLC

British Library Cataloguing in Publication Data
A catalogue record for this book is available from the
British Library

Library of Congress Cataloguing in Publication Data
A catalogue record for this book has been requested

ISBN 0-415-06025-7 (hbk)
ISBN 0-415-06026-5 (pbk)

CONTENTS

NOTES ON CONTRIBUTORS

Andrew Blake is the author of *Reading Victorian Fiction* (1989), *The Music Business* (1992) and *The Land Without Music. Music in twentieth-century Britain* (1996). He teaches in the Department of Cultural Studies at the University of East London.

Bob Chase is a Principal Lecturer in the Department of Cultural Studies at the University of East London, and is working on narrative theory and representations of history.

Catherine Hall is Professor of Sociology at the University of Essex, and the author (with Leonore Davidoff) of *Family Fortunes. Men and women of the English middle class, 1780–1850* (1987) and of *White, Male and Middle Class. Explorations in feminism and history* (1992). She is on the editorial collectives of *Feminist Review* and *Gender and History*.

Kenneth Parker is Professor of Cultural Studies in the Department of Cultural Studies at the University of East London. His publications include *The South African Novel in English* (1978) and the edited *Letters of Dorothy Osborne to Sir William Temple* (1987). He was formerly the editor of the *Southern African Review of Books*.

Gwyneth Tyson Roberts taught in the Department of Cultural Studies in the University of East London, and is now working on a full-length study of the language of the 1847 *Report . . . into the State of Education in Wales*.

Bill Schwarz is Reader in Communications and Cultural Studies at Goldsmiths College. He has co-edited *On Ideology* (1978), *Making Histories* (1982), and *Crises in the British State, 1880–1930* (1985), and he is on the editorial collectives of *History Workshop Journal* and *Cultural Studies*.

Couze Venn works in the Department of Cultural Studies at the University of East London, and is preparing a book on occidentalism and the emergence of modernity. He is the co-author of *Changing the Subject* (1984), and is on the editorial collective of *Theory, Culture and Society*.

1

INTRODUCTION
The Expansion and Contraction of England

Bill Schwarz

As the empire dies and England's decline continues apace, the inner forms of English culture are thrown into sharper relief. As we argue in the chapters which follow, that elusive, displaced notion of Englishness, apparently so insular and self-contained, cannot be grasped without seeing its intimate and complex connections to the wider imperial world. It is above all the external determinations which have been most vital. 'England alone' is a myth: potent, but false.

The historic connection between England and its colonial empire – and the separate but overlapping relations between white English men and women and their ethnic and racial Others – ineluctably lies at the very heart of the matter even, or perhaps especially, when it remains unspoken.

In the recent past these questions have assumed public prominence in many different arenas. Of particular significance were the debates about the appropriate forms of (national) history to be taught to school-children. What began broadly as another Thatcherite offensive – the imposition of a national curriculum – was quickly transformed into an issue of serious public debate. Some critics deplored the very idea of a national history. Though much can be said for this, the most commonly articulated objections fell for an easy cosmopolitanism, in which the story of the world's oppressed through the ages would define the historiographical project. In eschewing this, others argued for a national focus out of recognition of the global location of the British nations in modern history.[1] To justify the study of national history in this way has the advantage of appreciating that the empire has been, and inescapably still is, constitutive of English identity.[2] This indicates the need to relocate the formations of English culture within the larger compass of an imperial and global map.

But what these interventions miss is the degree to which there already exist valuable precedents. In the classics of colonial historiography one

1

can find powerful reconstructions of England in which the imperial determinations are primary and in which the idea of the nation is formed, immediately, by the spatial dimensions of territorial expansion and contraction. After the spate of microscopic, internal studies of the proclivities of the English, where the domestic frame determines and where an unnerving complicity between critic and object in the end always seems to prevail, to confront these older studies – their dogmatic conviction in their nation's destiny notwithstanding – is a relief, unfolding a larger map from which new routes may yet be charted.

One such text (amongst many) is Sir John Seeley's *The Expansion of England*. The book combines discussion of contending versions of historical inquiry, reflections on the relations between nation and empire, and an unembarrassed political purpose. Seeley himself, on the basis of bewildering credentials (his only substantial publication being an anonymous life of Christ), found himself appointed Regius Professor of History at Cambridge in 1869. He soon came to be influential in the professionalization of historical study both in the university (the historical tripos was introduced four years after his appointment) and more widely through the medium of working men's colleges. In 1881 he began to work systematically on colonial history most likely, it seems, lecturing in the first instance to would-be members of the Indian Civil Service. Initially determined that his lectures should remain unpublished he was persuaded otherwise in May 1882 by Florence Nightingale. His book appeared later that year, coinciding with the British occupation of Egypt; by 1885 some 80,000 copies had been sold. Thereafter it remained in print, its reputation as an imperial primer established, until 1956 – when Britain once more was bombarding Egypt, though on this occasion to less effect. Now it is hardly read at all.[3]

Seeley's lectures were delivered at a moment when it appeared as if the colonial frontiers could expand no further – or more accurately, when indigenous peoples were finally being quelled as a military threat. In this respect Seeley should be read alongside Frederick Jackson Turner whose more memorable lecture, 'The significance of the frontier in American history', was delivered to the American Historical Association in July 1893. In the American north it was only in 1890 that the native armies were finally defeated, in North Dakota; while at the other end of the continent, the Europeans of Buenos Aires and Santiago had put an end to regular indigenous attacks only as late as the 1880s, due largely to the arrival of the Remington rifle.[4] Global frontiers were closing in.

The expansion of the United States westwards, consolidating its power over the Pacific coastline, and the commensurate drive of Russia to the east, to its Pacific coast, posed the greatest threat, in Seeley's view, to the British empire. The political question was simple. England, as he saw it, had lost its first empire in the 1770s. A century later he

2

identified four great groupings of territories: the Dominion of Canada; the West Indian islands; the South African possessions; and the Australian colonies. To these he added India, 'subject to the Crown', 'ruled by English officials', but 'inhabited by a completely foreign race ... bound to us only by the tie of conquest'. Before long, he surmised, the colonial (that is, the white) population of the empire would be greater than that of England. Was the second empire to be lost too? Or was it possible to unify the empire sufficiently to compete with the USA and Russia? In fact, unusually for one of this temperament, Seeley was not overly swayed by a belief in an inherent national or racial destiny: it was for him a matter of contingency and politics – in sum, of history.[5]

In order to communicate what he saw as the political urgency of the imperial situation he organized his account of the nation in terms of its external dynamics: or better, he attempted to dismantle the dualism of 'internal' and 'external' altogether by insisting on the necessary unity of the two. 'It seems to be assumed that affairs which are remote from England cannot deserve a leading place in a history of England ...', he noted, complaining of a historiography 'much too exclusively European'. For Seeley the central issue of early imperial Europe was the presence of the New World, which 'does not lie outside Europe but exists inside it as a principle of unlimited political change'. Or as he put it more pithily: in the eighteenth century 'the history of England is not in England but in America and Asia'.[6]

In setting up the problem in this way he was able to avoid some of the more common, and the more arcane, hyper-idealizations of England. Of course, the idealizations are not absent: he contrasted the empire of the English to previous colonial projects precisely in terms of England's lack of 'violent military character' and he didn't – or couldn't – countenance anything other than a white empire. But by placing the colonial dynamic at the centre of his history he side-steps the usual story of England as the true home of well-regulated liberty. This is a history of England which pays scant attention to its monarchs, its parliaments, or the peculiar grace of its people. It is rather the authority of the English state which functions as the prime mover, an authority active as much in the colonies as in the metropolis. His own hopes were clear: that metropolitan rule would prove sufficiently benign, and colonialists sufficiently accommodating, for there to emerge throughout the empire a consensual unity founded upon a shared recognition of English ethnicity. 'If Greater Britain in the full sense of the phrase really existed, Canada and Australia would be to us as Kent and Cornwall'.[7]

To the degree that this had already occurred, it confirmed in Seeley's mind that strictly England possessed no empire, the colonies merely operating as an organic extension of the home-nation.[8] But this approach entailed a scepticism about the eternities of England which imperialists of his ilk, and at that time, generally were not keen to pursue. Seeley deplored an 'unhistorical way of thinking' which assumed England always to have been the same. 'That we might have been other than we are, nay that we once were other, is to us so inconceivable that we try to explain *why* we were always the same before ascertaining by any inquiry whether the fact is so'. 'The expansion of England', he continued, 'involves its transformation'. To be English promises no 'natural vocation, founded upon inherent aptitudes'. And it is for this reason that he could foresee a future for England akin to Holland or Sweden, its history, as he conceived it, 'wound up'.[9]

Seeley was also concerned that his lectures should stand as an essay in the practice of history. He drew a fine distinction between history and politics – both, as he saw it, principally concerned themselves with the examination and organization of the state – believing history should 'modify his (the reader's) view of the present'. His lectures on empire developed from his classes to young men who were about to administer the colonies, and the lectures themselves serve to fuse the categories of masculine and imperial authority.[10] He railed against a historiography which peddled only 'common sense' and worked by 'the drowsy spell of narrative'. He looked forward to a history based less on ethics and more on causes, which was analytical, rational and true. History bereft of these qualities, and bereft of a properly masculine concern with politics, became merely 'foppish ... aiming only at literary display, which produces delightful books hovering between poetry and prose'. A feminized history without politics could only alight upon such frivolities as 'the ladies thronging to the toy-shops'. Should history 'cease studying what sort of government our ancestors had and inquire rather what they had for dinner?' He had a number of malefactors in his sights. Scott was one, Macaulay another.[11] But Thackeray he condemned most of all precisely because it was he who proclaimed that fiction could be historically truthful and history fiction, denying the possibility (in Seeley's words) that 'history can establish any solid or important truths'. History in this scheme becomes only rhetoric. Thackeray, according to Seeley, 'does not deny that history might be important if it were true, but he says it is not true'. To this Seeley could only respond – one can imagine the tone – 'Make it true and trustworthy'.[12]

Seeley conceptualized England as constituted by its overseas posses-sions, and he was prepared to push this hard enough that the very differentiation between England and colony, internal and external, came to be questioned. But he did this in a cause palpably imperialist and racist. It is little wonder that subsequent liberal, radical and socialist historiographies ignored historians like Seeley, horrified that they constructed an England indistinguishable from its colonies. As a consequence, the chosen historiographical starting-point for an entire tradition of radical, popular history, far from being Seeley, came to fall on J.R. Green's *Short History of the English People*, first published eight years earlier in 1874; though a deal more generous in political sensibility than Seeley could ever imagine, it deployed an analysis of English history solidly internal, a forceful encoding of English ethnicity functioning both as object and means of study. The most famous passage reads as follows:

> The aim of the following work is defined by its title; it is not of English kings or English conquests, but of the English people ... I have preferred to pass lightly and briefly over the details of foreign wars and diplomacies, the personal adventures of kings and nobles, the pomp of courts, or the intrigues of favourites, and to dwell at length on the incidents of that constitutional, intellectual and social advance in which we read the history of the nation itself. It is with this purpose that I have devoted more space to Chaucer than to Creasy, to Caxton than to the petty strife of Yorkist and Lancastrian, to the Poor Law of Elizabeth than to her victory at Cadiz, to the Methodist revival than to the escape of the Young Pretender.[13]

While one can applaud the populism of this project, and see why it came about, the problems are palpable. The 'people' of England are treated as if they had no place in the sequence of 'English conquests', or as if they remained untouched by 'foreign wars and diplomacies'. As the historiographical emphasis on the people intensified, even as the nation's history was democratized, the emphasis on colonialism weakened: the two became incompatible approaches. The creation of a popular, democratic history in England brought with it a historiography parochial in texture, its frequent draughts from the cup of liberty inducing a deeper myopia.

For by underplaying the colonial dimensions, and by overplaying the long march of the freeborn Englishman, it could appear as if the two operated in distinct worlds, as if the full, complex constructs of English liberty did not carry inside them powerful exclusions which – amongst other things – were connected by an intimate set of relations to the workings of colonial rule. This conceptual separation of metropolis from colony incubated a belief common amongst radical political circles that once the shell of empire fell away there would remain the kernel of a benign England, untouched by its imperial past.[14] As a result the traditions of radical historiography could – invariably did – carry alongside them a passionate anti-colonialism. The problem was whether the silent codes of English ethnicity, in which the radical temper of the people could be pronounced, did not conceal more than they revealed.

As England contracts these things become clearer to see from within

5

the old metropolis itself. The chapters which follow explore the effects of the expansion of England on the 'internal' constitution of English ethnicities, paying careful attention to different locales.

But there is a second issue which runs just as powerfully through this book. This is the question of history: the practices of historical inquiry, the appropriate forms of historical narrative and the central issue of historical truth are all raised by Seeley. Indeed, he may suggest to us that the theoretical dilemmas of our own times are not so new. He was determined to establish a boundary between a hard (masculine) positivist truth and a more disconcerting (feminized) form of historical consciousness in which truth is less the issue than rhetoric and the imagination.

Very broadly, the collapse of historical positivism in conjunction with the arrival of many varieties of poststructuralism might suggest that today it is Thackeray rather than Seeley who is the more appropriate model. After all, it's easy enough to show the intimate connections between Seeley's conception of history and his conceptions of race and masculinity. With good reason, those who have now become dubbed postcolonial theorists expend great effort in showing how some of the most basic philosophical assumptions of 'Western' historical practice are part and parcel of the founding master-categories of race and nation, culture and sexuality.

As we show in the next chapter some of the more spirited renditions of postcolonial theory – in a burst of early enthusiasm – appeared to allow for no conception of history, of conceptualizing, past, present and future, which wasn't irretrievably contaminated by a debilitating Eurocentrism. Of course, there is no reason to believe that as the empires 'fell away' (in the rather quaint image of an earlier age) the philosophies of old Europe can simply be retrieved as the benign kernel, remaining as good to think with as they ever were. To read Seeley would confirm that at once.

But does that mean, in these putatively postcolonial times where irrationalisms and fundamentalisms stalk the globe, that notions of historical truth and received narrative forms have to be jettisoned? Does it make sense simply to invert Seeley's model, and opt for a feminized rhetoric rather than a masculine truth?

Or, as this division suggests, isn't there something spurious about that dichotomy itself, with truth counterposed to rhetoric, as if truth is not also (always) rhetorical? (The ferocity of Seeley's injunctions might make us suppose that even in his mind the two were in constant danger of collapsing.) But if history does have larger claims than being merely rhetoric, or a good story, how can we envisage categories of historical truth which aren't shot through with all the founding assumptions of the old imperialism?

These are the issues which we take up in the book. We work at many different levels of abstraction, in many different idioms, but the questions are shared. One thing we can be sure of: there is no general solution waiting to fall from the theoretical skies. To rethink historical practice for our own times we *have* to work with a variety of forms and procedures, moving across different levels of abstraction, thinking critically all the while of our own procedures.

The following chapters represent one attempt by a small group to come to grips with these questions. Any resolutions, we imagine, will necessarily be modest, tucked away in places which perhaps we are not even aware of. We hope the issues at least will become clear.

The book originates from one department in a single university, based in the first place on many informal conversations. That it ever came about is a measure of the intellectual vitality of our intellectual environment, and a tribute to the generosity of all – teachers, administrators and students – who work in it. More obliquely, it may be a more modest tribute to our publisher, Claire L'Enfant, who had faith in it from the start.

NOTES

1 Shula Marks, 'History, the nation and empire: sniping from the periphery', and Raphael Samuel, 'Grand narratives', both in *History Workshop Journal* 29, 1990.

2 The most explicit study comes from a Dane: Ulf Hedetoft, *British Colonialism and Modern Identity*, Aalborg University Press, Aalborg, 1985.

3 Deborah Wormell, *Sir John Seeley and the Uses of History*, Cambridge University Press, Cambridge, 1980; and Richard Aldrich, 'Imperialism in the study and teaching of history' in J.A. Mangan (ed.), *Benefits Bestowed? Education and British Imperialism*, Manchester University Press, Manchester, 1988. A modern empirical account on the epic scale, unjustly neglected, is Angus Calder's mighty *The Rise of the English-Speaking Empires, from the Fifteenth Century to the 1780s*, Dutton, New York, 1981.

4 Frederick Jackson Turner, *The Frontier in American History*, Henry Holt, New York, 1953; Dee Brown, *Bury My Heart at Wounded Knee. An Indian History of the American West*, Paladin, St Albans, 1978; and Alistair Hennessy, *The Frontier in Latin American History*, Edward Arnold, London, 1978. Of course, the frontiers between the New World and the Old are still operative; as recently as thirty years ago 'unknown' indigenous peoples were still being 'discovered' in Brazil: John Hemming, *Red Gold: the Conquest of the Brazilian Indians*, Macmillan, London, 1978.

5 J.R. Seeley, *The Expansion of England. Two Courses of Lectures*, Macmillan, London, 1883, pp.10–11.

6 Ibid., pp.121, 105, 103, 109.

7 Ibid., pp.43, 46. This sentiment was neither new then, nor had yet run its life. Clarendon had hoped to rule Massachusetts as if it were a corporation 'of Kent and Yorkshire', while the indefatigable Menzies delighted in the fact that 'the boundaries of Great Britain are not on the Kentish coast but at Cape

York and Invercargill'. See respectively Robert Bliss, *Revolution and Empire. English Politics and the American Colonies in the Seventeenth Century*, Manchester University Press, Manchester, 1990, p.132; and Judith Brett, *Robert Menzies' Forgotten People*, Pan Macmillan, Sydney, 1993, p.146.

8 Seeley, *The Expansion of England*, p.296. He still had difficulties with India within this scheme: pp.184, 203, 304. This fantasy that Britain had never really had an empire and that conquest had played no part in the accretion of territories, and the unease with regard to India in this respect – 'the exception which proves the rule' – was duplicated by Enoch Powell's mind-bending discoveries of 1964. See 'Myth and reality' in his *Freedom and Reality*, Batsford, London, 1969.

9 Seeley, pp.80–1, 84, 1.

10 Ibid., p.1. There are echoes here of Hegel's conviction that the process of becoming conscious of history was also the process of attaining 'true Manhood': G.W.F. Hegel, *The Philosophy of History*, Dover, New York, 1956, p.107.

11 Seeley, pp.166, 167, 173, 175. For Scott see Peter Burroughs, 'J.R. Seeley and British imperial history', *Journal of Imperial and Commonwealth History* 1:2, 1973, p.193. 'In Macaulay's hands', Seeley claimed, 'history resembled a romance and seemed almost to strive to become a ballad'; quoted in G.A. Reiss, *Sir John Seeley. A Study of a Historian*, Longwood, Wolfboro [New Hampshire], 1987 [first published 1912], p.39.

12 Seeley, pp.166, 167, 171–3, 175.

13 J.R. Green, *A Short History of the English People*, Everyman, Oxford, 1877, vol. I, p.xi. J.R. Green's *History of the English People* (4 vols), Macmillan, London, 1877–80, opens with 'the conquest of Britain by the English', p.1. For an earlier, profound, critique of Green along the same lines: Eric Williams, *British Historians and the West Indies*, Andre Deutsch, London, 1966, pp.38–9, 76–7.

14 For a good discussion of the politics, Stephen Howe, 'Labour patriotism, 1939–83' in Raphael Samuel (ed.), *Patriotism. vol. I, History and Politics*, Routledge, London, 1989; and more fully in his *Anticolonialism in British Politics. The Left and the End of Empire, 1918–64*, Clarendon Press, Oxford, 1993.

2

CONQUERORS OF TRUTH
Reflections on Postcolonial Theory
Bill Schwarz

Recently a number of studies have been published which focus on the first moment of encounter between Europe and the indigenous inhabitants of the New World, attempting to reconstruct the transformation in European cultures – the philosophical and moral effects of *self*-discovery – at the moment of first contact.[1] A powerful motif from this work emerges in the image of cartography. As the indigenous peoples and landscapes came under the control of the colonists, a system of thought evolved through which the emergent categories of mastery – of instrumental reason – could themselves be conceptualized. New dreams were possible. The process of mapping the colonial terrains and peoples created new structures of meaning – displacing or destroying previous meaning-systems – and indeed created a new truth. (One might reflect in passing that Mao Zedong, born in Hunan in 1893, did not even *see* a map of the world until he was twenty.)[2] With his usual eye for such things Conrad described the European explorers 'conquering a bit of truth here and a bit of truth there'.[3] This is a valuable insight. Out of colonialism developed new narratives and new epistemological categories which may still be our own. Conquest entailed not only mastery of peoples and ecologies, but also the conquest of truth itself.

In one sense, this is what postcolonial theory is about. A founding figure in this intellectual formation puts it this way:

> Conrad makes the point better than anyone, I think. The power to conquer territory is only in part a matter of physical force: there is the strong moral and intellectual component making the conquest itself secondary to an idea, which dignifies (and indeed hastens) pure force with arguments drawn from science, morality, ethics, and a general philosophy.[4]

As a starting-point one can say that postcolonial theory takes for its object colonial texts or discourses, reading or deconstructing them in such a way as to make evident the racialized effects or justifications for colonialism perpetrated by the particular text in question. More particularly it attempts to highlight the external determinations lodged in the interior of metropolitan narratives, even when these determinations appear to be absent, marginal or displaced. By focusing on the mechanisms of textual displacement – the linguistic procedures which establish the norms of civilization, and literally place outside those norms phenomena which become constructed as the Other – such an approach promises to bring to light that which remains present but unspoken or unspeakable within the colonial imagination. Thus Edward Said, for example, has posited the practice of 'contrapuntal' reading, while many speak of their determination to read 'against the grain'.

As I understand it in practice this has largely become a hermeneutic procedure, which begins with close reading – derived from the textual skills of literary interpretation – and then aims not merely to indicate surface influences or correspondences, but to reveal a deeper congruence between certain epistemological or narrative strategies (or in some more assured renditions, epistemology itself) and the colonial project. In this reading the co-ordinates underpinning the very notion of truth fall away, leaving old certainties exposed and vulnerable. At the same time all variants of postcolonial theory – drawing from well-rehearsed themes in poststructuralism – recognize the linguistic and discursive ordering of the real, the contingency of meaning, the fluidity of the text, and the ambivalent or contradictory properties of discourse itself, including all critical discourses. Truth is not so much reconquered as confronted by its own dispersal, the particular subsuming the universal.

The convergence between poststructuralism and critiques of colonialism has by now become a curious union. On the one hand, its upholders proclaim their conceptual audacity, delighting in their role as latter-day pioneers opening up new theoretical continents. On the other hand such a deluge of academic publication has appeared that work which boasts an intransigent radicalism too frequently has become subject to the tedium of predictability. Maybe this is simply due to the exigencies of intellectual production in late modernity; or it may result, paradoxically, from a certain parochialism or inwardness – one theory feeding off the next, ever-more self-referential, *ad infinitum* – such that a theoretical endeavour of this order becomes peculiarly susceptible to the institutional effects of academic organization. Either way, there is no denying the difficulty of this work. But it is too easy to condemn it all and turn one's back. For those engaged in the postcolonial critique are, it seems, attempting to write their way out of the hegemony exerted by the interlocking master-categories of race, nation, culture and sexuality which lie deep within the foundations of European thought. That these master-categories can seem so naturally and indivisibly one is an indication of the effort required to think in different terms.

At least potentially there exist within poststructuralism elements which offer a peculiarly productive way for understanding ethnicity. Race itself is a powerful symbolic force, profoundly and incessantly imbricated in the makings of social identity. It establishes territorial boundaries, sometimes of intoxicating power, differentiating us from Others, all the while categorizing and demarcating a vertiginous abundance of human groups into recognizable, classifiable social units. At one level this is achieved – in the cultural formations of modernity – by the equation of white with reason, order and civilization. At another level, on the terrain of lived experience, these structures of inclusion and exclusion are achieved and reproduced by means of a heady chaos of fantasy, irrationality and unconscious desire.

Poststructuralism offers a way into both these problems, and suggests some interconnections between the two. On the one hand its proponents seek to demolish a hard cognitive rationalism, identified above all with the long traditions of Western thought, which are indicted for generating the will to dominate, to establish boundaries, and to classify and calibrate. In its place are offered alternative, less authoritative and knowing modes of perceiving and understanding. This urge to break with the inherited epistemologies of rationalism is directly relevant to the political imperatives of a postcolonial culture, for the critique of rationalism can be mobilized to call into question the intellectual authority of all-knowing discourses of mastery, be it white over black, men over women, or capitalist over labourer.

On the other hand there are strands within poststructuralist theories – with antecedents stretching back to psychoanalysis, to critical theory, and to the aesthetic avant-garde of the early twentieth century – which typically valorize confusion, disorder and destabilization, invoke the fragments over the totality, revel in the implosion of boundaries and fixed identities, and commend allegiance to the periphery against real or putative centres. Or rather, far from proposing this as a desired outcome, the full force of poststructuralist critique is to demonstrate the degree to which the cultures – and *theorizations* – of modernity are, against all self-proclamations, constituted by what they disavow and repress, the repressed Other symbolically active in the internal histories of the colonial order. Much as the critical theory deployed by Adorno and Horkheimer was drawn to the dialectic by which reason tips into unreason, so a common theme in contemporary poststructuralism illuminates the irrationalities which shadow reason, the unconscious desires which run through habits of rational calculation, alerting us to the illusory, *impossible* quality of a transcendent, hypostatized reason.

To approach discourses of race and ethnicity from this vantage goes far in dispatching the essentialisms which remain securely attached to commonsense notions of racial identity, deconstructing the philosophical links in the symbolic chain of equivalence between white and civilization.

11

But a more particular interpretation coheres at this point. One reading of the dominant impulses of the philosophical heritage of the West suggests that its inner truths have been constituted on a determination to exclude those deemed incapable of mastering reason – women and children, the insane and the deviant, the lower orders ever about to raise Cain, and all those designated by the polite composite, natives. An elaboration of this argument, with a contemporary perspective, proposes a convergence between (on the one hand) the dismantling of Western reason 'from within' – heralded by the moment of deconstruction and by the arrival of a distinctly postmodern culture – and (on the other) a range of cultural and intellectual practices which have been generated on the peripheries of the world-system and which have sought to exclude themselves from the rationalist project of the West. Thus Robert Young can claim that 'deconstruction involves the decentralization and decolonization of European thought' – the notion of 'involvement' leaving much still to be said, while Gayatri Chakravorty Spivak suggests less opaquely if also less modestly that for Derrida deconstruction 'is the deconstitution of the founding concepts of the Western historical narrative'.[5]

Another way to argue this, as Cornel West does, is to broaden the terms of reference from philosophical postulates to the organization of the culture as a whole. Thus postmodernism, for West, 'is a set of responses due to [sic] the decentring of Europe – of living in a world that no longer rests upon European hegemony and domination in the political and economic, military and cultural dimensions which began in 1492'. In similar vein, though less troubled by temporal exactitude, Homi Bhabha understands postmodernism as an eruptive plurality of voices no longer subjugated to the logic of instrumental reason. 'The wider significance of the postmodern condition lies in the awareness that the epistemological "limits" of those ethnocentric ideas are also the enunciative boundaries of a range of other dissonant, even dissident histories and voices – women, the colonized, minority groups, the bearers of policed sexualities'.[6] In this view postmodernity represents not the staged successor to modernity, but the launching of genuinely new, hitherto repressed histories and the disruption of the historical time associated with the universal *telos* of the modern. The discovery of these histories, as Stuart Hall writes, is the moment when 'the world begins to be decolonized'.[7]

Here I can go back to the virtuoso founding text – Edward Said's *Orientalism* of 1978. The highbrow scholarly texture of Said's writing does nothing to conceal that the book's conceptual architecture is over-determined by a sense of historical formation – or as Fredric Jameson has suggested in another context, 'the historical "object" itself becomes inscribed in the very form'.[8]

12

Much has been written about this book: it has been reviewed, debated and become the object of any number of student assignments. Much too has been written about its author: we know about his family history, his cultural and conceptual tastes, his political engagements and his delight in embracing Manhattan high chic. There is no point in repeating all this here.[9] All that needs to be said for my purposes here can be summed up in the invocation of two names: Fanon and Foucault. Despite the complex cross-currents of the postwar intellectual milieu of Paris, and despite Foucault's espousal of a richly iconoclastic radicalism during the time of the Algerian war of independence, these have not been names commonly linked.[10] In writing *Orientalism* that – in part – was Said's point. Doggedly he places time and again on public record his frustrations with prestige intellectuals who refuse to think seriously about colonialism, denouncing Sartre for a prim, ignorant self-righteousness and Foucault for indifference, a denunciation extended – in more tempered terms – to Raymond Williams.[11] For Said, Fanon provided the necessary link back to the politics of decolonization, and also to an understanding of the need for the back-breaking dismantling and renovation of the intellectual formations of the metropolis. 'The whole point of Fanon's work', Said insisted, 'is to force the European metropolis to think its history *together with* the history of the colonies awakening from the cruel stupor and absurd immobility of imperial dominion'.[12]

Yet at the same time 'the whole point of Fanon's work' could not have been realized without his prolonged critical engagement with the philosophical foundations of the metropolitan order – including the putatively irredeemable traditions of the enlightenment. For in attacking the metropolis Fanon refused to affiliate to any simple – 'nativist' – nationalism which reproduced, as he saw it, the cultural and intellectual segregation of the colonized. In Said's words:

> To accept nativism is to accept the consequences of imperialism, the racial, religious, and political divisions imposed by imperialism itself. To leave the historical world for the metaphysics of enemies like *négritude*, Irishness, Islam or Catholicism is to abandon history for essentializations that have the power to turn human beings against each other. . .[13]

For Said, Fanon was *the* figure who condemned the epistemological conquests of Europe without compromise yet who – in the midst of military and political campaigns against colonialism – by virtue of his rejection of nativism was forced back into the intellectual systems he condemned, compelled to rework them for his own purposes.

This is how Said reflected on this process, heeding the historical break inaugurated by the early phases of decolonization:

13

The sense for Europeans of a tremendous and disorientating change in perspective in the West/non-West relationship was entirely new, experienced neither in the European Renaissance nor in the 'discovery' of the Orient three centuries later. Think of the differences between Poliziano's recovery and editing of Greek classics in the 1460s, or Bopp and Schlegel reading Sanskrit grammarians in the 1810s, and a French political theorist or Orientalist reading Fanon during the Algerian War in 1961, or Césaire's *Discours sur le colonialisme* when it appeared in 1955 just after the French defeat at Dien Bien Phu. Not only is this last unfortunate fellow addressed by natives while his army is engaged by them, as neither his predecessors were, but he is reading a text in the language of Bossuet and Chateaubriand, using concepts of Hegel, Marx and Freud to incriminate the very civilization producing all of them. Fanon goes still further when he reverses the hitherto accepted paradigm by which Europe gave the colonies their modernity and argues instead that not only were 'the well-being and progress of Europe – built up with the sweat and the dead bodies of Negroes, Arabs, Indians, and the yellow races' but 'Europe is literally the creation of the Third World', a charge to be made again and again by Walter Rodney, Chinweizu, and others. Concluding this preposterous reordering of things, we find Sartre echoing Fanon (instead of the other way round) when he says, 'There is nothing more consistent than a racist humanism, since the European has only been able to become a man through creating slaves and monsters'.[14]

It has now become a tired ritual to initiate discussion of Fanon not with Fanon himself but with Sartre's extraordinary Preface to *The Wretched of the Earth* in which he, Sartre, capitulated wholesale to the prevailing winds of 'Third Worldism' (and an accompanying programmatic catharsis of violence), announcing that European humanism comprised '*nothing but* an ideology of lies'. Thirty years on, from Khmer Rouge to Sendero Luminoso, Sartre's position is even harder to swallow – though the great irony is that Fanon himself, in the very text which followed Sartre's words, developed a more complex vision.[15] But while we may step back from the philosophical absolutism advocated by Sartre, the issues raised by Fanon remain both urgent and unresolved. Schooled in Martinique in the institutions of colonial education, migrating to Paris and the metropolis by way of the Free French Army (where he was decorated by Raoul Salan, who mutated later into the head of the OAS), as a Frenchman he was to discover that the universalist traditions bequeathed by the Revolution could in practice all too often function to maintain the system of colonialism. Furthermore as a psychiatrist at the Blida-Joinville hospital in Algeria from 1953 to 1956 he witnessed a medical profession founded on the precepts of a practical humanism working to abuse, abetting pain, misery and death. Although this is not always an easy stance to adopt from London, which can hardly boast clean hands, there is plenty of evidence to indicate that French decolonization – from Vietnam to the Battle of Algiers – was centred on a systematization of violence and torture to an intense degree. Nor was this confined to the colonies. On the night of 17 October 1961 – a few months after Fanon completed the draft of *The Wretched of the Earth* and only a matter of weeks before his death – approximately two hundred Algerian Muslims in Paris were murdered by the police, some fifty being garrotted at police headquarters. In Algeria's war of independence, from 1954–61, 141,000 FLN soldiers were killed by the French: the number of Muslim civilians who died at the hands of the French authorities is not recorded. It's little wonder that the theme of violence is prominent in Fanon's writings, and little wonder too that he felt impelled to strip away the mendacities imbricated in the idea of French civilization, recoiling from that which had formed him.

Fanon was active in a moment in the *longue durée* of decolonization when the deficiencies of nativism became thinkable, contributing to an anti-colonial political and theoretical project which found inspiration in many quarters. Given contemporary temptations to rely only on partial vision and to privilege 'postcolonialism' as a theoretical or textual strategy we should remind ourselves not only of its larger history, but of Fanon's explicit historical awareness of the forces which confronted him. The first page of *The Wretched of the Earth* is clear:

> Decolonization, as we know, is a historical process: that is to say that it cannot be understood, it cannot become intelligible, nor clear to itself except in the exact measure that we can discern the movements which give it historical form and content.[16]

In an abrasive, evocative imagery Fanon depicted a Manichean historical world, colonial and colonized, each inhabiting a separate space and time, a segregation externalized in the urban organization of the colonial city and internalized in distinct psychic structures. The dynamic of racial subjugation on which segregation was founded demanded, in Fanon's words, that 'Marxist analysis should always be slightly stretched every time we have to do with the colonial problem'.[17] Discussion of Fanon today is propelled by competing interpretations of what precisely this 'slight stretching' of Marxism – an intellectual formation impeccably European in its philosophical credentials – involves.

Arguably, Fanon's starting point was with what Said, and countless others, have subsequently denounced as part of the armoury of the 'enemy': the concept of *négritude*, associated pre-eminently with Aimé Césaire.[18] Fanon may initially have been sympathetic; he was close to its theoretical progenitors; and one can assume that for him it enabled certain issues to be voiced. It confirmed, precisely, an existential presence: some place to start. But from his earliest public writing it is evident that one of the defining intellectual dramas which sustained him was his determination to break through the impasse of a metaphysical Africa or blackness, and to translate the issues which *négritude* had opened into a more fully historical and political conceptual idiom. To retain affiliation to the category of *négritude* was, he warned, to dance 'without suspecting it . . . on the edge of a precipice'.[19] By the end of his short life, not many years later, he had implicitly arrived at a position in which he believed ethnic identity to be formed by political struggle (broadly understood), but which recurringly was 'interrupted' by the deeper interior forces of the psyche. Until the end Fanon projected a Manichean vision of the world: but he was always at pains to distinguish the contingent political forces drawn up, for or against colonialism, from what he described as the 'primitive Manicheanism of the settler – Blacks and Whites, Arabs and Christians' which derived entirely from pregiven ethnic determinations.[20]

In characteristically provocative, illuminating prose Fanon dwelt on the need to wrest history away from the colonial possessors: the effects of colonialism, he argued, worked as if to dispossess the colonized not only of their material wealth but also of their access to a precolonial past. 'The settler makes history and is conscious of making it'. To take the colonizers at their word it would have seemed as if the native had had no history until the colonialists arrived, and even then was excluded from the locations through which modern time moved, condemned to a perpetual present of dependent servitude.

> The colonialist . . . reaches the point of no longer being able to imagine a time occurring without him. His irruption into the history of the colonized people is deified, transformed into absolute necessity. Now a 'historic look at history' requires . . . that the French colonialist retire, for it has become historically necessary for the national time in Algeria to exist.[21]

Of course, the discovery of a pre-colonial past, asserting a presence independent of the colonial order, could lead straight to a philosophy of *négritude*. Fanon's power was that – while tracking this route – he all the while pulled away, looking to the future as much as to the past, and thinking relations between past and present dynamically.

In *The Wretched of the Earth* he recounted the shift which he had noted within the oral traditions of storytelling within Muslim culture in Algeria. Stories composed of 'inert episodes' restricted to an obscure past changed in their temporal structures. 'The formula "This all happened long ago" is substituted by that of "What we are going to speak of happened somewhere else, but it might well have happened here today, and it might happen tomorrow"'. The distinction is significant; it preoccupied Fanon, for it marks the difference between a folk antiquarianism, on the one hand, and – to borrow a term – 'a politically imagined possibility', looking from past to future, on the other. Or as he stated himself: his purpose was 'to use the past with the intention of opening the future'.[22]

Many issues arise from these points. I'll focus on merely one, which runs through the three central essays of *The Wretched of the Earth*: the emergence of the unreal or 'empty' nation in the postcolonial period, counterposed to the historic realities of the culture of the people, constituted by 'a hidden life, teeming and perpetually in motion'.[23] In the essay on 'Spontaneity' Fanon demonstrated the existence, as he perceived it, of two different realities in the independence movement. On the one hand there existed the Western, modernizing intellectuals who represented the public voice of the national party; on the other hand, there were 'the mass of the people' – largely unseen and silent, and even in the moment of most active liberation, still written out of history. In summary terms it could simply be said that Fanon's purpose was to create – in imagination and practice – a means of representation which could give voice to the colonized masses. If, a few decades on, this problem appears to be an obvious one there is no reason to suppose it was at the time. In this respect, Fanon himself represents a decisive moment in the reordering of the colonial world, which is why he remains contentious. Arguably, though, ambivalence is there in his very writing. In attempting to chart the development of national consciousness of the masses, for example, he could resort to an apparently unselfconsciously heroic imagery, depicting erstwhile criminal thugs acquiring a new self-discipline and marching 'shoulder to shoulder' in the vanguard of the new nation. Equally, however, he was as likely to stress – against this choreographed history where truth knows its place – a contrary reading, where history is more capricious and 'truths ... are only partial, limited and unstable'.[24]

In the celebrated essay which follows – 'The pitfalls of national consciousness' – he explored more fully the divide between the national elite and the popular classes. Suggesting that the Westernized leaders of the nation simultaneously were unable to break from the culture of the metropolis and to learn from the native masses, they were – he maintained – pushed into an ever-more precarious situation where the founding idea of the nation contracted: 'From nationalism we have passed to ultra-nationalism, to chauvinism, and finally to racism'. Thus: 'Everywhere where the national bourgeoisie has shown itself incapable of extending its vision of the world sufficiently, we observe a falling back towards old tribal attitudes, and furious and sick at heart, we

17

perceive that race feeling in its most exacerbated form is triumphing'.[25] The collapse of a secular vision – the 'hollow shell of nationality' – *produced* religious and ethnic sectarianism.

> Totally unexpected events break out here and there. In regions where Catholicism or Protestantism predominates, we see the Moslem minorities flinging themselves with unaccustomed ardour into their devotions. The Islamic feastdays are revived, and the Moslem religion defends itself inch by inch against the violent absolutism of the Catholic faith.

With a brutal logic, the nation transforms into the single party, and the party into 'the tribe', organizing 'an authentic ethnical dictatorship'.[26]

These are prophetic words. Maybe, with hindsight, a contemporary reader can legitimately complain that Fanon's aphoristic abstractions short-circuit too much. I would prefer to emphasize their prescience. Too often since his death we have seen a folkloric conception of the past in which a modern populace loses itself in myth, inaugurating variant nativisms of consuming powers, evident not only in the newly independent states but in the ruins of the old imperial heartlands too. In Fanon, the categories of nation and people – often so seductively coupled – are subjected to a critique which serves to dislocate as much as to connect, and which can be read as a kind of deconstructionism *avant la lettre*.

But in this lies a central problem, which reverberates through Edward Said's work and through the full corpus of postcolonial theory. It's here that all the controversies about enlightened reason – the philosophical source of all servitude, on the one hand, or the only possible antidote to barbarism on the other – converge. It's perfectly possible to follow one line of argument through, recruiting Fanon to the postcolonial, post-structuralist canon and establishing him as an enemy of Eurocentric reasoning. In an early essay Homi Bhabha, writing of Fanon's first book, *Black Skins, White Masks*, commended it for the fact that 'it rarely historicizes the colonial experience'. He went on: 'There is no master narrative or realist perspective that provides a background of social and historical facts against which emerge the problems of the individual or collective psyche... It is through image and fantasy – those orders that figure transgressively on the borders of history and the unconscious – that Fanon most profoundly provokes the colonial condition'. And further:

> Forms of social and psychic alienation and aggression – madness, self-hate, treason, violence – can never be acknowledged as determinate and constitutive conditions of civil authority, or as the ambivalent effects of the social instinct itself. They are always

18

explained as alien presences, occlusions of historical progress, the ultimate misrecognition of Man.

For Fanon such a myth of Man and Society is fundamentally undermined in the colonial situation where everyday life exhibits a 'constellation of delirium' that mediates the normal social relations of its subjects... These interpositions, indeed collaborations of political and psychic violence *within* civic virtue, alienation within identity, drive Fanon to describe the splitting of the colonial space of consciousness and society as marked by a 'Manichean delirium'.[27]

There are two arguments here, one running into the other; and they are followed by a third. The first, commending Fanon for his refusal to historicize and for his rejection of any 'master narrative or realist perspective', is the most strictly poststructuralist intervention. It comprises a very particular reading of Fanon but one – even accepting Bhabha's acute and helpful introduction of the psychoanalytically-derived idea of ambivalence – which in my view is too forced. To counter it, one could consider the following propositions: that the trajectory of Fanon's intellectual and political life moved from existential abstraction to a more conventionally historical mode of inquiry in *The Wretched of the Earth*, and in his writings, between 1957–60, in the FLN paper *el Moudjahid*; that his critique of 'ethnical dictatorship' and assorted nationalisms derived not from particularist interests but from some conception of enlightened universalism; that if he can be read as a proto-poststructuralist it was a position he arrived at, paradoxically, via Hegel; and similarly when Fanon – on a number of occasions – called for a new humanism, again in the image of a *reconstituted* enlightenment project, he meant what he was saying.[28] In this reading, where we see Fanon discussing the calorific intake of the Algerian *fellahs* or examining the most appropriate organization of FLN commando detachments, we are closer to Guevara or Giap than to the theoreticians of the 1990s. Maybe this is to bend the stick too far, but it serves a purpose.

Homi Bhabha's second argument is too easily conflated with the first. Here, his emphasis falls on the psychoanalytical component of Fanon, showing – rightly – that his appropriation of psychoanalysis throws into confusion overly-rationalistic interpretations of human agency, and supersedes an inherited, mechanistic divide between self and society. But formally, there is no reason to suppose that having recourse to psychoanalytical categories – whatever their deconstructive momentum – automatically accredits one as a poststructuralist *per se*. Even the most canny feminist appropriations of Lacan's appropriation of Freud might suggest an enlargement of historical inquiry rather than its formal, necessary deconstruction.

19

If this is right, to try to set Fanon up as a precursor of deconstruction doesn't have much going for it. But in fact I don't think this is where the key issue really lies; and it's here too that some imagined engagement between history, on the one hand, and poststructuralism, on the other, falls to pieces.[29] In practice poststructuralism has come to mean something quite different from obeisance to the last directives from Lacan or Derrida – which is as well, given their predilection for outflanking schools of epigones threatening to swim too close.[30] At this practical level poststructuralism has come to signify more a vigilance about the provenance and effectivity of conceptual categories, demanding we be on the look-out for the hypostatization of concepts and their elevation into self-confirming theoretical systems. 'It' – poststructuralism – hardly warrants nomination as a theory in its own right: if anything it has become a method, or perhaps more accurately a theorization of anti-theory, generating its own dispersal of truth. The moment of poststructuralism has passed, merging and dissolving into many different currents. Consequently it doesn't make much sense to worry away at 'its' relation to 'history' (especially, as often occurs, if history is cast in the most primitive role imaginable). Indeed, to accept this interpretation is to come close to a notionally Bakhtinian (or detotalizing) philosophy of history, whose principal enemy is conceptual stasis. In this respect historians might look fondly on poststructuralism, welcoming the reminder we should be aware of the consequences of our foundational explanatory and narrative procedures. We can see this practical poststructuralism at work in Bhabha himself – feted as a pre-eminent figure in the expanding universe of postcolonial theory – where traces of previous theoretical systems remain clearly in evidence, and where we can spot an almost Thompsonian urge to fashion concrete abstractions adequate to the complexity and historical movement of social life. We require a mode of theorization, Bhabha writes, where the key terms will be

> more complex than 'community'; more symbolic than 'society' . . .
> more rhetorical than reason of state; more mythological than
> ideology; less homogeneous than hegemony; less centred than the
> citizen; more collective than 'the subject'; more psychic than civility;
> more hybrid in the articulation of cultural differences and identi-
> fications – gender, race or class – than can be represented in any
> hierarchical or binary structuring of social antagonism.[31]

If *this* controlled eclecticism is what poststructuralist theory has become in practice, then the recovery of Fanon – not least the 'tremendous analogical virtues' of his psychoanalytic insights – is more convincing.[32]

This still leaves however the third strand of Bhabha's argument. He fully recognizes the allegiances of his own interpretation, and concedes that there are central ambiguities in Fanon which endorse contrary readings. Thus he identifies moments when Fanon 'lapses' back into the older, recidivist categories he had learned as a young existentialist; or when 'he is too quick to name the Other, to personalize its presence in the language of colonial racism'; or when he aimed 'to restore the dream to its proper political time and cultural space'. In sum: 'It is as if Fanon is fearful of his most radical insights'.[33] Thus, it seems, he is to be viewed as one who could only incompletely anticipate the radicalism of post-1968 poststructuralism. Yet accepting these antinomies, and accepting too his theoretical originality, it makes equal sense to turn Homi Bhabha's comments around so that they point in the opposite direction: not that Fanon was too timid to make the final leap into deconstruction but, confronted with immediate political imperatives, he knew when to stop. At some point, the theoretically mundane, incessantly qualified obligations of a 'realist perspective' assert themselves.

This is a roundabout way of coming to Said, for I think a similar set of antinomies and resolutions occurs here too. Fanon, in all his ambivalence, was crucial for Said, as he has been for all varieties of postcolonial theorist.[34] There is Foucault too. In the early 1970s Said was at his most Foucauldian.[35] The great insight derived from Foucault, which lies at the heart of *Orientalism*, is that discursive production *is* the production of power. To describe or represent is at the same time to demarcate, to include and exclude, in a word – to contain. Indeed, Said's very definition of culture is at one point palpably Foucauldian. 'Culture is a system of exclusions legislated from above but enacted throughout its polity, by which such things as anarchy, disorder, irrationality, inferiority, bad taste and immorality are identified, then deposited outside the culture and kept there by the power of the state and its institutions.'[36] From a stance such as this Said could approach Europe's long discursive preoccupation with the East and maintain that the Orient is itself the imaginative production of Europe and that this imaginative act functioned as a necessary, constitutive element in the consolidation of the imperial system. European representations of 'Orientals' and their ways served to contain and to colonize: not merely as a belated rationale or justification for the dirty work of empire, but in order to hold in place the phantasmagorical figure of Western civilization – rational man – by the systematic exclusion of his Other, the Oriental. Thus part of Said's thesis in *Orientalism* conformed closely to Foucault's ever-more spirited, extravagant battles against the forces of enlightened reason. *Orientalism*, to the extent that it was carried by this Foucauldian slipstream, portrayed an all-powerful Occident, internally free from competing ('non-Orientalist') definitions of Eastern and other civilizations, and free too from the inconvenience of the colonized speaking back. The grimmer, desolate cast of Foucauldianism, in which culture *per se* becomes a machine for repression, gets translated in *Orientalism* into an uncontested notion of the intellectual formation of the white metropolis switched on to perpetual motion, automatically reproducing the divisions between oppressors and oppressed. Merely to speak of the East is to condemn its peoples to oppression.

A paradox follows from this. If it really were the case that the discursive formations of the West were locked into this cycle of oppression, then the only alternative site for generating opposition would be the Third World. As one hostile critic has suggested: 'If the whole history of Western textualities, from Homer to Olivia Manning, was a history of Orientalist ontology, Third World literature was *prima facie* the site of liberationist practice'.[37] Sometimes, in Said's political writings, such a notion can be detected – when we see him, in other words, at his most beleaguered; sometimes too, with less justification, such beliefs can form an undercurrent in the more highly abstracted versions of postcolonial theory, protestations about the pitfalls of nativism and nationalism notwithstanding. But if present in Said's work it only ever occurred in minor key and, as I see it, was largely due to an unwarranted enthusiasm for a particular moment of Foucault – who in his intellectual journeyings stopped at many assorted stations of the cross. Just as in Fanon there existed a burning scepticism about the possibilities and realities of the European traditions of enlightened thought, and just as Fanon found himself thrown back to what he condemned, so too – in less fraught mode – with Said: a similar tension is at work. For James Clifford, 'Said's humanist perspectives do not harmonize with his use of methods derived from Foucault', while for Aijaz Ahmad this emerges more starkly as the 'impossible reconciliation' of *Orientalism*.[38]

Since the publication of *Orientalism* the shift in Said's theoretical sympathies has been clear. He has moved away from Foucault and from the characteristic ploys of poststructuralism, and has become much readier to uphold both a more straightforwardly empirical method and the virtues of reason.[39] Typically, he is now disarmingly matter-of-fact. 'I was always trying to abide by universalist principles and yet be concrete and critical at the same time', he now maintains. Or on aesthetics, in a move calculated to upset his more deconstructionist fans, he admits: 'I have this strange attachment, again it's a residual or vestigial consciousness, to what I consider in a dumb kind of way "great art"'.[40] In fact, these statements represent less a theoretical resolution to the dilemmas of *Orientalism* than a reaction against the academicization of theory, against 'the massive intervening institutional presence of theoretical discussion'. 'Metacritical' discourse he now indicts as 'hopelessly tiresome', echoing Benita Parry's early critique of postcolonial theory for its 'exorbitation of discourse'.[41] More particularly, he has felt himself driven to repeat rudimentary arguments about the historical location of texts, insisting that: 'Textuality has become the exact antithesis and displacement of what might be called history'. Indeed, for Said the move to a more or less philosophically conventional historiography, enlivened by purpose, curiosity and an agile historical imagination, appears to mark his final resting point.

> What really compels my attention outside the doctrinal boundaries of 'literary criticism', which I don't read any more, are interesting, daring, novel attempts to do something from a historical point of view, across discursive lines in often transgressive ways, in ways that try to connect politically and intellectually with other interventions.[42]

Respecting the differing imperatives and idioms in place, I'd suggest that this chosen practical resolution is not far removed from that of Fanon, when he too was confronted by a similar range of epistemological issues.

Up to this point I've made some general comments about postcolonial theory, without attempting to introduce any major objections. And I've also looked at Said's purpose in bringing together Fanon and Foucault, noting the theoretical ambivalence of his founding investigations and his subsequent move back, as I read it, to a more accommodating engagement with the given protocols of historiography. In doing this I suggested there might exist a weak rendition of poststructuralism which could be valuable in opening up the practices of historical exploration and explanation but which wouldn't at the same time obliterate the foundations of a low-gear conception of a textually conditioned external historical reality. Thus up to this point I've been arguing by implication that although the imperatives of the postcolonial epoch require the rethinking of historical practice, the more exhilarating suggestions that conventional historiography itself – by virtue of its complicity with the colonizing project – is damned, are more fanciful. But as everyone would agree, the issue is not based on the dichotomy of history – for or against – as on the degrees and forms of theoretical renovation required. Even so, my breezy tampering with poststructuralism, such that it turns out to be no more than a controlled eclecticism paying special attention to its narrative and explanatory forms, is unlikely to prove acceptable to those who have been more deeply formed by its modes of thought. With this in mind we need to look more closely at the specific critiques of historical narrative.

There are two places we might think to look. First, there is the momentary meeting of Gayatri Chakravorty Spivak with the 'Subaltern Studies' historians of South Asia who – in summary terms – on the basis of imaginative theoretical appropriation attempted to devise a historiography able to represent the putatively silent colonized masses. Their historical work is innovative and stimulating and exhibits a rich mix of hard archival empirical research with a dazzling array of competing high-theory paradigms.[43] Spivak's reputation in the global academic world falls just short of Said's; one need only turn to the number of published interviews to see just how insistently her authority is sought out. Despite her own misgivings, repeated often enough, she has come to personify the postcolonial feminist critic. Intellectually, since the early 1970s, she has associated herself with Derrida, and since then has come to be viewed as one of the principal architects of post-colonial theory. The importance of her response to Subaltern Studies lies in the extrinsic fact that it marks virtually the only occasion when a post-colonial critic of deconstructionist sympathies discusses historiographic work head-on.[44] The substance of her remarks, however, suggests that this promise remains unfulfilled. In sum, her thesis is unexceptional: she claims that the historiography is, due to its very objectives, compelled to be deconstructionist, but in practice doesn't quite make it. Here again, one might say that the emphasis on the conceptual intractability of historical work comes as no surprise, nor need it be deplored. Beyond that, the more local arguments are difficult to fathom: in a genre notor-ious for difficult writing, I find this article – entitled 'Subaltern Studies – deconstructing historiography' – an impossible mix of tangled abstrac-tion and terrible prose, in contrast to the energetic clarity of her spoken interviews, and think it wisest to move on. All that I might ponder, in mitigation, is whether rebarbative prose of this type – if that's what it is – hasn't something to do with the engagement between two such strikingly distinct cognitive forms?

A second instance can be found in Robert Young's influential *White Mythologies*. At one level the book functions as a commentary on the positions of other postcolonial theorists; at another – in marshalling these arguments under the banner of a strict deconstructionism – it deserves comment in its own right. His writing is sober, careful and clear, remi-niscent of the more mainstream traditions of English analytic philosophy: not for him the allusive poetics of an Adorno or Lacan. But the studied prose belies the extravagance of his conclusions. His arguments work by attrition. He takes his theorists; in an illuminating set of moves he gently but insistently knocks out the epistemological (metaphysical) supports of their positions, one by one; and with a subdued flourish he demonstrates the incoherence of all and sundry. Step by step this uneventful writing takes the reader on some extraordinary journeys – the passing suggestion that 'European philosophy reduplicates Western foreign policy' marking one such memorable example.[45]

He begins with a set of arguments which are challenging, but theoretically relatively uncontentious. First, history can only be known through discursive construction or abstraction: there are no processes by which history can spontaneously generate meaning. Second, European philosophies of history have intimately been connected to their colonized Others requiring, as he puts it, not the 'purging' of European thought but 'repositioning European systems of knowledge so as to demonstrate the long history of their operation as the effect of their colonial other'.[46] Third, a related point, he convincingly shows that it was along the axis of colonial critique – in the work of Barthes, Lévi-Strauss and Derrida – that effective engagement with the problems of theoretical humanism first occurred. Fourth, what we are presently experiencing is the dissolution of the West and of its historical imagination: this is what postmodernism or, in different register, poststructuralism, is about. And fifth, recognition of the centrality of the colonized serves actively to dislocate received notions of relations between theory and history, necessitating the elaboration of new cognitive frameworks. Thus in his closing pages he makes the following claim:

> Colonial discourse analysis is placed in the unique position of being able to examine English culture, literature, and indeed Englishness in its widest sense, from its determined position on the margins: not questing for the essence of Englishness but examining the representations it has produced for itself of its other, against and through which it defines itself, together with the function of such representations in a structure of power in which they are used instrumentally.[47]

A perverse reader might quibble at this point, and wonder whether a new subject of history – Englishness – has not insinuated itself, and speculate just how rapidly Sir Arthur Bryant is spinning in his grave. But the general issue is clear and, put like this, not far removed from my own thoughts spelt out so far.

But Young adopts an unflinchingly anti-realist stance which makes it difficult to see how any historical work can get started. In effect, in a revival of a theoretical vanguardism which appeared in the 1970s, historicism and historiography are systematically conflated: any historical endeavour, it would appear, is doomed to slide into the falsities of historicism. Thus when Fredric Jameson insists that historical inquiry necessarily works by abstraction, but equally insists that there is an irreducible historical reality, out there, Young has none of it, for this is to accord history (he believes) transcendental status.[48] This is a position which has its own logic. Needless to say, it's not one I share and to argue the point is futile. But we should see where it takes him. Ironically, given his taste for censuring historical narrative, he constructs a forceful story which he pursues with verve. As he sees it, the principal feature of contemporary Western philosophy has been its attempt to free itself from Hegel. Poststructuralism represents the most recent, most knowing, but also still necessarily incomplete instalment in this process. Yet inevitably, he continues, its practitioners remain caught in the epistemological systems they wish to dismantle, for there is no external space outside them which would allow critique to develop. It would seem a certain conceptual agility is called for, the work of deconstruction operating at the same moment that critique is initiated. This may have certain attractions, and carry certain pay-offs. But in Young's reading it comes at a heavy price. Said is condemned for his humanism, Bhabha for his commitment to the 'transcendent' categories of psychoanalysis, and Spivak for her (massively idiosyncratic, as I see it) Marxism. All fail. He quotes from Derrida's *Writing and Difference*, the emphasis in the original: a new concept of history '*is difficult, if not impossible, to lift from its teleological or eschatological horizon*'.[49] Here we can see how delicate is the divide between history and teleology, the elision ever-ready to happen. With Young, adherence to this position is strict: in an epistemological version of grandmother's footsteps, any attempt to think out of the present, imagining a step forward or back, into future or past, smacks of (Western) historicism or teleology.

And yet one has the sense that he wished it were not so. His rhetoric is one that positively values the idea of new historical thinking. His final sentence illuminates the hope for 'the new logics of historical writing'. (We might compare this to the closing sentence of Homi Bhabha's *Location of Culture*: 'What is crucial to such a vision of the future is the belief that we might not merely change the *narratives* of our histories, but transform our sense of what it means to live, to be, in other times and different spaces, both human and historical'.)[50] But in Young this remains rhetorical.[51] For fundamentally, a strong theoretical determinism is in place. Just as Jameson is (convincingly) criticized for his attempts at conceptual reconciliation, having Lukács, Sartre and Althusser link arms as they march together into History, so Young's critique works at the same level of abstraction but in mirror-image: Said, Bhabha and Spivak are all sent packing for the wistful look over their shoulders at earlier theoretical systems.[52] As we've seen before, the problem with this kind of determinism is that in practice it is accompanied by an uncontrolled pragmatism, for the means don't exist for any other kind of critical judgement.

This becomes clearly evident in the texture of his own argument. The book is shot-through with conventional historiographical consideration, from the mega (the historical connections between Western philosophy and colonial expansion) to the minor ('Althusser's influence declined in France after 1968, partly as a result of . . . '). He is, not surprisingly, aware of this and supplies a defence. 'The conditions of impossibility' of his argument, he avers, 'are also those of its possibility. If all history, in

Plato's terms, is a bad copy, then his stricture applies no less to this one: any history it offers is only a simulacrum of one, an historical pastiche'.[53] And there we have it: a Platonic ideal of history and an endless variety of bad historiographical copies with no means by which they can be differentiated.[54]

What this obliterates is any possibility of judging between different historical narratives: one narrative or rhetoric is as valuable as any other. This unnecessarily concedes too much. But to think of historiography in terms of a variety of bad copies (of some unknown Platonic ideal, if this sort of idiom appeals), is less of a problem. In fact, paradoxically, it sounds rather like the most conventional defence of their craft made by practising historians, whose claims for historical knowledge is often modest to a fault. One of the problems in these debates is that historiography acquires an image of scientificity, in an archaically positivistic mode, which rarely conforms to the ways in which historians work. Indeed, one could turn this argument around as well, and suggest that history – far from being the last bastion of positivistic science within the humanities – is to the contrary 'the most impermanent of written forms . . . a cognitive form that has no end'.[55] As we and our social world change so too does our relationship to the past, and new historiographies have to be invented. This is obvious enough. But this profoundly *contingent* quality of historical knowledge in itself should militate against imperiousness of any kind.

NOTES

1 There have been many of these, and many more after the quincentennial of 1492. I would mention three in particular: Stephen Greenblatt, *Marvelous Possessions. The Wonder of the New World*, Clarendon Press, Oxford, 1991; Peter Hulme, *Colonial Encounters: Europe and the Native Caribbean*, Routledge, London, 1992; and Paul Carter, *The Road to Botany Bay. An Essay in Spatial History*, Faber and Faber, London, 1987. For a gripping attempt to reconstruct the mental worlds of the conquered, Nathan Wachtel, *The Vision of the Vanquished. The Spanish Conquest of Peru through Indian Eyes, 1530–1570*, Harvester, Hassocks, 1971.
2 Stuart Schram, *Mao Tse-Tung*, Simon and Schuster, New York, 1966, p.31.
3 Joseph Conrad, 'Geography and some explorers' in his *Last Essays*, Dent, London, 1928, p.13. For those who like history in hypothetical mode, we might wonder what Orson Welles's first planned movie – of *Heart of Darkness* – would have looked like. In the event due to the vast expense involved RKO pulled the plug and we have *Citizen Kane* instead.
4 Edward Said, *The Question of Palestine*, Vintage, London, 1992, p.72. Conrad's allegories on the 'failure' of Europe are decisive anticipations of postcolonial theory. Said, in his *Joseph Conrad and the Fiction of Autobiography*, Harvard University Press, Cambridge (Mass.), 1966, dwells upon Conrad's own last imaginings of Poland 'as the outpost of Western civilization', p.81; though there is in the book another, less easily visible, intertwining of nineteenth-

century Poland and twentieth-century Palestine. See too Benita Parry, *Conrad and Imperialism. Ideological Boundaries and Visionary Frontiers*, Macmillan, London, 1983.

5 Robert Young, *White Mythologies. Writing History and the West*, Routledge, London, 1990, p.18; and Gayatri Chakravorty Spivak, *The Postcolonial Critic. Interviews, Strategies, Dialogues*, Routledge, London, 1990, p.31. Alternatively, on Derrida one could follow Gore Vidal's belief that as a child he must have overdosed on Krazy Kat: 'Surrealism and patriotism: the education of an American novelist', *New Left Review* 149, 1985, p.98.

6 He adds to this two further historical co-ordinates: the rise and decline of the US (1945–75); and the decolonization of the Third World: Cornel West, 'Decentring Europe: the contemporary crisis in culture', in his *Beyond Eurocentrism and Multiculturalism, vol.I, Prophetic Thought in Postmodern Times*, Common Courage Press, Monroe, Maine, 1993, pp.124–5; Homi Bhabha, *The Location of Culture*, Routledge, London, 1994, pp.4–5. This comes to assume that the oppressed – 'those who have suffered the sentence of history', p.172 – possess privileged access to knowledge by virtue of their oppression, an argument Bhabha would be unlikely to find persuasive in other contexts. In fact Bhabha echoes Foucault's 'insurrection of subjugated knowledges': Michel Foucault, 'Two lectures' in his *Power/Knowledge*, Harvester, Brighton, 1980, p.81. I've learnt much from Benita Parry's discussion of *The Location of Culture*, 'Signs of our times' *Third Text* 28/29, 1994.

7 Stuart Hall, 'Old and new identities, old and new ethnicities' in Anthony D. King (ed.), *Culture, Globalization and the World-System*, Macmillan, London, 1991, p.18.

8 Edward Said, *Orientalism. Western Conceptions of the Orient*, Penguin, Harmondsworth, 1985; Jameson's reference is to *Nostromo* – Fredric Jameson, *The Political Unconscious. Narrative as a Socially Symbolic Act*, Methuen, London, 1981, p.280. All I can do here is rehearse some key issues; for a 'review of reviews', Lata Mani and Ruth Frankenburg, 'The challenge of *Orientalism*', *Economy and Society* 14:2, 1985. *Orientalism* was written back-to-back with *The Question of Palestine*, and it shows. How else can one understand *Orientalism* opening with Balfour?

9 Some of these points are developed further in an essay in which I explore the formation of cultural studies in the larger historical context of decolonization: Bill Schwarz, 'Where is cultural studies?', *Cultural Studies* 8:3, 1994.

10 David Macey's wonderful biography, *The Lives of Michel Foucault*, Hutchinson, London, 1992, makes no mention of Fanon; until Foucault's experience of the Bourguiba regime in March 1968, North Africa appears more for its hedonistic than political possibilities.

11 By 1977 Williams was claiming that he should have opened *Culture and Society* (first published in 1958; Penguin, Harmondsworth, 1971) with Arnold's response to the Hyde Park riots and with Governor Eyre's actions in Jamaica: see *Politics and Letters*, Verso, London, 1979, p.109.

12 Edward Said, 'Representing the colonized: anthropology's interlocutors', *Critical Inquiry* 15:2, 1989, p.223.

13 Edward Said, *Culture and Imperialism*, Chatto and Windus, London, 1993, p.276.

14 Ibid., p.237.

15 Frantz Fanon, *The Wretched of the Earth*, Penguin, Harmondsworth, 1971, p.21, emphasis added. Much academic discussion of Fanon has remained frighteningly immune to the realities of violence which he discussed; for an important corrective, reflecting on the tyrannies which have emerged from

the neo-colonial states, Samir Al-Khalil (Karan Makiya), *Republic of Fear. Saddam's Iraq*, Hutchinson Radius, London, 1990, pp.xii–xiii.

16 Ibid., p.27.
17 Ibid., p.31.
18 The most revealing discussion I've come across is in an interview with Césaire conducted in 1967, reprinted in his *Discourse on Colonialism*, Monthly Review Press, New York, 1972.
19 Frantz Fanon, 'West Indians and Africans' (first published in 1955) in his *Toward the African Revolution*, Penguin, Harmondsworth, 1970, p.33. This essay marks a key moment in Fanon's trajectory.
20 Fanon, *Wretched of the Earth*, p.115.
21 Ibid., p.40; and Fanon, *Toward the African Revolution*, p.169.
22 Fanon, *Wretched of the Earth*, pp. 193 and 187. The phrase 'politically imagined possibility' comes from Raymond Williams, 'A lecture on realism', *Screen* 18:1, 1977, p.69.
23 Fanon, *Wretched of the Earth*, p.180.
24 Ibid., p.117.
25 Ibid., pp.125, 127.
26 Ibid., pp.128, 129, 132, 147.
27 Homi Bhabha, '"What does the black man want?"' *New Formations* 1, 1987, pp.118–28; Frantz Fanon, *Black Skins, White Masks*, Paladin, London, 1972.
28 For the contributions to *el Moudjahid*, Fanon, *Toward the African Revolution*; and for 'a new humanism', ibid., p.134, and Fanon, *Wretched of the Earth*, pp.252–4 – including the last sentence of the book which is, I guess, his last published writing.
29 Homi Bhabha does concede that Fanon's theorizations do not comprise 'a celebration of fragmentation, *bricolage*, pastiche or the "simulacrum"', *Location of Culture*, p.238. Indeed not: whatever else, Fanon is not Baudrillard.
30 Or to put this more formally, as Hayden White has noted of Foucault, the determination to deploy 'a discourse that dissolves its own authority', in John Sturrock (ed.), *Structuralism and Since. From Lévi-Strauss to Derrida*, Oxford University Press, Oxford, 1979, p.86.
31 Homi Bhabha, 'Dissemination: time, narrative and the margins of the modern nation' in Bhabha (ed.), *Nation and Narration*, p.292. For a riveting discussion of concrete abstraction, or the concrete in thought, which still holds: Stuart Hall, 'Marx's notes on method. A reading of the "1857 Introduction"', *Working Papers in Cultural Studies* 6, 1974.
32 Stephen Feuchtwang, 'Fanonian spaces', *New Formations* 1, 1987, p.127.
33 Bhabha, '"What does the black man want?"', pp.118 and 121; and Bhabha, *Location of Culture*, p.41.
34 Henry Louis Gates, 'Critical Fanonism', *Critical Inquiry* 17:3, 1991.
35 Edward Said, *Beginnings. Intention and Method*, Basic Books, New York, 1975.
36 Edward Said, *The World, the Text and the Critic*, Faber and Faber, London, 1984, p.11.
37 Aijaz Ahmad, *In Theory. Class, Nations, Literatures*, Verso, London, 1992, p.64. Despite his local insights and his frustration with the anti-historical bent of much current theory, Ahmad mounts a ferociously unwarranted attack on Said, his books and those influenced by him, suggesting all have been unwittingly captured by the intellectual advances of the New Right. Not unnaturally, the book has provoked vicious controversies. A long response from Benita Parry is published in *History Workshop Journal* 36, 1993.
38 James Clifford, review of *Orientalism*, *History and Theory* 19:2, 1980, p.212; Ahmad, p.164.

39 Contrast ch.5 of Said, *Beginnings* to the much more institutional or socio-logical interpretation to be found in the chapter entitled 'Knowledge and power' which closes his *Covering Islam*, Routledge, London, 1981. See too Edward Said, *Musical Elaborations*, Vintage, London, 1992, p.55.

40 Said, *Politics and Dispossession*, p.xix; Edward Said, 'Interview' in Michael Sprinker (ed.), *Edward Said. A Critical Reader*, Blackwell, Oxford, 1992, p.250; and see too Edward Said, *Representations of the Intellectuals. The 1993 Reith Lectures*, Vintage, London, 1994.

41 Edward Said, '*Orientalism* and after', *Radical Philosophy* 63, 1993, p.26; Said, 'Interview', pp.248-9; and Benita Parry, 'Problems in current theories of colonial discourse', *Oxford Literary Review* 9, 1987, p.43.

42 Said, *The Word, the Text and the Critic*, pp.3-4; see too Said, *The Question of Palestine*, p.56; and Said, 'Interview', p.248.

43 See especially, Ranajit Guha and Gayatri Chakravorty Spivak (eds), *Selected Subaltern Studies*, Oxford University Press, Delhi, 1988. A good introduction can be found in Terence Ranger, 'Subaltern Studies and "social history"', *Southern African Review of Books*, February/May 1990; and an indication of the groups's influence can be seen in Latin American Subaltern Studies Group, 'Founding statement', *Boundary* 2 20:3, 1993.

44 Gayatri Chakravorty Spivak, 'Subaltern Studies: deconstructing histori-ography' in Guha and Spivak, *Selected Subaltern Studies*.

45 Young, *White Mythologies*, p.14.

46 Ibid., p.119.

47 Ibid., p.174.

48 Ibid., p.101.

49 Ibid., p.66.

50 Ibid., p.175; and Bhabha, *Location of Culture*, p.256. One might note, from the same volume, Bhabha's unambivalent praise for Hobsbawm's militantly orthodox historiography: pp.139 and 266.

51 On the occasions he does substantiate he's forced back to a description of a perfectly recognizable historical practice. Here's one example. First the litany of bad practice (which Bhabha transcends): 'Bhabha does not in any sense offer a history of colonial discourse, nor even a simple historical account of it – for such historicization marks the very basis of the Europeanizing claims he is trying to invert'. Then the good practice, the text running on immedi-ately: 'Each text is both placed in its historical moment and gradually shifted from any single determination or linear development as Bhabha elaborates the complex problem of its reading', Young, *White Mythologies*, pp.146-7.

52 Ibid., p.93.

53 Ibid., p.vii.

54 Predictably, theory can't be lived at this pitch. His latest book is a deal jauntier, opening with *South Pacific* and a stroll round Greenwich Park. It contains much interesting historical material on the emergent category of miscegenation, working through the connections between race, nation, culture and sexuality in the nineteenth century. He now claims (wrongly, as I see it) that postcolonial theory never sought to exclude or replace other forms of analysis, but only ever determined to show how the structures of colonialism permeated all forms of knowledge, including purposively critical forms. The result is an acknowledged pluralism, a position he is apparently happier to embrace given what he himself identifies as the 'impasse' of post-colonial theory: Robert J.C. Young, *Colonial Desire. Hybridity in theory, culture and race*, Routledge, London, 1995, pp.163-4. For a further indication of the liveliness of the empirical and historical routes out of postcolonial theory,

see Gyan Prakash (ed.), *After Colonialism. Imperial histories and postcolonial displacements*, Princeton University Press, Princeton, 1995.
55 Carolyn Steedman, 'Culture, cultural studies and the historians' in Lawrence Grossberg, Cary Nelson and Paula Treichler (eds), *Cultural Studies*, Routledge, London, 1992, p.614.

3

HISTORY LESSONS

Formation of Subjects, (Post)colonialism, and an Other Project

Couze Venn

'It is possible to wonder if history itself does not begin with this relation to the other which for Levinas transcends history'.[1] The question I address prowls around this proposition of Derrida. I will pose it in the specific context of the emergence of the subject of modernity[2] and in this way interrogate the manner in which logocentrism in the 'ego's era'[3] has been sustained by the conditions which have accompanied colonialism and capitalism. Indeed, it is the complex and dynamic co-articulation of these phenomena in the history of modern times which frames my argument that the form of subjectivity which appeared with Descartes is founded on the systematic disavowal of the primacy of the relation to the other and the denial of the difference of the other. It could be argued, indeed, that the crisis in modernity, signalled by the troubled concept of the postmodern, is mirrored in the current vicissitudes of the subject, a subject clinging still to the debris of grand narratives, yet finding little purchase in the dissolution of the foundations which, until now, had harboured the signs of secure identities: race, nation, reason, progress and 'History' itself.

I will argue that it is not possible to imagine new foundations except by way of overcoming the metaphysics of presence that has crossed the discourses which constitute the autonomous, rational, unitary subject whose end we might be able to envisage[4] in the midst of the 'morbid symptoms' of 'late capitalism'.[5]

The different history of the subject which this implies proceeds from the view that resistance to oppression and the changing of circumstances are dependent on a politics which valorizes, but does not essentialize, difference and is informed by the rewriting of histories from the side of the oppressed and the dispossessed. It could be argued that the elements of such a history already exist, for example, in the important work - if often neglected by cultural theory - which the political economy of exploitation has accumulated concerning the mechanisms and the capillary ramifications of neo-colonialism and global or trans-national capitalism. Even so a theoretical insecurity does result from the weakening of the Marxist frameworks which shape these analyses and from the resilience of oppression. Power, as we know, operates on the basis of both domination and seduction, such that sections of oppressed groups collude in its efficacious exercise. It is through our subjectivity that we are ensnared in the stratagems of power, the obscure objects of our desire drawing us and binding us to that which secures our subjection. For this reason, the problem of the formation of subjects and all the classic debates about ideology need to be rethought beyond reductionist or essentialist models which have all but abolished the reality and meaningfulness of human lives.

We cannot, however, resolve these theoretical problems merely by way of a strategic switch to the point of view of the other, for example, by simply adopting the vantage of woman or the colonized.

I shall explain this by a brief reference to the work of the Subaltern Studies Group.[6] Guha makes this comment about the Group's effort to rewrite Indian history from the point of view of a 'subaltern con-sciousness': '. . . it is not possible to make sense of the experience of insurgency merely as a history of events without a subject'.[7] Spivak notes the Group's use of a notion of a unified consciousness in their effort to rewrite a history of colonialism which restitutes to the insurgent classes the degree of autonomy and agency denied them by dominant and elite historiography. She recognizes that such a consciousness is problematic from the point of view of 'First World anti-humanist post-Marxism', but argues that it is the index of a 'fracture of a discontinuity of philosophic levels, as well as a strategic asymmetry'.[8] From the point of a 'counter-history', the dilemma remains between granting the oppressed an 'expressive subjectivity' or condemning them to the 'unrepresentability' which is already the mark of oppression and a feature of the 'epistemic violence that constituted/effaced a subject that was obliged to cathect [occupy in response to a desire] the space of the imperialist self-consolidating other'.[9]

The problem is the correlation which exists between the imperialist subject and the subject of humanism, as I will discuss later. The use of Western intellectual figures as 'collaborators' can lead both to the repeti-tion of the discourse of agency attached to that of consciousness and totality as well as to a rupture from the discourses which have secured domination.

The poststructuralist critic thus runs the risk of being split between the project of deconstructing subject-centred teleologies and the 'wider narratives of imperialism', a predicament open to the danger of the pup of bourgeois individualism slipping between the legs of the decon-structionist.

So, how does one rethink agency without privileging either 'History' (and thus the structural determinations at work in social formations) or the humanist subject and its substitutes as origin of history? And how does one secure a space for the other to reinvent itself, an other whose assumed otherness is already defined by reference to the Western norm of subject? These are questions which we can re-examine in the light of several correlated developments.

First, we must take account of the critiques developed within structuralism and poststructuralism which target the key concepts which underwrite subject-centred accounts of history and culture. Derrida's deconstruction of the place of the logocentric subject is particularly useful to the extent that it destabilizes the Western ratio underpinning Europe's expansion; it indirectly reinstates a project of subjective becoming which follows Levinas in prioritizing ethics in the subject's relation to the other. Second, the Lacanian re-reading of Freud has provided some conceptual tools for historicizing the process of constitution of subjects and for thinking through the mechanisms by which the individual comes to be inscribed in the order of culture. Third, the work which interrogates colonial discourse from the side of the 'other' by people like Fanon and Said, then Spivak and Bhabha, has demonstrated the erasures and ambivalences, the psychic and epistemic violence, the suppressions and phantasies which have participated in the subjugative project of modern 'Western man'. This work has blown the cover of this would-be master of the universe and has opened the way for rewriting the history of Europe's others. Finally, feminist challenges to the authority of 'patriarchal' and 'masculinist' social relations and thought, as well as crises arising from the violence inflicted on nature and the human spirit through exploitative systems, add to the urgency and the possibility of thinking otherwise the history of humanity and its future.

HISTORICAL CONTEXT

The challenge to the founding principles of dominant Western consciousness has gathered momentum during a period which it is difficult to characterize except negatively by way of the 'post' of the postmodern. If we add to that the sense of a discontinuity conveyed in associated terms – postcolonial, postindustrial, postcapitalist, posthumanist – we are returned to the co-ordinates which framed the period of emergence of logocentrism and bourgeois individualism. In the wake of post-structuralist critiques no one finds shocking the claim that the grand narratives of modernity died with colonial liberation, with the ending of Europe's tragic Faustian adventure on the theatre of the world. Yet Sartre appeared particularly provocative when, thirty years ago, in the

Preface to Fanon's *The Wretched of the Earth*, he accused the whole of Europe of participation in the exploitation of the dispossessed and of guilt for the crimes against humanity which were integral to the advancement of the West: '... with us there is nothing more consistent than a racist humanism since the European has only been able to become a man through creating slaves and monsters'.[10]

Today Robert Young[11] can invoke Derrida, Levinas, Foucault and Jameson alongside Sartre as participants in the grand critique of the 'white mythologies' of modernity. It is tempting with hindsight to announce, as he does, that poststructuralism is not so much the product of May 1968 as it is that of the struggle for decolonization. We should remind ourselves though that the intellectual climate on the Left was rather more complex than Young implies in his reference to the recognition of Hegelianism and Eurocentrism. For even that recognition was in the name of a broad Marxism, whilst the critiques of the subject were aimed at the ideology of bourgeois individualism. It is true that the dreams of the (Kantian) 'long march of progress' faltered in the realities of the post-Second World War reassessment amongst the intellectual Left – the heirs of Enlightenment philosophy – yet, the aim remained that of the changing of circumstances to enable the emergence of the 'whole man, whom Europe has been incapable of bringing to triumphant birth'.[12]

Nineteen-sixty-eight, and not just May 1968, proved a turning point because it added to the disenchantment provoked by the realization that the longevity of the systematic inhumanity and irrationality of capitalism and imperialism owes its tenacity to certain features interior to the modern logos itself. It is a malaise which the *marginaux* felt more deeply in the bone than those who were persuaded that they never had it so good. The prospect of changing the world dimmed as the revolutionary lights went out throughout Europe and elsewhere. It is not poststructuralism itself which has occasioned the re-evaluation of modernity; nor is it the theoretical response to the crisis of modernity in any simple way. We need to bear in mind that a whole series of failures from the time of Nietzsche culminate in the postmodern condition. For Lyotard[13] Auschwitz has come to stand for the sign of the collapse of the project of modernity; equally, one could add Hiroshima, Algiers, the Gulag, Vietnam and much else. One feature of this condition is the existential crisis lived as a certain lack of being, *manque à être*, whose angst, for many, is assuaged in the compulsions and delights of consumerism. The 'Western individual' – who is not a geographical entity – is no longer called upon to prove and redeem himself in the project of becoming called 'History', but turns upon himself with a mixture of narcissism and disgust. It is in these circumstances – variously understood by writers like Lyotard, Baudrillard, Jameson – that the

35

reassessment of the modern period has been drawn towards a critique of what Lacan called the 'ego's era'. This era coincides with modernity and inaugurates an 'egology' which, for Levinas, is the index of an ontological error.[14] The connection with decolonization arises from the argument, proposed by Derrida, that the self-centred epistemology which supports 'egology' feeds into the 'appropriating narcissism of the West',[15] as I shall explain below. It is a thought which directs us to the theme of otherness and the struggle to break free from Europe's subjugating enterprise.

One other major ingredient of the historical context is the denunciation of the 'Man of Reason', inscribed as the authoritative subject at the heart of the discourses which claim to speak the truth of being everywhere and in every time. The rewriting of women's history and critiques of 'patriarchal' social order have made impossible the discursive recuperation of such a concept of the subject. At the same time, there is no clear conceptualization of the subject which is not simply an inversion, thus a repetition, of a subject-centred ontology.

There is thus a clear enough case establishing the complicity between logocentrism, ethnocentrism, phallocentrism and Western colonialism in the constitution of the specific form of subjectivity which has functioned to sustain modernity. A first step in moving away from this terrain is a critical engagement with the founding narratives which support that form of subjectivity. In the remainder of the chapter I will concentrate on two aspects of this critique, deriving first from Derrida, and secondly from Lacan.

THE LOGOCENTRIC SUBJECT

My discussion so far has summarized the elements which from the point of view of the present crises – of modernity, of identity, of political strategy – enable us to reconstruct a genealogy of the modern subject. I will attend to two moments of this genealogy: the birth of the modern subject and its anxious problematization, and protracted demise in our own times.

The logocentric subject is a category which appears at the centre of a tripartite system, acting as origin of the system, axed between a concept of writing which dissimulates its history in its production, a metaphysics which 'assigns to the logos the origin of truth in general',[16] and the concept of science as the possibility of a demarcation within knowledge which validates the privilege of the logos. Its development from the Greek discourse of being passes through medieval theology when its intelligibility is anchored to the notion of an absolute logos: 'In medieval theology, this absolute logos was an infinite creative subjectivity: the intelligible face of the sign is fixed upon the verb and the face of God'.[17]

I shall clarify this enigmatic statement by referring to Foucault's argument that in medieval thought no difference was made between the visible markings or signatures which God imprinted on the surface of things and the writings, illuminated by a divine light, preserved in scriptural and ancient texts which transmit their inner secrets: 'Everywhere there is but the same play, that of the sign and of similitude, and this is why nature and the verb can refer to each other indefinitely, constituting for those able to decipher it a kind of unique great text'.[18]

The subject of this knowledge derived its authority not from something like Reason, founded in the principles of mind, guided by the protocols of a method, but by reference to a revelatory discourse, whose authenticity transcended the human subject, and to a practice of reading validated by a hermeneutic tradition. It is the presence of the divine, activated by grace, that guaranteed truth and the possibility of knowledge.

My focus falls on the moment of the decisive break in the history of this concept of the subject which occurs with the birth of modernity, when there emerges 'at the same time as the science of nature, the determination of absolute presence as self-presence, as subjectivity'.[19] The denial of difference which this metaphysics of presence operates leads me to begin with the thematic of 'différance' and its implications for conceptualizing subjectivity and epistemology.

'Différance' in Derrida is a term which is used in order to rethink the founding oppositions in Western philosophy and operate a disengagement from them: for example, the difference between speech and writing, or between absence and presence inscribed in the sign. The sign represents the present in its absence: it takes its place; the sign emerges because of the detour forced by the impasse of presenting the thing which is signalled through it. The logic of this argument suggests that one can understand the sign as deferred presence, with the implication that signification is caught in the constant movement of the sign towards the deferred presence which it seeks to reappropriate, yet from which it must intrinsically differ. Thus, 'différance' can be thought as 'the movement according to which language, or any code, any system of referral in general, is constituted historically as a weave of differences'.[20]

Furthermore, 'différance' implicates spacing and temporalization, for, in the movement of signification which it makes possible 'each so-called "present" element, each element appearing on the scene of presence, is related to something other than itself, thereby keeping within itself the mark of the past element, and already letting itself be vitiated by the mark of its relation to the future element'.[21] The trace of history, it seems, inescapably leaves its mark on every statement. We need to work out how this happens. Since the speaking subject is inscribed in language, which itself is a system of difference, this means that the movement of signification and the movement of subjective identity are not only homologous but refer to each other in a constitutive compact. The historicity of both processes is something which foregrounds my analysis of this convergence.

The interesting connections Derrida makes between trace, 'différance' and subjective, psychic economy point the way to the manner in which the constitution of subjects and the process of signification are interwoven.

Trace (*Spur*) and *frayage* (*Bahnung*) – or the breaking of pathways – are indissolubly tied to 'différance'.[22] Derrida argues that differences in the production of unconscious traces can be interpreted as moments of 'différance'. The threat of loss or of dangerous investments is avoided through the breaking of pathways which, by a detour, defers them in an economy of 'différance' whereby they take the guise of something different. Thus it is that for the elements in the (Freudian) unconscious, 'one is but the other different and deferred, one differing and deferring the other . . . one is the "différance" of the other'.[23]

I have chosen to juxtapose these statements about psychic economy with the discussion of the process of signification because they provide the basis for thinking how the two can be correlated, precisely through Derrida's concept of 'différance', or, more generally, through a conceptualization of language. Lacan's claim that the unconscious is structured like a language motivates my juxtaposition. Equally, my exposition is guided by the view that signifying practice is intrinsically intersubjective and dialogical, that is to say, it belongs to the cultural and not the individual order. This is in contrast with the position underlying Cartesianism and logocentrism which prioritizes a self-centred subject, proclaims its unity and coherence to be self-evident and desires the abolition of an alterity of being that threatens the subject's insecure privilege as centre, as presence.

The concept of 'différance' helps to keep visible our relationship with that which we misrecognize. It overcomes the simple opposition of presence and absence through a play which ensures neither the irreparable loss of presence nor the instauration of pure presence. It is a play of alterity, 'to which Freud gives the metaphysical name of the unconscious',[24] which intrinsically escapes representation. However, 'The unconscious is not . . . a hidden, virtual or potential self-presence . . . it is woven of difference . . . it sends out delegates, representatives, proxies'.[25]

What Derrida has to say implies that identity is built on an ever-shifting, intractable chaos of psychic forces and their (libidinal)[26] representatives, a state of being which constantly threatens the fixity and stability of the subject. The temptation has always been to arrest the instability of the subject and of the sign through a metaphysics of presence, as in logocentrism, or through any device which enfolds difference into the

38

same. For logocentrism, this is achieved by founding presence in a return to itself, by establishing self-presence as the presuppositionless ground upon which being is constituted. The effect is to fix the subject in a definite position – as origin of history and meaning – or indeed as the teleological end of history which, in accomplishing the becoming of the logocentric subject, confirms its essential identity as, for example, in the Hegelian solution. Such an ontology of presence must seek to erase the trace of the other through the kind of epistemic violence Spivak has described, or through the dangerous antinomies of the supplement. The functioning of the other – the colonized – as supplement and the epistemic violence involved in this discursive stratagem will be addressed below.

What Derrida describes as the indifference of Western philosophy to 'différance' has important implications from the point of view of subjectivity, otherness and the historicity of the modern subject. Referring to Heidegger's discussion of the closure which is secured by the ontology of Being upon which logocentrism is founded, Derrida points out that this closure is achieved through the systematic forgetting of the trace which ensures that 'This trace quickly vanishes in the destiny of Being which unfolds in world history as Western metaphysics'.[27]

Furthermore, there is a drift in Derrida's elaboration of Heidegger which enables me to connect trace and 'différance' with the need for critique to recover the distinction between Being and beings, essence and existence, which a philosophy of presence suppresses in this act of forgetting. Such a recovery is possible because this distinction, which pluralizes the mode of existence of subjects, has left its trace in human history. It is not just on the basis of the 'alliance of speech and Being'[28] that this recovery is possible, through, for example, deconstructive analysis. Equally important is the fact that, for the other, difference and the memory of difference are lived in the everyday, for the trace of the making and the marks of difference have become engraved in cultural pathways, working at the level of the collective and the individual in systems of representations and practices of everyday life. We can examine this at two levels: first, that of the differentiations that operate as part of the strategies of disciplining and regulation which a dominating and normative power constructs; second, the differences which belong to the 'clandestine forms taken by the dispersed, tactical, and make-shift creativity of groups or individuals already caught in the nets of "discipline" . . . the procedures and ruses . . . deviousness, fantasy, or laughter',[29] which the 'subaltern' and the 'other' invent to deflect, displace, survive or oppose oppression.

We could for example, relate both 'history from below' and narrative practices in certain texts of the other to the process of recovery and reactivation of the elements which are excluded and marginalized in the normative plays of power. I am thinking here of the discursive devices and topos in Afro-American and African fiction which are rooted in the storytelling, the style, the tropes, the narratives which both mark a difference from dominant 'white' texts and revoke the names of unbelonging to which 'non-white' identities are banished.[30]

I have been arguing up to this point that the illusion of the self-centred subject is produced by a kind of short-circuit operated by shunting self-presence onto the idea of an ontologically prior Other who guarantees the subject's presence to itself. The discursive stratagem of logocentric discourse displaces and subsumes the constituting reality of others for subjects in the transcendent signifier Other/God. This God is imagined as the projected plenitude of being, at once origin, perfect form of the 'for-itself' and transcending finitude and death. It follows that the same move opens up the gap between the subject and its (transcendent) Other; it introduces an ontological difference measured by the irreducible void between the human being and that conceptualization of God. Thus, the metaphysics of presence hides, and by the same token, reveals the logocentric subject to be the subject of lack, the less than perfect, less than full, lacking plenitude. Indeed, what the logocentric subject lacks is the Other. This point finds support in the view that the critique of logocentrism, as Derrida has remarked, is the 'search for the "other"'.[31]

The Christian deviation has been to pin lack onto human error in the notion of sin and so inaugurate the thematics of imperfection, guilt and of (possible) redemption. It also inaugurates 'History', with a beginning, a process of unfolding and an end: the second coming, or else the path to a collective regaining of paradise, in which unity of the one with the other finally becomes possible. In philosophy, this theme takes the form of the problem of the unity with the One/Other – which is also the moment of identity of subject and object, a theme whose development and mystifications are charted in the (mis)adventures of the dialectic. Additionally, through the Church, Christian religion institutes the idea of a pastoral power, variously transformed in the modern era, as Foucault has argued.

Already, therefore, alongside the beginnings of European colonial expansion, an ontology of being emerges, tied to the metaphysics of presence attempting the reconciliation of the insufficiency of the human being in relation to a transcendent God, the reconciliation of the emergent notion of being as a totality and as a freedom with the requirement (for judgement) that there be principles underlying such a notion whose foundations are guaranteed outside the space and time of beings.[32] Renaissance humanism is caught in this problematic of the subject, inventing adjustments for the ethical and the epistemic subject, namely, by granting it a free will shepherded by Reason, yet retaining the foundation in Christian doctrine, privileging God as origin, truth and the good. Free-will burdens the subject of lack with a relative autonomy which intensifies the angst of being without resolving the question of self-presence and responsibility for speaking the truth of being.

What circumstances and what reasons combine to make such a fraught narrative of being appear compelling and soon become dominant? What transformations convert the anxieties and doubts of a Montaigne into the assertions of Descartes and, later, the certainties of Locke?

The answer at first takes us to Descartes and the way in which he resolves the dilemma by founding the subject on itself through a doubling which effaces difference: a classic sleight of hand much disapproved of since.

The Cartesian subject, exemplar of the logocentric subject, is established through a discursive stratagem which abolishes the movement of 'différance' in the constitution of the subject by erasing the space of difference between the subject and the other. This is achieved through the specular identity of the subject of knowledge with the subject of existence given in the principle: I think therefore I am. The Cartesian solution collapses the space between essence (the space of Being) and existence (the space of beings) in a presence ('I think') which is present to itself, that is, a self-presence, underwritten by God.

The (suppressed) other is conceptualized as absence, as non-presence, in other words, a non-subject, precisely in order for the logocentric subject who is positioned as its polar opposite to appear as presence. The self-presence of this subject is affirmed only by virtue of the other imagined as lack, as the subject deferred (because of so-called 'primitive rationality', 'backwardness', 'underdevelopment', and so on).

A crucial feature of the discourse is the way the Cartesian subject doubles as the modern epistemic subject by way of the functioning of reason in it. Reason comes to confirm the reality and worldliness of the subject by its identity with mind and the privilege and power which mind claims over matter. This is enshrined in the epistemological break in the emergence of modern science and mechanical philosophy whereby physical causality is replaced by rational necessity as the conceptual basis for understanding nature and indeed for the form of scientific explanation and of truth generally.[33] These shifts inaugurate a conceptual framework characterizing the modern episteme; they validate the universalizing implications of logocentrism and support its project of subjugation and domination. That this theory functions as a mythologizing subterfuge in Descartes and in postCartesian discourse finds support from Derrida who refers to 'the white mythology which reassembles and reflects the culture of the West: the white man takes his own mythology ... his own logos, that is, the mythos of his idiom for the universal form that he must still wish to call Reason'.[34]

Of course, the reason of the other, an other rationality, would seriously undermine the logocentric subject for it would pluralize or relativize the concept of rationality and thus reintroduce an irreducible difference inside the epistemological foundation. This is inconceivable within logocentrism. The only alternative is to exclude the possibility of other rationalities and knowledges, except as inferior to the Western form which functions as the norm. Within this logic, other forms necessarily appear to be primitive, regressive, feminine – at the very least erratic and deviant. In this way the disruptive reality of the difference of the other's otherness can be tamed by bringing it within the curve of normalizing discourses and the frame of technologies of regulation which define what they exclude to be a form of the normative subjectivity, aberrant certainly, but knowable and containable.

Thus, an effect of the discourse of self-centredness is the urge to reduce the other to the same, for example, by reconceptualizing the relation to the other within the framework of an abstract relation of, ideally, equally rational free subjects. Such a proposition makes possible all the forms of exclusion which it has historically engendered, namely of all those deemed to fall outside acceptable limits of the norm. An obvious example is the legitimation of colonial administration on the basis of the argument that the 'native' populations were not 'ready' for democratic forms of self-government.

It is clear, too, that this problematic of the subject is eminently compatible with the abstract subject of capitalist exchange and the legal subject of rights. It is allied to individualism in all its forms. It works precisely by suppressing its relation to the other; it imagines a universe in which all would be equally 'free' and equally 'in command'. As such, it is rooted in an intrinsic fallacy.

This problematic is sustained only by a process of disavowal and projection, psychically and discursively worked out through the introjection of the other into the general form of the ego and the projection of lack onto the other as site of otherness. The other is necessarily seen as imperfection: irrational, savage, immoral. In the context of colonialism, the other becomes the site of redemption: the taming of error in oneself lived through a projection which takes the form of a project elsewhere, namely, the notion of the civilizing-cum-Christianizing mission of 'Western man'. The other is the scene where the subject writes its history and 'History'.

Descartes' solution to the philosophical anxieties about the modern individual thus needed colonialism as a condition, since the New World made possible the material solution to the dilemma of the not-quite-subject of Renaissance humanism and the erasures operated by self-centred philosophies. The colonized becomes the object through which Western 'man' absolves and resolves himself. The conquest and mastery of otherness binds the one and the other, unites being into humanity. Violence is intrinsic to this project, epistemic (Derrida, Spivak), ontological (Levinas) and psychic (Fanon), adding to the brutality of conquest; together they collude to bend the other to that project. Western imperialism is the expression of this subjugative and subjectifying enterprise. It functions as proof of the power, righteousness and authority of the Western modern subject. Thus violence is not merely a contingent feature of Western civilization. It is, rather, its unspeakable dynamic.

What we have, then, is a unique historical conjuncture out of which emerged the specific conceptualization of otherness tied to the particular form of logocentrism elaborated with the beginning of modernity. The same conjuncture inaugurates the project of history as a history of progress and the project of the subject as the (rational) agent of that history. The building of empires of one kind or another is one way in which that project is given material expression. From the earliest moment of modernity, the destiny of Europe and that of its others become inextricably bound. More than this: the very process by which we become modern human subjects, Western or otherwise, has become enmeshed in that history.[35]

THE SUBJECT OF LACK: READING LACAN

Lacan's work has come to inform, directly or indirectly, the post-structuralist critiques of the certainties which had grown with the era of the triumph of the 'West' and the successes of the project of modernity. My reason for turning to him is not so much because of this recognition; rather, it is because of those things in this work which have not been sufficiently stressed and which support my analysis. For here is a theory of the subject which emphasizes the primacy of culture and language, of history and the space of intersubjectivity in the process of our formation, a theory, which, besides, anchors these elements in the soil of the philosophy of being and of subject-centredness elaborated in Western thought. Lacan ventures the idea that the subject belonging to the ego's era 'lives a lie'; this implies that there is a delusion at the heart of the subject imagining itself to be the constitutive sign of history, a subject who thereby misrecognizes its own and universal history.

I have suggested, established elsewhere,[36] the extent to which his theoretical project implicates the (im)possibility of the Cartesian subject, pointing out the references in his work which signal the modernity of that concept in its diverse manifestations: 'being-for itself', 'interior man', the Heideggerian self, and so on. Here I will simply underline those key elements of the Lacanian problematic that enable me to open up the question of identity and of otherness from the point of view of resistance and transformation. If the logocentric subject as well as its other are effects of specific discourses and practices, (the former appearing as origin of discourse through the 'metalepsis' described by Spivak),[37] then the demonstration of the historicity of that subject and its fractures participates in '. . . the intervention into those justifications of modernity – progress, homogeneity, cultural organicism, the deep nation, the long past – that rationalise the authoritarian, "normalising" tendencies within cultures in the name of the national interest or the ethnic prerogative'.[38]

That Lacan was centrally dealing with the problem of the subject which has appeared in philosophy since the end of feudalism is clear from the intertextual allusions in the *Discours de Rome* and his earlier essay on the mirror stage.[39] These texts both marked his break with orthodox Freudianism and aligned the psychoanalytic problematic of the self with the philosophical narrative of the subject which charts the will to recover for it the possibility of a plenitude, whether as a historical project of becoming or the Dionysian will for self-creation.

The difference which marks Lacan's interrogation of the 'philosophy of the subject' is that it reformulates the problem in terms of the psychic reality of the subject, which for psychoanalysis is inscribed in the domain of 'concrete discourse insofar as this is the field of the transindividual reality of the subject'.[40] Furthermore, psychoanalytic operations are those of history, not only because 'history . . . constitutes the emergence of truth in the real',[41] but equally because 'Events are engendered in a primary historicization, in other words, history is made on the stage where it is enacted once it has been written, deep inside oneself as much as outside the subject'.[42] In a very real sense history provides the stage upon which the subject appears. Indeed, 'it is history that we teach the subject to recognise as his unconscious',[43] an unconscious which, remember, 'is the discourse of the other'.[44] Three terms, as we see, have appeared which describe the co-ordinates of the subject: history, inter-subjective world, signification. Their interrelationship is revealed if we write that the historicity of the event and of subjectivity are woven together by means of the process of signification. Signifying practice itself is, as semiotic theory has taught us, mobile in relation to the temporal and spatial dimensions of intersubjectivity. In Lacan's formulation, the historical theory of the symbol, together with 'intersubjective logic and temporality of the subject', bind the subject's psychoanalytic experience.[45]

The signs in Lacan's text already point towards the territory of the phenomenology of being, in particular, Husserl's and Heidegger's attempts to reawaken for philosophy the ontology of *Dasein* – presence, the being-thereness of Being – which Heidegger argues is the essential omission in Descartes, and the measure of the Cartesian failure. What Heidegger restores to ontology is the (medieval) 'problematic of temporality' which treated 'the meaning of Being as . . . "presence"'.[46] Critique can then proceed to overcome the 'ontological tradition' as a way of bringing about the 'true concreteness of Being'.[47] In the same section he defines 'man's Being ... as that living thing whose Being is essentially determined by the potentiality for discourse.'[48] The resonances with Lacan – his emphasis on discourse, on the concreteness of the body, on the temporal dimension of subjectivity – are instructive.

One last remark to complete this brief excursion into Being and Time prompted by Lacan's textual intimations: Heidegger argues that the point of view of phenomenology forbids us from assuming the givenness of the 'I'. It demonstrates that 'a bare subject without a world never "is" proximally, nor is it ever given. And so in the end an isolated "I" without Others is just as far from being proximally given'.[49] If we connect the primacy of discourse with the primacy of the relation to the other within the narrative of being to which Lacan alludes, it becomes clear that Lacan follows Heidegger closely when he founds intersubjectivity in the symbolic relationship, and in the order of culture. The implication is that the Lacanian approach is indeed subversive of any theory of self-centred subjectivity, such as classical logocentrism. Additionally, the claim that the unconscious is the discourse of the other acquires its decisive importance from the point of view of rethinking otherness, as I shall discuss.

First I want to return to the tripartite relationship between the real, the symbolic and the imaginary in order to disaggregate some of the mechanisms at work, especially with regard to the emergence of the 'I' and the relation to the other. For Lacan, the imaginary, the symbolic and the 'lived' reality co-exist and intersect in the subject, but the latter can occupy the position of the 'I' only through the symbolic. However, this is not the case of a cogito, transcendent or otherwise, asserting its autonomous existence, for we are all from the beginning captured in the domain of the symbolic; it is only because of the specular relation to the Other in the stage of formation of the imago that the illusion of constitutive consciousness arise. Recognition in the mirror stage is not that of a previously constituted subject but is itself 'the transformation produced in the subject when it assumes an imago'.[50] This 'dialectic of intersubjectivity' occurs by way of the lack or 'béance' structuring the specular relation to the Other, the gap in which speech becomes inserted 'between the anteriority of the Subject and the beyond of the Other'.[51]

Since this takes place prior to identification with the other through objectification and the positioning of the subject in language, the process implicates primary alienation in the foundation of the subject, instanced in the splitting which opens up difference and lack, yet is the gap into which the subject becomes lodged. The process places out of reach the experience of primary formation. The subject, barred from entry into the place of the lost object, embarks on the search for 'the part of himself, lost forever, that is constituted by the fact that he is only a sexed living being, and that he is no longer immortal'.[52]

So, now a fourth term claims our attention, that of desire. This, as we know, is a ubiquitous and elusive term, open to every kind of investment, lodged in the cleft between need and demand, and charged with the force of the original loss. In the analysis of colonial discourse, as in the exploration of gender difference and sexuality, desire has become a central, if often vague, concept. This is because desire, as Lacan has often stated, is the desire of the other. Let us clarify this.

Lacan's problematic of desire appears in some respects to be faithful to Hegel's thought, or rather to Kojeve's interpretation whose translation of the *Phenomenology* makes clear that human 'desire . . . is the desire of the other'.[53] Its aim ultimately is recognition by the other, as a desired other in the play of desire for reciprocal recognition; indeed, 'human history is the history of desired Desires'.[54]

It is important to note the revision of Hegel which Lacan operates in his discussion of desire. For desire in Hegel belongs to the dialectic of master-slave in the emergence and realization of consciousness as self-consciousness and as history. In Lacan's system, desire is located inside the process of identification and the subsequent vicissitudes of the self arising from the specular structure of identification which, as I noted, is one of recognition/misrecognition, that is, a structure in which lack and splitting drives the infant to fill the void with the imaginary autonomy of the subject. In the economy of *jouissance*, of the sublime phantasy of plenitude in the relation to the Other, the latter is no longer the figure of the master but that of the lost object of (primary) identification.

Lacan's explanation of the dialectic of desire does indeed start with a reference to the *Phenomenology*, but this is a discursive tactic which signals the different terrain that provides the conceptual elements for operating a distance from the ground of 'ego psychology' as well as from the logicism of the *Aufhebung* (supercession). He instead highlights the relation to knowledge in the location of the subject, pointing out that it is in Hegel that desire is granted the responsibility for maintaining the link between the subject and 'the primal [*antique*] knowledge, to enable truth to be immanent to the realisation of knowledge [*savoir*]. The ruse of reason is to imply that the subject from the beginning and to the end knows what it wants'.[55] The crucial thing about psychoanalytic discourse is that Freud reopens 'the join between truth and knowledge' precisely because this is the place where 'desire binds itself to the desire of the Other, but within that knot dwells the desire to know'.[56]

The Lacanian narrative leads one to this interesting point where one can connect the will to know with the economy of desire and the relation to the other within the process of becoming of the subject, which is also the process of the realization of the 'truth' of the subject. That the question of power is interior to this system is a central point, relevant to the examination of the historicity of the subject from the point of view of the imperial project of modernity.

Let us go back to the hypothesis of an initial loss and separation, of splitting, in the emergence of the 'I', to the claim that there is primary alienation in the foundation of the subject whence desire becomes desire for the other. The account involves something else which is relevant to the history of otherness, namely, misrecognition and the related opacity of the signs of our formation.[57]

This passage of Lacan will provide an entry:

> If it is merely at the level of the desire of the Other that man can recognize his desire, as desire of the Other, is there not something here that must appear to him to be an obstacle to his fading, which is a point at which his desire can never be recognized? This obstacle is never lifted, nor ever to be lifted, for analytic experience shows us that it is in seeing a whole chain come into play at the level of the desire of the Other that the subject's desire is constituted.[58]

What is this whole chain? Does it belong to the 'symbolic matrix'[59] to which the 'I' rushes, and can one not propose that it links into language as the semiotic system that threads the chain into the fabric of culture?

One of the enigmatic statements of Lacan will help me develop the question, namely, when he says 'there can be no *fort* without *da*, one might say, without *dasein*'.[60] One could at first sight read this to mean no presence without absence; the addition of *dasein*, however, turns our thought away from any play of simple polarity toward a working out of *fort* and *da* through another term, the bobbin or as Lacan adds further on, the object 'a', the first in a whole chain of signifiers which writes the history of that working out, and thus also the experiential history of our becoming as specific subjects. It is impossible not to invoke 'différance' when we think about this process of the proliferation and doubling of signs, that is, a conceptualization of the signifying process as one that defers as it differs meaning: a dissemination. Furthermore, the proposition that the unconscious is structured like a language suggests that the imaginary and the symbolic matrix are constructed according to the economy of 'différance'. It is possible to imagine two signifying chains, the one curled round the other, formally homologous yet analytically distinct; one would form the system unconscious/ conscious and the other would refer to the 'individual' subject/culture system.[61] Indeed, I want to propose that it is the specific function of ideology to knit the one into the other.[62] I am tempted to think of the chain and its generation according to the model of the double helix, one element of the system spiralling around the other, linked to it by signifiers acting as '*points' de capiton*, effecting suture. We are all doubly inscribed. In this manner are constituted the 'monuments'[63] which the psychoanalytic experience seeks to recover or retrace.[64]

We can begin to glimpse in the light of what I have said the outline of the apparatus that enables us to connect desire, history and subjectivity in a constitutive compact, an apparatus which has some purchase for examining the (post)colonial subject and otherness generally. I want to draw several provisional conclusions in order to 'signpost' the terrain upon which a new problematic of subjectivity and identity can be constructed.

To start with, the illusion of a constitutive autonomous consciousness arises from the process of specular misrecognition. It could be argued that although the terms which describe the condition of the autonomous subject, like lack and angst, are the signs which appear in the gap opened up by the relation of difference, they become the signs of aggressivity and 'ressentiment' when we try to understand our experiences and ourselves by objectifying the other and centring everything onto the 'I' of narcissism.[65] The thought that beckons is that it is the suppression and denial of the difference of the other in a play of identity and repetition that produces, as effect, both the mirage of the autonomous self and the lack of being which only the recognition of the being of the other can abolish: one is but the 'différance' of the 'other'. The other is the degree zero of desire, measuring its limit and its liminality. It reappears in the 'defiles of the signifier' as the uncanny figure of the supplement shadowing our every move, the pale double banished from presence, yet psyching it out.

It may be too that castration is but the name for the split from and the misrecognition of the Other in the imaginary which opens up entry into culture, with all that is bundled up in this process of individuation – for example, disavowal and its consequences, and separation from our objects of desire and from those on whom our identity depends.

Second, entry into culture – precisely like original sin – is lived as a loss, a fall from plenitude which inaugurates a journey in search either of its recovery or its sublation. One could argue that the will to assert selfhood against the other, or as a difference from others, produces insecure, anxious subjects, for whom the insistent reality of dependencies comes to be invested in the substitutes that embody the displaced objects for the taming and binding of anxiety. Obsession and aggression, once again, are inherent in this process of emergence of the 'I' of the logocentric, self-referential, 'autonomous' subject, namely in the form of mastery (of oneself and others) and in a form of control founded in an instrumental rationality.

In the era of empire, it was possible for this would-be master of the universe to tame or else to invest the wild and the excessive forces unbound in the process of our formation by boldly going where no (white) man had gone before, to that other place where every phantasy could be lived out, as if in a dream, without threatening the stability of the ego. The ambivalence intrinsic to the discourse of logocentrism (and masculinism) is mirrored in the different strategies of self-realization and mastery of the subject which seek either to bring the chaos of these forces under control, to civilize and contain them within the bounds of the knowable and the known, or to assuage them within the libidinal but 'safe' – because objectified – space of otherness.

The tropes of desire are displaced through the projection of the subject's sensuous being onto the other as the being bounded by all that this subject must cast out and repress to remain within logocentrism or 'masculinism' at all. The other, as the site of projection, becomes the embodiment of the 'negative' qualities, the body to be conquered and tamed, the place of contamination and of the threatening return of the repressed.

Edward Said has amply demonstrated this in his analysis of the reality of the colonial presence in the 'Orient', while Catherine Hall's excavation of the story of Governor Eyre provides another interesting case, charting the ambivalences of space, time and identity for those (Europeans) caught up in the masterly discourse of empire.[66] The literature of the empire is full of examples of how failure to pacify the heart of darkness resulted in madness or 'going native', the apocalypse of the white Western male subject.[67]

Third, the question of power finds a point of entry in the theme I have just introduced. One narrative of power has its canonical expression in the Hegelian master–slave dialectic. Its many variants circulate in a diversity of discourses, though most do not appear to acknowledge the ironic implications drawn by Hegel, namely, that the recognition of the master as master is given by one – the slave – whose gaze is not the desired gaze and thus has no value for the unhappy consciousness of the master. The master–slave metaphor recurs in a wide range of analyses of colonial identity and colonial discourse – in Fanon for instance – but its ambivalent connotations mean that it is fraught with misunderstandings, while remaining bounded by the problematic of consciousness-for-itself. Nietzsche, interestingly, consigns the effort to resolve the contradictions while remaining within the narrative limits of this problematic to the 'misfortunes of consciousness', a consciousness mortgaged to the sorrow of 'ressentiment', its will blunted by the negative.[68] But, if we reject the philosophy of presence, is there no escape from the overman, that is, from the Dionysian project born from the wilful affirmation of the being of becoming, chancing its destiny beyond the grasp of the other?

The question I will address is whether there is something anterior to the economy of conflictual subjectivity[69] which, when taken into account, provides further means to deconstruct the problematic of the subject tied to the oppressive ontology of the Same and the One, of identity and repetition. I shall discuss this by considering what has been called 'the psychical phantasy of woman', that is to say, the doubling of the trope of woman in the (male) imaginary whereby she is split between the good and the bad woman/object or, in another register, the madonna and whore.

Teresa Brennan's interesting discussion[70] points out that cross-cultural evidence indicates that this dual idealization and denigration of woman is Western rather than universal, in spite of Lacan's implication that it is a universal feature of our entry into the symbolic order. The point is that the psychical phantasy of woman resolves the existential anxiety of lack in being, providing (negative) objects for projecting the ego's fear of the other – implicit in the master–slave dialectic – and for securing the stability of the autonomous subject, in an idealized other who grounds the truth of being. The dynamics of the process suggest that the urge to pacify, control, objectify and dominate the 'bad' object and its metonymies and the correlated wish to give oneself over to the idealized (loved?) object belong to the same economy of identification and desire.

Brennan attempts to bind together the psychical phantasy of woman and the additional anxieties which accompanied the emergence of the ego's era. These, according to Lacan, arose from the contracting physical space in which the urban environment (typical of emergent modernity) constricts the individual, resulting in increased aggressivity due to increased pressures on the spatial dimension of the ego and its ability to contain demands originating from others. The result is a greater territorial imperative, expressed in the will to dominate and in the reduction of difference to an already knowable sameness. The necessary counterparts of this feature of modernity are the economic and technological supplements, in the form of modern rational capitalism and the objectifying instrumental rationality of science.[71]

Brennan, drawing from Lacan, highlights the connection between the territorializing imperative of capitalism, colonial expansion, the totalizing gaze of instrumental reason and the 'white, Western masculine culture in which the [ego's] era originates'.[72] She argues that, within such a perspective, the psychical phantasy of woman participates in both the territorializing impulse of the West and acts as a trigger for social psychosis. I have located this, additionally, in the logic of logocentrism. The two establish a double-bind for the subject.

The story of the working out of the fractures of the autonomous subject is spun out in the vacillation between identification with the other, and disavowal of dependency and desire in the face of the dissolution of the ego implicated in identity with the other. This is what is partly theorized by the psychical phantasy of woman.

My analysis is consistent with the Lacanian account of subjectivity; psychosis, there, arises from the view that modern 'man' has managed to invent the means 'to forget his existence and his death'[73] but at a cost, for it paid out in the form of 'the most profound alienation of the subject of scientific civilisation', expressed in the paradox of the subject who has acquired the power to name the world, yet 'loses his meaning in the objectivisations of discourse'.[74] And so the evasions of the ego and the delusion of autonomy of the subject are played out in the stratagems of pacification and control. But these merely draw a veil over a culture of narcissism haunted by Thanatos.

That this destiny belongs to the fundamental mechanisms of subject formation becomes clear when we remember that the signifying process at the level of the unconscious and of consciousness are homologous and form part of the same economy of desire. The argument that the subject is a doubly inscribed historical being, once at the level of formation of the unconscious – the specificity of early 'lived' experiences organized within the signifying economy of 'différance' and primary identification, and somatically marked – and again in relation to the biography of the constituted self as it encounters specific cultural signs that become pinned onto the first system – means that the ambivalences and fractures interior to the process of our entry into culture in the place occupied by 'I' are necessarily mirrored in the vicissitudes of the subject. This view adds to and makes sense of how the solution to these contradictions which pass through the demand that Logos disowns Mythos inaugurates an age of profound sickness and astonishing triumphs, which in modern times is intensely exemplified in the history of colonialism and empire.

We must remember too that the body and sexuality are inextricably enmeshed at every level of the process. For a man in a 'patriarchal' culture identification passes through the symbolic token of power, namely, the phallus, not, however, by reference to its presence – it only exists in the gap of lack in being, its presence is always deferred, since the phallus is the mark of desire – but to its absence and thus to who lacks it: the woman, and the feminized other of colonial discourse.[75] The implication is that Dionysus ends up playing footsie with Ariadne: it is a sad tale.

THE POETICS OF DIS/ORIENTATION

When we come to analyse concrete historical events, we now need to acknowledge that subject positions exceed the places – gender, class, epistemic, ethnic – allowed in the enunciative positions constructed in totalizing theories. If the subject as centre is an effect sustained in the imaginary representations of self and other, and if the relation to the

51

other is in fact primary and sustaining in the formation of identity, then we can recognize the different belongings into which we are seduced or compelled by the conditions and different temporalities of modernity.

Additionally, the analysis of subjectivity is complicated by the fact that the discourses of power, sexuality, desire, identity and the narratives that reconstruct their relationships and their 'lived' reality establish rhizomic[76] signifying networks that are difficult to disentangle or apprehend because we are all caught up in them in our being.

This means that if we wish to avoid being ensnared within the specular maze of the philosophy of the subject, we need to take the standpoint of the other. This involves the 'affirmative deconstruction' of the texts of colonialism and the reconstitution of a history of resistance to the epistemic and psychic violence of colonialism, through a narrativization of history and a 're-memory'[77] that repairs the place and the space of otherness.

In this way, we engage with the conceptualization of the process of subjectification in the ego's era as a process constituting both colonizer and colonized, the Occidental and its others as subjects belonging together but differently to modernity.

The making of difference in the context of colonial subjugation is marked by a process of distortion, displacement and repetition that must be understood against the repressed knowledge of the violence of subjugation. Repression in the colonial instance motivated the displacement of this knowledge in the narrative of representation of the colonizer such that colonial presence appears split between its representation as original and authoritative and its articulation in forms of repetition and difference.[78] This is exemplified in the practice of history and narrative in the implantation of the Bible and English language in India in the nineteenth century,[79] which Homi Bhabha[80] makes visible through his interrogation of the texts, putting to work the Freudian concept of *Entstellung* – distortion as in the dreamwork. The term, as Lyotard reminds us,[81] is charged with the force of repression and desire at work in the dreamwork, and thus with the violence of censorship and the wish.

In colonial discourse what is repressed in the other scene of the stereotype of the colonized is invested in the tropes of savagery, anarchy, lust. They become the elements that construct the signs of both identification and alienation, desire and fear for colonizer and colonized. Bhabha[82] has analysed the play of recognition and disavowal of cultural and racial difference in terms of the stereotype functioning as fetish, that is to say, he explains how it works to effect a closure in the space of the representation of difference.

Bhabha argues that the disavowal of difference in the midst of its reality in the stratagems of colonial power produces ambivalence. What is disavowed is not repressed 'but repeated as something different – a mutation, a hybrid'.[83] Hybridity, however, is a 'metonymy of presence';[84] it 'terrorises authority with the ruse of recognition, its mimicry'.[85] Thus, mimicry is both 'resemblance and menace';[86] it produces a caricatured image of the colonizer which disturbs and disrupts the unitary gaze of surveillance in the exercise of power. The hybridity it produces repeats differently, it returns a gaze which resists subjugation, and so undermines colonial authority by participating in the 'strategic reversal of the process of domination'.[87]

It is possible, then, to understand a response such as mimicry as a mode of appropriation of colonial authority whereby the colonized or subaltern camouflages his or her resistance in the guise of an elusive sameness. It is here a tactic of power intrinsic to antagonistic relations within an agonistic space of signification.

Power, besides, is seductive, inducing and promising pleasures so that the masquerade of mimicry can equally be a veiled homage, a demand for recognition in the return gaze of the powerful. This scene, however, is ever open to the frustrations of mistaken identity. For there is this other specular misrecognition whereby the gaze of the colonized is fixed upon and transfixed by the imagined and desired identification with the other. It is only the reality, the presence of the other's challenging gaze – what are you staring at me for? – which interrupts the play of identification in the imaginary, introducing the alterity of power and provoking the violence of thwarted plenitude. Let us explore this through Lacan and Fanon.

Lacan's discussion of the basis of the subject's frustration relates it to the triadic binds of frustration, aggression, regression, and more interestingly, to the theme of the empty word and the full word, the theme that returns us to the duality of *béance* and *jouissance*, that is, to the experience of lack or void and to the desired plenitude of being. Lacan, we know, was speaking about the silence of the analyst emptying out the discourse of the subject, but, does not a similar silence confront the (ex)colonized when his or her Westernized discourse, seeking recognition from the knowing gaze of the (ex)colonizer, fails to find confirmation there and meets instead the equivocation of the 'not-quite' of hybridity? The colonized subjectivity disappears into the *béance* that measures the enormity of his or her dispossession, a double dispossession since there is, in any case, no adequate reply to the subject's discourse of being: 'We are the hollow men. . .'. Thus every word which participates in the play of misrecognition is added to the disappointment of mistaken identity, and becomes marked as the sign of the other's rejection and the insufficiency, indeed the castration and 'fading',[88] of the colonized as subject.

Here is Lacan's explanation:

Does the subject not become embroiled in an ever-increasing dispossession of that being of his, whereby ... he ends up recognising that that being has never been anything more than this construct in the imaginary and that this construct disappoints all his certainties? For, in the work he does to reconstruct this construct for an other, he finds again the fundamental alienation which made him construct it in the image of an other, and which has always destined it to be stripped from him by an other'.[89]

We can understand why when the mask of 'Westernized' identity is pulled off, self-disgust follows, and violence erupts, as Fanon perceptively described. Fanon argued that in a white world the black man's behaviour is oriented toward 'the Other in the guise of the white man, for the Other alone can give him worth'.[90] Or again: 'the native never ceases to dream of putting himself in the place of the settler ... [but] he is never sure whether or not he has crossed the frontier'.[91] Fanon explains that 'thwarted aggressivity' and the 'accumulated libido' are canalized and worked through in the ecstasy of collective dance or the transformative violence of uprisings. The place of the body as the site of this working out is a fundamental insight which has remained underdeveloped; it is consistent with Fanon's stress on the 'epidermal schema' in the process of formation of subjects, in addition to the Oedipal sexualization of the body. The two, of course, are conjoined, for 'As soon as I desire I am asking to be considered'.[92] I explained earlier how the desire for recognition is charged with the excessive force of primary repression and the lack of being which cries out to be overcome. It is not surprising that Fanon declares that: 'He who is reluctant to recognize me opposes me. In a savage struggle, I am willing to accept convulsions of death, invincible dissolution, but also the possibility of the impossible'.[93]

We know from the history of colonial subjugation and liberation that this is not merely rhetorical violence, for colonial history is a catalogue of excess. Today the new names of that excess, like Angola, Indonesia, Cambodia, South Africa and so many more, extend the list in the name of modernization/Westernization, often acting as a cover for continuing dispossession. In one way or another annihilation, fantasized or not, prowls around the hybrid being produced by colonial discourse and the material conditions of the formation of subject in (post)colonial spaces.

Not all colonized or subordinate subjects are caught to the same degree in these prisms. A subjugating power does not have to invest the whole of the colonial space for its authority or domination to be effective. Often a degree of collusion emerges such that the space is the site of multiple dominations and coercions and 'multiple subjectivities'.

Spivak's example of the double oppression of women, subject to colonial domination and to that of masculinist indigenous cultures, is a case in point.[94]

Resistance finds an anchorage in the places which a territorializing power either leaves untouched or has been unable to subvert. There are several examples one could cite. Guha's counter-narrative of insurrection in India, reconstructed from accounts of the Basarat uprising of 1831 and the Santal rebellion of 1855, and Panday's examination of peasant revolt in the context of the Indian nationalist movement, illustrate the discursive manoeuvres of power and resistance, the dodging and weaving, the tagging from one cultural lifeworld to another whereby struggles are relayed and interconnected, and spaces and identities defended and preserved or altered.[95]

In the urban environment of 'postmodernity', the counterpart of the instabilities threatening identity is the securing of spaces at the margins which counter-cultures can defend from colonization – for example through the play of masquerade and the incessant remaking of these imagined 'homelands', as Stuart Hall and Phil Cohen, amongst others, explore.[96]

Yet we know that for many of the disaffiliated, without a politicization, the burden of an exploitative culture will sap the strength of these spectacular and carnivalesque refusals.

If there are no comforting truths, no new grand narratives[97] to overcome the restlessness that the flaneurs of the diaspora live only too well, what basis informs politicization? If, as Bhabha declares, communities are neither homogenous nor horizontal, but form an interrupted and dispersed world,[98] what foundations are there for unifying projects? Whence this instability? If there is no place that desire may recognize as its lost object, or wilfully appropriate within the orbit of identity, are we repeatedly returned to our 'errances'?[99]

For the moment we are left with the fact that – because the other functions as supplement[100] in the discourse of mastery and domination – 'affirmative deconstruction' and 'restorative genealogy'[101] can contribute to the destabilization of narratives of power and superiority. They do so because, on the one hand, they affirm the agency of the dispossessed in an (unfinished) history of insurgency and resistance and, on the other hand, deconstructive strategies can join with the work of 're-memorization' – that is, the re-narrativization of the monuments that Lacan talks about – to constitute a poetics of dis/orientation. What I have in mind are the kind of textual practices which harbour the liminal presence of the place of desire and the space of the sublime – the co-ordinates of subjectivity and ideology – and which can loosen our certainties and cognitive frames ready for sublative transfiguration in the context of political struggles. They may, thus, be affiliated to other

55

narratives which support counter-ideological discourses and practices for which other subject positions and other options for the future find their conditions of possibility. The critique of the metaphysics of presence, as I noted at the beginning, is a vital part of moving beyond the oppressive and stupendous lifeworld which has provided the soil for its imagined realizations.

NOTES:

1 Jacques Derrida, *L'ecriture et la différence*, Editions du Seuil, Paris, 1967, p.139.

2 I will assume the first form of this subject to be the Cartesian rational being and thus locate modernity from that time, although the conditions which enabled the flowering of the 'man of reason' develop from the fifteenth century.

3 See Jacques Lacan's discussion in *Ecrits II*, Editions du Seuil, Paris, 1971, pp. 161–70, 275ff. Lacan argues that modernity begins with a decisive shift in European culture, marked by the privilege granted to the human being as centre of the new system of understanding and feeling which emerged with modernity. An obsessive concern for oneself and for one's individuality become the passionate emblem of the ego's era. The corollary of this self-centred culture is the neglect of the inter-individual sphere, both from the point of view of the proper recognition of the inter-subjective character of culture and language and the view which asserts, contrarily, that the foundation of understanding and feeling is grounded in the communitarian character of the process of production of knowledge and meaning and not in the notion of a self-sufficient rationality and a unity of being. Indeed, a key argument of the critique of the self-centred subject is that its plausibility rests on an unacknowledged metaphysics, whereby the centredness of the subject is guaranteed by the subject itself by virtue of some transcendent principle, for example the divine attribute (and gift) of reason to 'man'. I explore this 'metaphysics of presence' throughout this paper.

4 See Michel Foucault, *Les mots et les choses*, Editions Gallimard, Paris, 1966, p.398.

5 I refer here to Fredric Jameson's critique of the commodification of culture in which these symptoms are manifest in, for example 'Post-modernism, or the cultural logic of late capitalism', *New Left Review* 146, 1984; and to J.F. Lyotard's examination of the commodification of knowledge in his *The Postmodern Condition. A Report on Knowledge*, Manchester University Press, Manchester, 1984.

6 For examples of this work, see Ranajit Guha and Gayatri Spivak (eds), *Selected Subaltern Studies*, Oxford University Press, Delhi, 1988.

7 Guha, cited by Spivak, in Guha and Spivak, ibid., p.20.

8 Spivak, ibid. pp.19–20. In her discussion, the theoretical misgivings occasioned by the assumption that political action is given its meaning by consciousness and will are weighed against the political gains arising from the recognition of the effectivity and irreducibility of subaltern political activity in determining the course of events. The dangers are not thereby overcome, merely recognized. Furthermore, the problem cannot be divorced from its context in Western intellectual disputes about the category of the subject in humanism and in Marxism. For example, Spivak refers to

Althusser's argument that the concept of process without a subject is Hegelian to point out that the category of process – by implication, the concept of consciousness – is reinscribed differently in First Worldly anti-humanism and in subaltern Marxist historiography: it works to different ends in the two arenas. It seems that it is a matter of different strategic calculations of political effects.

9 G. Spivak, ibid. p.18.
10 Jean-Paul Sartre in Frantz Fanon, *The Wretched of the Earth*, Penguin, Harmondsworth, 1967, p.22.
11 Robert Young, *White Mythologies*, Routledge, London, 1990.
12 Fanon, *The Wretched of the Earth*, p.252.
13 J.F. Lyotard, 'Defining the postmodern', in *ICA Documents* 4, 1986, p.6.
14 Emmanuel Levinas (borrowing E. Husserl's term), in *Collected Papers*, trans. A. Lingis, Martinus Nijhoff Publishers, Dordrecht, 1987, p.50.
15 Jacques Derrida, *De la Grammatologie*, Editions de Minuit, Paris, p.11; and Emmanuel Levinas's analysis of knowledge and appropriation in 'Ethics as first philosophy' in S. Hand (ed.), *The Levinas Reader*, Basil Blackwell, Oxford, 1989, pp.76–86.
16 Derrida, *Grammatologie*, pp.11, 12.
17 Ibid., p.25.
18 Michel Foucault, *Les mots et les choses*, p.49.
19 Derrida, *Grammatologie*, p.29.
20 Derrida, *Margins of Philosophy*, Harvester Press, Brighton, 1986, p.12.
21 Ibid., p.13.
22 See the discussion by Derrida in *L'ecriture et la différence*, pp.298ff.
23 Derrida, *Margins of Philosophy*, p.18.
24 Ibid., p.20.
25 Ibid., pp.20–1.
26 The entry under 'libido' in J. Laplanche and J.B. Pontalis, *The Language of Psychoanalysis*, Hogarth Press, London, 1980, stressed that it is 'an expression ... of those instincts which have to do with all that may be comprised under the word "love"', p.239.
27 Derrida, *Margins*, p.25.
28 Ibid., p.27.
29 M. de Certeau, *The Practice of Everyday Life*, University of California Press, Berkeley and London, 1984, pp.xiv–xvii.
30 For example, the 'signifying monkey', discussed by H.L. Gates Jnr in H.L. Gates (ed.), *Black Literature and Literary Theory*, Methuen, New York and London, 1984.
31 Derrida in R. Kearney, *Dialogues with Contemporary Continental Thinkers*, Manchester University Press, Manchester, 1984, p.123.
32 See Levinas's analysis in *The Ego and the Totality*, in E. Levinas, *Collected Papers*, pp.25–45.
33 For work which establishes this point see Maurice Clavelin, *The Natural Philosophy of Galileo*, MIT Press, Massachusetts, 1974; and my discussion in Couze Venn, 'Beyond the Science–Ideology Relation', unpublished PhD thesis, University of Essex, 1982.
34 Derrida, *Margins*, p.213.
35 I have used the concept of occidentalism to describe this process.
36 C. Venn 'Subjectivity, ideology, difference: recovering otherness', *New Formations* 16, 1992, pp.40–61.
37 See Spivak, *Subaltern Studies*, pp.204–5.
38 Homi Bhabha (ed.), *Nation and Narration*, Routledge, London, 1990, p.4.

39 The 'Discours' was delivered in 1953 and published in 1956 as 'Fonction et champ de la parole et du language en psychanalyse'. It reappears in Ecrits, Editions du Seuil, Paris, 1966. For a classic exegesis of the text, see A. Wilden, *Speech and Language in Psychoanalysis*, Johns Hopkins University Press, Baltimore and London, 1981. Lacan, in his 1949 essay on the mirror stage, starts by pointing to the opposition between his account and any philosophy founded in the Cogito.
40 Lacan, *Ecrits I*, p.134.
41 Ibid., p.135.
42 Ibid., p.138.
43 Ibid., p.139.
44 Ibid., p.143.
45 Ibid., pp.169–70.
46 Martin Heidegger, *Being and Time*, Basil Blackwell, Oxford 1962, p.47.
47 Ibid., p.49.
48 Ibid., p.49.
49 Ibid., p.152.
50 Lacan, *Ecrits I*, p.90.
51 Ibid., p.67.
52 J. Lacan, *The Four Fundamental Concepts of Psycho-analysis*, Penguin, Harmondsworth, 1979, p.205.
53 Alexandre Kojève, *Introduction à la lecture de Hegel*, Gallimard, Paris, 1947, p.13.
54 Ibid., p.13. Note that Hegel's discussion claims that self-consciousness is desire in general. G. Hegel, *Phenomenology of the Spirit*, 1977, trans. A.V. Miller, Oxford University Press, Oxford, p.105 – though 'it is in fact something other than self-consciousness that is the essence of desire', p.109. Importantly desire is conceptualized within the master–slave dialectic.
55 Lacan, *Ecrits II*, p.162.
56 Ibid., p.162.
57 Symbolized by Lacan in the equation by which he suggests that the subject, S, is an unrepresentable, though conceptually intelligible element in the process of signification; *Ecrits II*, p.181.
58 Lacan, *Four Fundamental Concepts*, p.235.
59 Lacan, *Ecrits I*, p.90.
60 Ibid., p.239.
61 Julia Kristeva analysed the signifying process in terms of the semiotic chora and the symbolic, identifying the former with the unconscious level, a difference from the Lacanian model which is fruitful when examining the work of ideology in the formation of subjects: *La revolution du langage poetique*, Editions du Seuil, Paris, 1974.
62 A dual process is at work here, for the knitting or quilting mechanism takes the form of the narration of the subject as a particular 'self' in the symbolic form of language, and, at the same time, transposes the time of the 'self' into the temporality of the community, linking memory and history.
63 Lacan, *Ecrits I*, p.136.
64 Consider, too, Edward Said's point, emphasizing Gramsci's analysis, that an infinity of traces has become deposited in each of us, of which it is imperative that we compile an inventory: *Orientalism*, Routledge and Kegan Paul, London, 1978, p.25.
65 See Gilles Deleuze's discussion of 'ressentiment' in *Nietzsche and Philosophy*, Athlone Press, London, 1983, ch.4; and Lacan's reference to *Beyond Good and Evil* in *Four Fundamental Concepts*, p.241.

66 Catherine Hall, 'Imperial man: Edward Eyre in Australasia and the West Indies, 1833–66', in this volume.
67 See, for example, the discussion of Conrad by Tom Collits, 'Imperialism, marxism, Conrad: a political reading of *Victory*, *Textual Practice* vol.3, no.3, 1989, pp.303–22.
68 See also Deleuze, *Nietzsche and Philosophy*, pp.175–94.
69 The colonial context provides the exemplary case of the agonistic space of subjectivity. We might wish to keep open the question of whether subject formation and identity can occur on the basis of the principle of 'being-for-the-other', which Levinas prioritizes over the concept of 'being-for-itself'.
70 Teresa Brennan, 'History after Lacan', *Economy and Society*, vol.19, no.3, 1990, p.3.
71 It is a position that I develop in *Occidentalism and its Discontents*, New Ethnicities Unit, University of London, London, 1993.
72 Brennan, 'History after Lacan', p.297.
73 Lacan, *Ecrits I*, p.162.
74 Ibid., p.161.
75 Descriptions and representations of the New World emphasized the abundance of the flora and fauna, the natural wealth of the land, the wildness of geography and people which position the New World and its inhabitants as feminine, submissive, available, discovered. See P. Hulme. 'Polytropic Man: tropes of sexuality and mobility in early colonial discourse', in F. Barker, P. Hulme, M. Iverson, D. Loxley (eds), *Europe and its Others. Vol. II*, University of Essex, Colchester, 1985.
76 Gilles Deleuze and Felix Guattari, *Rhizome*, Editions de Minuit, Paris, 1976, p.21. Rhizome is a root-like network, a dispersed and chaotic arrangement that, nevertheless, forms a complex system.
77 Toni Morrison, *Beloved*, Plume, New York, 1987, p.36; Bob Chase. 'History and poststructuralism: Hayden White and Fredric Jameson', in this volume; Venn, 'Subjectivity, ideology, difference'.
78 Bhabha has illuminatingly explored the range of problems invoked in this statement from his earliest work on colonial discourse; in, for example, 'Difference, discrimination and the discourse of colonialism', in F. Barker, P. Hulme, D. Iverson, D. Loxley (eds), *The Politics of Theory*, University of Essex, Colchester, 1983.
79 Gauri Viswanathan, *Masks of Conquest. Literary Study and British Rule in India*, Faber and Faber, London, 1990.
80 Homi Bhabha, 'Signs taken for wonders: Questions of ambivalence and authority under a tree outside Delhi, May 1817' in F. Barker *et al* (eds), *Europe and its Others. Vol. I*, University of Essex, 1985, pp.89–127.
81 Jean-François Lyotard, 'The dream-work does not think', *Oxford Literary Review* vol.6, no.1, 1983, pp.3–34.
82 Homi Bhabha, 'The other question – the stereotype and colonial discourse', *Screen* vol.24, no.6, 1983, pp.18–36.
83 Bhabha, 'Signs taken for wonders', pp.96, 97.
84 Homi Bhabha examines this in several places, notably in 'Signs taken for wonders', p.99; and 'Of mimicry and man', *October* no.28, 1984, p.130.
85 Bhabha, 'Signs taken for wonders', p.100.
86 Bhabha, 'Of mimicry and man', pp.125–333.
87 Bhabha explains this in 'Signs taken for wonder', p.103.
88 I think we can understand 'fading' (aphanisis) to include both the covering of the subject by another and the forgetting of the subject in the Other: see Lacan, *Four Fundamental Concepts*, pp.207–8.

89 Lacan, *Ecrits I*, p.125.
90 Frantz Fanon, *Black Skin, White Masks*, Paladin, London, 1970, p.109.
91 Fanon, *Wretched of the Earth*, p.41.
92 Ibid., p.155.
93 Ibid., p.155.
94 G. Spivak, *In Other Worlds*, Routledge, London, 1988, pp.251–2; and 'Three women's texts and a critique of imperialism', *Critical Inquiry*, vol.12, no.1, 1985, pp.243–61.
95 In Guha and Spivak, *Subaltern Studies*, pp.45–84.
96 See Hall's discussion of identities in 'Minimal selves', in Lisa Appignanesi (ed.), *ICA Documents* 6, 1987, pp.44–6; and Phil Cohen, '"It's racism what dunnit". Hidden narratives in theories of racism, *Race', Culture and Difference*, James Donald and Ali Rattansi (eds), Sage Publications, London, 1992.
97 The great narratives 'imply that the future remains open as the ultimate aim of human history, under the name of emancipation. But they retain from myth the principle according to which the general course of history is conceivable ... Unlike myth, the modern project certainly does not ground its legitimacy in the past, but in the future' – Jean-François Lyotard, 'Time today', *Oxford Literary Review* vol.II, nos 1/2, 1989, pp.3–20. The difference is that with myth the future promises a repetition of the past, while the modern project promises a different future, although it is one which accomplishes what was promised in the past. The distance separating Mythos from Logos is that of a vanishing line.
98 Bhabha, 'A question of survival. Nations and psychic states', in Homi Bhabha (ed.), *National and Narration*, p.89.
99 Suggesting both wandering and error, the archaic time of investments and the present time of repetition.
100 Derrida, *Grammatologie*, ch.2, especially pp.203–18.
101 G. Spivak, *In Other Worlds*, p.207.

4

HISTORY AND POSTSTRUCTURALISM

Hayden White and Fredric Jameson

Bob Chase

INTRODUCTION

As a lapsed Christian of the generation of 1968, I have always found the narratives of historical materialism seductively attractive and reassuring: what better recuperation of one's childhood beliefs than to translate the fall from grace into a fall into class division and competitiveness and to view ourselves as struggling, under our own steam, towards a millennium of community, co-operation, and reconciliation with ourselves and with nature, all without the help of a perversely punitive deity? But I don't think I ever (or more than briefly, decades ago) tumbled into vulgar Marxist scientificity and entertained the belief that Marxist discourses were capable of representing the indisputable bedrock reality of the past (or the present). For me, as for most others, part of Marxism's appeal lay not in any putative claims to absolute verities but rather in the rigours of its heuristic methods for analysing social and cultural structures and histories. The long-term 'master'-narrative of historical materialism remained (and remains for me) as plausible as the Christian one, and seemed to beat its other competitors by daring to make an epistemological leap into an ethics which maintains that community and reconciliation are better for people than are competitiveness, oppression, and violence. Whilst acknowledging the force of our contemporary critiques of the underlying cultural and epistemological assumptions of Marxist humanism, I have resisted the blandishments of the deconstructive 'turn', always insisting that the dissolution of all perceived realities into sheer discursivity would leave us with no reason or motivation whatsoever to raise objections to suffering and oppression (the 'reality' of which would be similarly dissolved). Finally, I have to admit that I long ago discovered, to my chagrin, that I was a dyed-in-the-wool Anglo-Saxon empiricist, frightened by the excitements of poststructuralism, afraid of not being intellectually up to its theoretical rigours, and always in danger of recidivism. I have remained more or less a passive consumer

61

of theory, eschewing all attempts to invent, on my own, the rhetorical gestures of the innovating theorist.

But why all of this personal fuss? I suppose the main driving force behind my own private intellectual struggles to sort out exactly what was at stake in the poststructuralist challenge to conventional histori-ography was an acute sense of loss and epistemological crisis when I realized that those comforting tomes of 'history' were just possibly redundant – or worse. If all narrative continuities in historiography were nothing but spurious, culture-specific, discursive constructs with no epistemologically legitimate claims to any unbroken relation to putative referents in the realm of the real, then I was suddenly bereft of all that historical 'knowledge' I was using to orientate myself towards the future. What's more, if I was to take to heart the assaults on Western rationality and was to begin viewing it as yet another ruse of the white European male to establish and maintain mastery over our 'pre-Newtonian' sisters and brothers in the non-European, non-North-American world, I would have to consider seriously the degree to which I was part of the Western racist problem rather than a contributor to its solution. I have long accepted that our Western (liberal, empiricist) humanism has been deeply implicated in the long history of European colonialism – in ways analogous to its modes of legitimating intra-European social orders characterized by relations of domination and subordination. But I have had difficulty absorbing the notion that Marxism, surely the most powerful oppositional intra-European thought system for the last century or so, has been (and is) similarly implicated.[1] Of course Marx's own thinking was 'Eurocentric':[2] to describe it as such is tautological. If we accept as I do, however, that Marxist thinking carries within itself the conceptual tools for its own epistemological reconstruction and indeed embraces the intellectual imperative to conduct, relentlessly, precisely that self-reflexive process of self-criticism and self-revision, then it would seem unwise to jettison the whole undertaking when confronted with its Eurocentrism. Those of us who are capable of thinking only within the semantic and grammatical structures of European languages have only Eurocentric conceptual tools at our disposal anyway, even when we are carrying out the necessary operation of deconstructing those same structures. To think, given those inexorable constraints, is to be Eurocentric. But surely not all modes of European thinking are equally complicit in the enterprise of (neo-)colonialism. Margaret Thatcher and Raymond Williams may inhabit similar linguistic universes, but surely that needn't mean that all significant differences collapse. It may well be that the Hegelian 'philosophical structure' commits a sort of epistemological violence by 'appropriat[ing] ... the other as a form of knowledge', but surely *any* linguistic process of articulating and demarcating conceptual/semantic fields (the enabling conditions of thought itself) must do precisely that. I find it difficult to equate this process morally and materially with 'the geographical and economic absorption of the non-European world by the West'.[3]

A more serious objection is that Marx's grand narrative of human history presents itself as a history of the entire world and of all of its diverse cultures. One does flinch when one reads those passages in Marx's writings which half-celebrate, half-condemn the apparently inevitable success of the European bourgeoisie in its energetic project of battering down Chinese walls and civilizing barbarians.[4] It is indeed difficult to swallow the notion that the British were inadvertently doing India a favour by bringing it 'into the evolutionary narrative of Western history'.[5] Like Hegel, Marx would seem to be assuming that all real history is European history and that all other histories are not history at all. One might take the condescending tack and simply excuse Marx for his ignorance of other cultures, bewail his blinkered position within his particular historical and cultural context, and celebrate the potential, above-mentioned, self-correcting mechanisms (fuelled by enhanced empirical knowledge) within his thinking. No apology, however, is going to eliminate the fact that he seems incapable at times of imagining historical narratives incommensurable with his own. But now that we would appear to have entered an epoch of complacent *global* capitalism (a development hardly at odds with Marx's own analyses), it seems less unreasonable to speak in terms of Europe's global reach. If we still accept that Marxist thinking provides us with a starting point for a critique of capitalism, the argument about Marx's Eurocentrism carries less weight. Marxist analyses of capitalism provide us with our initial critical purchase, but the continuing critical project certainly demands that we in Europe learn more about other consciousnesses, other histories, and other historical temporalities and reflect critically on how we have imagined our own history. Disruption of dominant European rationality by its non-European Other does not render Marxist analyses redundant. To strive for socialism needn't entail striving for a homogeneous, Europeanized, socialist world.

Given my perhaps atavistic intellectual predilections, it will come as no surprise that I have found much of Fredric Jameson's writing a source of illumination in what I have felt to be a gathering, threatening, relativistic gloom. His insistence on the existence of a utopian impulse at the heart of all human storytelling seemed to offer the possibility of rescuing a progressive politics in the midst of our critiques of European narratives (grand or otherwise), whilst eschewing the philistine strategy of rejecting theory altogether. His bold attempt to restore meaningfulness to history has no doubt prejudiced me in his favour. At the same time, my meditations on narrative theory and historiography have led me ever deeper into the writings of Hayden White, whose lucid analyses of historical representations lead him to the diametrically opposed conclusion that we have to face up to the meaninglessness of history, that is, to accept that all meanings which we impose on the past are politically dangerous, culture-specific, discursive constructs. In order to concentrate my own mind, I have turned to the 'debate' between White and Jameson on the meaning of narrative in both historiography and fiction. In what follows, I shall be trying to reconstruct my own understanding of their basic arguments and their implications for a politics of forms of writing and modes of interpretation.

THE PROBLEM

It is difficult nowadays to defend grand narratives of history, when all historical narratives are seen as at best provisional and at worst epistemologically and politically delinquent.[6] But my hankering after meaning, and the conviction that I can't make sense of anything unless I turn it into a narrative, bring me back to those old stories that seemed to hold out the promise of some motivation for humane political action. I am uneasy with the fragmentation of long-term perspectives into a series of synchronous studies in depth, unless the latter are carefully integrated within a chronological framework of concurrent sets of contesting explanatory systems; otherwise we tend to suppress the very question of whether there is any story or stories to be told at all. But given that all of the great traditional master narratives of the West are now widely deemed to be – ultimately – epistemologically indefensible, it is often argued that fragmentation alone is intellectually and politically respectable. Choosing to resist a premature tumble into fragmentation, I already find an ally in Hayden White, who insists that

[t]hose historians who draw a firm line between history and philosophy of history fail to recognize that every historical discourse contains within it a full-blown, if only implicit, philosophy of history. And this is as true of what is conventionally called narrative (diachronic) historiography as it is of conceptual (or synchronic) historical representation. The principal difference between history and philosophy of history is that the latter brings the conceptual apparatus by which the facts are ordered in the discourse to the surface of the text, while history proper (as it is called) buries it in the interior of the narrative, where it serves as a hidden or implicit shaping device...[7]

This insight alone, however, provides us with no readily visible signposts to tell us which strategies of writing and teaching history are immanently progressive or reactionary. My problem is compounded by the fact that I am not at all sure that epistemological arguments alone, however rigorous, can be allowed to control decisions which are of a moral and ethical nature. After all, as Western philosophy never tires of telling us, no epistemological argument is going to prove that human life 'ought' to continue to exist at all. However, if we take as our one fixed point, as our *willed* transcendental source of meaning, as it were, our desire that human life *should* continue on earth in forms that enhance life-possibilities and reduce suffering and oppression, then perhaps the use of stories incorporating long-term perspectives may generate a politics of survival. The traditional master narratives or 'meta-narratives', however indefensible they may be in the last epistemological instance (which never comes), may still provide us with the framing arguments of a progressive politics. As Terry Eagleton points out,

> concepts of 'certainty', 'exactness', 'indeterminacy' and so on, like concepts of identity and difference, operate within practical forms of social life and take their force from that. It is just as trans-cendentally unhistorical to assert that all discourse is undecidable as it is to claim that all language is luminously clear. The post-structuralist devotee of undecidability is to this extent merely the prodigal child of the metaphysical father. ... *Of course* language is 'indeterminate': how could it work, how could we walk, if it were not? ... Is an indistinct photograph not a picture of a person at all, and is it always an advantage to replace an indistinct picture with a sharp one? 'Am I inexact because I do not give our distance from the sun to the nearest foot?'[8]

The signifier 'pain' does not hurt, just as the signifier 'dog' does not bark, but in the practical execution of our quotidian tasks, we perhaps needn't worry unduly about the reality of the referents. We may recoil from Eagleton's rambunctious rejection of some poststructuralist thinking, but I'm sure he has a point worth considering. Even though historical representations can never correspond to some hypothetical extra-discursive reality, surely we know enough about reality through experience (however culturally specific the construction of that experi-ence may be) to allow us to speculate that some representations may be better than others and may approximate sufficiently to general truths about oppression and exploitation to justify employing them as starting points for our approach to the question of history.

Even if we prefer to eschew the appeal to 'experience' (which can easily flip over into an illegitimate, universalizing attempt to assimilate the non-European to the European), we still need – and cannot escape from – representations of the past. Images of the past do shape our notions of what we think our 'human nature' may be and how we may decide to deal with our felt desires, urges, and wants in the future.

For the effectivity of the past, like that of any present event in the subject's life, is determined by the manner of its interpretation: it is the way we understand our past, for Lacan, which determines how it determines us. But since this understanding is itself intimately related to our orientation towards the future, it can be argued that, 'What is realised in my history is not the past definite of what was, since it is no more (this would be the objectivist view), or even the present perfect of what has been in what I am (as argued by Hegel), but the future anterior of what I shall have been for what I am in the process of becoming'.[9]

Whether any story of the past is convincing will depend largely on the rhetorical and structural devices of persuasion employed in the telling of it; of two or three narratives of human history, each one equally (in)defensible epistemologically, perhaps we will choose the one whose structure culminates in a denouement of survival. And if we *live* the narrative, of course it is true.

> ... the power possessed by history, whether that of the professional historian, the journalist, or the man-in-the-street, to sustain or to alter prevailing value systems depends on the success of the stories it tells. ... Not only do historical and theoretical narratives, if they are convincing enough, change the way we think and act, but the theories *about* them can do the same...[10]

The past can't itself reach forward and affect the present, but the present is always inhabited and modified by theories (or stories) of the past, popular and scholarly. It is not that we can or should attempt to constitute the 'truth' of the past retro-actively; it is retrospective *importance* that we are conferring on past events by way of our narratives. And that importance will most likely be internalized, become effective, only if embedded in stories which engage our attention and convince with their plausibility.

Peter Dews concludes that 'a wilful self-restriction of analysis to the fragmentary and the perspectival renders impossible any coherent understanding of our own historical and social situation'.[11] Hayden White speaks, rightly, of the moral or aesthetic grounds[12] for preferring one vision of history over another:

> It is not a matter of choosing between objectivity and distortion, but rather between different strategies for constituting 'reality' in thought so as to deal with it in different ways, each of which has its own implications. ... Such choices should be self-conscious rather than unconscious ones, and they should be made with a full understanding of the kind of human nature to the constitution of which they will contribute if they are taken as valid.[13]

HISTORIES AND STORIES

Since 'the past', by definition, does not exist, surely we can 'know' it only by way of representations. To what extent the representations may correspond to *'wie es eigentlich gewesen'*[14] (which we *can't* know), is the unsolvable epistemological problem. But, as I suggested above, the insolubility of the problem does not dictate that we collapse into helpless relativism. We know there is no way to escape the constraints of our (however nefarious) Western reason, even if we employ it to deconstruct notions of reason itself. My reason continues to tell me that, given the (however discursive) evidence we have of the past, some stories are going to be more plausible than others. If we assume (as I do) that narrative is, ultimately, the *only* way that human beings can make personal and collective sense of the kaleidoscopic flux of the universe, then only narratives are ever going to make sense, to have meaning, for most of us.

> And if this is true, then it follows that there are at least two levels of interpretation in every historical work: one in which the historian constitutes a story out of the chronicle of events and another in which, by a more fundamental technique, he progressively identifies the *kind of story* he is telling. . . .[15]

We see immediately that White's analysis of the 'plausibility effect' in historiography only deepens our epistemological problems. A representation of the past is going to appear plausible not because of its putative correspondence to any referents in the realm of the real, but because it follows 'narrative patterns of meaning similar to those more explicitly provided by the literary art of the culture[-] to which [it] belong[s]'.[16] Hence it is not the past itself which dictates the choice of the story to be told. This choice is going to be based on 'well-known, if frequently violated, literary conventions which the historian, like the poet, begins to assimilate from the first moment he is told a story as a child'.[17] And further:

> The historian shares with his audience *general notions* of the *forms* that significant human actions *must* take by virtue of his participation in the specific processes of sense-making which identify him as a member of one cultural endowment rather than another . . .[18]

> This is not unlike what happens, or is supposed to happen, in psychotherapy. . . . The problem is to get the patient to 'reemplot' his whole life history in such a way as to change the *meaning* of those events for him and their *significance* for the economy of the whole set of events that make up his life.[19]

Once again stressing the (in his view) primacy of literary models for historiography, White summarizes:

> historical narratives are not only models of past events and processes, but also metaphorical statements which suggest a relation of similitude between such events and processes and the story types that we conventionally use to endow the events of our lives with culturally sanctioned meanings. Viewed in a purely formal way, a historical narrative is not only a *reproduction* of the events reported in it, but also a *complex of symbols* which gives us directions for finding an *icon* of the structure of those events in our literary tradition.[20]

> It is frequently forgotten or, when remembered, denied that no given set of events attested by the historical record comprises a *story* manifestly finished and complete. This is as true of the events that comprise the life of an individual as it is of an institution, a nation, or a whole people. We do not *live* stories, even if we give our lives meaning by retrospectively casting them in the form of stories.[21]

By implication, White's arguments suggest that story-telling is a *universal* human cognitive device for making sense out of the chaos of phenomenal reality – however culturally specific the particular *kinds* of stories may be. To 'make sense' is to construct a narrative. We are left, to be sure, with the uneasy question regarding the cross-cultural (in-)commensurability of different kinds of narratives. Do the basic universal facts of human existence (birth, toil, copulation, death) generate stories with comparable underlying structures, or do the culture-specific discursive constructions of the meanings of those experiences result in stories which are utterly alien to one another? Regardless of how we answer these questions, the simple fact remains that narratives, if believed, do shape behaviour and beliefs. So perhaps we need to look again at which plausible versions of which master narratives might lead to a 'more convivial, ecologically responsible, more self-managing society',[22] bearing in mind White's assertion that 'the conviction that one can make sense of history stands on the same level of *epistemic* [as opposed to psychological] plausibility as the conviction that it makes no sense whatsoever'.[23] As we have seen, meanings are, ultimately, going to involve beliefs about 'human nature'.

We know that narrative is a cognitive device used not only in historical representations. For example, we use narrative, as White says, as an organizing principle in making sense of our own lives in our memories. But perhaps the most frequent present-day common-sense meaning of 'narrative' is something akin to 'fictional story'. Raymond Williams and

others have pointed out that 'in early English use, *history* and "story" ...
were both applied to an account either of imaginary events or of events
supposed to be true'.[24] (A look at words such as *histoire* or *Geschichte* etc.
in other European languages is instructive.) A clear distinction between
'history' and 'story' in English is a relatively recent development, and
becomes firm only with the rise of academic ('empiricist') history, roughly
concurrent with the process of articulating the conceptual terrain around
'romance' and 'novel'.

> Prior to the French Revolution [White maintains], historiography
> was conventionally regarded as a literary art.... [T]he crucial
> opposition was between 'truth' and 'error', rather than between
> fact and fancy, with it being understood that many kinds of truth,
> even in history, could be presented to the reader only by means of
> fictional techniques of representation.... In the early nineteenth
> century, however, it became conventional, at least among historians,
> to identify truth with fact and to regard fiction as the opposite of
> truth, hence as a hindrance to the understanding of reality rather
> than as a way of approaching it. History came to be set over against
> fiction, and especially the novel, as the representation of the 'actual'
> to the representation of the 'possible' or only 'imaginable'.[25]

The 'possible' or 'probable' or *'vraisemblable'* became the terrain of the
novel, over against the fanciful 'lies' of the romance. Paraphrasing
Roland Barthes, White points out that 'realism' in the nineteenth century
novel and 'objectivity' in nineteenth-century historiography 'developed
pied-à-pied'.

> What they had in common was a dependency on a specifically
> narrative mode of discourse, the principal purpose of which
> was to substitute surreptitiously a conceptual content (a signified)
> for a referent that it pretended merely to describe.... In contrast
> to the French discussion, in the Anglophone world narrative
> historiography was viewed for the most part not as an ideology
> but rather as an antidote for the nefarious 'philosophy of history'
> à la Hegel and Marx, the presumed ideological linchpin of 'totali-
> tarian' political systems.[26]

So there would seem to be historical connections between the rise
of the so-called realist novel ('stories' of a particular kind) and the
compartmentalization of the academic discipline of history. Indeed, the
narrative conventions we call 'realist' would seem to have made narrative
history possible (and/or vice versa). If we accept that we 'know' the past
(which no longer exists) only through discursive representations, then
the conceptual boundary between 'history' and 'fiction' is going to be
difficult to police. Any discussion of narrative on the level of form alone

is necessarily going to involve both academic historiography and the 'rise of the novel':

> Viewed simply as verbal artifacts histories and novels are indistinguishable from one another. ... The image of reality which the novelist ... constructs is meant to correspond in its general outline to some domain of human experience which is no less 'real' than that referred to by the historian. ... [I]f we recognized the literary or fictive element in every historical account, we would be able to move the teaching of historiography onto a higher level of selfconsciousness than it currently occupies.[27]

Given that I started this discussion with a sort of paean to historical materialism, it may seem odd that I have dwelt so long on Hayden White's arguments. After all, if we accept completely White's analysis of the epistemological status of all narrative, then the Marxist grand narrative dwindles into just another kind of Western story, deriving its plausibility from our most deeply rooted literary conventions. As I stated above, however, I am using the 'debate' between White and Fredric Jameson as a vehicle for my quarrels with myself as I attempt to come to terms with my personal predilections. It will readily be understood why Jameson is invoked in a defence of Marx, but White continues to serve as a potentially useful corrective. Once White (despite, or because of, his reverence for empirical historical research) has proved to his own satisfaction that all *meanings* bestowed upon historical facts and events by the tropological strategies of narrative discourse are epistemologically indefensible, he makes a political decision to renounce 'meaningful' narratives as a basis for social planning and political action in the future. Citing the ineluctably ideological nature of all seemingly coherent stories of the past, he argues that historical narratives, making sense as they do by replicating what any given social order decrees as making sense, can at best only reinforce the status quo. At worst they can lead, once dogmatized by reactionary or revolutionary authorities, to unacceptable coercion and tyranny. Despite the fact that White knows that the dissolution of all society-sustaining, functionally pre-cognitive, stories can lead to social crisis, disruption, and disintegration, he still advocates that we face, bravely, the ultimate meaninglessness of history. Aware, as well, that the embrace of meaninglessness can result in sheer voluntarism (read: terrorism), he expresses the hope, buttressed by Freud's notions of 'reaction-formation', that the contemplation of the sheer horror of the past will engender greater tolerance and pluralism, enabling us to avenge the victims of history by creating a more humane social order.

White can be particularly attractive for an Anglophone readership, since his intellectual career has not been characterized only by reactions to post-war intellectual developments in Paris. Many of his theoretical roots can be traced back to Vico and classic nineteenth-century historians and philosophers of history. Like all of us, he has been at pains to come to terms with the troublesome, contradictory, legacies of Saussure, but his positions have developed over several decades and he has been able to re-work, assimilate, and develop the work of the classic structuralists, the anti-humanist structural determinists, and the philosophers of power and/or desire, with no need to execute the abrupt swerves and recantations characteristic of some Anglophone avatars of the Parisian theorists.

HUMAN NATURE

In the 1990s I doubt that too many cultural theorists still need to be reminded incessantly that grand European Enlightenment notions of a universal human nature (corresponding remarkably to the European bourgeoisie's proud notions about itself) have been ideologically complicit in the subjugation of non-European cultures. It is also not difficult to theorize historical connections between the triumphalist liberal humanism of the nineteenth century (the victorious strand of thinking about human nature that emerges from the Enlightenment) and recent pronouncements about the 'end of history' that have accompanied the collapse of self-styled socialist regimes across the globe. To be sure, we might well pause to point out, as I frequently do (see my chapter on Walter Scott in this volume), that – at least since Vico – a counterstrain of Enlightenment thought has always insisted that human beings produce their own 'nature', in history, through their own social activities and institutions, but the fact remains that the victorious version of Western humanism managed to trample over non-European cultures, attempting to assimilate the different to itself by effacing all significant difference and congratulating itself for having brought the blessings of truly 'human' values and institutions to the hitherto unenlightened barbarian. That relentless ideological stress laid by official discourses on putative sameness and eternal human essences generated, quite rightly, a powerful deconstructive counter-strategy which has systematically dismantled Western myths of universal 'Man' and has relentlessly emphasized the historicity of all those human values and activities that the West had attempted to represent as nature. This process of 'de-centring' Western humanism surely represents a salutary intervention against the dominant discourses of sameness and must be continued. But in the 1990s, when – to coin a phrase – the globe has shrunk with alarming rapidity, we might ask whether an exclusive emphasis on cultural difference is the only way forward for a progressive politics of theory. If all human values, all human meanings, and all human stories about humankind are seen to be *only* culturally and historically specific,

71

it becomes difficult to see why we should worry about human suffering and oppression at all. There can arise a sort of relativism which strengthens the will to power by giving it a good conscience; we may end up with at best a sort of cheerful American pragmatism or at worst a twenty-first-century avatar of fascism. Surely it can still be argued that various versions of Western humanism at least made something like a life-preserving ethics possible; the sickening hypocrisy of the murderous colonialist was perhaps as much a sort of homage paid to morality as it was a logical extension of Western hubris.

Roland Barthes' astringent analysis of an American exhibition of photographs ('The Great Family of Man') has remained for the last thirty-odd years a touchstone for anti-humanist demystifications of humanist discourses.[28] Who could deny that an exhibition of that sort (I've never seen it, but I take Barthes' word for it) directs us to a 'myth of human "community"', which serves as an alibi to a large part of our humanism'? This postulation of a human essence underlying the 'diversity in skins, skulls, and customs' surely does indeed aim 'to suppress the determining weight of History'.[29] But perhaps we might argue that more than one lesson is to be learnt from this splendid little piece of journalistic polemic. After all, Barthes' assault on discourses and sentiments reminiscent of *Reader's Digest* and *National Geographic* is rather like shooting fish in a barrel. One admires his resistance to the massive assertion of Cold War American cultural hegemony over Western Europe, but one can still ask whether, in the 1990s, a positive political moment might not be recovered from such a photographic exhibition, once the sentimental humanist rubbish has been cleared away. Of course we all agree that the effacing of culture-specific meanings and values attached to the universal facts of birth, motherhood, toil, and death represents a sort of epistemological violence committed against cultural difference. But if unbridgeable difference and the utter relativity of cultural values are the only messages left to us, then we might well ask where we are to find the motivation (and the epistemological legitimation) to attack that violence. From where does Barthes himself get his sympathies for the parents of Emmet Till or for the North African workers of the Goutte d'Or district in Paris? We agree that if one removes 'History' from those 'facts of nature, universal facts . . . there is nothing more to be said about them; any comment about them becomes purely tautological'.[30] But just what is that 'determining weight of History' invoked by Barthes as that which does give meaning to 'the facts of nature'? It would seem that the early (Marxisant) Barthes is still insisting that there are politically valid stories to be told about humankind which are going to employ facts of nature as basic elements in their *fabulae*. Perhaps it is time that we returned to an emphasis on Barthes' (here untheorized) notion of 'History' as something transcending cultural difference. We might begin by hypothesizing that historical narratives may yet be the best form of discursive intervention against dominant beliefs, these narratives being effective by virtue of 'their ability to organise the consciousness and practice of historical agents',[31] that is, us and those who come after us.

After decades of widespread academic rejection of narrative as an appropriate device for representing the human condition, it may be time to return to the great master-narratives of Western culture. While we were busy denying the ultimate epistemological defensibility of any 'meta-language' used to represent human history, hosts of powerful metalanguages, usually of non-academic provenance, were asserting their social efficacy with apparently no need on their part to lay rigorous claims to absolute or transcendental validity. For reasons that I hope will become clearer, I am convinced that self-reflexive versions of historical materialism offer us perhaps the only appropriate narrative(s) for our threatened world. Needless to say, this must be an historical materialism shorn of any claims to absolute certainties or essential truths and aware of its own discursivity. But why this insistence on salvational narrative?

It would be too easy, and probably too tedious, to expatiate on the real threats to continued human life on earth. I have no intention of suggesting a checklist or setting a hierarchy of horrors and abominations, but surely the threat of annihilation by nuclear weapons or by nuclear fission in other forms is still going to be close to the top; or if that catastrophe is delayed (with the apparent disappearance of super-power rivalry), the palpable, almost measurable, destruction of the earth's ecosystems must demand a drastic revision of what many of us thought was the good life.[32] In the last decades it has become clear that our consuming passions just might kill us sooner than we thought. It seems unlikely that we shall remedy the situation if we choose to celebrate, a-historically, the contemporary Western human subject as 'a dispersed, decentred network of libidinal attachments, emptied of ethical substance and psychical interiority, the ephemeral function of this or that act of consumption, media experience, sexual relationship, trend or fashion'.[33] Abandoning ourselves to points of libidinal intensity, with the cheerful conviction that we may be transgressing social boundaries and liberating ourselves from the tyrannies of epistemologically indefensible versions of truth, falsehood, and ethics, would seem at the present juncture to be almost criminally frivolous. To survive, we are surely going to need another version of ourselves. This is where the master narratives come in. A story of humankind which represents human beings as *creating* their own 'nature', through material practice, over time, and arriving at the grand denouement of a communitarian, co-operative, non-antagonistic mode of living, in harmony with nature, must surely have more survival-value than does an embrace of chaotic discontinuity and meaninglessness. The sources of *jouissance* may be more various than we think. But where do we start?

If we were to believe our mistresses and masters in today's Britain; indeed, if we were to ask people in the street, we would presumably conclude that competitiveness is the most 'natural' component of 'human nature'. The old-fashioned Hobbesian struggle for room at the top and for income and possessions seems to belong as much as ever to every-day common-sense notions of what life is like. Just when many of us thought that styles of consumption were detaching themselves from traditional hierarchies of social status, the arrogance of conspicuous consumption re-asserts itself. Magnitude of appetite seems to correlate with perceived social position. The frugal lifestyle of our parents, who still inhabited a world of industrial capitalism, is seen by us, in the *société de consommation* (or the 'disaccumulative' moment of late monopoly or consumer or multi-national capitalism),[34] as a pitiable existence of repression and soul-destroying sublimation of natural desire. It is we who are free, we conclude illogically, as freedom must be the untrammelled pursuit of satisfaction of implacable appetites. But if satisfying our appetites is rapidly despoiling the earth and destroying even the human ecosystem, surely our notions of freedom and 'the natural' need revision.

NARRATIVE

If I were to stop the argument where I left it earlier and conclude that every effective present-day narrative representation of the past is effective by virtue of its plausibility and that all narrative plausibility is an effect in the mind of a 'realistic' replication of present-day common-sense notions of human nature, I would presumably be forced to concur with the familiar anti-realist bias of much poststructuralist thinking and agree that all seemingly objective narrative historiography is fatally tainted by its immanent tendency to reinforce prevalent beliefs about human motivation, values, and attitudes. In other words, I would be accepting Hayden White's position completely:

> The essence of nineteenth-century realism is to be found, whether in historical or novelistic discourse, in the representational practice which has the effect of constituting an image of a current social praxis as the criterion of plausibility by reference to which any given institution, activity, thought, or even a life can be endowed with the aspect of 'reality'.[35]

So, 'realism', whether in historiography, fiction, or other discourses about the world, would have to be seen as having the ideological effect of supporting the status quo. Since our beliefs about ourselves can only

be the effects in consciousness of a particular matrix of discursive formations in the present, when we attempt to make sense of the past by
means of plausible narratives, we are actually capable, cognitively, only
of talking about ourselves in the present. Since, therefore, the past is
unknowable, we should swear a vow of epistemological constancy and
stick to analysing the present – the only object of knowledge that can
be approached by observation. We would then be content to continue
with the post-Barthesian project of demythologizing and deconstructing
institutions and discursive practices which present themselves as 'nature'
rather than as historical constructions. After all, we might say, past events
no longer exist, and a politically progressive historiography surely has
to do with improving human life in the future. A non-existent past has
no effects on the future; only interpretation of the world in the present
will change it. Only by embracing the ultimate meaninglessness of the
past will we find the motivation and the epistemological legitimation to
will life-enhancing changes in the present and in the future.

In his more Althusserian formulations, Hayden White reaches
conclusions close to those adumbrated above. In the context of a lucid,
succinct summary of Althusserian discussions of ideology, he points out
that

> Historiography is, by its very nature, the representational practice
> best suited to the production of the 'law-abiding' citizen. This is
> not because it may deal in patriotism, nationalism, or explicit
> moralizing but because in its featuring of narrativity as a favoured
> representational practice, it is especially well suited to the produc-
> tion of notions of continuity, wholeness, closure and individuality
> that every 'civilized' society wishes to see itself as incarnating,
> against the chaos of a merely 'natural' way of life.[36]

The production of these notions, White argues, is the effect of

> a certain practice of representation whose function is to create a
> specific kind of reading or viewing subject capable of inserting
> himself into the social system that is his historically given potential
> field of activity. ... The ideological element in art, literature, or
> historiography consists of the projection of the kind of subjectivity
> that its viewers or readers must take on in order to experience it as
> art, as literature, or as historiography.[37]

In the essay quoted here, White demonstrates that Johann Gustav
Droysen, the nineteenth-century German historical theorist, brilliantly
anticipated Althusser's theories of discourse and ideology and embraced
wholeheartedly the implications of his own proto-Althusserianism for
the practice of historiography. Droysen knew that 'historical objectivity'
is and can only be partisan, so he devised a 'poetics' of historiography

('*Historik*') to explain how the partisan objectives can best be achieved. White himself, however, draws rather different conclusions for late-twentieth-century historiographers:

> If ... it is possible to imagine a conception of history that would signal its resistance to the bourgeois ideology of realism by its refusal to attempt a narrative mode for the representation of its truth, is it possible that this refusal itself signals a recovery of the historical sublime that bourgeois historiography repressed in the process of its disciplinization?[38]

White has moved towards the belief that 'a visionary politics' can proceed only on the conviction that history 'makes no sense whatsoever'.

As a relative neophyte, I confess that I often find Hayden White massively convincing in terms of epistemological purity. His are arguments that need to be incorporated into any open discussion of historiography and pedagogy. Be that as it may, however, I find myself, for whatever untheorized ideological reasons, still hankering after meaning in history. I am still not convinced that it is meaninglessness alone that 'can goad living human beings to make their lives different for themselves and their children, which is to say, to endow their lives with a meaning for which they alone are fully responsible'.[39] Of course I agree that the first, provisional, 'meaning' of history is the state of humankind in the 1990s. The ultimate meaning is, yes, going to be the denouement of the story being propelled forward by current tendencies, current practices, current beliefs. And yes, we must continue to de-mythologize (in the post-Barthesian sense) and deconstruct the ostensible natural-ness of our existing institutions and social practices, as a first step towards changing those beliefs and attitudes that make the denouement of our currently unfolding story so predictably catastrophic. But surely that process of analysis can be convincing, can have the force of plausibility and be politically effective, only if we can provide plausible historio-graphical narratives to explain the construction, over time, of those same beliefs and attitudes. So, we have come full circle and arrived again at the old familiar theoretical double-bind: we need stories about our-selves to motivate positive political action, but any plausible stories about our past are epistemologically indefensible. But if we limit ourselves to deconstructing every utterance and every deconstruction of the last deconstruction, exhilarating ourselves with the vertigo of infinite regress, we shall probably change nothing. So perhaps notions of epistemological purity must be bracketed if we are to change anything at all?[40]

I am convinced, like Peter Dews, that the poststructuralist impasse has made clear 'that critique is not a question of the arbitrary and coercive espousal of premises [sic] and precepts, but rather of commitment to that coherence of thought which alone ensures its emancipatory power'.[41]

Without mincing his polemic, Perry Anderson long ago came to similar conclusions, echoed by Terry Eagleton (in a moment of polemical exaggeration), to the effect that poststructuralism 'randomized history', 'strafed meaning, over-ran truth, outflanked ethics and politics, and wiped out history'.[42] In what seems perhaps to be a willed decision to transcend poststructuralism, Eagleton summarizes, with approval, a Wittgensteinian argument to the effect that in our functioning language-games notions of 'knowledge' and 'truth' are not worried about ultimate epistemological defensibility. Without committing unduly loutish violence against protocols of philosophical rigour we can and do make do with less. The way forward, I would argue, of course does not lie in the imposition of meaning where none is to be found. Given that even the most rigorous epistemological argument cannot conclude irrefutably that there is *no* meaning in history, and given that it seems highly likely that there is something in the motivational make-up of human beings (generated perhaps by those Barthesian 'facts of nature') that might justify the hypothesis of trans-cultural homologies and continuities in human existence over time, I am convinced that meaningful stories of the past need not be epistemological solecisms. Versions of historical materialism, I would maintain, are still capable of rendering those continuities into plausible narratives which can give meaning to the present and generate social beliefs and practices leading to a denouement of survival in the long-term history of humankind. I can see no other salvational narratives on the horizon.

CONTINUITIES

In the fourth section of this chapter ('Human nature') I argued that hope for a progressive politics of theory may lie in an emphasis on the shared humanity of human beings, even though our current stress on cultural difference should simultaneously continue to be seen as a necessary intervention against the powerful discourses of sameness which long seemed to legitimate Europe's conquest of its cultural others. I suggested that there may still be a progressive ethical moment in the narratives generated by some versions of Western humanism. I even dared to hint that there may be trans-cultural homologies in human histories, based on those Barthesian 'facts of nature'. It is clearly not enough, however, to justify the use of long-term historical narratives simply by shifting one's emphasis to some putatively shared human experiences. To embrace a long-term narrative as a story approximating to a usable version of human truth is to assume, as well, that there are long-term discursive continuities in human history. Faced with the epistemological insouciance of much conventional historiography, which still seems blithely confident that we can legitimately project our own conceptual universe back onto human beings who inhabited the past, it is right that we should continue to stress discursive *dis*continuities between us and the otherness of the past, just as we continue to foreground cultural difference in the present. At the same time, however, just as I would urge that we look again at our shared humanity in the present, I would also suggest that we need to shift our emphasis to continuities across time in order to underpin the plausibility of those potentially life-preserving narratives we should be telling ourselves about ourselves. Perhaps we needn't surrender completely to those claims of poststructuralists that all narrative continuities in historiography are nothing but spurious, culture-specific, discursive constructs with no epistemologically legitimate claims to any relation to referents in the realm of the real.

Although I can legitimately be accused of eschewing epistemological purity, of having my theoretical cake and eating it, I shall attempt here to justify – perhaps more polemically than analytically – my notion of continuities in human history. To do this, I shall have to tread some dangerous, shady, middle ground between, on the one hand, assumptions about the radical otherness and unknowability of the past and, on the other, the more traditional (bourgeois?) urge to efface differences in human consciousness across time. I can defend that ground best, I think, by starting with some undoubted (I hope), even banal, continuities in human life.

Leaving aside for now any questions regarding putative *discursive* continuities or discontinuities in history or in the history of human consciousness, perhaps there is no harm in impressing upon ourselves what we already know: the existence of vulgar *physical* continuities in human biological history. If this history is nothing else, it is at least an unbroken succession of female bodies, each giving birth to another female body (rather like Russian dolls), in an endless chain, extending down through the centuries and (we hope) into the future. Surely this uninterrupted reproduction of living tissue, the unending replication of DNA molecules, is a basic fact of biological continuity underlying everything else. All of this is painfully obvious, but when we read most standard textbook histories, or indeed most speculative theory about the construction of human consciousness, it is easy to get the impression that the basic fact of biological continuity has been suppressed. Raymond Williams,[43] in a critique of Timpanaro, long ago pointed out that while the physical and biological facts of human existence 'are never denied, within any relevant area of argument, they are quite often dismissed as banalities which have little practical bearing on the more interesting questions that lie ahead'.[44] I agree with Williams that once 'the sense of proportion imposed by this fundamental materialism is either forgotten or dismissed as a preliminary banality, the way is indeed open for every kind of obscurantism and evasion'.

78

To re-emphasize, as a fundamental materialism, the inherent physical conditions – a specific universe, a specific planet, a specific evolution, specific physical lives – *from which all labour and all consciousness must take their origins,* is right and necessary.[45]

This harping on biological continuity of course proves nothing. It does seem highly unlikely, however, that the unbroken existence over time of fleshly bodies, subject to more or less unchanging basic physical needs, is not going to be accompanied by something like continuity in motivational make-up. Far be it from me to imply that species-being somehow determines consciousness and human needs in some one-directional mechanical way, but it would surely be wilful to sever all connections prematurely. I wish to suggest here only that the assumption of an absolutely 'other', cognitively unapproachable, past consciousness sits uneasily with the vulgar fact of biological continuity over a relatively brief period of time. Discursive formations change rapidly, but can we legitimately leap to the conclusion that they are purely aleatory, that there is no sequentiality, no continuous process, no 'narrativity'? Williams is right to assert that 'the crucial question is the extent to which these fundamental physical conditions and processes affect or qualify the social and historical interpretations and projects which are the central specifications of Marxism'.[46] The 'elements of the biological condition are mediated by socio-historical experience and by its cultural forms'. But 'this mediation provides no basis for that still common kind of reduction, in which the biological is a mere datum and all the effective working social and historical'.[47] He goes on to assert that 'to restore this substance of human life to all effective social perspectives is a matter of great urgency'.[48] It is my contention here that this 'substance of human life' may have generated crucial discursive continuities which legitimate the use of long-term, non-trivial, historical narratives.

Perhaps we should look, next, at our everyday notions of time. I don't need to be told that my ways of experiencing and thinking about time are generated by the culture-specific discourses I inhabit. I don't think, in this post-Einsteinian age, that I am in danger of believing that my notions of time have any extra-discursive, 'real' referents out there in the natural world. Nevertheless, I am not going to 'make sense' of my lifeworld if the sense-making narratives around me do not embrace notions of time that are recognizable in my culture. And surely our histories, our stories of our culture and of ourselves, consist, minimally, of events arranged in temporal sequences. But everyone, not only poets and philosophers of existence, knows that the *experience* of time (as opposed to mechanically measured time) is utterly subjective. One hardly needs to add that different cultures and different areas within a single culture are going to change in accordance with different temporalities. None of these objections, however, has sufficient weight to cause us to jettison our everyday notions of chronological time, measured by clocks and calendars, which lend a sense-making coherence to our narratives.[49] We need, to be sure, to overcome our conventional rhetoric of aeons, ages, millennia, and Antiquity – a rhetoric which perhaps reflects culture-specific, quasi-precognitive thought patterns encouraging beliefs in permanence, cultural solidity, and organic development. It is this rhetoric that probably inhibits us from thinking in terms of narratives of rupture, innovation, planned construction of institutions, historically explicable social and economic advantages enjoyed by particular groups, and other potentially disruptive notions. If we accept that human history is remark-ably *brief*, surely we can argue with more force that continuities are more likely and that coherent stories are legitimate. There are people alive today who, as small children, heard aged relatives talk about hearing of the Battle of Waterloo. If twenty centenarians, each from a different century, were figuratively to join hands, they would connect the present moment with the birth of Christ. Twenty people are not a crowd. The segment of the biological continuum beginning with the Christian era is startlingly short – and might be felt as such if our standard stories of the past were couched in a different rhetoric. Absolutely unbridgeable cognitive chasms between us and the recorded past seem rather unlikely. Somehow we must hold on to the notion of continuity whilst still realizing that the past remains other. Despite traceable continuities, it remains cognitively impossible for us to inhabit an alien conceptual universe.

Of course, our common-sense notions of history have to do with more than just biological continuities. 'Prehistoric' refers usually to times before the existence of *written* artifacts. But if past writing is to have any meaning for us at all, we have to presuppose the continuity of language as well. Avoiding for the moment questions of semantic change and putative discontinuities in comprehensibility, we can take as given the fact that language (as a system of articulated sounds) does have a continuous history. Historical linguistics enables us to trace phonetic and phonemic development in European languages for the last few thousand years. If some schools of linguists are to be believed, computer-aided research, by feeding selected features of living languages into its programs, will be able to run backwards through all known phonemic evolution to arrive at the first syllables stammered by those ancestors of ours who, a few score thousand years ago, were the first human beings capable of articulate speech. This is indeed a specifically human continuity, and its length of duration, particularly since the invention of writing, is not very 'long'. If there is, then, a linguistic continuum, is there a continuum of meaning as well? Are there unbridgeable ruptures? Are there con-tinuities, over time, to be found among those longer discursive constructs we call narratives?

Nobody, I assume, doubts the facts of biological and linguistic continuity and the relative brevity of human history. But our common sense alone is, needless to say, insufficient warrant for legitimating the shaping of the past into discursive narratives emplotted in accordance with what is plausible to us in the present. To say the least, post-structuralism has taught us that it is perilous to harbour the assumption that any narrative 'shape' we may construct can 'correspond' in any way to any putative extra-discursive 'real' bedrock of the past. To suggest that the past had any shape at all is to court derision. Language, notoriously, has plunged us all into doubt. If we can no longer entertain a naïve mimetic theory of language, we are immediately going to question the adequacy of the story form of discourse to the representation of reality. As Paul Ricoeur would maintain,

> ... narrative discourse does not simply reflect or passively register a world already made; it works up the material given in perception and reflection, fashions it, and creates something new, in precisely the same way that human agents by their actions fashion distinctive forms of historical life out of the world they inherit as their past.[50]

But for Ricoeur, history does have meaning, 'because human actions produce meanings. These meanings are continuous over generations of human time'.

Ricoeur's embrace of continuity is welcome grist for my mills, but I'm afraid that the assumption of 'continuous meanings' needs to be inter-rogated further. Here is not the place to start with the basics of Saussurean linguistic theory, but we must not forget the important senses in which the linguistic sign is arbitrary. The link between verbal signifier and conceptual signified is not given by nature; the sign is constructed culturally in history. It is never stable, since meanings are always contested. As Bakhtin/Voloshinov has taught us, language is always 'dialogic':[51] any use of a sign is an attempt to assert a meaning to the exclusion of other struggling meanings. The success of the assertion will depend on the social position of the speaker/writer. Meaning always presupposes the existence of countermeanings.

No matter what explanation for semantic change we may prefer, it is perfectly obvious that meanings of words do change. A glance at an etymological dictionary will suffice to convince us, assuming that we are not already attuned to the *lived* experience of conceptual shifts. The meaning of a word is never some (mythical) 'original' meaning.[52] As Bakhtin/Voloshinov has theorized and Raymond Williams has so lucidly demonstrated in his *Keywords*, meanings have a *social* history. But the old question about continuity still remains: once concepts have evolved, changed their semantic shape, expanded, shrunk, bifurcated, disappeared, or become inextricably linked with other bits of the conceptual landscape previously experienced as discrete, to what degree can we say that we still 'understand' them? To what extent can our own culturally and historically specific cognitive structures penetrate, by way of theory, the alien universe of a past mentality? Can no-longer extant mentalities be represented in a language which maps the conceptual landscape with configurations incommensurable with the past? Have our own cognitive structures the power to reconstruct meanings that no longer exist? The answer to all of this is presumably, well, no, but we can certainly move *closer* to dependable knowledge through the work of theory and analysis. Our very ability to trace phonemic and semantic change convinces me of the existence of traceable discursive continuities. To assume radical rupture or purely aleatory change is to fly in the face of undoubted evidence. Human consciousness remains historically contingent, but stories of its development need not be epistemologically stupid. Our libraries are not redundant; the discipline of history need not cringe in the face of poststructuralist derision.

The narratives of historiography will never be able to lay claim to a mimetically accurate reproduction of 'the real', but the fact that they must remain culture-specific discursive constructs needn't bounce us into the conclusion that there are no ultimate referents out there in the real world. To construct stories of the past is not necessarily to invent lies about the past: we can retrospectively (and legitimately) bestow *importance* on past events in accordance with our concerns about the present and the future. I remain convinced that the story of human beings actively and continuously producing their own consciousness over time within determinate material conditions offers the best master-narrative. My conviction is, of course, ultimately a moral, political choice, and historical materialism remains, for me, the most plausible alternative to meaninglessness. Historical 'objectivity' is and can only be partisan.[53] So be it.

HISTORICAL MATERIALISM

Marxist narratives also derive their plausibility largely from a representation of common-sense beliefs, values, and social practices in the present. But there is a notorious difference. Because historical materialism proceeds from the assumption that beliefs, values, practices, etc. have been produced and are being produced within determinate historical circumstances which themselves include and are being produced by those same beliefs, values, and practices, its narratives disturb illusions of human fixity, of the stasis of consciousness, of the naturalness of what we perceive ourselves to be. On the level of quotidian consciousness, they produce habits of mind which, at the very least, impel us to ask *why* we are having the thoughts and desires we experience. The numbing feeling that our individual and collective senses of self are inexorably natural, is

– or can be – dissipated, to be replaced by the exhilarating conviction that we are in the process of *producing* ourselves and the social world which is our means of self-production. The plausibility of the master-narrative derives not only from the moment of self-recognition experienced in registering representations of ourselves, but also from the narrative coherence of the story of the historical processes that produced us. The task of demystifying and deconstructing our present-day beliefs and institutions remains paramount, and Roland Barthes (among others) has shown with a journalistic flourish how we can set about getting a theoretical purchase on those values and institutions that our culture represents as 'natural'. Post-Saussurean linguistic theory has supplied us with the conceptual tools we need to prise apart that illusory fit between language and the world, dispelling language's notorious bewitchment and revealing the historicity of all discursive systems. But only the explanatory story of historical materialism can move us beyond futile deconstructionist frenzies trapped in synchronicity. By convincing ourselves of the story of our self-production – willing backwards, as it were – we can organize the political desire to intervene in the narrative elements of the present to shape the progression of the story, into the future, towards a denouement of survival. Retrospective theory, the explanatory story, imposes its pattern through the minds of the living characters in the continuing narrative. In no way is the future seen to be determined by the past by means of some sort of historical machinery organized around a teleological principle. The concrete utopia of survival, the end of the story, is projected from an empirical analysis of the present; movement is generated by a political will, strengthened by the same utopian impulses that propel the narratives of the past, be they historiographical or fictional.

The redemptionist rhetoric of these pages may remind readers, depending on their intellectual provenance, of either Christianity or Marxism. Both attributions would be in a sense correct. For Fredric Jameson, all stories told by humankind to itself have as their ultimate meaning precisely the utopian impulse towards wholeness and collective safety, towards the reconciliation of human beings with themselves and with nature. 'Any comparison of Marxism with religion is a two-way street, in which the former is not necessarily discredited by its association with the latter.'[54]

> [Religion] has the symbolic value of wholeness . . .: but it is the wholeness of the older organic society or *Gemeinschaft* that it conveys. . . . [Its] linguistic and visual artifacts, thought systems, myths and narratives . . . look as though they had something to do with the forms in which our consciousness is at home, and yet which remain rigorously closed [to] it.[55]

If we have a sense of homelessness, we must believe on some level that there are, somewhere, 'forms' in which we are 'at home'. But 'home' is the place we have never experienced, although our aesthetic acts proleptically figure it. All narratives ultimately fail, of course, because the imaginary or formal solutions to unresolvable social contradictions[56] in any age are not only limited by what is capable of being thought in any age, but also founder on the (usually repressed) nightmare of 'History'. Even narrative closure, that structural necessity of 'realist' narrative in its classical form, damned by schools of poststructuralist criticism as evidence of 'contamination' of fiction 'by an idealizing and therefore duplicitous (bourgeois) ideology', is, for Jameson, justified 'insofar as it conforms to a vision of a humanity finally reconciled with nature and with itself, of a society finally delivered into the kind of community that both traditional religion and the Marxist master-narrative of history envision as a moral necessity'.[57] As long as class antagonisms persist, however, the 'closures' remain just that: 'visions', at war with themselves.

Jameson proceeds from many of the founding (post)structuralist assumptions he shares with Hayden White, but as I have pointed out already, his moral commitment to a Marxist master-narrative places him in opposition to anyone who would embrace meaninglessness in history. He knows that past events are available to us only in discursive representations (texts), but, like any Marxism or like any realist epistemology, he does not forget that every text has an ultimate referent,[58] however many mediating layers exist between it and the palimpsest of the extant text:

> One does not have to argue the reality of history: necessity, like Dr. Johnson's stone, does that for us. That history is *not* a text, for it is fundamentally non-narrative and non-representational; what can be added, however, is the proviso that history is inaccessible to us except in textual form, or in other words, that it can be approached only by way of prior (re)textualization.[59]

> History is what hurts, it is what refuses desire and sets inexorable limits to individual as well as collective praxis, which its 'ruses' turn into grisly and ironic reversals of their own intention. But this History can be apprehended only through its effects, and never directly as some reified force.[60]

So History is not a narrative, 'master' or otherwise, but it can be approached only by way of some prior narrative (re-)construction.[61] Narratives do not 're-present' history, in the sense of replicating sequences of events or 'reflecting' social forces and social contradictions. But the deep structures of narrative strategies project solutions, 'on the

84

aesthetic or imaginary level, to a genuinely contradictory situation in the concrete world of everyday social life'.[62] The stories of historiography and the stories of fiction (especially novels) remain the indispensable discursive figurations, the analysis of which leads us step by step back through various 'semantic horizons' to the specific forms of material and social necessity that obtained at the relevant moments of history. 'All literature must be read as a symbolic meditation on the destiny of community.'[63] History is not a narrative, but it is also not a discontinuous series of synchronic systems. The story of the successive modes of production, from primitive communism through slave and feudal economies to capitalism, the last stage of 'prehistory', represents the limits of our 'semantic horizon'. The modes of production are not empirically verifiable or representable forms of social and economic organization (capitalism is a special case); they are, crudely put, heuristic devices enabling us, by way of theory, to glimpse the limiting structures of necessity. So Marxism is the master-narrative of history, but it is not History itself. History is not a narrative, but Jameson is convinced of the essential narrativity of the historical *process*, that underlying struggle of human beings against the relentless pressures of necessity, toil and exploitation, a struggle which generates – through however many layers of cultural mediation – the elements of a *fabula* which becomes emplotted in stories of various shapes. The master-narrative of historical materialism, as the history of human desire pitted against necessity, with its ultimate historical perspective of reconciliation, of achieved socialism, of the end of 'prehistory' in Marx's sense, has inscribed itself in texts of various kinds since the beginning of 'prehistory', in the form of narrative movements towards a vision of wholeness, reconciliation, and satisfied desire.

Needless to say, Hayden White will have none of this talk about the 'narrativity of the historical process'. His epistemology would allow the hypothetical possibility that such is the case, but because the *fact* of narrativity can never be known for certain (and surely we must admit that he is right), all existing master-narratives, for White, represent merely partisan choices and are too risky to inspire conviction. As we saw above, *his* ethical choice is to embrace meaninglessness. He rebukes Jameson for 'simply ... sweep[ing] aside the theoretical relevance' of the 'fashionable conclusion that because history is a text, the "referent" does not exist'.[64] And, it has to be said, Jameson's arguably coy, often allusive discussions, sometimes of the Althusserian 'absent cause', sometimes of the 'nightmare of history', and sometimes of the 'meaningfulness of History', do breed confusion and the suspicion that Jameson is a bit touchy about his own case.

Oddly enough, however, both White and Jameson (the latter predictably) occasionally appeal to some sort of extra- or pre-discursive, pre-textual, bedrock of knowledge to lend weight to their arguments. For Jameson, that 'History' which hurts, that History which is the experience of Necessity, consists, in the end, of centuries of real human beings racked with the pain of backbreaking toil performed in contexts of violence and exploitation.[65] That is the repressed nightmare of the narratives of reconciliation, in which the labour of women and blacks is even more hidden than the fact of labour itself. Here we have Jameson's version of Dr Johnson's stone. Ultimately it is *experience* that impels one to the ethical decision not to embrace meaninglessness, not to take up permanent residence in the postmodernist phantasmagoria of the *société de consommation*, in which truth is the consumption of images of the truth, endlessly circulating in a world of commodities. To be progressive, theory must posit a bedrock of reality which generates human experience and which can be glimpsed, with the aid of theory, through the stories human beings tell about themselves. Those stories will always be culture-specific, but we must assume trans-cultural commensurability if we are to find the will to oppose oppression and exploitation. The notion of a shared humanity can serve as the basis for an ethics which still sees oppression and exploitation as unacceptable realities.

Hayden White, too, obviously stung by accusations of 'formalism', appeals to what is 'known' and devotes a long discussion to the Holocaust.[66] His vivid sense of horror makes clear that he, too, has not lost his European humanist ethics, even though to talk of 'horror' would seem to imply the surreptitious importation of epistemologically unjustifiable values into an argument which denies the existence of meaning in history. This move seems to support my own contention that a politics of progressive intervention against the continuing epistemological and material violence committed against Europe's 'others' requires the retention of the morality at the heart of progressive versions of European humanism. Given White's previous ethical choice, however, his conclusion is consistent: the Holocaust demands constant analysis and interpretation, especially in the face of present-day right-wing revisionist historiography; the Holocaust has no ultimate 'meaning', however, since history is ultimately meaningless. The horror is part of the 'historical sublime', that Burkean sense of an overwhelmingly irrational destructive power which throws the senses and powers of human judgement into confusion. It is this helpless sense of horror that White invokes as the potential impetus for us to start to *construct* humane social meanings from scratch. So both Jameson and White appeal to the existence of something which is pre-discursively real (however discursive the representations); the disagreement is over the moral and political effectiveness of narratives. White, the poststructuralist historian, does not tell us to forget the past. Both are concerned with the ways stories of the past are appropriated for ideological purposes in the present.

Most of us presumably orient our lives and thought without reference to any transcendental, religious, or metaphysical foundation. Hence, in a sense we don't need to be told that, ultimately, life on earth is meaningless. We do not assume that some sort of moral order is immanent in the universe. If we destroy ourselves, the universe will not grieve. Jameson's and White's meditations on narrative and historiography provide, for me, excellent starting points for thinking about the meanings human beings have constructed for themselves about their past. In the end, I plump for Jameson's attempt to harness precisely that (apparently universal) meaning-giving human activity of storytelling in the services of a contemporary politics which makes socialism thinkable, plausible, and desirable.

> [T]hat life is meaningless is not a proposition that need be inconsistent with Marxism, whose affirmation is the quite different one that History is meaningful, however absurd organic life may happen to be. . . . [I]n future societies people will still grow old and die, but the Pascalian wager of Marxism lies elsewhere, namely in the idea that death in a fragmented and individualized society is far more frightening and anxiety-laden than in a genuine community, in which dying is something that happens to the group more intensely than it happens to the individual subject. The hypothesis is that time will be no less structurally empty, or to use a current version, presence will be no less of a structural and ontological illusion, in a future communal social life, but rather that this particular 'fundamental revelation of the nothingness of existence' will have lost its sharpness and pain and be of less consequence.[67]

How profoundly unfashionable to be meditating upon one's death! I like the 'Pascalian wager'.

CONCLUSION

My earlier meditations on 'human nature' (and individual death) serve only to remind us that we remain in the empirical realm of physical necessity and that human beings have ineluctable species-specific bodily needs, the limiting constraints of which are going to impose a basic, coarse framework on any story of existence, regardless of the discursive meanings generated by any social formation. Historical and anthropological evidence would seem to indicate that the human psyche has the potential for an infinite variety of structures. Language, discursive formations, narratives, are probably our only highway to the past (and to the present, for that matter) of our species. And the manifest phonemic and semantic continuities of language allow us to hope that historical difference is not a result of a discontinuous series of synchronic

87

systems which remain, forever, cognitively unbridgeable. Whatever the ultimate origins of language (which we can never know), it surely arose in a dialectical interaction between the material experience of the social group and the relentless imperatives of physical existence and survival in nature. The continuity of work, of 'backbreaking toil' as Jameson would say, the production and reproduction of human life, have more than likely constituted a continuous core of experience around which successive cultures have constructed their meanings. If Jameson is right about narratives, then despite the manifest malleability of the human psyche there remains something trans-historical in the human motivational make-up, call it configurations of desire, libidinal economy, or whatever. Reading narratives through the Jamesonian theoretical apparatus, we conclude that human beings in all stages of 'prehistory' have not felt at home in the social and discursive structures they have inhabited. Once we have convinced ourselves that there is this basically utopian impulse at the heart of our desires, we will be enabled to will the narrative denouement of survival. If we are to cease destroying the lifeworld that sustains us, it would seem that we must save ourselves from our consuming passions, but that can be accomplished only by restructuring our psyches through the work of socialist practice, creating a place where we will finally be at home. It is inconceivable, to me, that a society of agonized individualism can ever be in harmony with the necessities of nature. As matters stand, compulsory renunciation of consumption would be experienced only as loss and coercion. Since only a fraction (albeit a large one) of the world's inhabitants, the so-called 'developed world', is ultimately responsible for the growing catastrophe, and since the vagaries of the great capitalist global system may, at any rate, soon force us to renounce what we can not yet do without, it would be wise to keep telling the narratives of socialism to ourselves in convincing, plausible ways. Once we have internalized the belief that the pain and paranoia of competitiveness, of the will to dominate, are but the effects of a pathological, aberrant social order, perhaps we shall be able to set the agenda for human progress.[68]

NOTES

1 For a strong version of this assertion, see especially R. Young, *White Mythologies. Writing History and the West*, Routledge, London, 1990, p.vii.
2 Ibid., p.2.
3 Ibid., p.3.
4 See for example K. Marx and F. Engels, *Manifesto of the Communist Party*, Lawrence and Wishart, London, 1983, p.19.
5 Young, *White Mythologies*, p.2 and note p.176.
6 For a recent airing of my old dilemma, see especially R. Samuel, 'Grand narratives', in *History Workshop Journal* 29, Spring 1990, pp.120–33.

7 H. White, 'The fictions of factual representation', in H. White, *Tropics of Discourse. Essays in Cultural Criticism*, Johns Hopkins University Press, Baltimore, 1978, pp.126–7.
8 T. Eagleton, 'Wittgenstein's friends', in T. Eagleton, *Against the Grain*, Verso, London, 1986, pp.103–4. (Emphasis in original.)
9 P. Dews, *Logics of Disintegration. Poststructuralist Thought and the Claims of Critical Theory*, Verso, London 1987, pp.66, 247, note 85. (Dews is quoting from J. Lacan, *Ecrits*, Paris, 1966, p.329.)
10 D. Attridge, 'Language as history/history as language: Saussure and the romance of etymology', in D. Attridge, G. Bennington, R. Young (eds), *Poststructuralism and the Question of History*, Cambridge University Press, Cambridge, 1987, p.201. (Emphasis in original.)
11 Dews, *Logics of Disintegration*, p.xiii.
12 H. White, *Metahistory. The Historical Imagination in Nineteenth-Century Europe*, Johns Hopkins University Press, Baltimore, 1973, p.433.
13 H. White, 'Introduction' to *Tropics of Discourse*, pp.22–3.
14 I am alluding of course to L. von Ranke's celebrated dictum in his *Geschichten der romanischen und germanischen Völker von 1494–1514*, 2nd edn (*Sämtl. Werke* 33–4), Leipzig, 1874, p.vii.
15 H. White, 'Interpretation in history', in *Tropics of Discourse*, pp.58–9. (Emphasis in original.)
16 Ibid., pp.58.
17 Ibid., pp.58–9.
18 H. White, 'The historical text as literary artifact', in *Tropics of Discourse*, p.86. (Emphasis in original.)
19 Ibid., p.87. (Emphasis in original.)
20 Ibid., p.88. (Emphasis in original.)
21 Ibid., p.90. (Emphasis in original.)
22 C. Taylor, review of P. Dews, *Logics of Disintegration*, in *New Left Review* 170, July/August 1988, p.116.
23 H. White, 'The politics of historical interpretation: discipline and de-sublimation', in H. White, *The Content of the Form. Narrative Discourse and Historical Representation*, Johns Hopkins University Press, Baltimore, 1987, p.73.
24 R. Williams, *Keywords*, London, Fontana, 1976, pp.119–20.
25 H. White, 'The Fictions of factual representation', in *Tropics of Discourse*, p.123.
26 H. White, 'The question of narrative in contemporary historical theory', in *The Content of the Form*, p.37.
27 H. White, 'The fictions of factual representation', in *Tropics of Discourse*, p.122; 'The historical text as literary artifact', in *Tropics of Discourse*, p.99.
28 R. Barthes, 'The great family of man', in *Mythologies*, Granada, London, 1983, pp.100–2. For a recent discussion of Barthes' essay, see R. Young, *White Mythologies*, pp.122ff.
29 Barthes, *Mythologies*, pp.100–1.
30 Ibid., p.101.
31 T. Bennett, 'Texts in history: the determinations of readings and their texts', *Poststructuralism and the Question of History*, p.68.
32 See P. Anderson, *In the Tracks of Historical Materialism*, Verso, London, 1983, pp.83ff.
33 T. Eagleton, 'Capitalism, modernism and postmodernism', in *Against the Grain*, p.145.
34 F. Jameson, *The Political Unconscious. Narrative as a Socially Symbolic Act*, Methuen, London, 1981, p.11.

35 H. White, 'Droysen's *Historik*: historical writing as a bourgeois science', *The Content of the Form*, pp.101–2. (For further relevant discussions, see T. Lovell, *Pictures of Reality*, BFI, London, 1980; C. Belsey, *Critical Practice*, Methuen, London, 1980.)
36 H. White, 'Droysen's *Historik*', in *The Content of the Form*, p.87.
37 Ibid., pp.86–7.
38 H. White, 'The politics of historical interpretation', in *The Content of the Form*, p.81.
39 Ibid., p.72.
40 See Note 8.
41 P. Dews, *Logics of Disintegration*, p.242.
42 T. Eagleton, 'Marxism, structuralism and poststructuralism', in *Against the Grain*, p.91. (See also P. Anderson, *In the Tracks of Historical Materialism*, pp.48, 64.)
43 R. Williams, 'Problems of materialism', *New Left Review* 109, May-June 1978, pp.3–17; reprinted in R. Williams, *Problems in Materialism and Culture*, Verso, London, 1980, pp.103–22.
44 Williams, *NLR* 109, 1978, p.6.
45 Ibid., p.7 (emphasis added).
46 Ibid. p.8.
47 Ibid., p.10.
48 Ibid., p.11.
49 See Young, *White Mythologies*, pp.55ff. for a recent discussion of notions of historical time.
50 H. White, 'The Metaphysics of narrativity: time and symbol in Ricoeur's philosophy of history', in *The Content of the Form*, pp.178–9.
51 See V.N. Voloshinov, *Marxism and the Philosophy of Language*, trans. L. Matejka and I.R. Titunik, Harvard University Press, Cambridge, Mass., 1986; M.M. Bakhtin, *The Dialogic Imagination*, ed. M. Holquist, trans. C. Emerson and M. Holquist, University of Texas Press, Austin, 1981.
52 See D. Attridge, 'Language as history/history as language', pp.187–8.
53 See H. White, 'Droysen's *Historik*', in *The Content of the Form*, p.95.
54 F. Jameson, *The Political Unconscious*, p.285.
55 Ibid., p.252. (In Jameson's text, the word '*Gesellschaft*' appears instead of the word '*Gemeinschaft*' which I have substituted for it. I have taken the unspeakable liberty of changing the passage, since I am convinced that there is an error in the original text. If I am wrong, I crave forgiveness.)
56 Ibid., p.79.
57 H. White, 'Getting out of history: Jameson's redemption of narrative', in *The Content of the Form*, p.165.
58 See also T. Lovell, *Pictures of Reality*, p.16.
59 F. Jameson, *The Political Unconscious*, p.82 (emphasis in original).
60 Ibid., p.102.
61 See F. Jameson, 'Marxism and historicism', in *The Ideologies of Theory. Essays 1971–1986*, vol.2: *The Syntax of History*, Routledge, London, 1988, p.150; and F. Jameson, *The Political Unconscious*, p.35.
62 F. Jameson, *The Political Unconscious*, p.225.
63 Ibid., p.70.
64 H. White, 'Jameson's redemption of narrative', in *The Content of the Form*, p.147; F. Jameson, *The Political Unconscious*, p.35.
65 F. Jameson, 'Marxism and historicism', in *The Ideologies of Theory*, vol.2, p.162.
66 H. White, 'The politics of historical interpretation', in *The Content of the Form*, pp.76ff. See also T. Lovell, *Pictures of Reality*, p.37.

During the time that has elapsed since I wrote this section on Hayden White, an intense and widespread debate has been conducted regarding the moral and political implications of White's putative 'extreme relativism' (Friedlander) and 'unlimited skeptical attitude toward historical narratives' (Ginzburg). A prime focal point for this debate was the conference on 'Nazism and the "Final Solution": Probing the Limits of Representation' held at UCLA in April 1990. An invaluable collection of papers presented at that conference appeared in book form in 1992, edited by Saul Friedlander and published by Harvard University Press (*Probing the Limits of Representation. Nazism and the 'Final Solution'*). In his excellent Introduction to the book, Friedlander poses the central queasy question: 'Can the extermination of the Jews of Europe be the object of theoretical discussions?' (p.1), and goes on to summarize, with consummate skill, the manifold positions taken up by the various contributors to the volume. I mention here only the virulent attack on White by Carlo Ginzburg ('Just One Witness'), in which he insists that '... White's contribution can be fully understood only in the framework of his intellectual development' (p.87), and traces this framework to the Italian neoidealism of, particularly, Benedetto Croce and Giovanni Gentile, the latter being seen as the prime philosopher of Italian fascism. Ginzburg, in the course of his impassioned plea for historical objectivity and truth, brings himself to the extremity of maintaining that 'White's argument connecting truth and effectiveness inevitably reminds us not of tolerance but of its opposite – Gentile's evaluation of the blackjack as a moral force' (p.94). In his own contribution ('Historical Emplotment and the Problem of Truth') to the volume, White offers what Friedlander calls 'a compromise position' (p.7): White invokes 'Roland Barthes's notion of "intransitive writing"...', a writing that 'denies the distances among the writer, text, what is written about, and, finally, the reader' (p.47), and, like Barthes (in *The Rustle of Language*), he relates this notion to the ancient Greek 'middle voice': 'Whereas in the active and passive voices the subject of the verb is presumed to be external to the action, as either agent or patient, in the middle voice the subject is presumed to be *interior* to the action'. (See p.48 and Note on p.342). As I understand it, this theorization of a voice supposedly appropriate for representations of the Holocaust does not represent so much 'a compromise position' (*pace* Friedlander), as, rather, another attempt on the part of White to explain why no historical meta-narrative which obeys the protocols of classic realism can ever represent the Truth of the Holocaust. There can only be the myriad local truths of those un-distanced 'middle voices' expressing their experiences of being immersed in the reality and/ or in their particular knowledges of that incomprehensible congeries of (undoubted) historical events we retrospectively call 'the Holocaust'. If I am reading White here aright, he has not significantly changed his long-standing epistemological position.

67 F. Jameson, *The Political Unconscious*, p.261.
68 The first version of this chapter was completed before the appearance of Fredric Jameson's most recent books. Although Jameson has moved on to a variety of newer concerns in his long-term project of 'cognitive mapping', I have chosen to let my discussion of his writings stand as it is. See F. Jameson, *Late Marxism. Adorno, or, the Persistence of the Dialectic*, Verso, London, 1990; *Postmodernism, or, The Cultural Logic of Late Capitalism*, Verso, London, 1991. For a recent trenchant critique of Jameson, see R. Young, 'The Jameson raid', in Young, *White Mythologies*, pp.91–118.

5

WALTER SCOTT
A New Historical Paradigm
Bob Chase

> The title of this work has not been chosen without the grave and
> solid deliberation which matters of importance demand from the
> prudent.
>
> Walter Scott, Waverley

The first sentence of Walter Scott's first novel sounds a note of bogus
gravitas which is perhaps not totally inappropriate for yet another
scholarly lucubration on Scott himself, that protean scribbler whose
inveterate mimicry rapidly becomes contagious and prevents one from
eschewing completely those hints of frivolousness which the prudent
normally banish from their own works of solid deliberation. Given the
present context of theoretical and historiographical concerns within
which the results of my grave efforts are to appear, I can't help but
think of a variety of conceivable titles which, analogous to Scott's playful
send-ups of literary conventions in 1805/14, would trigger off predictable
reader expectations in academics attuned to those issues which preoccupy
us in the 1990s.[1]

Had I, for example, entitled my work 'Walter Scott: The bard of internal
colonialism', what reader would not be reminded of those historical
narratives of Scott which can be read as legitimating and naturalizing
a convincing historical tale of England's imposition of its dominance
over its Celtic periphery?[2] That 'gradual influx of wealth, and extension
of commerce'[3] into the Highlands, celebrated by the narrator in the concluding chapter of *Waverley*, sounds for all the world like 'the essentially
colonial process by which English institutions and markets expanded
into the regions of the Celtic fringe'.[4] Textual evidence abounds, if taken
out of context, to support the view that Scott's narratives even share
that 'racist ideology which held that Norman Anglo-Saxon culture was
inherently superior to Celtic culture'[5] and thereby 'buttressed' English
military and political control in the peripheral regions. After all, does not
the petty-aristocratic Englishman Edward Waverley possess a 'general
philanthropy which render[s] it almost impossible for [him] to have
passed any person in ... distress', as opposed to those 'wild petticoat-

men' from the Highlands whose rigidly delimited solicitude extends only to members of their own clan?[6] We also know, of course, that this benighted Highland parochialism of sentiment can, with a slight adjustment of the cultural lens, be represented as a quaint, touching sort of unswerving loyalty to superiors (witness Evan Dhu's offer to be 'headed' or hanged in place of his 'Chief'),[7] a convenient trait in peripheral subalterns which will subsequently see service in a sort of 'subsidiary patriotism'[8] within the Empire, helping to explain those proverbial martial virtues of Scottish soldiers around the globe and supplying a sort of borrowed glory to compensate for the fact that, especially away from the Lowland commercial and industrial axis, 'the bulk of the peripheral population will be confined to subordinate positions in the social structure'.[9] This 'cultural division of labor' will continue to fester, however, and will contribute to a political climate in which 'aggregate voting patterns in the Celtic lands continue [-] to be largely determined by cultural rather than social structural factors'.[10] Small wonder that the Scots led the battle against the poll tax and needed to be reminded of their soldierly virtues and subsidiary patriotism by means of a service of thanksgiving and remembrance, in Glasgow, to commemorate their gallantry in the Gulf War! Perhaps old Trotsky was right to see in Scott nothing but 'the bard of the colonizing merchants'[11] (another conceivable title to conjure with).

But, my gentle readers might protest, Scott showed scarce interest in the Empire and was more concerned with stabilizing the Union. Had I expanded my notion of a 'racist ideology', and had I, borrowing from Edward Said,[12] entitled my work 'Sir Walter Scott, or Celticism (Gaelicism?) Revisited', what head so obtuse as not to image forth Scott as a profligate lackey of the English, determined to curry favour with a (largely) English readership by constructing an inferior Scottish Other much in need of the blessings of rational English culture and commerce? Before our very eyes we would witness the construction of a perfidious colonial discourse which would serve the English 'style for dominating, restructuring, and having authority over'[13] the Highlands. Within the overall discursive project, one might discern at least four conceptual nodal points which serve to anchor, structure, and lend coherence to the network of continuing knowledge-production: (i) I might start with Scott's representation in *Waverley* of the lamentable economic backwardness and under-productiveness of the region: evidenced by the banditry and cattle-rustling of the Highland 'caterans'; dominated by the elaborate protection rackets run by Highland magnates of the likes of Fergus MacIvor; and benignly neglected, in his anachronistic aristocratic indolence, by the jovial but addle-pated Baron of Bradwardine whose medieval lifestyle – legitimated by feudal tenure – battens on the labours of the dirty and half-starved residents of the hamlet of Tully-Veolan, whose agricultural methods have stagnated in the use of a 'common field, where the joint labour of the villagers cultivated alternate ridges and patches of rye, oats, barley, and peas, each of such minute extent, that at a little distance the unprofitable variety of the surface resembled a tailor's book of patterns'.[14] (Hereupon would follow a sober survey of contemporary official accounts and compilations of government statistics bewailing the 'over-population' of the Highlands, proclaiming the need for agricultural rationalization, and piously documenting and legitimating the notorious Highland Clearances.)[15] (ii) Next I might point out textual evidence for the 'noble savagery'[16] of the Highland Other by emphasizing, say, the child-like loyalty of Evan Dhu at his trial in Carlisle (see above) and by pointing to the depiction of his ilk as rather retarded, touching children (viewed, like all inferior races and like women, as stunted in their evolutionary development, imprisoned in a lower 'stage' of the progress of civilization), who need a better form of government than that provided by the machiavellian Highland lairds but who, simultaneously, embody a sort of natural simplicity against which a jaded civility might be criticized.[17] (iii) Then I would hypothesize that the text of *Waverley* constructs a libidinal threat to the rational, property-owning English*man*:[18] concentrating, firstly, on the eroticizing rhetoric[19] of the descriptions of 'sublime', disorderly Highland landscapes with their thrusting peaks, beshrubbed clefts (glens) and foaming streams, and associating this *locus amoenus* of romance with, say, Flora – that Celtic bundle of black hair and female wilfulness – whose sexual energies have been sublimated into her anachronistic political fanaticism and who must ultimately be replaced, in Edward Waverley's affections, by the docile, domesticated, Scottish/English Rose, whose 'very soul is in home, and in the discharge of all those quiet virtues of which home is the centre'.[20] (Yet another title suggests itself: 'Walter Scott: The reconstruction of gender identities in an age of imperial expansion'.) (iv) Finally I would trace the construction of 'the exotic' by the voyeuristic gaze of the touring Englishman: including the aforementioned child-like 'natives'; the 'sublime', disorderly, pre-industrial, un-English landscape (as opposed to 'English hedgerows, enclosures, and farmhouses');[21] and all of those quaint 'native' accoutrements such as tartans, kilts, sporrans, and bagpipes which now adorn our picture postcards and whisky labels and, in their day, prefigured our penchant for Navaho blankets, native dances, and African sculpture.

Or again, this time listening to the perhaps more important resonances of Scott beyond these islands, if my work had been entitled 'Walter Scott: The creator of nationhoods', wouldst thou not, gentle reader, have demanded from me a dashing sketch of those literary imitations of Scott which arguably contributed to senses of imagined communities in North America and on the Continent of Europe? Fenimore Cooper, with his doughty Anglo-Saxon republic of tidy hamlets inhabited by ruggedly individualistic yeoman farmers, defining themselves over against a haunting world of virgin forests beyond the frontier which separates them from developmentally anachronistic noble savages and savage treachery alike, would make his appearance,[22] followed by his epigonal imitators in Hollywood, who continued to contrast settled agricultural life (including caring women back at the ranch) with that anachronistic but heady sort of lawless all-male freedom beyond the bounds of civility, until it was decided that the cowboy and the farmer should be friends. One would also need to assess the effect of Scott himself upon the American South:

> [Mark Twain] makes poor Sir Walter responsible for the gimcrack Gothic of the Louisiana state capitol, the flowery style of Southern newspaper reporters, and finally for all the benighted feudalism and reaction of Southern life. Indeed he says that Scott did so much to form Southern character, that he was 'in great measure responsible for the [Civil] war'.[23]

If Mark Twain was right, this would mean that Southerners managed to identify with the side that *loses* in all the Waverley Novels. For those of us brought up on *Gone With The Wind*, this thesis seems to have a lot to recommend it: all of those stilted, drawling, 'aristocratic' Southern ladies and gentlemen with their faithful black 'feudal' retainers, threatened by the influx of Yankee industrial wealth and the extension of commerce and in fear of losing their feudal tenures through things such as emancipation proclamations.

And we would then move on to the European Continent: Balzac's wild re-creation of the Scottish Highlands in Brittany (*Les Chouans*, 1829),[24] where a backward, benighted Breton peasantry, suitably led by disguised priests and a dashing, handsome aristocratic emigré à la Bonnie Prince Charlie, rebel against a rationalistic republican Paris and envisage a sort of capital in Fougères, which becomes in Balzac's prose the rhetorical equivalent of Edinburgh and later supplies the setting for a breathless denouement of sexual passion and slaughter in scenes of voluptuous Catholic sensuality and morbidity. (If one can believe what one reads in the papers, Breton nationalists still look to *Les Chouans* for inspiration before blowing up electricity pylons.) And on the tamer side, Theodor Fontane discovers yet another *locus amoenus* as a focal point for, this time, Prussian nationalist community feeling[25] when he transfers the attractions of Scott's Highlands to the Mark Brandenburg (*Wanderungen durch die Mark Brandenburg*, 1862–82; *Vor dem Sturm*, 1878) and constructs a solid sort of earthy 'Prussianness' in opposition to the fashionable French (and frenchified Berlin), locating – like Scott – much of his writing in an imagined space existing, discursively, somewhere between the fashionable world of the society novel and the exotic never never land of the old romance.[26] Finally, one might mention Adalbert Stifter, beloved by W.H. Auden, who, in a ponderous attempt to imitate Scott (*Witiko*, 1865/67), essayed to compose a national prose epic for Bohemia by transplanting the literary landscape of Scotland into the heart of Europe, where it changed into an attractively anachronistic nation of stolid, sword-swinging Bohemian worthies in the process of being assimilated reluctantly into the more prosaic but advanced culture of the medieval German empire.[27] Analogous to England's expansion, the ascendancy of the Reich is viewed as historically inevitable, necessarily overwhelming smaller cultural entities, the obliteration of whose anachronistic features can be viewed with melancholy resignation. (Stifter's travesty of Palacky's *History of Bohemia* was intended as a propagandistic palliative in the post-1848 period of nationalist unrest within the Habsburg empire, and continued to serve analogous, Hitlerian, purposes before and after 1938.) This list of Continental appropriations or discursive modifications of Scott could be extended at will – to include perhaps even Manzoni's *The Betrothed* or Tolstoy's *War and Peace*, but I am perhaps tyrannizing unnecessarily long over the impatience of my reader.

But damn the impatience of readers! If we want to take the (epistemologically dubious) position that the meanings of texts are fixed for all time by the discourses putatively in circulation during the period of their composition, then – borrowing from recent historiographical reconstructions of the growth of the British Empire – I might suggest another title or two. 'Walter Scott: Empire and agrarian patriotism' has a good solid historian's ring to it, and suggests Bayly's emphasis on contemporary official encouragement of 'tributary patriotisms' in Britain which would be compatible with empire.[28] Within the Union, this meant for Scotland, *faute de mieux*, the assertion of patriotism by assimilation, since the Scottish nation was felt to be in decline.[29] In practice, it proved to be a celebration of the patriotic aspect of agrarian improvement, especially in the Highlands and Islands, and was expressed to a great extent in dry statistical compilations on Scotland which were tantamount to an elaborate plan of assimilation and control.[30] Bayly sees all of this as part of the colonialist imperial strategy: fostering subordinate forms of nationalism within the empire by rediscovering indigenous languages, literatures and customs. 'This policy was seen at its most successful in the case of Scotland with the invention by Walter Scott and his generation of a Scottish mythology of national identity under the Crown.'[31]

Scott's personal stage-managing of the tartan charade of a be-kilted George IV landing in Leith from over the water in 1822 bears sufficient witness to the truth of Bayly's assertion.[32] And sure enough, the

Waverley Novels abound in examples of industrious yeoman farmers and a flourishing agrarian capitalism, enforced by paternalistic gentlemen (think of Scott himself at Abbotsford!) and contributing to the wealth of the puissant nation/Union. In *Old Mortality*, King William's 'peace' after 1689 enables Cuddie Headrigg and his faithful Jenny to flourish in bucolic (pre-Union) comfort among hedges, flourishing orchards, cattle and strutting chickens.[33] In *Guy Mannering*, the eponymous English army officer, returning to Scotland after having sorted out affairs of state in colonial India, befriends the doughty yeoman farmer Dandie Dinmont, who presides benignly but effectively over his dogs, his women and his agricultural enterprise. In *The Heart of Midlothian*, read by James Kerr as a 'romance of national regeneration', Jeanie Deans finds happiness and prosperity with Reuben Butler on the experimental farm at Knocktarlitie under the aegis of 'the improving spirit and agricultural skill' of the Duke of Argyle, that 'embodiment of the enlightened aristocracy Scott saw as the right ruling authority of the nation'.[34] Again, the list of examples could be expanded at will. But before we leave off this potentially endless game, perhaps I should just mention another catch-all title: 'Walter Scott: The avuncular sage of victorious capitalism'. It was Lukács, of course, who first tried systematically to re-construct Scott as the great novelistic forerunner of historical materialism and stressed his (Scott's and his own) bourgeois humanistic credentials as part of the Comintern's popular front strategy in 1937. Accordingly, 'Scott endeavours to portray the struggles and antagonisms of history by means of characters who, in their psychology and destiny, always represent social trends and historical forces'.[35]

The 'struggles and antagonisms', not surprisingly, are those between the aristocracy and the revolutionary bourgeoisie, the ruling classes in the opposed historical modes of production. Into his flattering portrait of 'the age-old steadfastness of English development amidst the most terrible crises',[36] Lukács inserts Scott's 'mediocre' heroes, who allegedly embody the good old British middle way between warring extremes and recapitulate in their careers the grand Hegelian synthesis of an historically redundant feudalism and a victorious capitalism. The petty aristocrat Edward Waverley, for instance, being by virtue of geography and the accidents of education a malleable person caught between the anachronistic values and relationships of feudal Scotland and the ascendant *contractual* relations of commercial England, ultimately becomes a staunch Hanoverian and settles down into a sensible middle-class ménage in a house that has been bought and paid for – and he has the deed to prove it. Alexander Welsh, on the other hand, although he would doubtless endorse my proffered title, will countenance no highfalutin' talk of Hegelian historical progress in Scott. In his Reichian-Freudian zeal to convince us that all restraint of libidinal impulses is bad

97

for our psychic health and serves only the interests of capitalism, Welsh insists that those passive, wimpish, up-tight Waverley heroes project only a timeless image of the self-restrained British property-owner and serve as a compositional thread through Scott's 'romance of property, the myth that property (real happiness) automatically devolves upon those who respect the existing arrangement of things'.[37] 'The hero is not precisely Everyman, but every gentleman – not in some supercilious social sense, but in the profound conviction that society is a compact of independent owners of property.'[38]

The odd thing about my game with titles is that all of it or none of it may be true, depending on how we choose to read Scott's texts.[39] The problem hitherto, however, is that I have usually been tacitly denying the fictionality of those texts and disregarding their status as constellations of invented narrative voices which just may not add up to any coherent statement about any putative extra-textual realities whatsoever. I have been behaving as if the 'content' of a Scott text had nothing to do with the deployment of narrative conventions and devices. It is as if I had decided that there existed and exists (in his texts) a knowable (by us) writing human subject (called Scott) who, in his liberal humanist epistemological certainty, surveyed the social and political issues of his day and shaped them into some sort of politically loaded representation by means of his recuperable (by us), consistent, coherent, non-contradictory, unitary narrative voice.[40] I seem to have been assuming that, by assimilating a modicum of (extra-discursive?) knowledge of political and cultural history, I too could, if I wished, reconstruct the 'meaning' of Scott's texts – a meaning which would be anchored referentially in the reality of Scott's own world. As Kerr reminds us, 'we know that in Scott's own time, the popularity of the Waverley novels rested largely on the perceived reality of his writing'.[41] So the ideological pressures which, I have playfully been suggesting, were possibly exerted upon readers by Scott's texts, were perhaps very real indeed and deadly serious in their effects. But I can't really *know* that, and I still find it hard to believe that Scott's 'inveterate mimicry' (which has infected my own writing) went totally unnoticed by all of his contemporary readers. If Scott's texts are – even in part – a tissue of parody, pastiche and mimicry, who am I to assert that one particular narrative voice (some putatively 'privileged' discourse?) has pretensions to being the 'real voice' of the 'real' Scott, as he constructs his novelistic colonialist programme? James Kerr (whose arguments intersect with mine in a number of places) claims that

By eliding the historical referent he had supplied in the earlier novels [before *Redgauntlet*], Scott shifts the emphasis of his writing, to a greater degree than ever, towards the processes of making historical narrative. He makes the fact of the novel's fictionality its defining feature ...

... Scott's self-conscious playing with the procedures of historical representation anticipates a more modern preoccupation with the power and limits of the imagination as an instrument for writing history and with the problematic relationship between language and reality. Scott is at his most modern in *Redgauntlet*, where the accurate observation of historical conditions is deemphasized in favour of metafictional reflection.[42]

My only quarrel with Kerr would be one of emphasis: I suspect that the 'historical referent' is equally elusive in *all* of Scott's novels. In another context, Kerr insists that he is not suggesting 'that Scott was a meta-historian in the ironic mode of Hayden White'.[43] I still suspect that such a 'suggestion' might have a lot to recommend it.

Were we still celebrating the rather shopworn triumphs of high post-structuralism, I would venture to suggest yet another title for my work: 'Walter Scott, or self-consuming discourses'. It would simply be too easy, however, to count the number of times Scott's narrative voices: (i) address the reader, (ii) append silly 'historical' footnotes calling attention to the fictionality of the fiction, and (iii) meditate on the processes of constructing plots, withholding information, misleading the reader, and arriving at a 'satisfying' novelistic closure; needless to say, devices are continuously bared, the textuality of texts is always being rubbed under our noses, and the constructedness of constructed historical and fictional worlds can never be far from our lazy readers' consciousnesses. Any novel by Scott is fully as much 'about' the technique of its own making as is Shklovsky's beloved *Tristram Shandy*. Scott cannot be accused of composing any perfidious 'classic realist text' which ideologically ensnares its hapless reader in the toils of a self-telling 'privileged' discourse or woos him/her with the blandishments of 'illusionism'. Scott's texts are clearly 'interrogative' and 'writerly' – liberating the reader to romp among the 'polyphonous' voices that assure us of the construct-edness of all ideologies by demonstrating the conventionality of all signifying conventions.[44] Any sensible reader must scorn all of my cheap gibes about 'colonialist discourses' and 'agrarian patriotism'. The texts are about themselves.

Despite my flippant tone, I am not yet willing to surrender all of the hard-won theoretical insights of the last few decades. Our continuing critique of 'expressive realism', proceeding – at a distance – from the original structuralist theories of language, must not be allowed to collapse back into a flaccid sort of neo-liberal empiricist model of textual analysis, however critical our intentions may be. If there is a villain among nineteenth-century historians and novelists, surely it is not Scott (or any other individual), but rather our notorious subject of liberal bourgeois humanism who, in the arrogant assumption that he/she possesses an autonomous, unified, extra-discursive self capable of registering and re-presenting the past (or the present) *'wie es eigentlich gewesen'*[45] (or is), constructs knowledges of other peoples in order to dominate them. It is our empiricist epistemology, underpinning our 'progressive' liberal ideology, that has enabled England to expand and still enables the West to dictate to the East and to the South. Edward Said supplies some telling quotations from Henry Kissinger's essay 'Domestic structure and foreign policy' which hardly require further comment:

> [The West] is deeply committed to the notion that the real world is external to the observer, that knowledge consists of recording and classifying data – the more accurately the better ... Cultures which escaped the early impact of Newtonian thinking have retained the essentially pre-Newtonian view that the real world is almost completely *internal* to the observer ... [Consequently], empirical reality has a much different significance for many of the new countries than for the West because in a certain sense they never went through the process of discovering it.[46]

Regardless of what position we take up vis à vis Kissinger's arrogant epistemological certainties, I want to argue in what follows that Scott harboured a subversive 'conservative' strain of epistemological thinking that refused to embrace the triumphal liberal 'progressiveness' of his contemporaries and resulted in texts which constantly disrupt and subvert any comfortable assumptions that the world and its history can be represented in language and in 'realist' narratives. I would assert that Scott remained closer to that Renaissance humanist position which accepts the possibility of different but equal rationalities on the basis of differences in cultures and histories, as Montaigne did.[47] Hence Scott, along with a remnant of others stretching from, say, Vico to Marx, was not 'the white man [who] takes his own mythology ... his own *logos*, that is, the *mythos* of his idiom, for the universal form that he must still wish to call Reason'.[48] He resisted that 'project of history as a history of progress and the project of the subject as the (rational) agent of history'; his counter-epistemology subverts the truth/power of the colonialist subject. Were I willing and able to pursue this line of Derridean theoretical argument further, I might suggest one last alternative title for my work: 'Walter Scott, or refusing to change the subject', but I scorn to tyrannize longer over the impatience of my reader, who is doubtless anxious to know why I have the temerity, despite everything, to associate the name of Walter Scott with 'a new historical paradigm'.

Accidents in my own life and education have led me to consider this strange case of Walter Scott – that massively best-selling author of the early nineteenth century whose name was once mentioned in one breath with Shakespeare and Milton and who was banished, by means of a brief footnote, from F.R. Leavis's Great Tradition.[49] Not even the voracious critical machinery of poststructuralism, which has managed to deify, say, Laurence Sterne for his defamiliarizing anti-realism and to damn most of the 'classic realists' for their putative collusion in a stabilizing bourgeois ideology, seems to have found time to turn its attention to the – arguably – socially and politically most significant author during Britain's period of greatest industrial and imperial expansion.[50] Despite a handful of admirable exceptions, traditional and anti-traditional academic criticism seems to consider Scott beneath its dignity – rather like Zane Grey or Mills and Boon romances. I am at a loss to explain the mechanisms of this strange exclusion.[51] In what follows, I have no intention of attempting to shake up the canon by re-inserting Scott (though it might not be a bad idea). Nor am I driven by any missionary zeal to prove that Scott was somehow more humanely progressive than other nineteenth-century novelists (he surely was not). I am interested, however, in exploring the 'conservative' narratives of Scott, with a view towards buttressing my own hypothesis that it was precisely his 'radical conservatism' that resulted in his critical eclipse by the 'progressive' narratives of nineteenth-century 'realism'. It is my view that it was his 'conservative ideology', refusing to embrace the triumphant 'progressivist' liberal empiricism of his century, that led him to foreground narratives of history which project an alterable and culturally contingent 'human nature'. At the moment when the protocols of a newly academicized discipline of 'history' were distancing themselves, in the wake of the French Revolution, from 'fictional' compositions and over-arching stories of human development,[52] Scott refused to accept the conceptual distinctions between 'story' and 'history', 'history' and 'philosophy of history', 'romance' and 'novel'. It is my opinion that it was this refusal that resulted ultimately in his undoing at the hands of academic criticism.

Before I continue to bandy about words such as 'conservative' and 'progressive', however, perhaps I should explain a few terms. Most useful for me, I have found, is the dialectical historiographical argument underlying Michael McKeon's monumental book, *The Origins of the English Novel, 1660–1740* (1987).[53] If nothing else, McKeon has demonstrated brilliantly the ultimate inseparability of a reigning epistemology and the social order it sustains and is sustained by. 'Questions of truth' in a society are deeply implicated in the 'questions of virtue' regarding the legitimacy of any social hierarchy characterized by relations of domination and subordination. In what follows I shall be attempting to recapitulate, in a necessarily distorting, fragmented summary form,

McKeon's richly elaborate dialectical 'story' of early modern England's cultural and political history, a story which is structured by a series of discursive reversals and counter-reversals. For my own purposes, I shall be extending his story into the nineteenth century and extrapolating conclusions applicable to Walter Scott and to my own notions of historical narratives capable of projecting a vision of human self-transformation and ultimate reconciliation.

Once upon a time (I summarize crudely), the worth of a person was determined solely by his or her birth, validated by a punctilious attention to lineage. Noble birth was the guarantor of a person's inner worth – of the personal 'virtue' that legitimated a position of power and dominance in the social hierarchy. Ancientness of lineage, bodying forth the sanctions of a necessarily divinely ordained tradition, was the objective correlative of a belief that all knowledge of the world and humankind had been revealed to the Ancients, the writers of the Bible, and to the Church Fathers. Truth was known, *a priori*, on the basis of discursive apparatuses that had the sanction of tradition and authority. Error was usually the result of presumptuous human reliance on the evidence of fleshly sense experience, seen by dominant discourses as no more than a snare set by the forces of Evil in a post-lapsarian human world. The existing feudal social order was hence an earthly manifestation of divine truth; a corrosive individualistic analysis of the absurdity of inherited social honour by the likes of Gloucester's bastard son Edmund was clearly a sign of evil and un-truth (although the social categories had presumably become sufficiently destabilized by Shakespeare's time to give Edmund's social critique a subversive ring of plausibility). Inherent 'aristocratic nobility' was of course never an unthreatened, static, social category: the steadily decreasing importance of military prowess as a sign of inner nobility, and the rise of Renaissance humanist notions of '*true* nobility' being discoverable (or capable of being cultivated) in men of lesser birth, sufficiently destabilized social categories and created sufficient anxiety about status inconsistencies to generate countless romances which attempted to resolve discursively the social contradictions thrown up by a destabilized 'aristocratic ideology' ever more hard-pressed by the failures of 'idealist epistemology' to generate satisfactory explanations for social change. As proto-capitalist economic activities increasingly destabilized the inherited social order in early modern England, prompting the early Stuarts to distribute noble titles with ever increasing frequency, an 'inflation of honors'[54] resulted that threw the 'questions of virtue' – questions regarding the correspondence of social station to inner personal worth – into embarrassingly sharp relief. 'The inflation of honors helped fuel the critique of aristocratic ideology that I [McKeon] call[s] "progressive ideology", a critical posture that bears an analogous relation to naïve empiricism.'[55]

102

Francis Bacon's injunction to his fellow human beings to shake off the oppressing mental chains of received discursive structures sanctioned by tradition and authority[56] was hence not containable within some purely epistemological realm. The rejection of the authority of the Ancients and of ecclesiastical certainties by Bacon's natural philosophy, indeed the rejection of empirically untested *a priori* truths *tout court*, was inseparable from the rejection of any automatically assumed correspondence between noble birth and inner worth. Hence, the Baconian epistemological revolution necessarily questioned that status-specific personal 'virtue' of aristocrats which alone justified their position of dominance in the social order. If birth was no longer the *a priori* sign of worth, then there must be some other way of ascertaining 'real' personal and social virtue. The new criteria for measuring individual merit ('progressive ideology') would include the observable worldly accomplishments of a person and his (almost always his) degree of worldly success. That Protestantism, particularly in its introspective Puritan variants, supplied a mediating set of explanatory discourses for this massive ideological shift, has been thoroughly argued since the days of Weber and Tawney and, more recently, by Christopher Hill.[57] The 'romance' discourses of aristocratic ideology, underpinned by an idealist epistemology, find themselves increasingly embattled and intertwined with the 'realist' ('novelistic') discourses of the new progressive ideology, generated by the strengthening commitment to a 'naïve' empiricism in the process of being buttressed by its manifest success in unlocking the secrets of the natural world and in enabling the creation of ever more efficient methods of supplying the needs and wealth of a new capitalist society. Romances are being replaced by allegedly '*true* histories'. 'For progressive ideology, the experience of disenchantment with titles of nobility ... might seem the necessary prelude to the replacement of the old and outworn fictions by the new truth.'[58] As we know with the benefit of hindsight, these notions of 'true histories' will finally emerge victorious in the institutionalized discipline of academic history in the nineteenth century and in the narrative epistemology of the triumphant 'realist' novel.

Even before we pursue McKeon's story to its provisional denouement in the 1740s, one is struck by the parallels between his account of the consequences of the epistemological revolution and the manifest content of numerous novels by Scott, who was clearly never able to rest easy with the notion that the post-Baconian world represented unalloyed progress over the old aristocratic world of Romance. It was Scott, indeed, who was most likely responsible for popularizing a particular version of the Baconian 'revolution' (a considerable accomplishment for a novelist), although he was never content to allow that revolution an uncontested victory. In his very first novel, *Waverley* (1814), which appeared during the Napoleonic wars, at a time when conservative hysteria in England against radical agitation in the wake of the French Revolution was running high, Scott (or one of his narrating personae) portrays the leaders of the Jacobite uprising of 1745 as labouring within a pre-empiricist mental framework, whilst his Whiggish Hanoverian characters are motivated by a stolid sort of English pragmatism. Fergus MacIvor, the great aristocratic Highland magnate, has 'an intellect which was sharpened by the habit of acting on a preconceived and regular system'.[59] That system stands or falls, of course, on the *a priori* first principle of a political legitimacy based on the inherited rights of the House of Stuart (clearly a latter-day version of McKeon's 'aristocratic ideology', underpinned by an 'idealist epistemology'), but MacIvor's own 'idealism' proves to be shot through with tainting traces of personal ambition and the jealous desire for power and political aggrandizement (his coveted Earl's patent). This same Fergus is, of course, captured before the ultimate Jacobite defeat at Culloden and executed in a grisly manner by the English. In the context of 1814, this portrayal of the defeated Jacobites is richly ambiguous, even contradictory: Scott's nostalgia for his beloved aristocrats, evident in almost all of his novels, comes to the fore particularly in his portrayal of MacIvor's death, but his description of MacIvor's intellect, which in the thematic economy of the novel belongs to the superseded past of a pre-Baconian 'aristocratic' rationalism, is also reminiscent of that dread of abstract systems which the French *philosophes* (and Thomas Paine) inspired in Edmund Burke.[60] In MacIvor's case, however, that 'abstract system' is based ultimately on an idealist notion of inherited 'virtue', whereas Burke's attack is directed against abstract principles of government based on the empirically derived 'knowledge' of a putatively universal human nature.

Both Scott and Burke recoil from embracing the 'progressive ideology' of a Tom Paine, which would unleash the energies of entrepreneurial activities, but Scott continues to narrate a process of political and social *change*, shaped by determinate economic and social circumstances. In 1814, Scott's ideological tensions are manifest: like Burke before him and Macaulay after him, Scott is a great upholder of the putative achievements of the Glorious Revolution of 1688; but – also like Burke – he has a hankering for an old aristocratic world of traditional, habituated principles of thought and behaviour. In 1814, with the French Revolution still inspiring ideologically dangerous versions of 'liberty' and 'human nature', it is a risky undertaking to divide one's narrative sympathies between defeated aristocrats and triumphant, 'progressivist' Hanoverians and to narrate – with whatever ambivalences of tone and perspective – the historically necessary defeat of an 'aristocratic' undertaking ('The Forty-Five') which sought to undo the results of William III's *coup d'état*. Scott, it seems, can pull it off only by making his Jacobite 'dark hero'[61] pathologically obsessed with abstract principles of honour and legitimacy which belong simultaneously to a lost but not emotionally repudiated past and, by rhetorical suggestion, to a present threatened by newer, abstract notions of liberty and democracy. It is the tortuous attempts to square the circle that make the novel politically interesting.[62] It's small wonder that Scott spent the rest of his writing life exploring and re-exploring that great cultural revolution which transformed the old, ostensibly static, aristocratic mental universe of feudalism into our modern bourgeois world of thrusting individualism and pragmatic commerce. And of course, at the centre of his entire novel-writing enterprise, Scott is worrying away at the ultimately unanswerable questions regarding the degree to which human nature is an a-historical given and the extent to which it is a product of particular historical and social circumstances. The contradictory answers offered in the first and last chapters of *Waverley* (of which more below) set a sort of writing agenda which Scott never abandoned for very long.

The Baconian epistemological revolution itself is perhaps the most obvious thematic concern of *The Fortunes of Nigel* (1822), a novel seldom mentioned nowadays, but one of which seven thousand copies were sold 'before half-past ten o'clock'[63] on the day of its publication. Set in the reign of James I of England, the novel constructs a world in which 'some beams of chivalry . . . continued to animate and gild the horizon', but

> . . . the hour was already arrived when Bacon was about to teach the world that they were no longer to reason from authority to fact, but to establish truth by advancing from fact to fact, till they fixed an indisputable authority, not from hypothesis, but from experiment.[64]

The passage would seem not to leave much doubt as to where the narrator's sympathies lie in the great epistemological upheaval; indeed, there is an odour of the free-thinker about these 'fictional' remarks which seems distinctly dangerous at a time (1822) so close to Peterloo (1819), when Scott, in the real world, defended the actions of the Manchester authorities passionately and publicly.[65] Of course the narrative voice does say that 'hypothesis' without experimental proof is an insufficient warrant for truth – and presumably for action as well – so one might also conclude that untried political 'hypotheses' (for example democratic institutions being fitting for universal, natural 'rights of man'), with no tradition behind them, are to be eschewed. However, there remains the ambiguous message that the accumulation of 'facts' can lead to new truths and, thereby, presumably to new political arrangements and institutions. As usual, however, we must be wary of Scott's inveterate irony and mischievous mimicry; after all, the narrative 'voice' quoted is but one of many. The sense of any piece of text can, particularly in the case of Scott, always easily tumble into its reverse. 'Indisputable authority', in the broader context of the moral and political economy of an entire novel, can turn out to be eminently disputable. We are far from the moral certainties of a Dickens or a George Eliot.

In this novel, though, it seems fair to conclude that the overall thematic structure culminates in a comfortable sort of compromise between rationalism and empiricism (as opposed to the stark, irreconcilable, tragic contrasts in, say, *The Bride of Lammermoor*). Parallel to and directly connected with the thematic revolution in epistemology are the final decay of chivalry, with its *a priori* dictates for human behaviour, and the rise of the commercial middle class, whose sole criterion for judging the merit of an idea or action is its practicability. Opposing epistemologies are embodied in sets of contrasting characters: in the very first chapter we are presented with two apprentices, one of whom (Francis Tunstall) considers himself to be of 'ancient and proud descent' and pays particular attention to the 'abstract principles of science', whereas his counterpart (Jin Vin) is a born-and-bred Londoner who knows 'every lane, blind alley, and sequestered court of the ward better than his catechism', and 'beat[s] his companion beyond the distance-post in everything like the practical adaptation of thorough practice in the dexterity of hand necessary to execute the mechanical branches of the art, and double-distance[s] him in all respecting the commercial affairs of the shop'.[66] Further contrasts are provided by the figures of already-anachronistic courtiers who no longer have a social function (such as Sir Mungo Malagrowther and the vain Duke of Buckingham), viewed against successful men of commerce such as George Heriot and David Ramsay. In the end, the merging of the two epistemological universes is symbolically consummated by a marriage: Nigel, the down-at-the-heels Lord of Glenvarloch, weds Margaret Ramsay, 'the daughter of a Lonnun mechanic'.[67] The implication for the future is, I suppose, that down-to-earth English empiricism will be tempered by inherited Scottish principles of honour and probity. This is presumably a comforting compromise for the captains of nineteenth-century industrial capitalism, but it can hardly be taken as licence for unbridled *laissez-faire* economics.[68]

Other, powerful, Scottian images of historical transition may not have been so comforting for many nineteenth-century contemporaries. In an unabashed return to the old romance motif of the lost heir of a noble family (in *Guy Mannering*, 1815), Scott creates a youthful hero, Harry Bertram, whose superior human qualities become manifest while he is yet a wandering commoner (birth = worth) and who returns to claim the estate of Ellangowan from the scheming parvenu Glossin. The moral economy of the novel makes it clear that the old paternalistic, symbiotic relationship between heritable lairdships and dependent, unproductive gypsy settlements was humanly superior to the new, calculating, ambitious world of upstart Glossins. The new legalistic society of 'improving' landlords has made the world a harsh place for the great eccentric characters of the likes of Meg Merrilies, who inhabits a mental universe shaped by unbreakable bonds of personal loyalty and filled with magical beliefs beyond the comprehension of a mechanical philosophy. It must not be forgotten, however, that it is the wise (but unbending) *English* officer, Colonel Mannering, whose ministrations in Scotland bring about the desired resolutions, after he has brought about order while doing duty in the colonial service in India. And it is the productive yeoman farmer, Dandie Dinmont, proud possessor of an idyllic cottage complete with doting wife and daughters, who clearly provides an object of unwavering narrative adulation. It seems to have been Dandie who inspired the fan-mail to the author of Waverley, often requesting puppies from the fictional dogs.[69]

The Bride of Lammermoor (1819), however, offers no such consolations. The Heathcliffe-like Master of Ravenswood, unversed in the devious-ness of post-1689 property law, has been deprived of his ancestral estate by the parvenu Ashton, the Lord Keeper, and has secluded himself in the castle of Wolf's Crag, a veritable parody of a half-ruined baronial pile. There he dwells and sulks in conditions of acute privation, sustained by the waning sentimental charity of erstwhile family retainers and comforted – only half ironically – by the comically strenuous efforts of an old butler (Caleb Balderston) – the Sancho Panza figure who, in comic reversal, inhabits the quixotic mental world of the old romance and who strives and always fails to resurrect an empirical world of aristocratic meals, plate, hospitality, and noble accoutrements to correspond to the discursive world of an aristocratic ideology which has lost all episte-mological moorings. This fictional situation would remain little more than a nostalgic, tragicomical narration of the decline of an old, lost way of life, were it not complicated by the unabashedly 'romantic' and melodramatic clash of the sexual passion (conceived of as a sort of, well, elemental force), shared by Ravenswood and Lucy Ashton (the daughter of the Lord Keeper), with the exigencies of the cash-and-property nexus of the new social order which dictates that women should be objects of profitable exchange in a male world of competition, political manoeuvre, and self-aggrandizement. Lucy's frenzied attempt, on her bridal night, to murder the bridegroom foisted upon her by her calculating parents, her madness and convulsive death (seized upon by romantic opera composers), followed by Ravenswood's ghastly demise in quicksand (swallowed up, as it were, by the elemental forces that had seemed to sustain him), all create an effect – however melodramatic – that leaves the reader with the impression that the social changes that have been narrated are not just the consequences of some drab, necessary historical 'progress', but are, rather, constitutive of a murderous social order that sacrifices all human ties to ambition and greed. Whatever compromises, prevarications, and spurious narrative solutions Scott may resort to here and in other novels, his narratives are always circling round a queasy suspicion that social values and human personalities may be merely historically contingent. It is not surprising that he was one of Marx's favourite authors.

Consideration of Scott's narrative solutions to his tortured narratives of historical transition, solutions which vary and hesitate as they do between half-comforting compromises (*Waverley*, *Nigel*), stark tragic loss (*The Bride of Lammermoor*), and parodistic send-up and pastiche (*Old Mortality*) of the conventional endings of 'realist' novels (whose plausibility depends on the common-sense acceptance of the 'progressive ideology' underpinned by our liberal empiricism),[70] brings us back to McKeon's historiographical 'story' of dialectical discursive reversals and counter-reversals, which – if I read it correctly – actually *predicts* Scott's 'conservative' narrative rejection of the blandishments of 'progressive' liberal ideology, which McKeon represents as never having managed to dispel completely the old suspicion of individualistic empirical assessment of personal worth and the nature of reality. By the end of the seventeenth century, to be sure,

> the argument of true nobility has ceased definitively to work as a stabilizer of aristocratic nobility – the exception proves the rule – and come to represent instead an alternative system of social ethics; ... in the traditional sense of the term, as a quality susceptible of inheritance, honor is no more credible than the fictions of romance.[71]

The idealist conventions of romance continue to radiate their nostalgic glow, however, and serve as the necessary dialectical antithesis against which novelistic discourses will increasingly be defined. More crucially (for my purposes here), however, the thrusting new progressive ideology generates (or better: has long been incubating) its own dialectical reversal. As we know from Weber and Tawney, that intensely introspective Protestant conscience, which sought to convince itself of its own individual merit and justification in the eyes of its threatening and personal god and looked for external signs of personal Election in the success of worldly enterprises, soon traversed the relatively short psychic distance from luminous, militant spirituality to the conviction that worldly success and wealth alone were sufficient signs of inner worth. It did not escape contemporaries (particularly aristocratic ones) that manifest greed, ambition, and aggressive competitiveness in upstart entrepreneurs and speculators were often masquerading as signs of inner spirituality and divine Election. The time was not yet come when totally open aggressiveness and avarice would be 'naturalized' as socially necessary, dynamic elements in an unchanging 'human nature'.[72] In progressive ideology, worldly success was replacing noble birth as a sign of socially legitimating inner virtue, but there existed still-powerful public discourses which still demanded something like a spiritual sanction for social-climbing – corresponding to something like pre-capitalist inborn personal merit – to legitimate the social power achieved through the accumulation of wealth. A social hierarchy based on *achieved* status, or better: positions of social power and domination achieved through the unleashing of greed and appetite, those ancient human failings traditionally regarded as 'unnatural' side-effects of the Fall from Grace, must surely be unnatural deviations from the divine order and abominations in the face of God, Man, and Nature. So progressive ideology, tending as it did to confuse ruthless ambition and greed with inner merit, generated in turn its dialectical reversal: 'conservative ideology'. Like its progressive adversary, conservative ideology also attacked the transparent fiction that noble birth is a guarantor of inner worth (aristocratic ideology) and rejected the fanciful idealistic 'lies' of romance, based on an idealist epistemology, which attempted discursively to legitimate a social order which seemed patently absurd and unjust; but it also struggled to grasp – or conserve elements of – a more humane social order which would somehow be based on notions of human worth representing a less catastrophic break with traditional truths and social values – a sort of 'translation' of public pre-capitalist values into terms of communitarian concerns and personal integrity organized around values generated by particular, common, regional, and national traditions. (At a later date, Scott is clearly trying to do something like this in his narrated clashes between traditional, pre-capitalist – usually Highland – Scottish cultural values and the upstart commercial enterprise culture from the South.) In terms of traditional notions of divine – or natural – justice and equity, conservative ideology was unable to comprehend why a new social system, which doomed people to suffer domination and exploitation because they happened to lack the 'unnatural' failings of greed and personal ambition, should be considered more 'just' than the traditional order, which placed people in the same unenviable position as the result of their lowly birth. The injustice of the arbitrary accidents of birth seemed less reprehensible than the public rewarding of unnatural desires.

Analogous to this 'conservative' assault on the 'progressive' assumption that empirically manifest individual abilities should legitimate a position of power within society, these conservatives also questioned the overweening confidence of the triumphalist empiricists that human beings would eventually comprehend all of reality through the agency of their unfettered sense experience and would be able to represent – indeed replicate in a sort of verbal simulacrum – the very structures of the natural, social, and psychic worlds in a carefully controlled use of language – that

109

clothing of thought which, if properly tailored, was believed to correspond perfectly to the contours of reality communicated to the mind by the objective apparatus of the senses. The dyspeptic prose of a Jonathan Swift, the subversive discursive horse-play of a Laurence Sterne, and the often convoluted, self-referential texts of Walter Scott bore witness to the conservative belief that an infinitely complex and kaleidoscopic human reality and the reality of the natural world could not be captured in linguistic strategies which must needs select, exclude, and shape by means of ultimately arbitrary principles of emphasis and the granting and withholding of human significance.[73] The confidently labelled 'true histories' of the 'progressive' empiricists were simply the old lying romances in modern guise. This recognition on the part of the 'conservative' ideologists that there was no necessary correspondence between 'the real' and human sense experience and linguistic strategies, resulted in what McKeon calls 'extreme skepticism', a dialectical reversal of empiricism and, simultaneously, a rejection of the older 'idealist' epistemology. 'Truth', for the conservative ideologist, can never be the function of universal, unchangeable, rational principles, but must remain – as Burke so passionately maintained – locally and temporally particular.

If truth – and, with it, moral and political values, human aspirations, and indeed human nature itself – is seen as culturally and historically contingent, we are of course plunged into that treacherous but fertile epistemological quagmire of historicism which underlies the philosophical efforts of, *inter alia*, Vico, Herder, Hegel, Marx, and many exponents of our contemporary anti-empiricist theory – many of whom hold out a vision of human self-transformation over time, within determinate material and social circumstances. It was this vision, and its agonizing uncertainties and contradictions, that preoccupied Walter Scott throughout much of his writing life. In his playful 'Introductory' chapter to *Waverley*, full of parody, pastiche and astute literary criticism (making the old poststructuralist point that the acceptability of any narrative is a function of the fit between reader expectations and various sets of storytelling conventions), Scott – or his narrative persona – informs his readers that he is going to throw the force of his narrative upon the characters and passions of the actors:

> those passions common to men in all stages of society, and which have alike agitated the human heart, whether it throbbed under the steel corslet of the fifteenth century, the brocaded coat of the eighteenth, or the blue frock and dimity waistcoat of the present day. Upon these passions it is no doubt true that the state of manners and laws casts a necessary colouring; but the bearings, to use the language of heraldry, remain the same, though the tincture may be not only different, but opposed in strong contradistinction.[74]

110

Here, as countless critics have pointed out,[75] is (or seems to be) Scott the belated Enlightenment sage, asserting the essential uniformity of human nature across ages and cultures. History would seem to be peopled at all times by the same creatures, putting on various sorts of fancy dress to suit the fashions of successive periods. The basic configuration of passions, like the armorial bearings in a family scutcheon, remains fixed and immutable; only the coloration, the 'tincture', of passions/bearings – that is, the mode of expression of inborn passion – changes in accordance with changing social arrangements and practices ('manners and laws').

In the final chapter ('A Postscript, Which Should Have Been A Preface') of *Waverley*, however, Scott seems to be contradicting the very premises upon which he announced his tale would be based:

There is no European nation which, within the course of half a century, or little more, has undergone so complete a change as this kingdom of Scotland. The effects of the insurrection of 1745 – the destruction of the patriarchal power of the Highland chiefs – the abolition of the heritable jurisdictions of the Lowland nobility and barons – the total eradication of the Jacobite party, which, averse to intermingle with the English, or adopt their customs, long continued to pride themselves upon maintaining Scottish manners and customs – commenced this innovation. The gradual influx of wealth, and extension of commerce, have since united to render the present people of Scotland a class of beings as different from their grandfathers as the existing English are from those of Queen Elizabeth's time.[76]

Whether becoming a different 'class of beings' also entails a rearrangement and/or replacement of the bearings in the scutcheon of human passions, remains an unanswered question. But without a doubt, the emphasis of these concluding comments by Scott has shifted massively away from the old-fashioned Enlightenment uniformitarianism expressed in his 'Introductory'. In important ways, people who live in a money economy and carry on commerce are creatures very different from those who live in patriarchal feudal clans dependent for their living on marauding and subsistence agriculture. Scott is saying that Scotland has moved from one stage of society (feudalism) to another (capitalism) and that people have changed accordingly. Scott would, of course, be the last person to deny the existence of some unchanging inner human 'substance', but he has clearly moved, in the course of writing his *Waverley*, to a more environmentalist view of human nature. Indeed, one can read *Waverley* as a protracted meditation on precisely that issue. And as was maintained above, he never departed for long from his agenda of exploring in narrative the extent to which human nature is a product of particular historical and social circumstances.

We hardly need to be a Marxist philosopher such as Lukács to be able to conclude that Scott is structuring his narratives of history around something like successive 'modes of production', each with its concomitant and intertwined psycho-social mental structurations. Fredric Jameson has reminded us again, recently, that the emergence of the new concept of a mode of production is part of what he sees as 'new discursive paradigms', the existence of which is reinforced by the presence, in the literary sphere, of the 'new historical paradigm in the novels of Sir Walter Scott'.[77] And it is no accident that it is Scottish society in the late eighteenth century which generates these new discourses of history in a recognizable modern form:

> Scotland is in many ways a more complex and interesting case [than France], for, as last of the emergent First World countries, or first of the Third World ones (to use Tom Nairn's provocative idea, in *The Break-up of Britain*),[78] Enlightenment Scotland is above all the space of a coexistence of radically distinct zones of production and culture: the archaic economy of the Highlanders and their clan system, the new agricultural exploitation of the Lowlands, the commercial vigour of the English 'partner' over the border, on the eve of its industrial 'take-off'. The brilliance of Edinburgh is therefore not a matter of Gaelic genetic material, but rather owing to the strategic yet eccentric position of the Scottish metropolis and intellectuals with respect to this virtually synchronic coexistence of distinct modes of production which it is now uniquely the task of the Scottish Enlightenment to 'think' or to conceptualize. Nor is this merely an economic matter: Scott, like Faulkner later on, inherits a social and historical raw material, a popular memory, in which the fiercest revolutions and civil and religious wars now inscribe the coexistence of modes of production in vivid narrative form. The condition of thinking a new reality and articulating a new paradigm for it therefore seem to demand a peculiar conjuncture and a certain strategic distance from that new reality, which tends to overwhelm those immersed in it . . .[79]

Jameson goes on to argue, of course, that 'the waning of our sense of history, and more particularly our resistance to globalizing or totalizing concepts like that of the mode of production itself, are a function of precisely that universalization of capitalism'.[80]

To overcome our 'postmodern moment, [which is] the cultural logic of an enlarged third stage of classical capitalism', Jameson seems to be implying that the discursive paradigm offered by Scott can serve as a homologous model for our own conceptualization of our 'transitional period between two stages of capitalism'.[81] Rejecting the notion that the postmodern can be thought of only on the level of its apparently 'sheer heteronomy and the emergence of random and unrelated subsystems of all kinds',[82] Jameson acknowledges the political indispensability and unavoidability of 'local struggles and issues', but insists that 'they are effective only so long as they also remain figures or allegories for some larger systemic transformation'.[83] It is on that latter 'semantic horizon' that Scott has apparently conceptualized a 'master' narrative of history, the continuation of which will enable us to 'think' the logic of the post-modern (as the cultural logic of the latest distinct stage of capitalism), in order that we may begin 'to "master" history in whatever ways turn out to be possible: the escape from the nightmare of history, the conquest by human beings of control over the otherwise seemingly blind and natural "laws" of socioeconomic fatality . . .'.[84] So it turns out that the conservative, curmudgeonly old Sir Walter remains part of a 'Marxist heritage' (as Marx himself presumably knew), a discursive pioneer in the emergence of the narratives of historical materialism, which – needless to say – project a vision of humankind reconciled with itself and with nature – beyond the 'progressive ideology' underpinning a mental universe of possessive, consuming, individualism. Jameson's position on postmodernism remains, of course, highly contentious and continues to fuel academic debate. Here we must return to McKeon's story of dialectical discursive reversals and Scott's place in the discursive 'mastery' of Scotland.

It should be more than clear by now that Scott's historicist view of human nature, with its accompanying assumption of the cultural and historical contingency of truth, places him firmly within the ambit of McKeon's 'conservative ideology', which rejects 'naïve empiricism' by asserting an 'extreme skepticism'. The trouble with 'extreme skepticism', however, is that it is – by definition – unable to posit any immovable first principles of its own upon which an edifice of binding social, moral, and political principles might be erected. It can only analyse, criticize, and deconstruct principles already in place, without being able to advance a confident political programme to replace them – something our own latter-day postmodernist political theorists know to their cost. Swift's witty and withering satirical attacks on the social and political assumptions of his own day led him, arguably, nowhere except to a proto-Stalinist Houyhnhnm utopia and a sour, despairing, crabbed misanthropy.[85] Sterne's ebullient *jeu d'esprit* ultimately could not refer to anything tangible beyond itself; it remained an epistemological time-bomb, waiting to detonate in the twentieth century,[86] while in the meantime the discourses of 'progressive ideology' conquered the intellectual landscape. Burke's insistence on that 'second nature' of human beings, generated and shaped by life in 'civil society',[87] tended to be forgotten, whilst his critics, including Marx,[88] stressed his hysterical defence of patriarchal privilege. Walter Scott was somehow turned into an obscurantist glorifier of the Middle Ages (which he most assuredly was not) and was finally dismissed from the canon, by F.R. Leavis, as the epigone of 'the bad tradition of eighteenth-century romance'.[89] For writers McKeon would label 'conservative', it is difficult to defend values when all values are seen to be epistemologically relative. (We need think only about the never-ending debates around the theme of 'Marxism and morality'.) As we saw above, the conservative ideologists were forced to fall back upon something like *traditional* human values, however much the older notions of human worth might have been discredited by the irreversible rejection of aristocratic ideology in its purer forms. After all, had not the Christian tradition resulted in a commonsense view that all human beings are spiritually equal and mutually responsible for the welfare of each other? Had not feudal society, despite its idealistic 'lies' about the divine sanction of a hier-archical social order, sustained public discourses reinforcing a sense of reciprocal social responsibilities and a notion that all people are part of an inter-locking, interdependent, Christian community? In the face of the victory of those 'progressive' ideologists who equated liberty with the freedom of the ambitious and the greedy to achieve positions of social power, some 'skeptical' conservatives were even willing to cling to the old aristocratic notions of inborn personal worth, concluding that such fictions were, *faute de mieux*, necessary to prevent humanity from preying upon itself. One could easily trace a line from Shakespeare to – *mutatis mutandis* – Fielding's 'instrumentality of belief',[90] to Burke, and – occasionally – to Scott.

Both aristocratic and progressive social hierarchies continued (and continue) to present moral contradictions. However virtuous a person of ancient lineage may happen to be, our sense of natural justice recoils from consigning plebeians, whose virtue may be equal to that of any aristocrat, to a life of toil and exploitation. But our progressive meritocracy is equally fraught with moral contradictions. McKeon puts it succinctly:

> Within progressive utopianism there is a potential conflict between the righteous impulse to overcome status inconsistency by effacing all stratification whatsoever, and the recognition that the progressive ideals of industry and merit depend for their very meaning on the possibility of mobility and relative achievement within some existing system of social rank.[91]

If our achievements, acquisitions, and upward mobility are to be considered morally justified, we must at least tacitly grant moral authority to the social order which confers positions and rewards. But as we know to our cost, it is primarily individualistic ambition, competitiveness, greed, and guile which inspire us to embrace those 'progressive ideals of industry and merit' which propel us upward. It is those traits, frequently clothed in a rhetoric of IQ, dynamism, alertness, and social skills, which become the measure of human worth. 'Freedom' is a state of not being unjustly thwarted (owing to class, gender, race, sexual orientation, etc.) in the exercise of one's competitive abilities. People who advocate meritocracies have a way of believing that they themselves will come out on top, given their confidently held evaluations of their abilities. Measured against traditional communitarian values, total freedom, in this 'progressive' sense, would be a totally 'natural' Darwinian selection of the vile. Tom Paine remains trapped in McKeon's 'progressive' ideology; Burke and Scott, with their 'radicial skepticism', are McKeon conservatives.

The 'righteous impulse to efface all stratification whatsoever' may indeed be hopelessly utopian, and it certainly was not an impulse actively entertained (or even thought of) by the 'progressive' ideologists or even by most of the conservative 'skeptics' in the early modern period. However, if conservative ideology is pressed to its logical extreme – beyond the humanizing influence of instrumental fictions – it is going to analyse what amounts to the real material basis for social power and domination: control over the land and (in a later period) other means of production. 'Progressives' were, logically, prepared to countenance the abolition of feudal tenures, but – after Locke's tortuous arguments – they were scarcely prepared to contemplate the abolition of private property *tout court*. Ownership of land and capital was, after all, what they were after. It was an 'extreme skeptical' analysis of social power, conducted by a variant of conservative ideology, that concluded that humankind could be returned to its Edenic, communitarian, egalitarian values only if the 'Fall' into private property were reversed by making the earth once again a 'common treasury' for all humans. It was the Digger Gerrard Winstanley who, with his True Levellers, imprinted this 'conservative' political programme upon the English conceptual landscape by writing his theoretical tracts and by ploughing up St George's Hill in Surrey.[92]

> Passing tumultuously through the secularization process that would take their culture several centuries to experience, these sectarians by-passed the stage of capitalist ideology altogether. So if Calvinist Protestantism gave a vital impetus to the growth of progressive ideology, it also fed, through the distinct modes of Marvell and Winstanley, a vital counterstrain that would contribute to the emergence of conservative ideology.[93]

Needless to say, this 'vital counterstrain' by-passes Tom Paine completely. Burke, who shares a latter-day version of that conservative strain of 'extreme skepticism', still clings to the 'landed interests' and the 'instrumental belief' in their ultimate benevolence. Scott, internalizing the emerging concept of a 'mode of production', generated discursively by the likes of Adam Smith and Adam Ferguson, both of whom saw human society as advancing through four distinct socioeconomic 'stages' of development, narrated the processes of historical transition, dwelling upon the historical contingency of human motivations and worrying away at the issue of property – sometimes hinting at the possibility of its dissolution by pushing the rhetoric of deeds and contracts to the point of self-destructing parody.[94] (The obsession with property can be read as a sign for the problem of property.) Whatever Scott's own ideological conclusions, his narratives – even when read as conservative 'romances of property' – arguably have contours like those of the stories of historical materialism, those discourses generated by Marx, the ultimate 'conservative', who pushes his 'extreme skepticism' to its necessary conclusions. Given the palpable fact that our own latest contemporary dialectical swerve of 'progressive ideology', this time in the guise of a triumphalist enterprise culture, is hell-bent on destroying the very basis of human life on earth, we might do well to resurrect those corrosive 'conservative' narratives which question the virtue of meritocracies based on competitiveness and which share with the discourses of historical materialism a vision of humankind reconciled with itself and with nature.

But what forms do these conservative narratives take? As was always implicit in the above discussion, each of McKeon's dialectically intertwined ideologies, together with its necessary and concomitant epistemology, implies and generates its own story of human history and its own set of discursive practices in imaginative writing. The old 'aristocratic ideology', as we have seen, equated noble birth with inner worth, and underpinned its notions of human 'virtue' with an 'idealist' epistemology which presupposed that all truth and knowledge existed eternally and inalterably in the mind of God and manifested itself to human beings, however imperfectly, through revelation and the natural world – the latter including the divinely ordered traditional social hierarchy, presided over by those of ancient lineage. An unchanging human nature partook of the eternal divine nature, but had been rendered imperfect and erring as a result of the original Fall from Grace. Human history, being the eternally present story of the plan of salvation, consisted of moral examples and monitory disasters, all events being types, pre-figurations, and fulfilments of other events. Romance 'truth' embodied these 'idealist' divine truths, representing human beings as already-made, undeveloping, static types of the eternal human substance, continually undergoing stereotypical tests and adventures in a timeless unlocalized landscape and never growing older in the process. Questions of empirical truth or probability would have been irrelevant; fanciful, fantastic episodes embodied romance truth fully as well – or rather: better than did tales accommodated more closely to the ordinary, vulgar train of human events. The upstart 'progressive ideology', on the other hand, scorned the fanciful 'lies' of romance and rejected those monumental 'types' of virtue and evil who populated traditional narratives. Turning to the actually existing records and artifacts from the past, progressive ideology attempted to arrive at 'true histories' of the world and human-kind, aiming to displace those romance 'lies' which clouded human understanding and prevented humans from arriving at firmer truths based on induction from the putatively objective data of sense experience. Its naïvely empiricist epistemology presupposed an inalterable, universal, trans-historical human nature which, once it was liberated from the shackling tutelage of received authority, would see the world as it truly was and would advance and increase its knowledge, thereby generating material progress and relieving 'man's estate'.[95] Its story of human history was one of verifiable deeds of real individual human beings, enmeshed in a familiar matrix of ordinary, everyday, empirically observable causes and effects. 'Fancy' was no longer a source of truth. The 'fictions' of progressive ideology were anxious to distance themselves from the 'lies' of romance; fictional 'truth' – if not a true replica of what had *actually* happened – at least had to be sufficiently plausible to generate the belief that the narrated fictional events *could have* happened. 'True' fiction was 'factual fiction',[96] approximating to the truth itself by means of its 'probability' and 'verisimilitude'. Narrative movement was generated by the plausible motivations of individualized human characters moving through real clock and calendar time in recognizable physical settings.[97] Language was a transparent window onto an empirically verifiable world.

As we have seen, the next dialectical reversal – 'conservative ideology' – rejected the 'mechanical philosophy' of the progressives, but shared the progressive scorn for the idealist lies of romance. Attempting to transcend the new 'lies' of naïve empiricism, it ridiculed the belief of the progres-sives that parochial sense experience and the man-made artifice of language could comprehend the world, and embraced an epistemology of extreme scepticism that subversively dismantled all claims to immovable truths. Eschewing any notion of a fixed, eternal, human nature, con-servatives tended to embrace historically contingent versions of the truth, often attempting to reclaim more traditional notions of a humane social order and implying the necessity of redeeming humankind from its progressive fall into individualistic empiricism. 'History' tended to be the story of the fall from Edenic community, accelerated by the guileful ruses of the powerful – be they corrupt aristocrats or thrusting capitalist speculators. The discursive methods of the conservatives tended towards the corrosive strategies of parody and satire – destabilizing and defamiliarizing the confident, plausible narratives and social categories

117

of progressive ideology. For McKeon, the dialectical interaction of these ideologies and epistemologies (which are separable only in the abstractions of theory) reaches a level of conscious self-awareness in the 1740s, in the rivalry between Richardson (the 'progressive') and Fielding (the 'conservative'),[98] giving rise to the abstract concept of 'the novel', under which rubric the dialectical pattern of discursive reversal and counter-reversal will continue its course until the present day. At any rate, it is clear that these rival stories of human history were firmly in place in the second half of the eighteenth century and set the agenda for the competing historiographical representations of, especially, the French Revolution. Indeed, it is arguable that the lived experience of the Revolution and its contemporary representations were shaped by the pressures of McKeon's competing ideologies. Paine and Burke provide convenient exemplars. Marx, subsequently, articulates the full flowering of 'conservative ideology', in dialectical conflict with the triumphant 'progressive' institutionalized academic discipline of 'history', the very *raison d'être* of which may be seen in its 'objective' empiricist attempts to construct 'true' plausible stories of humankind which portray revolutions as aberrant, irrational, unnecessary, and preventable.[99]

When we turn, in conclusion, to examine some brief samples of Scottian 'conservative' narrative, we perhaps need first to clear away some of the conventional critical underbrush that has grown up around notions of 'socialist realism' – that mode of literary representation long ago imposed upon writers in the name of historical materialism, the stories of which, I maintain, are in opposition to any theory of 'realist' writing which could reinforce the discourse of a 'progressive ideology' underpinned by a naïvely empiricist epistemology. If truth is historically contingent, and if human nature itself is a function of history, then conservative narrative must reject the notion of any a-historical correspondence between 'reality' and any period-specific discursive forms. Reality itself can only be known discursively; discursive forms are specific to the social formations that generate them, always retelling their stories of human lack and desired reconciliation against the ultimate semantic horizon of the nightmare of History.[100] As was suggested above, the conservative epistemological stance suggests that, in the first instance, quotation, juxtaposition, parody, and – hence – subversion of existing discursive forms can undermine the commonsense assumption that competitive individualism is somehow an a-historical 'natural' component of an unchanging 'human nature'. It is these strategies which enable us to 'think' the historicity and alterability of human consciousness and behaviour. In his coded references to the ideological perils of an undialectical 'socialist realism' which largely preserved the narrative strategies of the nineteenth-century bourgeois humanist 'realist' novel, Lukács long ago pointed out that a narrative stance of 'objective' observation and description of the surface experience of things leads to a conceptual freezing of the social and historical landscape, a 'naturalizing' of social forms, human psychologies, and economic practices.[101] It should now be no surprise to us that Lukács chooses, instead, (*inter alia*) Walter Scott, the virtuoso of parody, pastiche, and mimicry of narrative voices, as his exemplar of 'Great Realists'. Lukács, perhaps unwittingly, was an ally of Brecht, perhaps the best example of a Marxist writer who is prepared to use *any* received discursive forms in a distancing mélange of jarring, dissonant voices which comment upon and criticize each other – all for purposes of exposing the bad fit between official ideologies and the exigencies of capitalist economic structures and social relations.

Mentioning Brecht and Scott in one breath may not be as far-fetched as it sounds, as Scott expounds a curiously modern notion of an ideal 'middle' aesthetic distance which will encourage his reader to contemplate the historical alterability of human psychology.[102] His *Waverley* is set 'Sixty Years before the present 1st November 1805',[103] since he intends to deliver 'neither a romance of chivalry, nor a tale of modern manners'. Had he set his story in a more distant past, his readers would bring to the text the conventional expectations associated with the old romance; if his tale were set in the present, his readers would be seduced by the recognition of the familiar and away from the task of contemplating 'men'. So there seem to be two sorts of 'interest' which must be thwarted before active reading can take place:

> ... the object of my tale is more a description of men than manners. A tale of manners, to be *interesting*, must either refer to antiquity so great as to have become venerable, or it must bear a vivid reflection of those scenes which are passing daily before our eyes ...[104]

Since Scott is clearly rejecting both the conventional (nostalgically outmoded) 'aristocratic ideology' of romance and the 'progressive ideology' of the 'tale of modern manners', he chooses his 'middle' narrative time which will 'distance' his readers from both of the sets of conventional responses. He believes (perhaps naïvely? perhaps disingenuously?) that the generation of our grandparents will always hold the least 'interest' for us and will hence serve best to throw the force of his narrative 'upon the characters and passions of the actors'. The distancing effect will be maintained by using slightly out-of-date forms of language and a style slightly more formal than the popular prose of the day. The persona (or personae) speaking the narrative voice(s) will never pretend to be a hypothetical, neutral, 'contemporary' observer of the narrated events. Instead, pretending to be the chatting contemporary of the reader, the voice of the narrator(s) will continually thwart any potential illusion that the past of the tale is somehow being experienced 'in the present', by employing a rhetoric of 'at that time', 'at that period', 'sixty years since', etc.[105] It should be almost superfluous to note that the narrator is also constantly chatting about the process of composition itself, inviting the reader to play with the evidence revealed and withheld, and making intertextual references to the devices of other authors ('Shall this be a long or a short chapter?').[106] It remains puzzling to me that poststructuralist criticism has not yet digested these patently self-referential texts of Scott.[107] Had Shklovsky perhaps happened upon *Waverley* instead of *Tristram Shandy*,[108] the course of recent anti-traditional literary criticism might be rather different. At any rate, it becomes increasingly clear why the dominant aesthetics of 'realism' banished Scott from the Great Tradition and from the canon as a whole.

Waverley begins, of course, with that outrageously po-faced sentence which has presumably prompted many a reader to close the book immediately: 'The title of this work has not been chosen without the grave and solid deliberation which matters of importance demand from the prudent'. (The celebrated first sentence of *Pride and Prejudice* clearly has more zip!) Scott's 'Introductory' then proceeds, however, to send up most of the existing conventions of fiction of his day, all of which are seen to be related to reader expectations triggered off by the sounds of titles.[109] But what conventions are left for Scott himself? All of them, we must conclude before we finish the book, despite the fact that he seems to be indicating in the passages about 'middle distance' that he is striking out on a new path. Even one of his parodistic plot summaries in the 'Introductory' repeats itself in one of the crucial episodes in the career of Edward Waverley:

> Or if I had rather chosen to call my work a 'Sentimental Tale', would it not have been a sufficient presage of a heroine with a profusion of auburn hair, and a harp, the soft solace of her solitary hours, which she fortunately finds always the means of transporting from castle to cottage, although she herself be sometimes obliged to jump out of a two-pair-of-stairs window, and is more than once bewildered on her journey, alone and on foot, without any guide but a blowzy peasant girl, whose jargon she can hardly understand?[110]

In this case, to appreciate the full force of Scott's playful cross-referencing and his games with narrative point of view, we would need to look at Chapter Twenty-Second ('Highland Minstrelsy') in its entirety, but perhaps a few selected passages[111] will serve our purposes here:

> Una [ah, *The Faerie Queene*, romance!], having received instructions in her native language [Scots Gaelic, of course. Remember the jargon of the blowzy peasant girl.], conducted Waverley out by a passage different from that through which he had entered the

apartment. At a distance he heard the hall of the chief still resounding with the clang of bagpipes and the high applause of his guests.

(All of this sounds suspiciously like the clichés of some hack writer's imitation of a 'romance'. But we know that little Edward has spent half of his childhood in an old Gothic library, revelling in romantic fiction and in the 'pages of Froissart, with his heart-stirring and eye-dazzling descriptions of war and of tournaments'.[112] Waverley *thinks* in the clichés of bad romances; Scott's use of 'free indirect focalization'[113] has caused the narrative voice to take on the cadences and vocabulary of Waverley's thoughts.) Waverley continues his twilight stroll in the direction of Flora's appointed meeting place:

> These streams were different also in character. The larger was placid, and even sullen in its course, wheeling in deep eddies, or sleeping in dark blue pools; but the motions of the lesser brook were rapid and furious, issuing from between precipices, like a maniac from his confinement, all foam and uproar.

Perhaps we, in our Freud-infested epoch, should draw a veil over the sexual connotations of Edward's mental associations with the stream; it suffices to know that he is stumbling up a narrow valley to meet a beautiful woman. But we know already that he has a penchant for 'sublime' landscapes, and is busily shaping the Highlands into his own personal *locus amoenus*, one fitting his mental world of romance scenes and personages, in the manner of Don Quixote.

> It was up the course of this last stream that Waverley, like a knight of romance [or so he sees himself. The ironic condescension of the narrator towards 'our hero' has prepared us for this crashing cliché.], was conducted by the fair Highland damsel, his silent guide. A small path, which had been rendered easy in many places for Flora's accommodation, led him through scenery of a very different description from that which he had just quitted. Around the castle, all was cold, bare and desolate, yet tame even in desolation; but this narrow glen, at so short a distance, seemed to open into the land of romance.[114]

So Waverley finally has the empirical referent for his mental discourses of romance. He, poor soul, does not yet know that this whole 'romantic' scene has been stage-managed by the machiavellian Fergus and his sister Flora in order to seduce him politically into joining the Jacobite cause. They know, long before he does, that his 'idealist epistemology', fed by a surfeit of 'romance truth', has prepared him psychologically to embrace the 'aristocratic ideology' of Bonnie Prince Charlie. We are invited to revel in the scene, but the cruel rhetoric of cliché must distance us from any naïve acceptance of Waverley's perception of it. And after further 'sublime' landscape experience:

> Here, like one of those lovely forms which decorate the landscapes of Poussin, Waverley found Flora gazing on the waterfall. Two paces further back stood Cathleen, holding a small Scottish harp, the use of which had been taught to Flora by Rory Dall, one of the last harpers of the Western Highlands.

So now we even have the promised harp, which has been transported at great risk over a rickety bridge spanning a chasm 150 feet deep – and in the uncertain light of the setting sun. In later editions, Scott appends a footnote assuring his reader that a very similar waterfall actually exists 'at [a] farm . . . on the northern side of Lochard, and near the head of the Lake, four or five miles from Aberfoyle'.[115] So, we 'know' now that this outrageously romantic scene has its referent in empirical reality. The depicted scene, therefore, just might be within the bounds of probability – soothing reader expectations in a dawning 'realist' age. But, of course, the existence of the ironically pedantic footnote only calls our attention to the fictionality of the fiction and distances us (if we still needed it) yet more from the narrative discourse.[116]

Flora duly carries out her duty of political seduction by plunging into Ossian-like rhetoric:[117]

> To speak in the poetical language of my country, the seat of the Celtic muse is in the mist of the secret and solitary hill, and her voice in the murmur of the mountain stream. He who woos her must love the barren rock more than the fertile valley, and solitude of the desert better than the festivity of the hall.

With a queasy feeling, we can predict the Victorian illustrations of this scene in later editions and see the racks of present-day picture postcards all catering to pre-constructed tourist expectations of Celtic kitsch. Scott himself may have had something similar in mind, given that the Highlands had long since been opened to the tourist trade by 1814. In case his readers have not registered the fact that his 'Introductory' parodies have – proleptically – rendered the 'harp scene' rather ludicrous, he continues in his footnote on the waterfall:

> The appearance of Flora with the harp, as described, has been justly censured as too theatrical and affected for the lady-like simplicity of her character. But something may be allowed to her French education, in which point and striking effect always make a considerable object.

This outrageous 'explanation' (surely only a very obtuse reader would find 'lady-like simplicity' in the active, passionate, political fanaticism of Flora) gives us cause to suspect that many post-1814 reader expectations were already not up to the vigorous games of self-parody and self-referentiality generated by Scott's conservative narrative discourses. His narratives hardly radiate that high seriousness about 'Life' which gains one admission to the canons of great traditions.[118] But, needless to say, the use that we make of his narratives is our affair.

It has been argued here that Scott's conservative ideology, based as it is on a sceptical epistemology founded on the assumption that truth and human nature are culturally and historically contingent, is generated by the particular historical moment of the Scottish Enlightenment, when two distinct modes of production co-existed for a time within a relatively circumscribed geographical space. It has also been suggested, relying heavily on Fredric Jameson, that Scott's 'new historical paradigm' can perhaps serve as a homologous model for our own conceptualization of our 'transitional period between two stages of capitalism'. I myself have been at pains to make clear why I think the narratives of conservative ideology, in McKeon's sense, can help us to overcome our sense of 'the end of history' and to disrupt our 'naturalized' notions about our competitively individualistic human nature. Although Scott's narratives were arguably generated out of the situation of 'internal colonialism'[119] which obtained (and obtains) in the Celtic periphery of Britain, however, I see no hope of recuperating his narratives for a politically progressive 'Scottish' identity which might challenge the complacent discourses of Englishness/Britishness in these islands.[120] Attempts to do that will presumably always founder on the obvious facts that (i) Scott himself was (usually) a passionate advocate of the Union and (ii) his nostalgic antiquarian portrayals of a 'lost' Scottish culture have probably contributed to that kitsch 'Scottishness' of tartans, kilts, sporrans, bagpipes, whisky labels, Highland Games, and the whole unbearable ambience of Balmoral. (Victoria's enthusiasm for Scott presumably had something to do with that last-mentioned phenomenon.) Rather, I would suggest that Scott's 'extreme skepticism' contains a radical potential to disrupt the 'progressive ideology' which has helped to legitimate the subjugation by England of its Celtic periphery and continues to view 'Europe' as a threat to the commonsense decencies of 'Englishness'. Scott's narratives of change and (usually) reconciliation may have had a function of reassurance and comforting explanation during England's period of greatest industrial and imperial expansion, but the underlying epistemology arguably asserts its radical potential in a period of complacent global capitalism. Scott's attempt to narrate the clash between two distinct modes of production may never inspire the militant politics of an aggrieved national identity, but perhaps it can generate discursive strategies which could contribute towards the construction of a 'post-conventional identity'[121] beyond the narrow particularities of nation and destructive competitiveness.

NOTES

1 In what follows I was unable to deal in detail with work published after 1991. Of the various relevant works that have appeared since then, I should like to call attention to the following four in particular: R. Crawford, *Devolving English Literature*, Clarendon, Oxford, 1992; D. Elam, *Romancing the Postmodern*, Routledge, London, 1992; F. Azim, *The Colonial Rise of the Novel*, Routledge, London, 1993; and F. Robertson, *Legitimate Histories. Scott, Gothic, and the Authorities of Fiction*, Clarendon, Oxford, 1994. In the notes to my own text I have tried where possible to note their relevance.

2 R. Crawford makes a point of anchoring Scott and *Waverley* firmly in the category of 'Scottish Literature', which 'offers the longest continuing example of a substantial body of literature produced by a culture pressurized by the threat of English cultural domination', and maintains that 'Scottish writing has often formed a model for writers in other countries concerned to escape from being England's cultural provinces' (Crawford, *Devolving English Literature*, p.8). 'Scott, attempting to ensure and articulate Scotland's distinctive place in Britain in *Waverley*, is conscious of the need both to construct and to reconstruct images of cultural identity that are other than Anglo-centric' (ibid., p.15).

3 W. Scott, *Waverley*, Penguin, Harmondsworth, 1980, p.492.

4 M. Hechter, *Internal Colonialism. The Celtic Fringe in British National Development 1536–1966*, Routledge & Kegan Paul, London, 1975, p.342.

5 Ibid., p.342.

6 Scott, *Waverley*, p.329.

7 Ibid. p.465.

8 C.A. Bayly, *Imperial Meridian. The British Empire and the World 1780–1830*, Longman, Harlow, 1989, p.109.

9 Hechter, *Internal Colonialism*, p.344.

10 Ibid., p.345.

11 G. Lukács, *The Historical Novel*, trans. H. and S. Mitchell, Penguin, Harmondsworth, 1981, p.52.

12 E.W. Said, *Orientalism*, Harmondsworth, Penguin, 1985. D. Cairns and S. Richards use the term 'Celticism' (in my sense of the word) in their book *Writing Ireland: Colonialism, Nationalism and Culture*, Manchester University Press, Manchester, 1988, pp.47ff.

13 Said, *Orientalism*, p.3.

14 Scott, *Waverley*, p.76.

15 See, for example, G. McMaster, *Scott and Society*, Cambridge University Press, Cambridge, 1981, ch.4.

16 F. Azim, *The Colonial Rise of the Novel*, pp.39–42, devotes a brief section (the noble savage) to the history of this notion.

17 My formulation is indebted to P. Brown, 'This thing of darkness I acknowledge mine: *The Tempest* and the discourse of colonialism', in J. Dollimore and A. Sinfield (eds), *Political Shakespeare. New Essays in Cultural Materialism*, Manchester University Press, Manchester, 1985, pp.48–71. R. Crawford (*Devolving English Literature*), among others, points out that Scott's Gaelic Highlanders and Fenimore Cooper's American Indians share the same 'grave and splendid rhetoric' (pp.127–8; see also pp.190ff.).

18 My thinking here was inspired by A. Welsh, *The Hero of the Waverley Novels*, Atheneum, New York, 1968.

19 F. Azim, *The Colonial Rise of the Novel*, pp.37–9, speaks of the 'sexualisation of the land'.

20 Scott, *Waverley*, p.183. For a witty analysis of Scott's female characters (including Flora and Rose), see D. Elam, *Romancing the Postmodern*, pp.16ff. and pp.104ff. According to Elam, 'gender ... becomes unfixed in Scott's romance' (ibid., p.109).

21 Scott, *Waverley*, p.406.

22 For an elaborate recent discussion of Scott's massive influence on Cooper, see R. Crawford, *Devolving English Literature*, ch.4 ('Anthologizing America').

23 J.T. Hillhouse, *The Waverley Novels and their Critics*, University of Minnesota Press, Minneapolis and London, 1936, p.318 (summarizing from chs 40, 45, 46 of Mark Twain's *Life on the Mississippi*). See also R. Crawford, *Devolving English Literature*, p.215; F. Robertson, *Legitimate Histories*, pp.10, 21, 24.

24 See Lukács, *The Historical Novel*, pp.92ff.

25 See P. Demetz, *Formen des Realismus: Theodor Fontane*, Hanser, Munich, 1964.

26 Ibid., p.34.

27 R. Chase, 'Adalbert Stifter as historical novelist', unpublished PhD thesis, Yale University, 1968, pp.13ff.

28 Bayly, *Imperial Meridian*, p.109.

29 Ibid., p.82.

30 Ibid., pp.121ff.

31 Ibid., p.200.

32 H. Trevor-Roper, 'The invention of tradition: the highland tradition of Scotland', in E. Hobsbawm and T. Ranger (eds), *The Invention of Tradition*, Cambridge University Press, Cambridge, 1983, pp.29–31.

33 W. Scott, *Old Mortality*, Penguin, Harmondsworth, 1980, p.402.

34 J. Kerr, *Fiction against History. Scott As Storyteller*, Cambridge University Press, Cambridge, 1989, pp.62ff.

35 Lukács, *The Historical Novel*, p.33. For a recent discussion of the transformation of Scott criticism in the 1960s, see F. Robertson, *Legitimate Histories*, pp.47ff.

36 Lukács, *The Historical Novel*, p.37.

37 A. Welsh, *The Hero of the Waverley Novels*, p.150.

38 Ibid., p.57.

39 Fiona Robertson also focuses on Scott's 'disquisition on the implications of titles in the first chapter of *Waverley*'. Her book as a whole sets out to study 'the relationship between Scott's texts and the narrative strategies and conventions of late eighteenth- and early nineteenth-century Gothic, in order to elucidate the narrative complexities of the Waverley Novels, their interplays of different forms of narratorial and historical authority, and the special narratorial status of the "Author of *Waverley*"'. She speaks of 'the literary transgressiveness of the Waverly Novels, defined as the narrational and descriptive processes by which they both suggest and continually redefine generic vocabularies'. (F. Robertson, *Legitimate Histories*, pp.2ff.).

40 Firdous Azim remains stuck in much of our current (postcolonial) orthodoxy, when she asserts that 'the novel' is primarily *about* the notion of a putatively coherent, consistent narrating subject. (See F. Azim, *The Colonial Rise of the Novel*, ch.1: 'The subject/s of the novel', pp.10–33, and ch.7: 'Rereading feminism's texts', pp.172ff.). Azim shows few signs of having read Scott. According to F. Robertson, *Legitimate Histories*, p.19, '... the elevation of the rational voice of the "Author of *Waverley*" into the sole voice of Scott is a misrepresentation of the conflict of styles and tones characteristic of his fiction'. I agree.

41 J. Kerr, *Fiction against History*, p.2.

42 Ibid., pp.102–4. See also F. Robertson, *Legitimate Histories*, pp.246–64. Robertson picks up the analysis of *Redgauntlet* more or less where Kerr leaves off, calling it 'Scott's most widely admired essay in metafiction' (ibid., p.254).

43 J. Kerr, *Fiction against History*, p.15. See also D. Elam, *Romancing the Postmodern*, pp.13ff.

44 This is, of course, a travesty of C. Belsey's excellent arguments in her *Critical Practice*, Methuen, London, 1980. See also D. Elam, *Romancing the Postmodern*, p.51: 'Scott's texts explode in a welter of textuality: marginalia, footnotes, parodic scholarship'. Elam prefers to call Scott's novels 'postmodern romances'.

45 I am alluding to L. von Ranke's celebrated dictum in his *Geschichten der romanischen und germanischen Völker von 1494–1514*, 2nd edn, (*Sämtl. Werke* 33–34), Leipzig, 1874, p.VII.

46 Said, *Orientalism*, pp.46–7 (emphasis in original).

47 My formulation echoes Couze Venn's argument in his contribution to this volume.

48 J. Derrida, 'White mythology', in *Margins of Philosophy*, trans. A. Bass, Chicago University Press, Chicago, 1982, p.213.

49 F.R. Leavis, *The Great Tradition*, New York University Press, New York, 1973, pp.5–6.

50 J. Kerr, *Fiction against History*, and the works listed in Note 1 (excepting Azim) have gone a long way towards rectifying this situation.

51 Crawford suggests a rather cynical explanation for this omission: 'If literary theorists have largely ignored Scottish writing, this may be another instance of poststructuralism's tendency in practice to do little to upset the status quo.' (R. Crawford, *Devolving English Literature*, p.10).

52 My thinking here is indebted in part to H. White, 'The fictions of factual representation', *Tropics of Discourse*, Johns Hopkins University Press, Baltimore, 1978, pp.121–34. See also D. Elam, *Romancing the Postmodern*, p.8: 'Scott . . . does not so much romanticize the history of Scotland as render that history "unreal", writable only as romance.' And further: '. . . Scott's novels provide a way to rethink the relationship between narrative and the legitimation of historical knowledge, to think otherwise than in terms of a simple opposition of real(ist) history to romance', (ibid. p.54). See also F. Robertson, *Legitimate Histories*, p.6, pp.14–15.

53 M. McKeon, *The Origins of the English Novel, 1660–1740*, Johns Hopkins University Press, Baltimore, 1987, (reprinted: Radius, London, 1988).

54 Ibid., pp.150ff.

55 Ibid., p.153.

56 See especially F. Bacon, 'The refutation of philosophies', trans. B. Farrington, in B. Farrington, *The Philosophy of Francis Bacon*, Liverpool University Press, Liverpool, 1964, p.131.

57 The literature on the so-called 'Weber thesis' is of course vast. I am referring here to the basic texts: M. Weber, *The Protestant Ethic and the Spirit of Capitalism*, trans. T. Parsons, Allen and Unwin, London, 2nd edn, 1976; R.H. Tawney, *Religion and the Rise of Capitalism*, Penguin, Harmondsworth, 1980; C. Hill, 'Protestantism and the rise of capitalism', in *Change and Continuity in Seventeenth Century England*, Weidenfeld and Nicolson, London, 1974.

58 McKeon, *The Origins of the English Novel*, p.153.

59 Scott, *Waverley*, pp. 201–2.

60 E. Burke, *Reflections on the Revolution in France*, Penguin, Harmondsworth, 1988; T. Paine, *Rights of Man*, Penguin, Harmondsworth, 1987.

61 I have borrowed the epithet from A. Welsh, *The Hero of the Waverley Novels*, pp. 58–70.
62 For a discussion of the political relevance of the Waverley Novels in the post-1814 period, see F. Robertson, *Legitimate Histories*, pp.8ff.
63 Quoted in the Editor's Introduction, in W. Scott, *The Fortunes of Nigel*, ed. F.M. Link, University of Nebraska Press, Lincoln, 1965, p.x. F. Robertson goes a long way towards rescuing poor old *Nigel* from neglect. See her 'Phantoms of revolution: *The Fortunes of Nigel*' in Robertson, *Legitimate Histories*, pp.225–33.
64 Scott, *The Fortunes of Nigel*, p.xxi.
65 See G. McMaster, *Scott and Society*, 'Appendix' pp.228–41.
66 Scott, *The Fortunes of Nigel*, pp.4–6.
67 Ibid., p.419.
68 See D. Elam, *Romancing the Postmodern*, p.50, regarding the 'uncertainty of historical knowledge' that surrounds the account of 'the progress of capitalism that Scott preaches'.
69 W. Scott, *Guy Mannering*, Dutton, New York, p.160 (note).
70 F. Robertson devotes the final paragraph of her book to reflections on the endings of the Waverley Novels (Robertson, *Legitimate Histories*, p.273).
71 McKeon, *The Origins of the English Novel*, pp.155–6.
72 See ibid., ch.9: 'Parables of the younger son (I): Defoe and the naturalization of desire', pp.315–37.
73 Fiona Robertson sees this extreme scepticism as a defining element of the Gothic in general. One of her aims is to demonstrate that Scott – contrary to the received truths of nineteenth-century Scott criticism – is an integral part of the Gothic tradition. (See F. Robertson, *Legitimate Histories*, especially ch.2: 'Gothic: the passages that lead to nothing'; also pp.161ff. and pp.244–5).
74 Scott, *Waverley*, pp.35–6.
75 The discussion of this passage in P. Demetz, *Formen des Realismus*, pp.41ff., probably remains unsurpassed.
76 Scott, *Waverley*, p.492. This passage from *Waverley* has an important part to play in D. Elam's discussion of Scott's 'postmodern romances'. See Elam, *Romancing the Postmodern*, pp.61ff.
77 F. Jameson, 'Marxism and postmodernism', *New Left Review* 176, July/August 1989, p.38.
78 See T. Nairn, *The Break-Up of Britain. Crisis and Neo-Nationalism*, 2nd, expanded edn, Verso, London, 1981, (esp. chs 2–3).
79 F. Jameson, 'Marxism and postmodernism', pp.38–9. See also R. Crawford, *Devolving English Literature*, pp.16ff.; D. Elam, *Romancing the Postmodern*, pp.13, 35, 40.
80 F. Jameson, 'Marxism and postmodernism', p.39.
81 Ibid., p.44.
82 Ibid., p.34.
83 Ibid., p.44.
84 Ibid., p.34.
85 See McKeon, *The Origins of the English Novel*, ch.10: 'Parables of the younger son (II): Swift and the containment of desire', pp.338–56.
86 See V. Shklovsky, 'Sterne's *Tristram Shandy*: Stylistic commentary' (1921), in L.T. Lemon (ed.), *Russian Formalist Criticism, Four Essays*, trans. L.T. Lemon and M.T. Reis, University of Nebraska Press, Lincoln, 1965.
87 Burke, *Reflections*, p.299.
88 See, for instance, K. Marx, *Das Kapital*, Dietz Verlag, Berlin (East), 1986, Erster Band, p.788.

89 See Note 49 above.
90 See McKeon, *The Origins of the English Novel*, ch.12: 'The institutionalization of conflict (II): Fielding and the instrumentality of belief', pp.382–409.
91 McKeon, *The Origins of the English Novel*, p.251. F. Azim, *The Colonial Rise of the Novel*, includes McKeon in her bibliography, but does not appear to have read him. Her 'Enlightenment' remains monolithic – with no room for 'counterstrains' or 'extreme skepticism'.
92 See C. Hill, *The World Turned Upside Down*, Penguin, Harmondsworth, 1976, ch.7; McKeon, *The Origins of the English Novel*, pp.77–8.
93 McKeon, *The Origins of the English Novel*, p.198.
94 The long-winded Bailie Macwheeble supplies the first example. See Scott, *Waverley*, ch.71.
95 F. Bacon, *The Advancement of Learning*, ed. G.W. Kitchin, Everyman's University Library, Dent, London, 1973, p.35.
96 I have borrowed the term from L.J. Davis, *Factual Fictions: The Origins of the English Novel*, Columbia University Press, New York, 1983. See also H. White, 'The fictions of factual representation', *Tropics of Discourse*, pp.121–34.
97 I am referring, of course, to I. Watt's definition of 'formal realism'. See I. Watt, *The Rise of the Novel*, Penguin, Harmondsworth, 1979, ch.1.
98 For a fuller discussion of the Richardson–Fielding relationship, see McKeon, *The Origins of the English Novel*, 'Conclusion', pp. 410–21.
99 See especially H. White, 'The politics of historical interpretation: discipline and de-sublimation', in *The Content of the Form. Narrative Discourse and Historical Representation*, Johns Hopkins University Press, Baltimore, 1987, pp.58–82.
100 See F. Jameson, *The Political Unconscious. Narrative as a Socially Symbolic Act*, Methuen, London, 1981, pp.74ff., p.261, pp.289ff. Also: F. Jameson, 'Marxism and historicism', in *The Ideologies of Theory. Essays 1971–1986*, vol.2: *Syntax of History*, Routledge, London, 1988, pp.162ff.
101 Lukács's now classical distinction between 'narration' and 'description' gets an accessible airing in G. Lukács, 'Narrate or describe', in *Writer and Critic and Other Essays*, ed. and trans. A. Kahn, Merlin Press, London, 1978, pp.110–48. (Reprinted in A. Kettle (ed.), *The Nineteenth Century Novel*, Heineman, London, 1982, pp.62–79).
102 My thinking here is greatly indebted to P. Demetz, *Formen des Realismus*, pp.28–32. See also R. Crawford, *Devolving English Literature*, pp.117–18, p.124.
103 Scott, *Waverley*, p.34.
104 Ibid., p.35 (emphasis added).
105 Demetz, *Formen des Realismus*, pp.17ff. See also R. Crawford, *Devolving English Literature*, p.124. Crawford maintains that 'the intrusive, self-mocking, and elaborately self-conscious tone of Scott's editorial voice is a new one' (ibid., p.125). See also F. Robertson, *Legitimate Histories*, pp.117ff.
106 This Shandy-esque flourish is the first sentence of *Waverley*, ch.24 (p.186).
107 As previously mentioned (see Note 51), R. Crawford puts this neglect of Scottish writing down to 'poststructuralism's tendency in practice to do little to upset the status quo' (Crawford, *Devolving English Literature*, p.10). J. Kerr (*Fiction against History*) is one of the first serious critics to bring Scott into the ambit of debates generated by Hayden White's poststructuralist analyses of historiography. D. Elam (*Romancing the Postmodern*), who finds a kindred spirit in Scott and his textual high jinks, wants to reclaim *Waverley* and other 'postmodern romances' by Scott for her own Derridean project. For Elam, '. . . romance, by virtue of its troubled relation to both history and novelistic realism, has in a sense been postmodern all along' (Elam,

Romancing the Postmodern, p.3). F. Robertson has produced the most recent and, arguably, most astute analysis of Scott's 'fluid strategems of authenticity and fictionality'. She points out that '. . . recent Bakhtin-inspired interpretation . . . has made the Waverley Novels model instances of dialogism, setting out as competing discourses the (several) official voices of authoritative narrators and the unofficial voices of local gossips, incompetent antiquarians, minstrels, poetic or prophetic amateurs'. (See especially ch.3: 'Fictions of authenticity: the frame narratives and notes of the Waverley Novels', in F. Robertson, *Legitimate Histories*, pp.117–60).

108 See Note 86 above.
109 F. Robertson, *Legitimate Histories*, p.62, speaks of Scott's 'theory about contracts of expectation between writers and readers'. See also Robertson, ibid., pp.119, 145, 151.
110 Scott, *Waverley*, p.34.
111 The following passages are taken from W. Scott, *Waverley*, pp.174–80. (My own interpolations are enclosed in square brackets.) One of the best recent analyses of this 'waterfall scene' is to be found in J. Kerr, *Fiction against History*, pp.29ff.
112 Scott, *Waverley*, p.49.
113 I have borrowed the term from M. Bal, *Narratology. Introduction to the Theory of Narrative*, trans. C. van Boheemen, University of Toronto Press, Toronto, 1985, p.113.
114 In a witty discussion of the same passage, D. Elam is less reticent than I am in pointing out the blatant sexual imagery 'in the scene of romance and of female sexuality, in Flora's "narrow glen"' (Elam, *Romancing the Postmodern*, pp.67–8).
115 Scott, *Waverley*, p.502.
116 See Demetz, *Formen des Realismus*, pp.21–2. F. Robertson, *Legitimate Histories*, pp.159–60, provides a brief history of systems of annotation in epic romances and historical novels.
117 For an exhaustive recent discussion of Scott's indebtedness to the 'Ossianic stimulus', see R. Crawford, *Devolving English Literature*, pp.119ff.
118 Scott himself speaks of his 'hoity toity, whisky frisky' pertness (quoted by F. Robertson, *Legitimate Histories*, p.150).
119 See Note 4 above.
120 Crawford, on the other hand, sees Scott as defining a distinct Scottish identity within the broader category of 'Britishness'. 'Scott's novel [*Waverley*] (his novels, in fact) is about the construction of a new, culturally eclectic unity – Great Britain – but it is also about the need to preserve cultures within that unity' (R. Crawford, *Devolving English Literature*, p.130). Tracing a Scottish tradition from Scott (and earlier writers) to the troubled present, Crawford concludes: 'If literature was important in the attempted formation of a British mentality, then it is also playing its part in the search for a post-British identity which has grown in twentieth-century Scotland, particularly in the wake of Hugh MacDiarmid' (ibid., p.302).
121 I have borrowed the term from Jürgen Habermas. See his polemical essay 'Eine Art Schadensabwicklung' in the documentation of the recent German 'historians' debate': *Historikerstreit*, Piper, Munich and Zürich, 1987, p.75.

6

IMPERIAL MAN

Edward Eyre in Australasia and the West Indies 1833–66

Catherine Hall

The pride to rear an independent shed
And give to lips we love unborrowed bread;
To see the world from shadowy forest won,
In youthful beauty wedded to the sun;
To skirt our home with harvests widely sown,
And call the blooming landscape all our own;
Our children's heritage in prospect long;
These are the hopes, highminded hopes and strong,
That beckon England's wanderers o'er the brine
To realms where foreign constellations shine.

(Popular poem of the 1830s)

In October 1865 a riot occurred outside the court house in the small town of Morant Bay on the south-eastern coast of Jamaica.[1] Months of tensions between blacks and whites over land, labour and law erupted after an unpopular verdict from magistrates which led to a demonstration and attempted arrests. The police had been resisted, an angry crowd had gathered and marched on the court house. The Volunteers had been called up in anticipation of trouble and were marshalled as the crowd came into the square. The local official had already asked the British Governor, Edward John Eyre, for troops and they were on their way by sea. Stones were thrown, sticks brandished, the Riot Act read and the Volunteers fired. Several people in the crowd were killed. In the subsequent violence eighteen officials and members of the militia were killed, thirty-one wounded. The next day Eyre received a message, 'the blacks have risen'.[2] The 13,000 whites on the island had constantly feared a rising from the 350,000 blacks. More troops were immediately sent in and martial law declared. In the month that followed horrific reprisals took place. Despite the absence of organized resistance, troops under British command executed 439 people, flogged more than 600 men and women and burnt over 1,000 homes. A mixed-race member of the Jamaican House of Assembly, George William Gordon, was hanged.[3]

The initial response from the British government was cautiously to endorse Eyre's actions. Jamaica, conquered almost by chance by the troops of Oliver Cromwell in 1655, had become the jewel in the British crown during the halcyon days of Caribbean slave-sugar in the eighteenth century. By the 1780s, however, the anti-slavery movement was challenging the permanence of the plantation economy built on slave labour and the island increasingly became a source of difficulty and dispute for the Colonial Office. The abolition of the slave trade in 1807, and of slavery and apprenticeship in 1833 and 1838, put Jamaica, as the largest of the British Caribbean islands, at the heart of the great experiment of the abolitionists – the attempt to construct a successful free-labour economy with black labour. By mid-century this experiment looked, from the British line of vision, as less than successful and Jamaica increasingly appeared in Britain as a source of trouble and strife, its black population lazy, its planter class decadent and archaic. The riot in Morant Bay, following in the wake of the Indian Mutiny, was further evidence for the Colonial Office and the Liberal government of the day of the rebellious nature of 'native' populations and the need for strong government.

The government's initial support for Eyre soon came under attack, however, from abolitionist and dissenting groups. Delegations were organized to petition the Colonial Office, public meetings were held following lurid newspaper reports of the actions of the British troops, questions were asked in Parliament. The government was forced to establish a Royal Commission to inquire into the events in Jamaica. Meanwhile, a Jamaica Committee had been set up, chaired by Charles Buxton, the son of that veteran anti-slavery leader, Sir Thomas Fowell Buxton, in order to monitor the official inquiry and keep the British public informed of the issues.[4]

The Royal Commission report, based on evidence collected from witnesses in Jamaica, was published in April 1866. It claimed that the initial violence had presented a genuine danger and that Eyre had been right to react vigorously in order to prevent the spread of the disturbance. However, the report also concluded that martial law had continued for too long, that deaths had been unnecesarily frequent, that the floggings had been excessive and in some instances 'barbarous' and that the burning of so many homes was 'wanton and cruel'.[5] Faced with this critical report, the new Tory government decided that since Eyre had already been suspended, a resolution in the House of Commons deploring the excessive punishments would be an adequate response. This official leniency provoked the Jamaica Committee to consider serving a private prosecution on Eyre, a move which alarmed Buxton and led to his resignation. He was replaced by the doyen of liberal intellectuals,

John Stuart Mill. The threatened prosecution of Eyre caused a backlash and led to popular mobilization in his defence, culminating in the formation of an Eyre Defence Committee, pledged to raise money for any necessary legal action.[6]

For months the debate over the Eyre case raged in Britain. On either side were leading intellectuals and public men. Behind John Stuart Mill were the cream of the liberal intelligentsia – Charles Darwin, Charles Lyall, Herbert Spencer, Thomas Huxley, John Bright and Frederick Harrison. They believed that martial law had been misused and British subjects, regardless of colour, denied their ancient right to the rule of law.[7] Spearheading the defence of Eyre was Thomas Carlyle, the prophetic voice of mid-nineteenth-century England, backed by Charles Dickens, John Ruskin, Charles Kingsley and Alfred Lord Tennyson. Carlyle argued that Eyre's actions had been heroic, that he had saved the whites from massacre and that, more fundamentally, blacks were in any case born to be mastered.[8] Between the summer of 1866 and 1867 respectable public opinion swung away from the Jamaica Committee to the supporters of Eyre. By the time the third, last and still unsuccessful attempt was made to prosecute Eyre it was clear that the defence of black Jamaican rights was no longer a popular cause. Only a small core of middle-class radicals was left, led by a disillusioned and disheartened Mill and relying for support on working-class radicalism. The respectable middle class had arrived at the view that blacks were, essentially, different from whites and thus could not expect the same rights.

At stake in this debate were issues about the relations between the 'mother country' and 'her' colonies, the place of martial law and the rule of law, and the very nature of black people. But also at issue were questions about the nature of Englishness itself. Ethnic identities depend on an 'imagined community', a sense of self rooted in a collective consciousness of 'us' compared to 'them'.[9] Neither the 'us' nor the 'them' are fixed but rather constantly negotiated and re-worked. The debate over Eyre marked a moment when two different conceptions of 'us', constructed through two different notions of 'them', were publicly contested. Mill's imagined community was one of potential equality, in which 'us', white Anglo-Saxon men and women, believed in the potential of Jamaican blacks to become like 'us' through a process of civilization. Carlyle's imagined community was an hierarchically ordered one in which 'we' would always master 'them'.

In each of these imagined communities the identities constructed for men and women, for blacks and whites, were distinctively different. Mill and Carlyle were particularly preoccupied with contesting each other's notions of white, male middle-class identity – for Mill, Eyre was the villain, for Carlyle, the hero. In constructing their villain and hero they demonstrated their commitment to certain definitions of 'good' manliness, the kind of man they could or could not identify with, the kind of man they wanted to be themselves and wanted others to be.

For identities are historically specific, not essentially given; they are never completed but constantly in flux. Identities are the fictions, the representations, the stories that we tell ourselves about who we are. The process of forming cultural and social identities, as Stuart Hall argues, is 'the construction of a sense of belonging which draws people together into an "imagined community" and the construction of symbolic boundaries which define who does *not* belong or is excluded from it'.[10] But that imagined community is historically specific too and who is defined as belonging shifts and turns. Since self is not so much a core as a process, the varied fragments of self are in play in different ways at different historical moments. But particular identities will be structured in dominance: politically validated and institutionally legiti-mated.[11] In 1866–7 it was the discourse of the white middle-class man as master, as superior in essence and for all time, to inferior blacks which eventually emerged as the dominant discourse.

In this chapter I explore some of the shifting elements in nineteenth-century, male, middle-class identities using the biography of Edward Eyre as my starting point. Eyre's own account of his early manhood represented his masculinity in deeply conventional terms. By 1866, however, his identity as narrated by himself, by Carlyle and by other supporters, was part of a distinctively new discourse of middle-class masculinity which, by the later decades of the nineteenth century, was to achieve hegemony.

AUSTRALIA

In the 1830s respectable English middle-class men supported the anti-slavery movement and emancipation. To be a supporter of the weak and the dependent – women, children, slaves and animals – constituted precisely the 'independence' of middle-class masculinity. True manliness was derived not from property and inheritance but from 'real religion' – the faith born from religious conversion and a determination to make life anew. True manliness also encompassed a belief in individual integrity and freedom from subjection to the will of another. Such beliefs were in part rooted in a refusal of aristocratic patronage, a conviction that client relationships were demeaning and that 'a man must act'.[12] True manhood was defined by the capacity to work for oneself in the world, to trust in the dignity of labour, and to make money rather than to live off an existing fortune. Such a definition rested on fragile foundations in a society in which economic crises were frequent – when banks collapsed and bankruptcy constantly threatened – and when for many men the activities of the market brought not sturdy independence

133

but fearful anxieties. The very vulnerability of manhood was repressed in the ideological fictions of integrity and independence – whether in the marketplace, the political arena or the home, but arguably it was this unspoken vulnerability which gave ideologies of masculinity in this period their dynamic intensity.[13]

In the troubled decade of the 1830s, when opportunities for young men with only a modest capital were limited, the empire beckoned as a source of riches, opportunities and adventure. The American and French Revolutions had profoundly affected attitudes to the colonies and had convinced many that colonies would eventually become self-governing. The consensus on colonial policy deriving from the political economy of the late eighteenth century – emphasizing above all the expense and burden of the colonies – was, by the 1820s, beginning to unravel. Of strategic importance in challenging the old consensus was a group which called itself the Colonial Reformers, advocating empire-building as a necessary, indeed vital, response to the serious internal problems faced by Britain. Systematic colonization and the development of responsible government in the settler colonies they believed to be essential both for the maintenance of unity in the empire and the economic wealth of Britain.

The chief theorist of this group was Edward Gibbon Wakefield, grandson of Priscilla Wakefield, the celebrated philanthropist and writer for the young; son of a man with many interests but no fixed occupation, farmer, land agent, writer, and friend of Francis Place and James Mill. Wakefield had no independent income and had to find ways of making a living. In 1827 he was confined to Newgate for three years as a result of one of his less respectable ventures, the abduction of an heiress to Gretna Green. In prison he occupied himself initially with writing on questions of penal reform, but increasingly he became fascinated by the colonies and their potential. In his unfettered imagination Australia became a new and better England, a construct of desire.[14] In his *A Letter from Sydney*, initially published anonymously in 1829 as a series of letters to the *Morning Chronicle*, he transported himself from his prison cell to Australia, a land he had never seen and which he assumed to be empty with no indigenous population, and imagined himself as a farmer with a large tract of land which could not be worked because of the dearth of labour. He addressed himself to 'young men of rank and connections' and those 'in the intermediate ranks of life' and argued that the colonies provided 'the most certain means of obtaining a comfortable settlement'. Reflecting on the importance of a proper balance between land and labour he saw Australia as the solution to over-population in England and eloquently developed the case for an organized system of emigration for both the middle and the working classes. As a modern man Edward Gibbon Wakefield rejected both slavery and the convict system (a 'system full of evil') as solutions to the labour problem. He maintained that planned emigration was possible if colonial lands were sold at a reasonable price and the proceeds of the land sales used to pay for working-class emigration. The effect of this would be to transform 'a waste country' into a profitable and civilized extension of Britain.[15]

In 1833 Wakefield published *England and America* which developed the case he had made in the earlier volume, but emphasized that improving the conditions of the working classes was crucial if social revolution was to be avoided at home. Empire-building provided a key and properly planned colonization, which meant supporting the emigration of young couples so that each colony would become 'one immense nursery', would furthermore contribute to the ending of slavery in America which arose because of the need for labour.[16]

Wakefield, a brilliant publicist, touched vital nerves in these years of reform and emancipation and was successful in making systematic colonization a public issue. His insistence on mixed class emigration was central to breaking the link between Australia and convicts, making it a respectable place for the middle classes.[17] He converted both Bentham and John Stuart Mill to his views, the latter insisting that,

> There needs be no hesitation in affirming that Colonization, in the present state of the world, is the best affair of business, in which the capital of an old and wealthy country can engage.[18]

Wakefield's scheme also became part of the Radical programme articulating the Radical alternative to the old colonial system.

Thomas Carlyle also came to be convinced of the virtues of systematic colonization.[19] He saw emigration as a solution to the problem of 'over-population' and as a way to deal with the economic ills of the time. With characteristic hyperbole he conceptualized the non-European world as a 'vacant earth', calling to be tilled, and white European man as miraculously benevolent:

> If this small western rim of Europe is overpeopled, does not everywhere else a whole vacant Earth, as it were, call to us, Come and till me, come and reap me! Can it be an evil that in an Earth such as ours there should be new Men? Considered as mercantile commodities, as working machines, is there in Birmingham or out of it a machine of such value? 'Good Heavens! a white European Man, standing on his two legs, with his two five-fingered Hands at his shackle-bones, and miraculous Head on his shoulders, is worth something considerable, one would say!'

Malthusians, he argued, should stop being so gloomy and encourage emigration, which promised such riches both for Anglo-Saxons and the rest of the world. It was time to revive the heroic actions of a Clive, to send the 'iron missionaries' – the wonders of Britain's industrial revolution – into the wilder vineyards of the Lord. The time was ripe for another major expansion, conceived of by Carlyle in what was rapidly becoming a conventional narrative of the nineteenth century, the fantasized fiction of imperialism as masculine triumph over femininized colony.[20] For Carlyle the emphasis is on white European man, the powerful and phallic 'fire-pillar', bursting forth from 'swelling, simmering, never-resting Europe' and planting his seed which would bring forth new men from painful labour. Here indeed was conquering, imperial man at work.

> Is it not as if this swelling, simmering, never-resting Europe of ours stood, once more, on the verge of an expansion without parallel; struggling, struggling like a mighty tree again about to burst in the embrace of summer, and shoot forth broad fondant boughs which would fill the whole earth? A disease; but the noblest of all – as of her who is in pain and sore travail, but travails that she may be a mother, and say, Behold, there is a new Man born! ... Alas, where now are the Hengsts and Alarics of our still-glowing, still-expanding Europe; who, when their home is grown too narrow, will enlist and, like fire-pillars, guide onwards those superfluous masses of indomitable living Valour; equipped, not now with the battle-axe and war-chariot, but with the steam-engine and ploughshare.[21]

Mill's vision was certainly different, but both men were united in the Radicalism of the 1830s which believed colonization to be a key to a better world.

The proselytizing of Wakefield, the support he mobilized and the organizing activities of the Colonial Reformers were to bear fruit. Until the early 1830s Australia had mainly been colonized as a convict settlement on the East coast. By 1834, after several years of agitation and organization, a South Australia Association was formed to encourage British settlement and after long negotiations with the Colonial Office an act was passed in the same year which opened South Australia to British colonization with a system of land sales and free passages, as Wakefield had proposed. South Australia was to be a land for free men, enjoying civil liberties, social and economic opportunities and religious toleration. Great efforts were made to encourage the right kind of people to emigrate, 'proper men' who would establish an appropriate, serious, hard-working ethic for the colony.[22]

Edward Eyre was destined to be one of these 'proper men'. Born into a clerical family in Yorkshire in 1816, the third son of a rector without land he soon learnt that:

There was no landed property for me to inherit and my attention was in consequence early directed to the necessity of engaging in some employment as a means of providing for myself.[23]

His autobiography, written in the Caribbean in 1859, describes his early years in Australia. Through his writing he retrospectively constructed himself for himself as a man whose manhood was properly expressed through action, independence and work. In his early forties when writing, he narrated his young manhood as a success story. Through hard work, duty and determination he had made his way in the world with only superior character and Christian gentility to support him. Born into a good family but with no other resources he had found a place for himself, a way of being English in the colonies, a way of belonging to his imagined community.

Eyre himself had originally been intended for the army but his father was seized with the notion that his son could go to Australia, which 'was then just beginning to be known ... [as] a desirable field for a young man commencing life'. In 1833, aged only seventeen, Eyre set out, armed with modest capital and some letters of introduction. He cherished the idea that soon he was to be his 'own master, free from all contracts and taking an independent position in life'. In his later account of these years he conveys the certainty that he would do well, blessed as he was by Providence and possessing those providential characteristics – duty, diligence, abstemiousness, pride in physical hardship – which would enable him to prove his manhood and return with a fortune. While the disappearance of the 'white cliffs' of Dover brought many tears to his eyes, he recorded later that, 'I never once regretted that I had not chosen an easier and less solitary path; whilst the very impossibility of my now turning back or my receiving aid from others made me feel more reliance on myself and determined me to spare no efforts to make my own way in the world'.[24] A man, after all, must act.

On the lengthy voyage Eyre enjoyed the company of his fellow first-class travellers, especially the pretty Mrs Abell who sang 'Home, Sweet Home' to the assembled group on Christmas Day, read Madame de Stael on the commencement of a career alone, quoted Byron to the sea on the beauties of the rainbow and the Bible on the wonders of the deep. He also learnt all he could 'from books relative to the new regions which were so soon to become at once our home and the theatre of our struggles to advance ourselves in life'.[25]

On arrival in Sydney he found no lucrative government post opening to him despite his letters of introduction. Taking advice from a colonist who befriended him he decided to become a farmer. He entered into an agreement with a gentleman settler, Mr Bell, for a year to learn the trade. During that year he bought sheep and land, and was assigned convict labour under the government scheme. Setting up his own farm (which he named 'Woodlands') together with his work with Mr Bell required continuous, intensive labour and Eyre soon discovered the worries which came with the ownership of property. 'With the possession of property', he noted, 'came an increase of care and anxiety'.[26] Brought up amidst the comforts of a Yorkshire vicarage, accustomed to having his food prepared, his washing miraculously done, his fires laid, Eyre learnt not only how to care for stock, build and carpenter, and grow food supplies, but also how to sew on buttons and care for his clothes, cook, often after catching the fish or fowl first, render down fat, make candles, salt beef and bread, twist up tobacco, make his own wool bags for the wool from his first shearing. In what spare time he had he liked to follow those favoured pursuits of middle-class men in an age when the spirit of scientific inquiry was widespread, reading, writing, stuffing birds and catching and classifying insects and butterflies. This was English masculinity with a difference.

Eyre's later narration of these years is structured through a powerful sense of the proprieties of English middle-class gentility, which for him included both a commitment to hard work and a recognition of the need for the deferral of gratification. 'A man must act' if a small capital is to be converted into an income. A colonist must look to his farm first and the comforts of his home second; but he must also struggle to maintain the civilities of English life, to hold on to English notions of respect-ability which served to distinguish him from those convicts and 'natives' who were his daily companions. Remembering Christmas Day 1834, a bright, hot day just after the first shearing, Eyre bemoaned the lost comforts of home and evoked the delights of English paternalism in comparison with the harsh life of master and men in the colony:

Christmas Day at last arrived ... but how unlike Christmas at home. There were no solemn chants to awake you from your rest at the approach of the sacred day, no greetings in the morning, no affectionate wishes, no kind presents, no peel of merry bells, no cheerful voices of village children loud and clamorous in their greetings of the season as in their solicitations for the customary remembrance of it ... there was no anticipation of pleasure, no prospect of meeting kind friends, no expected enjoyment of any innocent recreation or amusement. All that the men wished for or cared for was that they might have grog and get tipsy. If they could accomplish this they were satisfied to remain dirty and comfort-less and miserable in all other respects.[27]

Thus Eyre separated himself from those men on whom he had to rely in daily life, underpinning his own self-esteem by denigrating the lack of self-control, the base impulses, of those around him.

Eyre was convinced that the system of convict labour was valuable and that transportation provided a solution to the problem of punishment, both freeing Britain of criminals and reforming them. 'For the most part', he argued, 'the convicts, or Government men as they liked to be called, were well and kindly treated from the natural feelings and kind disposition inherent in Englishmen'. 'It was also', he noted, in 'the masters' interests to make them comfortable and contented'. He was impressed by the care, industry and trustworthiness of many of the convicts and believed that the combination of a healthy rural life and the prospect of freedom brought out the best in most Englishmen. There were, unfortunately, instances of tyranny on the part of the masters; he was shocked by the sight of men being flogged, a punishment which the colonists insisted was an absolute necessity. Writing in 1859 Eyre recalled that, 'It was a sickening sight to see the scarred and bleeding backs of human beings, convicts tho' they were. Could I ever divest myself', he asked himself rhetorically (little knowing what his answer would be in 1865), 'of the impression that the punishment of flogging was not only revolting and degrading but hardening also?'[28] In the early 1830s, however, as a young man bred in the enlightened, serious Christianity of the Evangelicals, Eyre's identity was shaped by the emphasis on the sensitive, responsible man, caring for, encouraging and correcting dependents, all of whom had the potential to become new men and women. Physical brutality should be something of the past, a form of punishment no longer necessary in a rational and enlightened age. That other voice in Eyre, which reminded him of the absolute necessity of harsh punishment, a voice so easily discarded in the 1830s and 1840s was, by the 1860s, to be more insistent.

After a year Eyre left Mr Bell and set up on his own. His experiment with sheepfarming went well until he entered an unwise partnership, impelled primarily by his desire for companionship, tired of a life where his everyday contacts were only with convicts and 'natives'. This proved financially disastrous and he decided to try his hand as an overlander, taking sheep and cattle across the country to the new settlements in South Australia. Despite the hardships of the life he was able to make a considerable amount of money, for as one observer remarked, 'The first entrance of an Overlander into a district, may be compared to the rising of the Nile upon the thirsty land of Egypt; then does the country bear fruit and the land give forth her increase'. Overlanding required some capital and plenty of confidence; it was an exciting, romantic and dangerous life. As the explorer and colonial administrator George Grey described it:

> The life of an Overlander in the bush is one of great excitement, which constantly calls every energy into action, is full of romantic and novel situations, and habituates the mind to self-possession

and command. The large and stately herd of cattle, is at least a fine, if not an imposing sight. The fierce and deadly contests which at times take place with the natives, when two or three hardy Europeans stand opposed to an apparently overwhelming majority of blacks, call for a large share of personal courage and decision; whilst the savage yells, and diabolic whoops of the barbarians in their onsets, their fantastically painted forms, their quivering spears, their contortions, and shifting of their bodies, and their wild leaps, attach a species of romance to these encounters, which affords plentiful matter for after meditation.[29]

Eyre thrived on the travelling life and became increasingly interested in the land, its potential for wealth and its mysteries. While overlanding Eyre took on two 'Aborigine' boys (the European term), intending to educate and civilize them.[30] From his first contacts with Aborigine people Eyre had been fascinated by their differences from Europeans, both physically and culturally. Eyre had left England in the year of the great Reform Act, just before the new Parliament, elected by its wider franchise, finally passed emancipation, that statement of faith from the anti-slavery public in the potential of blacks to be brothers. A true child of the era of emancipation, Eyre carried that faith to Australia and while never doubting the European right to possess the land, he firmly believed in British responsibility towards those they had dispossessed, denouncing those settlers who 'think as little of firing at a black, as at a bird'.[31]

By 1839 Eyre had made a considerable amount of money from overlanding and he decided to devote his energies to an exploration of parts of the north and west of South Australia, impelled by 'an innate feeling of ambition and a desire to distinguish myself in a more honourable and disinterested way than the mere acquisition of wealth'.[32] Australia remained the vast unexplored continent, a field of adventure for the ambitious. 'Over the centre of this mighty continent', wrote Charles Sturt, Eyre's friend and fellow explorer,

> there hangs a veil which the most enterprising might be proud to raise. The path of it, I would venture to say, is full of difficulty and danger, and to him who first treads it much will be due ... I shall envy that man who shall first plant the flag of our native country in the centre of our adopted one.[33]

Both overlanding and exploration were quintessentially male activities – indeed, exploration can be interpreted as the ultimate expression of frontier masculinity, the extension in the European mind of man's conquest over 'virgin' territory. In an article in the *South Australian Register* of 1840 Eyre's metaphorical language of conquest, like Sturt's, and Carlyle's, evokes the psychic links between power over other men, over women and over nature. Thus the web of connections established in the first encounters between the European and the 'new world' and later richly elaborated in the popular fictions of African conquest, were spun for Australia too.[34] Once again making use of what had become a conventional sexualized narrative of conquest Eyre noted:

> In a geographical point of view it will be exceedingly interesting to know the character of the intervening country between this colony and theirs, and to unfold the secrets hidden by those lofty, and singular cliffs at the head of the Great Bight ... It is possible that a light party might, in a favourable season, force their way across ... I would rather, therefore, turn the public attention to the Northward, as being the most profitable point from which discoveries of importance may be made, or such as are likely to prove beneficial to this and the other colonies, and from which it is possible the veil may be lifted from the still unknown and mysterious interior of this vast continent.[35]

When Eyre's second expedition set out from Adelaide, following the writing of this article, Charles Sturt presented him with a Union Jack, worked by the ladies of the town as their contribution to exploration – a manifestation of their particular relation to the public world of men – which he was to plant in the centre of the mighty continent 'as a sign to the savage that the footstep of civilised man has penetrated so far'; an evocative moment in the complex of relations between English middle-class men and their 'others', whether black or white female.[36]

Overlanders would occasionally have a woman with them, explorers never. The men had to survive on their own and the skills that Eyre had learnt as a bachelor-farmer – cooking, washing and repairing his clothes, dealing with sickness – were quite as essential as those associated with the driving of stock, the keeping of journals and charts, the daily observation of the barometer, the thermometer, the winds and the weather. When times were hard Eyre, trained in the ways of cleanliness and godliness, found there was nothing better than 'a good wash' to make himself feel better.[37]

The entire land of Australia had been claimed by the British crown in 1788 but only relatively small areas had been settled by the 1830s, providing, in the words of Charles Sturt, a 'girdle of civilisation'.[38] Since Aborigines did not share the Western concept of property and were hunter-gatherers with no fixed settlements, no arable farming, nor stock raising, they were utterly strange to the settlers.[39] The British saw the land as theirs to take, to improve and, in their terms, to make valuable. The introduction of sheep farming, profitable for the colonists, was a disaster for the Aborigine, resulting in the destruction of the traditional hunting environment. Aborigine resistance to the invasion, once they understood that this was what it was, was considerable, but the combination of guns, the ravages of new diseases and the destruction of the traditional means of survival resulted in the deaths of tens of thousands. For many of the settlers it became a self-fulfilling orthodoxy that the Aborigine were doomed to extinction.

As a farmer Eyre had been glad to employ casual Aborigine labour, making use, for example, of traditional Aborigine skills in stripping bark which could then be used for building sheep pens.[40] As an overlander he again had need of Aborigine skills and was dependent on their knowledge of the countryside. As an explorer this knowledge was even more essential and on his expeditions into the heartlands of South Australia Eyre would not have survived without Aborigine help. At numerous points on his ill-fated exploration of the Great Bight it was Aborigine knowledge of the water holes which saved at least some of the party. 'In how strong a light does such simple kindness of the inhabitants of the wilds to Europeans travelling through his country (when his fears are not excited or his prejudices violated) stand contrasted', he noted, 'with the treatment he experiences from them when they occupy his country, and dispossess him of his all'.[41]

Eyre's expeditions were not successful, failing to discover new lands which could be settled and farmed; indeed, in one Australian school textbook Eyre appears in a chapter titled 'Explorers who did not find things'.[42] On his return, however, he was invited by George Grey, then governor of the colony, to stay in South Australia and become Protector of the Aborigine for four years, in an area in which there had been considerable trouble between blacks and whites. Grey had become fascinated during his explorations by the Aborigine and in 1840 submitted a memorandum to the Secretary of State arguing for a different approach to the 'native problem'. He argued that the Aborigine 'are as apt and intelligent as any other race of men I am acquainted with' and that the future must lie in their amalgamation into settler society. Drawing on his observation of their 'peculiar code of laws' he insisted that until these 'barbarous' laws were dispensed with there was no hope for civilization. A programme of regular employment and improvement should be combined with subjection to British laws. South Australia was to be the testing ground for this new policy.[43]

In 1845 Eyre returned to England and on the voyage followed the example of Grey and wrote up the journals of his expeditions. Having produced the land as landscape for an English audience he followed the textual practices of the period in relation to travel writing and wrote an ethnographic portrait separate from the narrative proper – the *Manners and Customs of the Aborigines of Australia*. As Mary Louise Pratt points out this was the conventional way of producing 'non-European subjects for the domestic audience of imperialism', homogenizing 'the people into an iconic "he"', codifying and ordering the practices of another society.[44] Eyre's account of the Aborigine was a powerful plea

> on behalf of a people, who are fast fading away before the progress of a civilization, which ought only to have added to their improvement and prosperity ... It is most lamentable to think that the progress and prosperity of one race should conduce to the downfal [sic] and decay of another.

Both men relied on the new discourse of anthropology to give shape to their accounts and both were actively intervening in the continuing struggle by the emancipationist and humanitarian lobbies to insist that blacks were men and brothers and should be treated as such. Eyre's narrative, a narrative of 'anti-conquest' in Pratt's terminology, a strategy of representation whereby European bourgeois subjects sought to secure their innocence at the same time as asserting European hegemony, argued from the conviction 'that the Australian is fully equal in natural powers and intelligence, to the generality of mankind'.[45] The state of the 'generality of mankind', was in his mind coterminous with white Western society, always the benchmark against which other peoples could be measured.

Eyre believed that the interests of both settlers and Aborigine could co-exist. He insisted that in his experience the Aborigine were 'generally of a very inoffensive and tractable character', and could be 'rendered peaceable and well disposed by kind and consistent treatment'. We must remember, he reminded his readers, 'That our being in their country at all is, so far as their ideas of right and wrong are concerned, altogether an act of intrusion and aggression.'

Settlement meant dispossession. The Aborigine had become 'strangers in their own land' – subject to summary violence from settlers, while the law – 'which merely lays down rules for the protection of the privileged robber' – offered no protection.[46]

While acting as Protector of the Aborigine on the Murray River Eyre had developed a system which he strongly recommended was worthy of general notice. The area had been one in which considerable violence had taken place between the Aborigine and the overlanders. Under Eyre's control it had become peaceful. In his account of events he hoped to convince his readers of the capacities of the Aborigine and of the failure of the white settlers to raise these 'children of the wilds', these 'poor untutored children of impulse', higher in the scale of civilization. Eyre did not doubt that the Aborigine were 'savages' in that, for example, they treated their wives as slaves (always a key index for the Victorian Englishman as to the scale of a civilization). He was also quite ready to denounce them as 'silent and cunning in all they do', needing to be watched all the time. He doubted, however, that they were cannibals.

143

They had, he was sure, no thought of the morrow, a natural taste for a rambling and indolent life, and no idea of temperance and prudence. In other words they lacked those characteristics which the middle-class Englishman valued, the belief in the deferral of gratification, the commitment to the values of labour and discipline. In his writings Eyre described with amazement and disapproval the capacity of the Aborigine, having caught a kangaroo, to eat vast quantities of meat, just like his white, male working-class companions who drank gallons of water having been deprived of it, while he, ever prudent, ate only a modest amount of his share keeping the rest for another day, content with his usual pot of tea.[47] Nevertheless, he recognized that contrary to many European assumptions the Aborigine had their own relation to the land, their own feelings, their own value system, their own legal code, their own marriage customs, their own religious ideas, their own language. In Eyre's view their culture was different from and inferior to that of the English; the proper response to this was to make it genuinely possible for them to become 'like us'.

'Englishmen have ever been ready to come forward to protect the weak or the oppressed', he believed. English men must make the Aborigine into dependents. The twist within this thinking lay in the way in which the native was constructed as victim only as long as he/she was docile and compliant. But natives were also intemperate, unreliable, untrustworthy, always in danger of acting on these impulses. Eyre, at the time of writing his tract in 1844, was firmly contained within the discourses of philanthropic humanitarianism, exuding a degree of optimism. Typically he argued that having deprived the Aborigine of their subsistence 'we' must provide for them, and give them blankets, food, must separate the children from the parents and the boys from the girls, teach them entirely in English, educate them for work, find jobs for them so that they would not be tempted back to the wandering life, take them to church on Sundays, and give presents to those parents who were willing to abandon 'savage or barbarous ceremonies' on their children. Eyre argued that, 'we', the collective white English 'we', 'must adopt a system which may at once administer to their wants, and at the same time give us a controlling influence over them.'[48]

English men must act to protect the savages from their own savagery and make them anew as men and women in their own – English – image. Co-existence meant that blacks could be like brothers as long as the brothers were in their brothers' image. Once they were not, the seeds of other ways of perceiving the native were already contained in the interstices of the philanthropic mind.

NEW ZEALAND

Eyre left Australia in 1845 hoping he would find employment in the colonial service. He returned to England taking with him the two Aborigine boys that he was educating and 'civilising', his personal experiment in the construction of 'new men'.[49] While in England he met Ada Ormond, the daughter of a captain, a meeting that 'eventually became the turning point of my own destiny and led to the most important occurrence of my whole life.' Miss Ormond was not only socially highly suitable, being the daughter of a Captain in the Royal Navy, she was also 'a fair and beautiful girl, then in her teens, with all the attractive charms of incipient womanhood, the freshness, grace and loveliness of the rosebud ere it expands into the opening flower'.[50] Like many middle-class men Eyre preferred to marry a younger woman, whose adulthood would be formed in relation to him. In November 1846, after a year spent visiting friends and family, he was appointed Lieutenant Governor of the South Island of New Zealand, under the governorship of George Grey who had been transferred from South Australia. He set out for New Zealand at the beginning of 1847.

New Zealand had become an object of public concern in Britain in the late 1830s, when the Aborigine Protection Society was founded and the House of Commons Select Committee Report on Aborigines in British settlements was published. The Report, articulating the concerns of the anti-slavery lobby, argued that the expansion of the empire must involve the trusteeship of 'native races', protecting them from the worst effects of uncontrolled European contact. New Zealand, still only in the early stages of settlement, seemed to offer the possibility for a happier outcome than Australia, the amalgamation of Maori society with the settler community.[51] This was the hope of the Aborigine Protection Society and the New Zealand missionaries who were closely connected with it.

In the 1830s, however, Edward Gibbon Wakefield and the Colonial Reformers also sought the ear of the Colonial Office with a very different agenda. Disappointed with their unfulfilled desires in Australia they turned their attention to New Zealand, seeing it as a land rich in opportunities. Increasing French interest in New Zealand lent force to Wakefield's proposals that the territory should be seized for Britain. Wakefield himself was active in promoting the cause of systematic colonization through his evidence to the Parliamentary Inquiry on colonial lands in 1836, for which he was the chief witness, and to the Select Committee of the House of Lords on New Zealand, which took place in 1838.[52] In 1837 the New Zealand Association was formed, soon to be transformed into a joint stock company, the New Zealand Land Company, which acquired land and sent ships and settlers out to New Zealand, with Wakefield's son and brother on the first ship. The

Company was anxious to force the government to declare sovreignty, concerned to protect settler interests and dismissive of any conception of a Maori culture as in need of protection. In this vision, as in that of Carlyle, the islands were of no value until the settlers were there. 'Wilderness land', the company argued in its prospectus,

> is worth nothing to its native owners, or worth nothing more than the trifle they can obtain for it. We are not therefore to take much account of the inadequacy of the purchase money according to English notions of the value of land. The land is really of no value, and can become valuable only by means of a great outlay of capital on emigration and settlement.[53]

The missionaries who provided vital information on events on the islands, were extremely hostile to the naked commercial greed, as they saw it, of the Company, and they had the support of Lord Glenelg at the Colonial Office, who had been Vice-President of the Church Missionary Society. By 1838, however, the Colonial Office had become convinced (despite the wishes of the missionaries) that more intervention was essential in order to protect Maori interests from the settlers and ensure that colonization proceeded in an orderly, civilizing fashion. The official view had moved from the idea of 'a Maori New Zealand in which a place had to be found for British intruders' to 'a settler New Zealand in which a place had to be found for the Maori'.[54]

The Treaty of Waitangi of 1840 was the government's attempt to resolve the competing claims of the New Zealand Land Company, on the one hand, and the missionaries on the other. The government persuaded a substantial number of Maori chiefs to cede their sovereignty to the Queen and give the crown exclusive rights to the pre-emption of such lands as the Maori people wished to sell. In exchange, the Maori were granted full rights of ownership of their lands, forests and fisheries. They were also granted 'the rights and privileges of British subjects' and royal protection.[55] The government relied on substantial help from the missionaries – many of whom had built up a relation of trust with Maori chiefs – to conclude this treaty. They translated the terms of the treaty, taking care to interpret the agreement in the most favourable possible light, paying minimal attention to the loss of sovereignty. At the meeting called to conclude the treaty, 'There was considerable excitement amongst the people', one missionary recalled,

> greatly increased by the irritating language of ill-disposed Europeans, stating to the chiefs, in most insulting language, that their country was gone, and they now were only taurekareka [slaves]. Many came to us to speak upon this new state of affairs. We gave them but one version, explaining clause by clause,

showing the advantage to them of being taken under the fostering care of the British Government, by which act they would become one people with the English, in the suppression of wars, and of every lawless act; under one sovereign, and one Law, human and divine.

As each Maori chief signed the treaty the British representative shook hands and said in Maori, 'We are now one people'.[56] That 'we' was to prove somewhat more troublesome than it sounded.

The Treaty of Waitangi broke new ground in British colonial history in that the 'native' population was officially recognized as owning the land: Maoris were no longer to be 'strangers in their own land'. In this sense it was a triumph for the humanitarian lobby and an experiment akin to emancipation – were the blacks capable of emulating the British? The detailed interpretation of the clauses of the Treaty was a subject of dispute from the very beginning, however, and has remained so ever since. Rights over land were at the heart of conflicts between the Maori and the settlers and these conflicts erupted into open violence at several points in the early 1840s, most dramatically in 1845. George Grey, fresh from his successes in saving South Australia from financial ruin and racial conflict, was appointed to control the situation. New Zealand was to provide a more ambitious site for his policy of racial amalgamation.

It had been Grey who had appointed Eyre to be a Protector of the Aborigine in South Australia, part of his planned programme of 'native civilization', teaching savages the ways of civilized life and showing them the benefits which they could accrue. In his report on the Aborigine Grey had argued that the Aborigine were both like and unlike other men. The dissimilarities arose from their system of law which not only made it impossible 'that any nation subject to them could ever emerge from a savage state', but also meant that 'no race, however highly endowed, however civilized, could in other respects remain long in a state of civilization, if they were submitted to the operation of such barbarous customs'.[57] Grey believed that British laws, British missionaries, British education, British patterns of work, British culture, would transform Australian Aborigines or New Zealand Maoris and allow their underlying intelligence to flower. It was this belief which underpinned the policies which Grey and Eyre followed in South Australia and New Zealand. They were the protectors and guides who would bring their charges into full manhood or womanhood.

Eyre was active in attempting to foster amicable relations between black and white, and to raise the level of Maori civilization, in accordance with the framework which Grey had set out. On one of his trips, for example, he took with him a Maori chief and his wife, 'to show the feelings and intentions of the White people towards the native race'. He was quite prepared to be seen kneeling at services with natives rather than pompously dispaying his power. Most strikingly, his own marriage was a double ceremony in which the other couple were Maori and the lunch and the singing were shared, a symbolic expression of the brotherhood of man.[58] This policy of friendship and assimilation was combined with an energetic programme of land buying by the Crown from the Maori, in order significantly to reduce their overall holdings. Grey envisaged that in time the Maori would be 'trained to become useful labourers for the colonists'. He was convinced that they were 'a people quite equal in natural sense and ability to the mass of the European people'.[59]

The policies of Grey and Eyre were vigorously opposed by many settlers who were alienated by the autocratic style of government and also by many Maori who recognized the limitations of their own autonomy. Grey's private relationship with Eyre became very strained, due in part to an episode in Eyre's courtship of Ada, and then broke down completely despite their common approach to the 'native question'. Grey deprived Eyre of any power and Eyre returned to England in 1853, now with a wife and two children and looking for a new post.[60]

The 1850s saw a hardening of attitudes on all sides. The Maori were increasingly resolved to resist the imposition of British supremacy. The settlers were intolerant of what they saw as soft attitudes to the natives and anxious to extend their land-holdings in the north, which meant a further challenge to the Treaty of Waitangi. The Colonial Office and public opinion in Britain were moving away from the influence of the humanitarian lobby, with its emphasis on native welfare, and were increasingly preoccupied with settler development and self-government.[61] The dream of 'one people' was beginning to look outdated, the 'we' collapsing into 'them' and 'us'.

ST VINCENT AND ANTIGUA

Eyre spent some time in England before being appointed as Lieutenant Governor for the Caribbean island of St Vincent. The England he encountered was changing. The respectable, emancipationist orthodoxy about blacks as brothers and sisters was breaking up and ideas about 'race' and racial inferiority more openly discussed. The great experiment of emancipation in the West Indies had not been entirely successful from the British point of view. Anxieties focused around the collapse, as it was seen in Britain, of the plantation economy. While the planters' lobby loudly bemoaned their ruin at the indolent hands of lazy blacks, abolitionists were increasingly defensive in their accounts of the West Indies. Reflecting the signs of the times and articulating new thoughts on the relations between black and white Carlyle published his 'Occasional Discourse on the Negro Question' in 1849, re-published as a pamphlet and re-titled in 1853 an *Occasional Discourse on the Nigger Question*. This piece, instantly repudiated by the abolitionist press, marked the moment when it became legitimate for respectable, influential men publicly to profess a belief in the essential inferiority of black people, and to claim that blacks were born to be mastered and could never attain the level of European civilization.[62] By mid-century, it had become the fashion within scientific discourse to aver that distinct and fixed racial types provided the key to human history.

As Nancy Stepan has argued, the battle against slavery might have been won but the war against racism was lost. Indeed, it was emancipation which provoked the rise of new forms of racism, for it raised the spectre of black peoples as free and equal. It was in this context that 'race' became more, rather than less, important. In the 1830s and 1840s it was class (always inflected with gender difference) which had formed the primary language of self and group identification. By the 1850s, '"Race" increasingly became a primary form of self and group identification'.[63] In 1845 Robert Knox, soon to be celebrated as the author of *The Races of Men*, travelled the country visiting major provincial cities and lecturing on his personal obsession, race. He noted that while the provincial press reported him, the national press did not. By 1850, when his lectures were published as a book, he noted retrospectively that the situation was very different. The world had moved on and the climate had changed. Race had indeed become an issue. As he argued from his own bizarre radical and anti-imperialist position in 1850,

> ... that race is in human affairs everything is simply a fact, the most remarkable, the most comprehensive, which philosophy has ever announced. Race is everything: literature, science, art – in a word – civilization depends on it.

Knox believed that races were organically distinct and 'not convertible into each other by any contrivance whatever'; races could not amalgamate, and hybridity could only result in withering and death.[64] Civilization depended, in other words, on racial purity, on the separation of races, not on their harmonious integration.

It was in this climate that Eyre began to write his autobiography, working from his old journals. While Knox, holding to the radical tradition of the Norman Yoke, believed that the Norman conquest of England had been a disaster, Eyre was anxious to demonstrate his Norman origins as the roots of his gentility. 'The family of Eyre or le Eyre', he wrote, 'is an ancient and honourable one, said to have come to England with William the Conquerer'.[65] This good stock from which he claimed descent had by the eighteenth and early nineteenth centuries turned from land to the professions and Eyre combined his aspirations to nobility (entirely rejected it should be said, by the Jamaican whites who were outraged that a 'nobody' should be made their Governor)[66] with a conviction that it was his personal characteristics of hard work, duty and temperance which made it possible for him to succeed to fame and fortune. 'Although beginning life under great disadvantages, I have ever maintained the character and standing of a gentleman', he told himself and others, even in the strange conditions of the colonies which offered a career to 'the steady, the energetic and the persevering'.[67] It was providential in his eyes, just as for classical Weberian bourgeois man, that his superior characteristics allowed him to succeed, while improvident blacks and convicts had the habit of wasting themselves.

The optimistic tone of his narrative may well have been re-thought not long after as he languished in a public silence unbroken between 1868 and his death in 1901. But his account of his daring exploration, his determined disciplining of his 'men', his social conquests, sit ill-at-ease with the description of him in his thirties as having a badly proportioned head, a narrow chest, a speech impediment and a tip-toeing awkward gait, and with stories of his difficult courtship of Ada and his troubled times socially in New Zealand and Jamaica.[68] The retrospective, fanciful tale of his years in Australia, in other words, has to be seen as part of the persona he desperately wanted to present to himself and others in 1859, as he sat in the heat of St Vincent and hoped against hope that the Colonial Office would see fit to send him back to Australia. For Knox that land was one of the few colonies in which Europeans might hope to thrive since the climate was temperate and the blacks would soon have disappeared, for 'by shooting the natives as freely as we do crows in other countries, the population must become thin and scarce in time'.[69] Climate and natives were the twin challenges to the equilibrium of the white 'fire-pillar' of Carlyle's imagination. For Eyre the parts of Australia he liked best were those which were well watered, like England. His notions of beauty were entirely conventional, the landscape valued according to its potential for wealth. His determination was to remain an Englishman, to maintain 'the good old traditions of the English race' – never, in other words, to be a stranger in his own land.[70] Blacks might conceivably be able to become like 'us' – 'we' were certainly not going to become like 'them'. Australia offered more hope of such a scenario in the 1830s and 1840s than did the Caribbean twenty years later, to an older and less confident man.

Eyre arrived at the end of 1854 in St Vincent, one of the tiny islands of the Caribbean, with his wife, his two small children, a private secretary, a manservant and three women servants – a profoundly English middle-class party.[71] He was shocked by the contrast between the settler colonies of Australia and New Zealand and the tropical world of the plantation economy with its long established white population and its black freed slaves. He found the financial state of the colony 'deplorable', with a large debt and the annual expenditure exceeding the revenue. Public services were 'most unsound and unsatisfactory' with the hospital closed, the jail dilapidated, no aid being given to schools, no refuges for the destitute or orphans, no mental institution, indeed, the island lacked 'the most essential laws and the most necessary institutions'. His own residence was 'deficient in many of the essentials and commonest conveniences of an ordinary English dwelling'. A child of the Reform Act, who had strongly supported the establishment of an elective legislative council in New Zealand and saw himself as 'a great admirer and strong advocate for representative institutions in the Colonies', he swiftly determined that those institutions were not workable in St Vincent. With a population of over 30,000 only 293 electors were registered and in the previous election only 130 had voted for the nineteen members. At various times, he discovered,

> four members have been returned by ten votes, three members by four votes, three members by three votes, one member by one voter and in one instance a single voter actually returned two out of the nineteen members.

Furthermore those members who were returned were not up to their duties for there were, in his view, 'few persons of intelligence, education and respectablity' willing to take up public service. The Speaker of the House at the time Eyre was there wrote:

> During the time I have been Speaker, it has scarcely been possible to find a member who could, as chairman, conduct the business of a Committee of the House – Very many cannot read a manuscript at all – some cannot read a manuscript law bill at all – and on one occasion a gentleman in the chair could neither read nor write.[72]

Eyre pressed for intervention from the British government believing the island incapable of effecting reform for itself. Henry Taylor, who had long been responsible for the West Indies at the Colonial Office and had been arguing for direct crown rule since 1839, commented that: 'there is nothing that the Home Government can do to bring about a more prosperous state of things'. His colleague Herman Merivale, after reading one of Eyre's depressed despatches thought that despondency, 'strikes him the more forcibly as coming so recently from a new and rising colony'.[73] The comparison between the virgin lands of Australia and New Zealand and the decrepitude of a failing sugar economy was indeed striking. The young enterprising middle-class English settlers, whose presence was seen as so vital by Wakefield, were certainly not to be found in St Vincent. Indeed, as a visiting American was to comment a few years later, 'the island was utterly destitute of the spirit of enterprise'.[74] The absence of whites and the dependence on coloured shopkeepers and tradesmen for public office was responsible, in Eyre's view, for the prevailing decadence. 'Persons of this class', he informed the Colonial Office, 'cannot be expected to act from very pure or very enlightened motives'. These were men lacking in talent and 'greatly deficient even in ordinary education and information'.[75] Whereas in Australia and New Zealand natives were children to raise up, the uppity coloureds of St Vincent, whether in the House of Assembly or acting as magistrates, special constables or volunteers, occupied a different space in the imperial imagination. Long established patterns of racial inter-mixing and the existence of a coloured middle class brought Eyre problems he had not previously encountered.

Eyre complained: 'public opinion has no influence or can scarcely be said to exist amidst the proverbial apathy and indolence of West Indian colonists'.[76] It was public opinion, public spirit, a responsible press, which had, in the eyes of liberal reformers, created the conditions in which democratic institutions could flourish in England. While the Colonial Office had long been contemptuous of the capacity of white planters to supersede self-interest, Eyre bemoaned the absence of them on the island, an absence which resulted in the prominence of urban coloureds. He compared the island unfavourably with Barbados, where there were more resident whites 'interspersed amongst the coloured population and above all there is the moral influence of a large body of disciplined European troops'.[77]

The missionaries and their allies in England had long been preoccupied with building a black middle class which would be capable, in their eyes, of conducting responsible government.[78] Given Eyre's historic attachment to the protection of native races it might have been expected that he would have aligned himself to just such a policy; but this was not to be. Just as the presence of coloured merchants, tradesmen and newspaper editors troubled him, so the blacks that he encountered in St Vincent were disturbingly different from the indigenous natives he was familiar with, those 'children of the wilds' or 'strangers in their own lands' who were to be pitied as victims and made into dependents. The blacks of the British Caribbean were freed slaves, still riven with the memory of slavery and ever watchful of any attempt to reimpose that hated institution, whether in the guise of new penal codes or the importation of indentured labourers from Asia. They had been brought forcibly from Africa but were now independent peoples with property, skills and aspirations. On Spanish territory, all too close, slavery still flourished. Their children had never experienced slavery, but had been raised in its shadow. Numerically the blacks outnumbered the whites on St Vincent by twenty to one and had the potential, if they achieved the vote, to provide the electoral majority. Thousands of acres were being cultivated by small independent black proprietors, enjoying unparallelled prosperity.[79]

Eyre's first encounters with blacks left him disappointed with the extent to which, for him, they were 'so little improved a race'.[80] The promise of emancipation had not been realized; and far from considering any extension in the franchise to raise the degree of representation he was convinced that the executive should increase its powers at the expense of the elected bodies, a conviction which he was able to translate into new constitutional legislation.

Eyre's fears about public order, in an island on which no white troops were stationed and boasting 'so excitable a population', were stirred by riots over the case of a coloured woman accused of stealing canes in 1855. On attempting to swear in special constables Eyre found that few coloured men would volunteer, his first recognition of the bond between people of colour which overrode class divisions. In describing this event to his superior Eyre complained that the coloureds 'were resolutely banded together for the purpose of preventing the awards of law being carried out in cases where they disapproved of the decisions'. He needed white soldiers to exert a 'moral influence' and 'to keep within proper bounds that innate conviction of their own power which is so often apt to mislead a population such as that of St Vincent in cases where they imagine ... their interest as a class to be concerned'. His fears were seen as exaggerated by his Governor-in-Chief in Barbados, however, who firmly told him that 'there is no reason to mistrust the black population when properly appealed to'.[81] But Eyre became increasingly nervous as to the 'mine' upon 'which all the West Indian colonies rest'; the 'mine' being the 'very excitable and easily misled' people, the non-European population.[82]

Eyre sailed to England on six months' leave in 1857, the year of the Indian Mutiny, when the middle-class public which had proved so liberal on anti-slavery identified with the whites in what was speedily constructed on the most simple of narratives: a racial and religious war in which the whites were victims. 'How little we know of the heart of the native!' was the cry on every lip.[83] The abolitionist public, still ready to defend Christian blacks, was silent on the persecution of Hindus and Moslems. As Macaulay noted in his diary:

> The cruelties of the Sepoy natives have inflamed the Nation to a degree unprecendented within my memory. Peace Societies, Aborigines Protection Societies, and societies for the reformation of criminals are silent. There is one terrible cry to revenge ... The almost universal feeling is that not a single Sepoy within the walls of Delhi should be spared, and I own that is a feeling with which I cannot help sympathising.[84]

Eyre returned reluctantly to the Caribbean on his own, his wife's health having suffered severely from the tropics. He hoped for an appointment in Australia so he could be reunited with his family. Having a limited private income he also desperately wanted a better paid post as his constant correspondence with the Colonial Office made clear. The impact of the Mutiny spread to St Vincent after a suggestion that 'mutineers' of a less dangerous kind could be transported to provide labour for the desperate West Indian planters. Eyre was in favour of this provided a small garrison of white troops were available, and that wives and children came too in order to establish proper family life and

> always supposing that they are of a class from which a reasonable amount of labour may be obtained: for I am not sufficiently acquainted with the character of the high caste Mutineers of India to be able to judge how far it would be practicable to get them to apply themselves cheerfully to manual labour in the fields.[85]

This suggests a clear recognition of the different understanding of India within the imperial imagination, as a place with an ancient civilization and its own established hierarchies – a far cry from the un-educated and 'excitable' negroes.

At Christmas and New Year there were riots in the capital of St Vincent again. With the experience of the Indian Mutiny behind him and an increasing sense of the island as a 'small and isolated colony', Eyre did not hesitate to interpret the dangers in racial terms. The riots had begun with drunken British sailors rampaging in the town, offending local inhabitants. An angry crowd collected, 'nearly the whole population of Kingstown'. Eyre's only available peace-keeping force were volunteers drawn from this very same crowd and 'just as much excited as the rest of the people'. He envisaged an ugly confrontation between 'resolute English sailors' and the 'excited crowd'. 'It was evident', he reported to his superior, 'that in the event of any collision taking place it would become one of race – the coloured against the white man'. He concluded that without white troops there could be no security.[86]

It was in the midst of all this that Eyre was writing his autobiography, sending bundles of it back to his wife who was in Plymouth with the children. Alone in the heat of the tropics, cut off from ordinary social intercourse by his position as Lieutenant Governor, and from England by the absence of white settlers and the irregularity of the mail, surrounded by – as he increasingly interpreted it – hostile coloureds and blacks, it is hardly surprising that his young manhood seemed deeply enticing. At the same time he was penning regular letters to the Secretary of State for the Colonies, asserting his qualifications for any posts which he heard about in the hope of escaping his predicament. These letters focused on his long-term experience with the different native peoples of the empire, and also served, alongside his autobiographical writing, to heighten his sense of his own identity as 'a white Englishman'. His persistence demonstrated that he was, as Taylor noted, 'certainly a very urgent and indefatigable suitor'. The Colonial Office, however, judged him as rather less capable than he would have liked. In April 1859, however, a reasonably satisfactory solution was found when he was offered a slightly better temporary post in Antigua.[87]

This promotion, together with his pleasure at leaving St Vincent in a more orderly state than he had found it, may account for a more optimistic note in his first comments on Antiguan blacks. His first task was to attempt to form a local militia. He discovered that the whites were afraid to arm the blacks even against a common enemy but reported that, 'I do not in the least share this feeling; for however excitable or disposed to occasional excesses whilst under excitement the labouring classes of the West Indies are, I believe, as a Body both truly loyal and fully alive to the advantages of living under British rule'.[88] Such a positive note was soon subsumed, however, in more gloomy comments on the fall in population which was occurring on the island. Eyre explained this odd phenomenon in 'a people naturally so prolific as the Negro race' in terms of their lack of proper family life, their neglect of their children and their desperate need for 'respectable and influential residents in their neighbourhood', who could improve by their moral example. While 'excitable' almost always signified black, 'respectable' meant white, with all its imagined meanings.[89]

In 1860 Eyre returned once more to England and had to wait eighteen months before he was appointed Deputy Governor of Jamaica. The Maori wars had replaced the Indian Mutiny as the major source of colonial disillusionment, Eyre's old colleague Grey, sent back to New Zealand from South Africa in order to save the situation, was now ready to describe the Maori as 'a semi-barbarous race, puffed up with the pride of an imagined equality'. New Zealand whites bemoaned the fact that:

> We have dealt with the natives of this country upon a principle radically wrong. We have conceded them rights and privileges which nature has refused to ratify ... We have pampered ignorance and misrule, and we now experience their hatred of intelligence and order. The bubble is burst. The Maori is now known to us as what he is, and not as missionaries and philanthropists were willing to believe him. [In reality the Maori is] a man ignorant and savage, loving darkness and anarchy, hating light and order; a man of fierce, and ungoverned passions, bloodthirsty, cruel, ungrateful, treacherous.[90]

As the intensity of discourses of racial difference deepened, so the connotation of 'native' with 'irredeemable savage' became more common and immovable. In New Zealand Grey's erstwhile philanthropy toward the Maori could not survive intact. In Jamaica, where a similar dynamic

155

was being played out, the commonsense of the planter class – negroes no longer held in check by violence would revert to savagery – began to touch more closely the 'official mind' of the empire. In the Parliamentary debates on emancipation and apprenticeship those who were fearful of sudden freedom argued that it might result in the adoption of 'primitive habits of savage life', habits which had been contained only by a regime of the whip.[91] For English officials the fight against encroaching Africanisms was a constant one, whether in the form of attacks on John Canoe festivities or revivals of obeahism. This was the kind of English commonsense which Eyre increasingly had recourse to from his early days in Jamaica. The language of brotherhood had disappeared. The fear now articulated was that blacks would sink back into the barbarism from which they had been briefly lifted, by their enforced enslavement and encounter with Europe. The confidence and enthusiasm which had permeated Eyre's account of his young manhood and his successful years with the Aborigine was gone. Public and private disappointments, the responsibility of supporting a growing family of five, his wife's ill-health and his separation from her and his children, all combined with the new racial discourses of the 1850s and 1860s to construct a more threatened, defensive, disturbed identity, one which depended on an assertion of established white authority.

Mill, reflecting on debates in England on the American Civil War and observing the absence of a strong tide of anti-slavery feeling, pointed to the generational change which had taken place: those who had fought for abolition and believed slavery to be an issue which went right to the heart were no longer active in public debate. Eyre was only too ready to ponder on a different generational change which had occurred in Jamaica. Whites on the island widely agreed that the most respectful blacks were those who had been born into slavery; it was their children who had become idle and profligate.[92] And it was they, who had not felt the whip, who were the future.

Furthermore, whereas Eyre's early ideas about the Aborigine had been formed through daily contact and dependence, as sheep farmer, over-lander and explorer, his life as a colonial dignatory was very different. Surrounded by white servants his household included a white man-servant, two women servants and a tutor for his children – in other words the most personal tasks demanding direct contact were done by whites – and, like the white and coloured upper and middle classes of the Caribbean islands, he probably rarely encountered blacks in any personal way. On the occasions that he did, for example on his tour of the island in 1864, he could still recognize warmth and hospitality before retreating into the certainties of an ever harsher vocabulary of race. Jamaican blacks, as he constructed them in his imagination through the lens of Maori wars, Indian Mutinies and the newly popular discourses of racial difference, were much more fearful and dangerous than those Aborigine whose help he had once relied upon for his survival.

Eyre's first months in Jamaica convinced him of the centrality of race to an understanding of the society; it was a place where every opportunity was taken 'to make the question one of colour'. With a population of thirty-two blacks and coloureds to every white this could appear very threatening, especially when the vast majority were, in Eyre's terms, 'uneducated and excitable' and 'always liable to be easily imposed upon by designing persons'. The declining white population was a source of serious concern to him, as it had been in St Vincent, for colonists with 'ability and intelligence' were leaving or dying off with the consequence that the executive had to rely on 'a very different class of persons'.[93]

That 'different class of persons' was predominantly coloured and fairly well represented in the House of Assembly. When coloureds united with Jews (there was a significant Jewish mercantile presence in Kingston) in the House they could often form a majority. Eyre found many of the middle-class coloured men exceedingly difficult to deal with, especially George William Gordon, the son of a planter and a slave who had become a planter himself and was a prominent member of the House of Assembly and severe critic of the Governor on many counts.[94] But nor could he count on the support of the whites. He was convinced that 1863, for example, was a good year economically for the colony since – though the planters had not done well – the small settlers, the black independent peasantry, had. The planters, however, 'will not recognize and do not like to be told of a prosperity in which they are not sharing'. The *Jamaica Guardian* admiringly quoted Eyre as providing evidence which would tell against the prejudices of Carlyle:

> Mr. Eyre is the first Governor we have had who has recognised the small settlers of the country, as forming an important element in the industrial activity and enterprise of Jamaica ... We rejoice to have such convincing evidence afforded us, and to be able to put forth such proof to the world, that they are making creditable progress in those pursuits which become a people worthy of freedom. Carlyle and his disciples will see that the pumpkin-eaters of this island – the men 'up to the eyes in pumpkin' as he has described them – are not such lazy worthless fellows after all.[95]

Eyre's clashes with the House led him speedily to the same conclusion he had reached in the other Caribbean islands: representative institutions could not work in such societies. In a recent election forty-seven members had been returned by 1,457 voters, out of a population of 441,264, so that the vast majority of the population 'had no voice in returning their so called Representatives'. He was not, however, in favour of increasing the franchise, since he regarded the 'general population' as 'quite unfitted for the exercise of political privileges'. Representative institutions were the 'great bulwark of British liberty and British greatness' – but Jamaica was not Britain and the Jamaican population were not black Anglo-Saxons.[96]

In May 1864 Eyre was finally made Governor, against the wishes of many prominent Jamaicans, after a long period of uncertainty which he felt deeply undermined his authority in 'this most troubled colony'. Under attack from many sides, with his own position 'anomalous and doubtful', suffering again from the absence of his wife and children who could not stand the climate and had returned to England, with no proper 'establishment' or 'Lady' to dispense the hospitality which might have eased his isolation, he felt that only his sense of duty sustained him.[97] In his new and more prestigious capacity, however, he decided on a tour of the island. His response to the addresses of the peasantry detailing their distress, reported to the Secretary of State was, as Thomas Holt puts it, 'laced with classic mid-Victorian platitudes and irrelevancies'.[98] He instructed the small settlers that the Queen was 'most anxious that you should progress in civilization, in education, in morality and in material prosperity' and that such improvements must depend on their own efforts, particularly in relation to their children. It was their lack of proper family life, as he defined it, which ensured that there was no base from which 'civilization', meaning English society with its particular gender order, could develop. 'All Ages and all Sexes promiscuously occupy the same apartment', he disapprovingly noted. 'The natural and necessary result is that all sense of propriety or decency, all morality and all cleanliness are utterly wanting'. Whilst he was impressed by the relative prosperity of the small settlers with their lands, carts, horses and Sunday clothes his final judgement of them as 'a people' was that in 'their own homes, and in their social habits and relations', they were 'little better than absolute savages'.[99]

Having in his own mind constructed the population of the island as 'absolute savages', the shift to a highly coercive regime appeared quite logical. Theft, for example, had become a serious problem. The culprits, it appeared, were not the old and the needy but the young and able-bodied of both sexes, 'those who are well able to work'. 'I fear', argued Eyre, moving towards the logic of Carlyle and the planters, 'it is rather an indisposition to labour than an inability to procure work' which led them to steal. Far from feeling shamed by imprisonment such offenders, Eyre believed, returned home to 'their people' with no stigma attached to them. From June 1864 Eyre began to inquire of the Colonial Office whether the treadmill had ever been officially banned; and after his tour of the country he pressed for the re-intoduction of the whip, together with a system of enforced apprenticeship. The proposed number of stripes was well in excess of those allowed within the British army or under the old apprenticeship system. Given 'the peculiar state of things' in the West Indies, Eyre maintained flogging had become a necessary remedy, though not one that he had expected to have to resort to in his younger days. He insisted that propertied blacks, indeed all classes of the community, were in favour of such action, a view with which Gordon, for one, dissented.[100]

In March 1865 Eyre received a letter forwarded to him by Cardwell, the Secretary of State at the Colonial Office, from the Secretary of the Baptist Missionary Society, Edward Bean Underhill. The Baptists had long been active in Jamaica and had been powerfully identified as 'the friend of the negro'.[101] Underhill's letter expressed great concern at the level of want and starvation on the island and asked for action. Eyre, a committed Anglican, had previously, maintained reasonable, if not warm, relations with the Baptists on the island; but the letter outraged him. Allying himself with the white establishment, he collected reports on the state of the population, emphatically denied Underhill's claims and placed responsibility for all ills squarely on the shoulders of 'excitable' blacks and dangerous agitators. At the heart of the problem, he was now convinced, was race – the character of the Creole labourer, born in Jamaica, and the 'difficulty of elevating him'. 'It must ... be borne in mind', he argued, reproducing exactly the rhetoric of the slave-owners of the 1830s and Carlyle in the 1840s,

> that even when he does work, the Creole labourer requires an amount of direction, supervision and watching unknown in other Countries, and detracting greatly from the value of his services; and this remark is equally applicable to the best and most intelligent tradesman and mechanics as to the mere field labourer ... If he can obtain a bare subsistence by little effort or exertion, he will not extend his labours to secure comfort or independence.

'The people' suffered from 'an utter want of principle or moral sense', a 'total absence of parental control or proper training of children', 'incorrigible indolence, apathy and improvidence' and a 'degraded and immoral social existence'. They were 'easily misled' by 'political agitators or designing Men'. At the core of their degradation lay immorality, most sharply signified by promiscuity, parental irresponsibility, and the neglect of the old and the sick by familial networks. These were all indices, for the evangelical Christian, of a culture in disintegration; for only a Christian household with a proper division of labour between the sexes and a proper sense of responsibility for the awesome duties entailed by parenthood could provide the fundamentals for a good society. 'Deterioration, Decadence and Decay' were everywhere apparent with the whites leaving and no 'fresh influx of European energy, intelligence, experience, enlightened views and moral principles' replacing them, 'qualities which are so essential as examples to stimulate and influence races, only just emerging from, and without such influences likely to fall back rapidly into a state of barbarism.'[102]

For Eyre, utterly convinced as he was and always had been of white superiority, the notion contained in his early memorandum on the Aborigine, the respectful recognition of their separate, and different culture with its own rituals, laws and institutions, was no longer possible. West Indian negroes were 'savages' and 'barbarians' without culture, unable to adapt to the requirements of civilization. Mastery and control were the only solutions.

Given this construction of 'them' as essentially, utterly different from 'us', of the Caribbean islands as mine-fields, and whites as beleaguered and in great jeopardy, it became inevitable that Eyre could see the rising in Morant Bay only as the preordained fulfilment of his worst fantasies, in which the whites of Jamaica faced extinction and all manner of torment. His first despatch recounted horrific brutalities committed by the black rioters – later proven by the Royal Commission never to have occurred – which 'could only be paralleled by the atrocities of the Indian mutiny'. The women, he asserted, 'as usual on such occasions, were even more brutal and barbarous than the men', a clear signifier for the English middle class that the last remnants of civilization had been torn away. Only white troops (with the help of loyal black Maroons who had cooperated with the whites for many years in return for relative free-doms) could save the white population from the 'evil passions' of black savagery, wickedly stirred up by 'wolves in sheep's clothing' (as Eyre perceived the Baptist missionaries) who found it easy to sway the rioters but 'impossible to guide, direct, or control them when once excited.' 'It is scarcely necessary to point out', Eyre insisted to the Colonial Office when he first heard intimations of criticism from England,

> that the negro is a creature of impulse and imitation, easily misled, very excitable, and a perfect fiend when under the influence of an excitement which stirs up all the evil passions of a race little removed in many respects from absolute savagery.

By such a logic justice could only be meted out by the imposition of the most severe retribution.[103]

Morant Bay finally convinced Eyre that he had been right in his political assessment: Jamaica was not capable of self-government, the people were 'incompetent to judge for themselves'. Only direct rule from Britain was possible. The terrified white population concurred. Despite the objections of some of the coloured members, the House of Assembly and the Legislative Council abolished themselves.[104] Jamaica became a crown colony, ruled from London, until the struggle for independence eventually proved successful in 1962.

Soon after the rebellion had been repressed Eyre greeted the Maroons at a celebration in their honour in order to thank them for the help they had given in defeating the rebels. 'Maroons of Jamaica', he proclaimed,

it is in times of difficulty and danger like the present that the true character of individuals, or of races, becomes prominently brought to light ... may you carry away with you a pleasant recollection of this day's proceedings; and when, in long after years, you talk of them to your children and your children's children, tell them that the welcome we now offer, and the reception we have given, was intended to shew them, that the Queen of England, and all in authority under her, respect and honour the brave and loyal of every country, whatever be their race or colour.[105]

The ordinary blacks of Jamaica might be forgiven for thinking differently.

By the time that Eyre left Jamaica in 1866, suspended from duty, he was immensely popular with the whites on the island; his departure provided an opportunity for grateful addresses, thanking him for saving the colony from anarchy. The shared commonsense of the white population was clearly adopted and articulated by Eyre in his despatches to the Colonial Office, and in his subsequent evidence to the Royal Commission. Negroes, in this view, were not black Anglo-Saxons; indeed, 'there are feelings of race within the black man's breast impenetrable to those without', preventing many in England from understanding the true 'character and tone of thinking of the negro population'.[106] There were powerful echoes here of the arguments of the planters in the 1830s, the insistence that only people who knew blacks could 'know', and that 'Nigger-Philanthropists', to use Carlyle's term (a term which placed the enemy firmly within), were deluded in their fantasies of black equality.[107] 'I know of no general grievance under which the negroes of this colony labour', insisted Eyre.[108] Their pursuit of a rebellious plot against the whites could, therefore, only be blamed on designing others. The enemy, it turned out, was within as well as without. The uncivilized and ignorant blacks had been misled and encouraged by 'pseudo-philanthropists' from England, who could not be aware of what terrible harm they were causing, by 'political demagogues' and, evil-minded men' who excited the blacks to 'rebellion, arson, murder'. There was an unresolved tension in the thinking here, as there had been in the Indian Mutiny, between the notion of blacks as incapable of acting for themselves, puppets on strings, and blacks as a source of conspiracy and evil, awaiting only white surveillance to be lifted to explode into the light of day. Blacks at one and the same time were objects of contempt – effeminized and made dependent – and objects of terror and fear – rapists, torturers and murderers.

For the supporters of Eyre in England, shocked at the unrelenting persecution of him, as they saw it, by the Jamaica Committee, it was vital to make the British public understand the true character of the negro as it had been revealed all too clearly by the events at Morant Bay. Thus a key protagonist of Eyre's, Commander Bedford Pim, presented a paper to the Anthropological Society of London (a new society of which Eyre was a founder member, that combined 'science' with politics) in February 1866, in which he stated that the rebellion meant that 'my countrymen, whether they liked it or not, were brought face to face with the negro'. Pim gave himself the task of laying out the 'negro's peculiarities' to his respectable, enthusiastic audience. Reminding the crowded room that 'We do not admit equality even amongst our own race, as is proved by the state of the franchise at this hour in England', Pim asserted that, 'to suppose two alien races can compose a political unity is simply ridiculous. One section *must* govern the other.' 'The principles', he continued,

> on which alien and dissimilar races ought to be governed, is not yet understood by our rulers. Jamaica is not the only proof of this: the state of St Vincent, Antigua, New Zealand, the Cape of Good Hope, to say nothing of India, attests that 'how to govern alien races' has yet to be learnt. Let us take the negro as we find him, as God designed him, not a white man, nor the equal of a white man ...[109]

Similarly Hamilton Hume, the contemporary biographer of Eyre who was closely involved in establishing Eyre's Defence Fund, sought to vindicate his hero and show the real nature of the dangers he had faced. His descriptions of the events at Morant Bay, heavily laced with fantasy, dwelt on

> those fearful and bloody acts which were scarcely paralleled by the massacre at Cawnpore. The cries for mercy, the savage yells of the women hounding on the men as each new victim was discovered, and the heavy thuds of the cutlasses on the bodies of the butchered, were heard even above the rattle of the musketry and the hissing of the devouring flames ... Captain Hitchens ... was slowly hacked to death by a negro with a cutlass, who sat down to his diabolical work as coolly and as slowly as if he had been chopping wood.

The negroes were 'drunk with blood' and 'mad with excitement', all of which justified the view that

> Nothing can be more absurd than to compare a negro insurrection with a rebellion in England. The negroes, from being in the very lowest state of civilization, and under the influence of superstitious feelings, can never be dealt with in the same manner as might the peasantry of an English county.[110]

The supporters of Eyre felt compelled to defend their own *race*, to counter the tendency of those who 'in their desire to whitewash the black man, too often blacken the white man'.[111] William Finlason, in his desire to provide an accessible, edited version of the hundreds of official papers dealing with the events, published several books, all attempting to exonerate Eyre. His heavy-handed comments on the Jamaica Committee focused on their preocupation with

> the oppressors of 'subject and dependent races'. As if anybody wanted to oppress them. As if, now-a-days, there was any disposition; at all events among men likely to be in authority, to injure or oppress them! As if the current were not running rather in the opposite direction, and the tendency rather to oppression of our own fellow-countrymen by classes prejudiced against them, on the plea of their pretended oppression of dependent races![112]

It was time for real men to speak out, to end the fantasy of racial equality, to accept reality, and govern with a strong hand. This was what Eyre had done, and it was this which deserved their support and celebration. In narrating Eyre as hero – 'one of the very finest types of English manhood', who had 'preserved the lives of 7,000 British men, and the honour of 7,000 British women, from the murder and the lust of black savages', who 'put to proof some of the very highest qualities that ever in a man ... have been considered meritorious', – Carlyle and his acolytes were determined to destroy earlier visions of equality, whether of the races, the classes or the sexes. And in large part they were successful. In his defence of Eyre Carlyle poured scorn on the humanitarians, effeminizing them just as he had done in his *Occasional Discourse*. He celebrated Eyre as the manly hero, the silent doer, who had responded to threat and acted with strength, saving the whites from 'black unutterabilities'.[113] The constant struggle over the meanings of English male identity took another turn: 'we' must be seen to assert proper forms of hierarchy and power, 'we' must defend 'our own'. The magazine *Punch*, which actively supported Eyre, greeted the first failed prosecution against him, which took place in Market Drayton, Shropshire, with immense glee. 'FREE AS EYRE!' they trumpeted. 'Well done, old Shropshire! Well done, Market Drayton ... English good sense is seldom appealed to in vain. We really cannot murder a man for saving a colony'.[114] 'We' could no longer be one people with those of the colonies. 'We' had returned to a much narrower definition of the imagined community – one that was exclusively white.

Eyre himself must have been profoundly shocked by his return to England and his discovery of the bitter controversy attached to his name. His only public statements after his return aimed to demonstrate his

163

sense of himself as a faithful public servant, a man who had done his Christian duty as he had seen fit. Having spent the vast majority of his adult life in the colonies, dreaming of an England that was more active in memory than reality, it must have been a bitter experience to return to live in retirement, his pension secured only after long negotiation, his reputation high with many but his figure burnt in effigy by working-class radicals.[115] His response to the personal prosecution by the Jamaica Committee, Finlason claims, 'echoed throughout England'.

> I have only this to say, that not upon me, but upon those who brought me here, lies the foul disgrace that a public servant who has faithfully discharged his duty for upwards of twenty years, has been now, after two years and a half of persecution, brought to a criminal court and committed for trial for having performed his duty at a trying moment, and thereby saved, indubitably, a great British colony from destruction, and its well-disposed inhabitants, white and black, from massacre or worse ... I am satisfied that the large majority of my fellow-countrymen do not sanction these proceedings against me, and to their sense of justice, and to their common sense, I may say, I confidently entrust my honour as a gentleman and my character as a public officer.[116]

He was correct in his judgement. Successive prosecutions were thrown out by the juries of 'twelve good men and true' who determined that an Englishman's rights and liberties were more important than those of black Jamaicans.

NOTES

1 This chapter is part of a larger research project on race, ethnicity and the English middle class between 1833 and 1868. I am grateful to the Economic and Social Research Council for its financial support for this project, Ref. no. R000232169. Versions of this paper have been given at the University of Sussex, the History Workshop seminar in London, Thames Polytechnic, King's College, Cambridge, the University of Michigan at Ann Arbor, the Centre for Research on Sex and Gender at Columbia and Barnard and the Johns Hopkins University, Baltimore. I would like to thank the members of those seminars, Cora Kaplan, the contributors to this book, especially Bob Chase, and most of all Bill Schwarz, for their comments.

2 *Parliamentary Papers*, 1866, vol. L1, Papers Relating to the Disturbances in Jamaica, no.251, 20/10/1865, Eyre to Cardwell, p.152.

3 Some of the major sources for Morant Bay and its aftermath are: *Parliamentary Papers, Report of the Jamaica Royal Commission, 1866,* Eyre and Spottiswood, London, 1866; Hamilton Hume, *The Life of Edward John Eyre, Late Governor of Jamaica,* Richard Bentley, London, 1867; William F. Finlason, *The History of the Jamaica Case founded upon official or authentic documents, and containing an account of the debates in Parliament, and the criminal prosecutions, arising out of the case,* Chapman and Hall, London, 1869; Edward Bean

Underhill, *The Tragedy of Morant Bay: A Narrative of the Disturbances in the Island of Jamaica in 1865*, Alexander and Shepheard, London, 1895; Sydney S. Olivier, *The Myth of Governor Eyre*, Leonard and Virginia Woolf, London, 1933; Philip D. Curtin, *Two Jamaicas: The Role of Ideas in a Tropical Colony, 1830–1865*, Harvard University Press, Cambridge, Mass. 1955; Douglas Hall, *Free Jamaica, 1836–65: An Economic History*, Yale University Press, New Haven, 1959; Bernard Semmel, *The Governor Eyre Controversy*, MacGibbon and Kee, London, 1962; Douglas Lorimer, *Class, Colour and the Victorians: English Attitudes to the Negroes in the Mid-nineteenth Century*, Leicester University Press, Leicester, 1978; Geoffrey Dutton, *The Hero as Murderer: The Life of Edward John Eyre, Australian Explorer and Governor of Jamaica, 1815–1901*, William Collins, London, 1967; Christine Bolt, *The Anti-Slavery Movement and Reconstruction. A Study in Anglo-American Cooperation 1833–77*, Oxford University Press, Oxford, 1969; Gad J. Heuman, *Between Black and White. Race, Politics and the Free Coloureds in Jamaica 1792–1865*, Greenwood, Connecticut, 1981; Abigail B. Bakan, *Ideology and Class Conflict in Jamaica. The Politics of Rebellion*, McGill-Queen's University Press, London, 1990; Thomas C. Holt, *The Problem of Freedom: Race, Labor and Politics in Jamaica and Britain 1832–1938*, Johns Hopkins University Press, Baltimore, 1992; Gad Heuman, *'The Killing Time'. The Morant Bay Rebellion in Jamaica*, Macmillan, London, 1994.

4 Jamaica Committee, *Jamaica Papers*, nos 1–6, Jamaica Committee, London, 1866–7.

5 Parliamentary Papers, *Jamaica Royal Commission*, pp.40–1.

6 Hume, *Edward John Eyre*; Finlason, *History of the Jamaica Case*.

7 Jamaica Committee, *Jamaica Papers*, especially no.1.

8 For Carlyle's most substantial interventions on race see his 'Occasional discourse on the nigger question', a revised version of his original polemic of 1849, in *English and Other Critical Essays*, vol.2, Dent, London, 1964 and 'Shooting Niagara: and after?', in *Critical and Miscellaneous Essays*, vol.5, Chapman and Hall, London, 1899. For a discussion of the debate between Carlyle and Mill see Catherine Hall, 'Competing masculinities: Thomas Carlyle, John Stuart Mill and the case of Governor Eyre' in *White, Male and Middle Class: Explorations in Feminism and History*, Polity, Cambridge, 1992. On the problems associated with Carlyle's masculinity see Norma Clarke, 'Strenuous idleness. Thomas Carlyle and the man of letters as hero', in Michael Roper and John Tosh (eds), *Manful Assertions. Masculinities since 1800*, Routledge, London, 1991.

9 Benedict Anderson, *Imagined Communities. Reflections on the Origin and Spread of Nationalism*, Verso, London, 1983; Stuart Hall, 'New ethnicities', *Black Film, British Cinema*, ICA Documents 7, London, 1988.

10 Stuart Hall, in Stuart Hall and Bram Gieben (eds), *Formations of Modernity*, Polity, Cambridge, 1992, p.6.

11 On self as process see Trinh T. Minh-ha, 'Difference: "a special Third World women issue"', *Feminist Review* 25, 1987. For a discussion of the construction of masculinities see Lynne Segal, *Slow Motion. Changing Masculinities, Changing Men*, Virago, London, 1990.

12 Rev. Isaac Taylor, *Self Cultivation Recommended; or, Hints to a Youth Leaving School*, T. Cadell and Son, London, 1817, p.17. For discussions of early nineteenth-century masculinity see Leonore Davidoff and Catherine Hall, *Family Fortunes: Men and Women of the English Middle Class 1780–1850*, Hutchinson, London, 1987; and Leonore Davidoff, 'Adam spoke first and named the orders of the world', in Helen Corr and Lynne Jamieson (eds), *Politics of*

Everyday Life. Continuity and Change in Work and the Family, Macmillan, London, 1990.

13 For an illuminating discussion of the ideological work associated with this fiction, see Mary Poovey, *Uneven Developments. The Ideological Work of Gender in Mid-Victorian Britain*, Virago, London, 1989, especially ch.4.

14 R. Garnett, *Edward Gibbon Wakefield. The Colonization of Australia and New Zealand*, T. Fisher Unwin, London, 1897; C.A. Bodelsen, *Studies in Mid-Victorian Imperialism*, Scandinavian University Books, Copenhagen, 1960; Bernard Semmel, *The Rise of Free Trade Imperialism. Classical Political Economy, the Empire of Free Trade and Imperialism 1750–1850*, Cambridge University Press, Cambridge, 1970.

15 Edward Gibbon Wakefield, *A Letter from Sydney*, J.M. Dent, London, 1929, pp.4, 17, 48.

16 Edward Gibbon Wakefield, *England and America*, Richard Bentley, London, 1833, vol.2, p.216.

17 Douglas Pike, *Paradise of Dissent. South Australia 1829–57*, Longman, Green and Co., London, 1957.

18 John Stuart Mill, *Principles of Political Economy*, Books IV and V, Penguin, Harmondsworth, 1985, p.337.

19 One of Carlyle's favourite pupils, Charles Buller, was important to this process. See David A. Haury, *The Origins of the Liberal Party and Liberal Imperialism: The Career of Charles Buller, 1806–48*, Garland, New York, 1987, pp.48, 164.

20 For a brilliant account of De Quincy's version of this fiction see John Barrell, *The Infection of Thomas De Quincy. A Psychopathology of Imperialism*, Harvard University Press, London, 1991.

21 Thomas Carlyle, 'Chartism', first published 1839, in *Thomas Carlyle: Selected Writings*, Penguin, Harmondsworth, 1971, pp.228–9, 214, 232.

22 The phrase is George Fife Angas's, a great enthusiast for South Australia, in a letter to Edward Gibbon Wakefield, quoted in Pike, *Paradise of Dissent*, p.131.

23 Edward John Eyre, *Autobiographical Narrative, 1832–39*, edited with an introduction by Jill Waterhouse, Caliban, London, 1984, p.1.

24 Eyre, *Autobiography*, pp.1, 3.

25 Ibid., pp.29, 7, 3, 31.

26 Ibid., p.46.

27 Ibid., p.73.

28 Ibid., pp.47–8.

29 George Grey, *Journals of Two Expeditions of Discovery in North-West and Western Australia During the years 1837, 38 and 39*, T. and W. Boone, London, 1841, vol.2, pp.185, 190.

30 'Aborigine' was a term coined by the colonists for the large numbers of peoples with different languages who had been living on the Australian continent for at least 40,000 years before the arrival of the British in 1788. Unfortunately it remains the only term for the indigenous peoples generally. I am grateful to Ann Curthoys for clarifying this for me.

31 Edward John Eyre, *Journals of Expeditions of Discovery into Central Australia and Overland from Adelaide to King George's Sound in the Years 1840–1*, T. and W. Boone, London, 1845, vol.1, p.170.

32 Eyre, *Autobiography*, p.194.

33 Eyre, *Journals*, vol.1, pp.8–9.

34 On the sexual and psychic meanings of the first encounters see Peter Hulme, *Colonial Encounters: Europe and the Native Caribbean 1492–1797*, Methuen,

London, 1986. For one of the richest examples of the elaborations of these connections in Africa see H. Rider Haggard, *King Solomon's Mines*, Cassell, London, 1891.

35 Eyre, *Journals*, vol.1, p.7.
36 Ibid., p.20.
37 Eyre, *Autobiography*, p.42.
38 Charles Sturt lectured at the Mechanics' Institute in Adelaide in support of Eyre's expedition. Eyre, *Journals*, vol.1, pp.8–9.
39 There is a very considerable debate amongst anthropologists as to the nature of Aborigine systems of landholding; for a summary of the debate, see Henry Reynolds, *The Other Side of the Frontier*, James Cook University Press, Townsville, 1981.
40 Eyre, *Autobiography*, p.55.
41 Eyre, *Journals*, vol.1, p.224.
42 Quoted in Malcolm Uren and Robert Stephens, *Waterless Horizons*, Robertson and Mullens, Melbourne, 1945, p.25.
43 George Grey, *Journals*, vol.2, p.374.
44 Mary Louise Pratt, *Imperial Eyes. Travel Writing and Transculturation*, Routledge, London and New York, 1992, pp.63–4.
45 Eyre, *Journals*, vol.1, p.x; vol.2, p.423; Pratt, *Imperial Eyes*, p.7.
46 Eyre, *Journals*, vol.1, p.xi; vol.2, pp.167, 172, 175.
47 Eyre, *Journals*, vol.2, pp.111, 156, 255; vol.1, p.288; *Autobiography*, pp.133, 147.
48 Eyre, *Journals*, vol.2, pp.458–9, 489, 479.
49 One 'proving of a vicious temper' was sent back to Australia, the other died of pneumonia at seventeen; see Hume, *Edward John Eyre*, p.95.
50 Eyre, *Autobiography*, p.213.
51 Claudia Orange, *The Treaty of Waitangi*, Allen and Unwin, Wellington, 1987.
52 Orange, *Waitangi*; Garnett, *Edward Gibbon Wakefield*; William P. Morrell, *British Colonial Policy in the Age of Peel and Russell*, Oxford University Press, Oxford, 1930; Morrell, *British Colonial Policy in the Mid-Victorian Age*, Oxford University Press, Oxford, 1969.
53 Quoted in Garnett, *Edward Gibbon Wakefield*, p.194.
54 Orange, *Waitangi*, p.31.
55 *Parliamentary Papers*, Despatch from Hobson to Gipps and Treaty of Waitangi, in Kenneth N. Bell and William P. Morrell (eds), *Select Documents on British Colonial Policy 1830–1860*, Oxford University Press, Oxford, 1928, pp.557–63.
56 Quoted in Orange, *Waitangi*, pp.51, 53.
57 Grey, *Journals*, vol.2, p.374.
58 Dutton, *The Murderer as Hero*, pp.181, 182, 187.
59 Quoted in James Rutherford, *Sir George Grey. A Study in Colonial Government 1812–98*, Cassell, London, 1961, pp.221, 224, 226; Morrell, *British Colonial Policy in the Age of Peel and Russell*; Earl H.G. Grey, *The Colonial Policy of Lord John Russell's Administration*, Richard Bentley, London, 1853, 2 vols.
60 Dutton, *The Hero as Murderer*, has a brief account of Eyre's time in New Zealand. Grey also left New Zealand in 1853, this time for South Africa.
61 Orange, *Waitangi*; Morrell, *British Colonial Policy in the Mid-Victorian Age*; James Belich, *The New Zealand Wars and the Victorian Interpretation of Racial Conflict*, Auckland University Press, Auckland, 1986.
62 Carlyle, 'Occasional discourse on the negro question', *Fraser's Magazine*, vol. 40, Dec. 1849; Carlyle, *Occasional Discourse on the Nigger Question*, Thomas Bosworth, London, 1853.

63 Nancy Stepan, *The Idea of Race in Science: Great Britain 1800–1960*, Macmillan, London, 1982, p.xii.

64 Robert Knox, *The Races of Men: A Philosophical Inquiry into the Influence of Race over the Destinies of Nations*, 2nd edn, Henry Renshaw, London, 1862, pp.v, 8, 20, 44.

65 Knox, *The Races of Men*, p.379; Eyre, *Autobiography*, p.219. Eyre's claim to Norman lineage was primarily concerned with proving his gentility. He does not appear to be making claims for the Norman race as the progenitors of English greatness – claims which would put him seriously at odds with his later supporters Carlyle and Kingsley, who were enthusiastic supporters of 'Saxonism'. Christopher Hill in his seminal essay 'The Norman Yoke', traces the myth of the Yoke and the different ways in which it was articulated to varieties of radicalism between the seventeenth and nineteenth centuries. 'The Norman Yoke', in *Puritanism and Revolution. Studies in Interpretation of the English Revolution of the Seventeenth Century*, Secker and Warburg, London, 1958. Eyre's genealogical claim was taken up by his contemporary biographer Hume who argued in 1867 that those who had attacked him over his conduct in Jamaica had 'also represented him as a man of no birth and without connections'. Hume also made clear, however, that he was a self-made man. *Edward John Eyre*, p.1.

66 See, for example, the outrage occasioned by Eyre travelling on an omnibus, C.O. 137/376, Eyre to Newcastle, 24/12/1863.

67 Eyre, *Autobiography*, pp.218, 219.

68 Dutton, *The Hero as Murderer*, p.175.

69 Knox, *The Races of Men*, p.145.

70 Quoted in Jill Waterhouse, 'Introduction', Eyre, *Autobiography*, p.xxviii.

71 C.O.261/81, Eyre to Colonial Office, 30/10/1854.

72 C.O.260/82, Colebrooke to Grey, 19/1/1855, no.9, enclosure no.1; C.O.260/83, confidential letter Choppin to Eyre, 28/6/1855.

73 C.O.260/82, Colebrooke to Grey, 19/1/1855, no.9. On Taylor and the West Indies see Henry Taylor, *Autobiography of Henry Taylor 1800–1875*, Longmans, Green and Co., London, 1885. On the constitutional questions see C.V. Gocking, 'Early constitutional history of Jamaica. With special reference to the period 1838–66', *Caribbean Quarterly*, vol.6, 1960.

74 William G. Sewell, *The Ordeal of Free Labour in the British West Indies*, Harper and Bros, New York, 1861, p.76.

75 C.O.260/82, confidential letter, Eyre to Colebrooke, 2/5/1855.

76 Ibid.

77 C.O.260/84, confidential letter, Eyre to Colebrooke, 10/12/1855.

78 On the desire for a black middle class see, for example, Edward Bean Underhill, *The West Indies: Their Social and Religious Condition*, Jackson, Walford and Hodder, London, 1862.

79 Sewell, *The Ordeal of Free Labour*, p.80.

80 C.O.260/83, Colebrooke to Russell, 7/8/1855, no.43, enclosure no.1.

81 C.O.260/84, Colebrooke to Grey, 10/12/1855, no.66, enclosure no.1; Colebrooke to Grey, 19/12/1855, no.67, enclosure no.1.

82 C.O.260/87, Hincks to Labouchere, 1/11/1856, no.67, enclosure no.1.

83 The quote is from the Baptist *Missionary Herald*, a bastion of support for emancipation and the blacks in the West Indies; October, 1857. Both Baptist missionaries in India and the abolitionist public they addressed were deeply shocked by events in India and saw more English government, more English troops and 'more Englishmen of the right sort' as the only possible solution for India.

84 Quoted in Semmel, *The Governor Eyre Controversy*, p.21.

85 C.O.260/91, Hincks to Stanley, 7/5/1858, no.23, enclosure no.1.

86 C.O.260/91, Hincks to Stanley, 5/6/1858, no.30, enclosure no.3; C.O.260/92, Hincks to Lytton, 20/1/1859, no.7, enclosure no.1.

87 C.O.7/113, confidential letter Eyre to Newcastle, 20/10/1859.

88 C.O.7/112, Eyre to Lytton, 27/5/1859, no.52.

89 C.O.7/114, Eyre to Newcastle, 20/3/1860, no.35.

90 Quoted in Belich, *The New Zealand Wars*, p.328.

91 Stanley, quoted in Green, *British Slave Emancipation*, p.119; Curtin, *Two Jamaicas*.

92 John Stuart Mill, *Autobiography*, Oxford University Press, Oxford, 1963, p.288; CO 137/390, Eyre to Cardwell, 19/4/1865.

93 C.O.137/367, Eyre to Newcastle, 7/8/1862, nos. 56; 8/9/62, no.80; C.O.137/368, Eyre to Newcastle, 9/10/1862, no.88.

94 On the role of coloureds in Jamaican politics see Heuman, *Between Black and White*.

95 C.O.137/375, Eyre to Newcastle, 4/11/1863, no.260, enclosure no.1.

96 C.O.137/390, Eyre to Cardwell, 19/4/1865, no.90.

97 C.O.137/380, Eyre to Newcastle, 18/3/1864, separate communication; C.O.137/381, Eyre to Newcastle, 23/4/1864, no.132.

98 Holt, *The Problem of Freedom*, p.273.

99 C.O.137/384, Eyre to Cardwell, 12/8/1864, no.237; Eyre to Cardwell, 24/8/1864, no.240.

100 C.O.137/384, Eyre to Cardwell, 10/9/1864, no.256; C.O.137/388, Eyre to Cardwell, 2/3/1865, no.40; C.O.137/390, Eyre to Cardwell, 15/4/1865, no.89, enclosure no.1.

101 Mary Turner, *Slaves and Missionaries. The Disintegration of Jamaican Slave Society, 1787–1834*, Urbana University Press, Illinois, 1982; Catherine Hall, 'Missionary stories: gender and ethnicity in England in the 1830s and 1840s', in *White, Male and Middle Class: Explorations in Feminism and History*, Polity, Cambridge, 1992.

102 C.O.137/388, Eyre to Cardwell, 2/3/1865, no.40; C.O.137/390, Eyre to Cardwell, 19/4/1865, no.90.

103 *Parliamentary Papers*, 1866, vol.L1, 'Papers relating to the disturbances in Jamaica', Part 1. Eyre to Cardwell, 20/10/1865, no.251; 28/10/1865, no.257; 8/12/1865, no.321.

104 *Parliamentary Papers*, 1866, vol.L1, Eyre to Cardwell, 7/12/1865, no.313.

105 *Parliamentary Papers*, 1866, vol.L1, Eyre to Cardwell, 20/11/1865, no.292, enclosure no.1, C.O. 137/395.

106 *Parliamentary Papers, Report of the Jamaica Royal Commission*, 1866, pp.16, 157, 158.

107 Thomas Carlyle, 'Shooting Niagara: and after?', first published August 1867, re-published in *Critical and Miscellaneous Essays*, Chapman and Hall, London, 1899, 5 vols, vol.5, p.12.

108 Parliamentary Papers, 1866, L1, p.313.

109 Commander Bedford Pim, *The Negro and Jamaica*, Trubner and Co., London, 1866, pp.v, 35, 50. On the Anthropological Society see J.W. Burrow, *Evolution and Society. A Study in Victorian Social Theory*, Cambridge University Press, Cambridge, 1968, p.125; Ronald Rainger, 'Race, politics and science: the Anthropological Society of London in the 1860s', *Victorian Studies*, vol.22, no.1, Autumn 1978.

110 Hume, *Edward John Eyre*, pp.201–2, 217.

111 Hume, *Edward John Eyre*, in his dedication to the Earl of Shrewsbury, p.vi.

112 Finlason, *Jamaica Case*, p.634.
113 Pim, *The Negro and Jamaica*, p.vi; Prof. John Tyndall, quoted in Hume, *Edward John Eyre*, p.272; Thomas Carlyle, draft petition for the Eyre Defence Committee held in the Institute of Jamaica, quoted in Olivier, *The Myth of Governor Eyre*, p.336; 'Shooting Niagara'. For a longer discussion of Carlyle's position see Catherine Hall, 'Competing masculinities: Thomas Carlyle, John Stuart Mill and the Case of Governor Eyre' in *White, Male and Middle Class*.
114 Quoted in Dutton, *The Hero as Murderer*, p.370.
115 For an account of the events around this see Semmel, *The Governor Eyre Controversy*.
116 Finlason, *Jamaica Case*, p.562.

7

'UNDER THE HATCHES'

English Parliamentary Commissioners' Views of the People and Language of Mid-nineteenth-century Wales

Gwyneth Tyson Roberts

We all call barbarism that which does not conform to our own usages.

Montaigne, Of Cannibals

Wales is unique in its official relation to England: it is attached to the larger country for many purposes of civil administration in a way that Scotland, for example, is not, but its status is sufficiently distinct to require this inclusion to be specified (as in 'the legal system of England and Wales', 'the education system of England and Wales') in a way that Cornwall's, for example, does not. Descriptions of this relation during the nineteenth century have ranged from seeing Wales as part of 'the British Empire in Europe'[1] to 'junior partner' 'within Imperial Britain'[2] to 'internal colony';[3] this chapter will, rather, focus on the relationship as a clash between two cultural systems unequal in power and status as well as in their self-images. John Berger has usefully distinguished between 'cultures of progress' which envision ever-expanding horizons for themselves, and 'cultures of survival' which see their future as safe-guarded only by the deliberate maintenance of their distinctive cultural practices;[4] this chapter will suggest that the mid-nineteenth-century English 'culture of progress' regarded the deliberate maintenance of the distinctive cultural practices of Welsh-speaking Wales as a threat, by its very existence within a supposedly unified Britain, which must be removed in the interests of both communities. Superficial cultural differences which merely offered an enlivening touch of local colour were, of course, acceptable; subordinate nationalisms could be tolerated and even encouraged as long as they operated within a framework that offered no real challenge to the authority of the state or loyalty to the Crown (Bayly, for example, has demonstrated how cultural difference was acceptable in the subaltern states of British India because it operated within 'the broad framework of loyalty to the Crown and a notion of natural aristocracy' to establish a 'tributary patriotism';[5] nearer home from a Welsh point of view, the vogue for tartans, kilts, bagpipes and other outward and visible trappings of the culture of the Scottish Highlands, encouraged by Queen Victoria and her descendants, was only possible because any real political threat from the Highlands had been defused by the smashing of the clan system and the enforced emigration caused by the enclosures of the eighteenth century.)[6] To find fundamental cultural differences where only superficial ones had been expected was, however, felt to be profoundly disturbing and potentially dangerous; something clearly had to be done.

I wish to argue that what was in fact 'done' represents a prime example of the way a dominant culture represses a minority culture by degrading it in the eyes of members of both cultures, through a discourse whose ideological aim was to crush the challenge to the hegemony of Englishness within Britain. I shall take as the focus of my argument the 1847 *Reports of the Commissioners of Inquiry into the State of Education in Wales*, which played an important part in the construction of English representations of the Welsh and Welsh representations of themselves for generations, and which was described by a dominant figure in Welsh twentieth-century cultural and political thinking as 'the most important nineteenth-century historical document we possess';[7] I will attempt to show that this text can be fully evaluated only by locating it within the parameters of a discourse that asserts the hegemony of Englishness by naturalizing unequal power relationships between two national cultures and the languages through which they worked – relationships that are established and naturalized by those with power.[8] In my view, a great part of the *Report*'s significance lies in its capacity to locate within such parameters a people whose territory was contiguous with England's, which at an institutional level had been officially joined to England for over three hundred years, and whose ancestors were popularly supposed to have put the 'British' in 'British Empire'. It was the discovery from an official English perspective of an alternative hierarchy of cultural values (with direct political implications and consequences) that fuelled official English anxieties: the realization that a battered but surviving sense of cultural identity had combined with the legacy of the process described by a sixteenth-century writer as 'those rigorous laws which were provided against the Welshmen [sic] to keep them poor, to deprive them of good education, and to make them uncivil and brutish',[9] to produce a distinct and separate people.

Wales was conquered militarily by England in the late thirteenth century, and incorporated into England for legal purposes in the sixteenth. The first of the Acts of Incorporation (later called the Acts of Union) for Wales (1536) can be seen as a paradigm of official English attitudes to the country: its preamble declared that:

172

the Dominion Principality and Country of Wales justly and righteously is and ever hath been incorporated annexed united and subject to and under the Imperial Crown of this Realm [the last two words refer to England throughout].[10]

and then proceeded to recognize difference between the two countries only to remove it. Because the Welsh had 'divers Rights Usages Laws and Customs [that] be far discrepant from the Laws and Customs of this Realm' and the people 'do daily use a Speech nothing like nor consonant to the natural Mother Tongue used within this Realm', the King had decided that 'this his said Country or Dominion of Wales shall be and continue for ever from hence forth incorporated united and annexed to and with this his realm of England.' (Some indication of the severity of the penal laws previously in existence against the Welsh is provided by the fact that earlier in 1536 Welsh landowners had petitioned the king for English common law to be extended to Wales; it was an advance in Welsh civil rights not to be discriminated against because of one's nationality.)[11] The Act thus presented English as 'the natural Mother Tongue' within the King's dominions, with implications that others were less than 'natural', and it also declared that the incorporation was being carried out in the best interests of the King's Welsh subjects – he had decided 'utterly to extirp all and singular the sinister Usages and Customs' that differed from those of England because of 'the singular Zeal Love and Favour that he beareth' to them. It has been argued[12] that the emphasis of this Act, as of those relating to other parts of the British Isles, was on royal authority and legal reform, not on differences of nationality; its basis, however, was the frequently recurring paradox that differences needed to be explicitly acknowledged in order for them to be declared officially non-existent, and the clause of the legislation which formally annexed Wales declared that historically it had been united to England 'for ever' – which, if true, would have rendered the entire piece of legislation redundant. As these quotations suggest, language was seen as a crucial marker of this difference, and the official attitude indicated here remained constant through the succeeding centuries (except for three years during the civil war, when legislation treated Wales as a separate entity in order to allow for the removal of Anglican ministers from Welsh parishes: in the Act for the Propagation of the Gospel in Wales of 1650, the criteria for dismissing clergymen included their inability to preach in Welsh).[13]

In the early part of the nineteenth century two very different English images of Wales were current, and both images can be traced in the perceptions of the English Commissioners who drew up the *Report*: it was seen variously as a land of romantic landscapes and less romantic peasants, and as a hotbed of dangerous political subversives continually erupting into open rebellion against the established (and, to the official English mind, 'natural') order. To those who held to the first of these images, the Welsh language was an interesting touch of local colour that sometimes created communication problems, whereas to those who subscribed to the latter it provided simultaneously an easy means for the Welsh to conceal subversion and a barrier to the dissemination of English values and civilization.

The first image cohered indirectly as a result of the difficulties in European travel caused by the French Revolution and the Napoleonic wars: English middle-class tourists discovered the landscapes of rural north and west Wales at a time when romantic attitudes to nature made them particularly attractive, and in the last quarter of the eighteenth century and the first half of the nineteenth more than one hundred accounts of tours in Wales were published.[14] The travellers tended to look for romantically magnificent scenery: for example, the 1833 edition of William Gambold's *Grammar of the Welsh Language*, first published in 1727, contains such indispensable phrases for English tourists as 'Is not there a waterfall in the neighbourhood?'.[15] There were often complaints if the inhabitants were insufficiently decorative: one travel-writer described some begging children as 'not quite ragged enough to be picturesque'.[16] (Achieving the precise degree of raggedness to be considered picturesque by English tourists clearly required delicate calculation.) There was a considerable growth of antiquarian interest in Welsh matters during this period, in which old traditions were rediscovered and sometimes invented: traditional Welsh harp music was famous but effectively dead, so English songs were translated and pressed into service to take the place of the Welsh folk songs that had vanished in the previous century; folk tales such as the story of Llywelyn and his touchingly faithful hound Gelert were fabricated to attract visitors to tourist spots such as Beddgelert; Lady Llanofer developed the (female) 'Welsh national costume' from various aspects of Welsh peasant dress (Prys Morgan comments acidly that since Lord Llanofer was not interested in wearing fancy dress, the menfolk of Wales were spared); Iolo Morgannwg – poet, antiquary, visionary and forger – reinvented the eisteddfodau which had died out in the sixteenth century. These outward and visible signs of Welshness were presented as examples of a cultural distinctiveness[17] that was entirely compatible with the demands of loyalty to the Great British state, a phenomenon that fitted into the pattern of early nineteenth-century (and later) British imperial policy, since it contributed to a 'tributary patriotism' on the Scottish model.

Such cultural distinctiveness was presented as essentially superficial, and therefore non-threatening as long as it did not open the door to the awareness of difference at a deeper level which could lead to challenges to English authority. The second view of Wales saw such challenges in the civil unrest in Wales in the early nineteenth century – particularly in the industrialized areas of the south-east, which it regarded as a particularly subversive territory – and in the threat it posed to public order. Not only did the early years of the nineteenth century see a series of strikes and public protests (the whole of the Glamorgan and Monmouthshire coalfield came to a halt in 1816, 1822, 1830, and 1832)[18] and the emergence of secret organizations which acted against strike-breakers, against bailiffs (the Scotch Cattle),[19] and against toll-gates and workhouses (the Daughters of Rebecca),[20] but in addition there were two major incidents of insurrection against the civil authorities in which towns were held (however briefly) against police and militia. To add to official concern, both were driven by political motives (Merthyr Tydfil in 1831 in support of the 1832 Reform Bill as well as a protest against wage-cuts and mass dismissals;[21] Newport in 1839 in support of the Charter, and believed by *The Times* to be 'for seizing the whole of South Wales to erect a Chartist kingdom'),[22] and Wales in the 1840s has been called 'the most militarized zone in Britain'.[23] English commentators, particularly alarmed by the social and political threat which Chartism posed to the established order, attributed the success of the secret planning for the Newport rising to the difference in language: the London *Morning Chronicle* commented that 'in no part of the country could an organization be formed, with so little interruption, as in a district where the lower orders speak almost universally a language unknown to the educated classes.'[24]

Similar views were expressed both in a report to the newly-created Committee of the Privy Council on Education in 1840 on the state of education in the mining districts of south Wales,[25] and in the 1844 report of the Commission of Inquiry for South Wales. The latter investigated both the effects of the 1834 Poor Law Amendment Act in the area and the Rebecca Riots,[26] citing 'among the causes which affect the social condition of the people, the ignorance of the English language which pervades so large a proportion of the country' which was described as 'a serious impediment to the removal of those evils which most require correction.[27] Such comments reveal the official English perception that education was the remedy for working-class political disaffection and that the English language was a necessary part of that education; English not only emphasized the official status of Wales as incorporated into, and subordinate to, England, it was also perceived as the means by which English culture and civilization could be internalized. These beliefs underpin the 1847 *Reports of the Commissioners of Inquiry into the State of Education in Wales* 'and especially into the means afforded to the Labouring Classes of acquiring a Knowledge of the English Language'.

EDUCATION

The provision of working-class education in Wales during the early nineteenth century was differentiated by religious affiliation and the language of instruction. The Sunday School movement, emerging at the end of the eighteenth century, was closely associated with the non-conformist churches, especially the Independents and Baptists. They operated in Welsh, concentrated on catechizing the children and teaching them to read, and put great emphasis on rote learning. (There is an anecdote of a child of five-and-a-half who, having already memorized a hundred chapters of the Bible, was forging ahead at the rate of one more each week.)[28] However, the economic advantages of a knowledge of English were sufficiently strongly felt for many of the most enthusiastic workers for the Welsh-medium Sunday School to support strongly English-language day schools,[29] and although in the eighteenth century Anglican schools (the 'Circulating Schools' founded by Griffith Jones) had used Welsh, from the early nineteenth century the prevailing language of the schools of the 'National Society for promoting the Education of the Poor in the principles of the Established Church' was English. However, no provision was made for actually teaching the children English, and many of them left these schools able to recite long passages of scripture in English with only the haziest understanding of what they were saying.[30] English had prestige as the language of education and social advancement, but Welsh had other claims:

Would you a child should speak some foreign tongue?
First let him know the language which has rung
  Familiar by his own fireside . . .

Children have conned with pain your English lore,
In dull toil sick at heart; and as of yore
  Have cherished still their father's tongue . . .[31]

English was also the medium of instruction in the schools established in Wales by the British and Foreign Schools Society, which were technically non-sectarian; and when, in 1843, the educational clauses of Graham's Factory Bill were felt to give the Anglican Church control over the 'British' schools, as they were known, Welsh non-conformists rose in fury in defence of their religious liberty, and the Bill was withdrawn.[32] In the same year, Hugh Owen, the major figure in Welsh education in the nineteenth century, put forward a plan (in a letter in Welsh to the Welsh non-conformist periodicals) for schools on the 'British' model to be supported by local committees throughout Wales,[33] which received an enthusiastic response: between 1843 and 1847, seventy-nine British Schools in Wales were added to the twenty-nine already in operation.[34]

Education in early nineteenth-century Wales was thus the object of considerable interest and concern, and the subject of much debate in the years leading up to 1846 (it has been suggested[35] that the provision of elementary education for the working class attracted more public attention in Wales than any other issue during the whole of the nineteenth century). In these debates, religion and language were crucial issues.

RELIGION

Religious belief became an increasingly important shaper of group and national identity during the nineteenth century in Wales. Many Welsh believers regarded themselves as a people chosen by God to receive a unique religious revelation in the Welsh language:[36] popular Welsh views on the language still showed the influence of earlier beliefs on the origins of human language, which were closely tied in to the story of creation in Genesis. These held that every language on earth was derived from one of the languages which had sprung into existence at the building of the Tower of Babel, and which were known as the cardinal or mother languages. The eighteenth-century Welsh grammarians had demonstrated to their own satisfaction (if to that of few others) that Welsh had close and direct lines of descent from the Hebrew spoken before Babel, and had retained its original purity.[37] The language was thus an important aspect of the divine revelation the Welsh had been chosen to receive: one essayist wrote in 1825 that God must have given the Welsh, as a nation, such a wonderful language for a special purpose.[38] This sense of having been chosen was overwhelmingly expressed through varieties of Christianity which the Anglican Church viewed with great suspicion, not least because of their great popularity: in the religious census of 1851 there were nearly two and a half times as many non-conformist as Anglican places of worship in Wales, and although there are some difficulties in estimating relative numbers of worshippers, it seems likely that around three-quarters attended non-conformist places of worship.[39] Welsh, as the language of religion, literary culture, and the home and family, offered a space in which Welsh-speakers could assert the power of their community and their own personal dignity against the pressures of the English-dominated forces of industrialization: 'to cherish the language was no more than a necessary act of self-respect'.[40] This Welsh view of Welsh was diametrically opposed to the view of the English Commissioners who compiled the 1847 *Report*.

LANGUAGE

An increasingly detailed academic debate among European philologists in the first half of the nineteenth century focused on the historical development of languages, using the analogy with natural selection. The comparative analysis of the structures of languages initiated by Sir William Jones towards the end of the eighteenth century was explored and developed in the early nineteenth century by many philologists in continental Europe (for example, by Rasmus Rask in Denmark and Franz Bopp, Jacob Grimm, August Schleicher, Friedrich and August von Schlegel in Germany). By the 1830s this 'new philology' had reached Britain (via two Englishmen who had studied under Rask and Grimm), and provoked wide interest; the Philological Society of London, for example, was founded in 1842 as a forum for debate.[41]

A system of classifying languages had been developed (by August von Schlegel in 1818) which assigned them to one of three broadly-defined groups. One group included those languages in which component parts (for example syllables) could be put together to form compound words whose separate elements remained clearly distinct: they were known as *agglutinating* languages. A second group was that in which the forms of the words changed to indicate grammatical relationships, but in which the elements of meaning could not be equated with distinct parts of a word in the same way as with agglutinating languages; these were called *inflecting* languages, and included Welsh. The third group was that where the forms of the individual words remained (relatively) unchanged, and grammatical relationships were indicated by forming strings of words in a particular order: these were called *isolating* languages, and included English. This classification did not imply that a language showed the distinguishing marks of its category in each word, but it indicated the most important elements of the differences between language structures.[42]

Since nineteenth-century linguists assumed a progression from the lower to the higher in the historical development of languages, the question then arose: which came first, and which later? For example, were inflecting languages higher or lower in the evolutionary chain than the isolating group? Earlier in the century both language groups had had their partisans, but by the late 1840s August Schleicher argued for the following evolutionary development: in the very early stages of human existence, language was simple; as human intellect developed, languages developed in parallel, and so were able to express more complex concepts and relationships; as human intellect developed even further, it no longer needed the prop of complex forms of language to support it, and could thus move into a third stage of evolution, one that was apparently simpler in form but of a simplicity that was refined and 'purified'.

The attraction of this theory was that it seemed to fit with contemporary anthropological observation, and suggested a line of progression: first came so-called 'primitive' tribes with 'simple' forms of language, often described by European travellers in terms of grunts or other animal-like noises; then followed a later stage of development that produced inflecting languages such as Latin and Classical Greek, regarded as the bedrock of western civilization; finally came (modern) isolating languages such as English, whose speakers could feel that the structures and forms of their national languages demonstrated that they had reached a higher stage of development in language as in other cultural fields: a 'highly-developed' language was a clear marker of a 'highly-developed' society, and a 'highly-developed' society would of course have a 'highly-developed' language. Predictably, this theory was bad news for speakers of 'less highly evolved' languages: the progress of civilization and the spirit of the age required that they should slough off the 'lower', 'more primitive' language and acquire a 'more advanced' one, which would take them to a higher stage of intellectual activity, scientific progress, social advancement, and the greater material prosperity that inevitably went with them.[43]

BACKGROUND

This view of the relationship between a language and the community that speaks it is clear in the proposal for a report on current educational provision for the 'labouring classes' in Wales moved in the House of Commons on 10 March 1846 by William Williams, MP for Coventry and a self-made millionaire from a poor Welsh-speaking background. The events of the previous years, he argued, (especially the Rebecca Riots and the Merthyr and Newport Risings) had demonstrated that all was not well with Wales: the solution was 'a good sound system of education' through the medium of English, which was 'the road to improvement, civilization ... and advancement to the poor Welshman [sic].' Such an education would not only 'raise up an intelligent population' but promote public order – 'the moral power of the schoolmaster was a more economical and effectual instrument for governing this people than the bayonet' – and would be more cost-effective in the long run: he was 'sure, whatever might be the cost, it would be saved tenfold at the expense of the army, police and prisons'.[44] Williams's argument when proposing the Report encapsulates its conclusions.[45]

The inquiry was to be conducted under the authority of the Committee of the Privy Council on Education; the Commissioners who were to carry it out were instructed by the Secretary to the Council, Kay-Shuttleworth, to report in detail on the schools, the teachers and the children as well as the educational provision and the children's attainments. They were also instructed to 'form some estimate of the general state of intelligence and information of the poorer classes in Wales, and of the influence which an improved education might be expected to produce, on the general condition of society and on its moral and religious progress.'[46]

The three Commissioners appointed by Kay-Shuttleworth were all upper middle-class lawyers and Anglicans, who had had no experience of teaching in or administering any system of education and did not speak Welsh (they were, however, provided with Assistants who interpreted when necessary): they were thus separated from those whose lives they investigated by language, culture, educational experience, religious denomination and class. They were young men with promising futures: R.R.W. (later Lord) Lingen went on to serve for twenty years as the Secretary to the Committee of the Council on Education, and later Secretary to the Treasury; J.C. Symons, apparently undeterred by his experiences in Wales, later became an Inspector of Schools; H.V. Johnson was made Secretary to Lord Chancellor Campbell (his father-in-law).[47]

They met and conferred at Builth Wells on 1 October 1846, began their deliberations with discussions with the Bishops of Hereford and St David's, and then went their separate ways to begin their investigations, Lingen to Carmarthenshire, Glamorgan and Pembrokeshire, Symons to Brecknockshire, Cardiganshire, Radnorshire and Monmouthshire, and Johnson to 'North Wales' (which covered everywhere else). The *Report* – in three volumes and 1,252 folio pages – was published in the autumn of 1847. Each of the three Parts of the *Report* consists of the relevant Commissioner's report on 'his' area, followed by appendices which contain the accounts of visits to schools by the Commissioner or one of his Assistants and evidence of witnesses on which the report is based (and frequently cites). Many of the quantifiable data (population figures, number of schools in a parish and children in a school, etc.) are given in statistical tables, presenting this information as incontrovertible 'facts' and increasing the authority with which the *Report*'s judgements are made.

The authority and confidence in the correctness and completeness of its own judgements is one of the most notable features of the *Report*, and an important property more generally of official discourse.[48] This variety of discourse works by emphasizing its own thoroughness (the breadth and depth of its investigations, the volume of material received, and its 'penchant for detail'), and by assuming the truth of the 'commonsense' position that those in command of most facts are best situated to judge them. A major guarantee of the correctness of the findings is the privileged position of the author(s), entitled to adjudicate precisely because of the amount of knowledge acquired through the above mentioned thoroughness. Above all, this presents the relation of its author(s) to those whose lives are investigated as entirely natural and beyond question; in the 1847 *Report* the greatest omission – the fact that cannot be contemplated since even to deny it would imply the possibility of its existence – is that the people whose lives the Commissioners investigated operated not merely within a different class but within a different national culture, and that this culture was just as autonomous and viable as that of the Commissioners. It could not be acknowledged that Wales had a national identity separate from, and of equal validity to, that of England: the *Report* could not acknowledge this possibility in any way, since to do so would have fatally undermined the English perception of Britain as the seat of a unified and coherent English national consciousness.

THE REPORT

I shall consider the ways in which the Commissioners presented themselves and the Welsh by examining the language of the *Report*; in order to give a sharper focus, the examples will be drawn from the three Commissioners' reports and not from the appendices, so that the language under examination is either that of the Commissioners themselves or of quotations from witnesses which they used in their reports to establish points and which they frequently employed as irrefutable proof of the 'truth' about a situation. I shall look at their use of personal pronouns, the grammatical cases used of themselves and of the Welsh, their use of the active and passive voices, and their lexical choices, since all these elements reveal the Commissioners' construction of themselves as knowledgeable and authoritative subjects and the Welsh as objects of their knowledge.

The Commissioners' presentation of themselves through their use of the first-person personal pronouns (especially *I*) communicates effectively their view of themselves as authoritative doers who hold knowledge of 'the truth'. Lingen, in Part I, makes greater use than the others of *I*, particularly with verbs indicating decisive action ('I found/I regard/ I laid down the following rules/I made the teacher repeat the names'), while Symons in Part II tends to shelter behind the collective responsibility of 'my colleagues and myself/we', and his references to himself tend to be more tentative ('I am enabled to state/I have requested permission'). This does not mean, however, that he is any less certain of the rightness of his own judgement; for example, he makes great play with his hypothesis that the extent of a pupil's knowledge is to be discovered by the lure of ready money, offering a penny to the first child to give a correct answer to his questions, 'not only in cases of bashfulness, in order to counteract it, but in cases of gross ignorance, in order to test the reality'.[49] This certainty that 'the reality' can be discovered by authoritative and knowledgeable people who ask the right questions in the right way underlies the whole *Report*. Johnson, in Part III, avoids personal responsibility for his opinions by another technique: rather than emphasizing his own role in collecting information and making judgements on it, his report shows relatively few cases of *I* as the main subject of a sentence, but has far greater use of authoritative third-person statements, which in conjunction with his extensive use of statistical tables (thirteen pages out of the sixty-five in his report), presents his views not as the (possibly partial) findings of an individual, but as 'the truth', not to be disputed or modified but accepted without question. (He comments on the lack of school lavatories: 'It is a fact significant of the Welsh character, that 417 schools [71.5 per cent of the entire number] are destitute of sufficient outbuildings: 210 [or 36 per cent] having no sort of provision of any kind. The germs of the barbarous and immoral habits which disfigure Welsh civilization are thus implanted in the minds of children, together with the first elements of education.')[50] All three Commissioners make generalized and authoritative comments on the inhabitants of 'their' respective areas: on people (the teachers are 'ignorant and petulant',[51] 'the children are generally self-willed and indulged by their parents'),[52] on schools ('the school is held in a ruinous hovel of the most squalid and miserable character')[53] and on morals ('The morals of the people are of a very low standard'),[54] and this confidence in judgement extends not only to the children's mind-set ('The ideas of the children remain as helplessly local as they might have done a thousand years ago'),[55] but to that of their forebears – in the same passage Lingen writes of the backwardness 'not only of the children's minds but those of their remote ancestors'.

Similarly, when the Commissioners make particular groups of Welsh people or the nation as a whole the subject of a clause, they do so either after introductory remarks which establish their own authority as sociological commentators, or with negatives and limitations ('The Welsh element is never found at the top of the social scale';[56] 'The Welsh children require [moral training] perhaps more than any other children in the kingdom ... and are destitute of it';[57] the Welsh may be better than the equivalent English social class at theological debate, but 'they remain inferior in every branch of practical knowledge and skill'.)[58] This assumption of a distinctively Welsh type of mental inferiority is reflected in the Commissioners' frequent use of the passive voice to talk about the Welsh, particularly when advocating the major recommendation of the *Report*, that the Welsh working class should as soon as possible learn English and forget Welsh: Symons, for example, declares that the need for translation into English of the testimony in a court of law of a Welsh-speaking defendant 'abets fraud' and 'makes a mockery of justice', and that this situation 'must continue until the people are taught the English language'.[59] Here the choice of 'are taught' rather than 'learn' suggests that the Welsh are imagined as passive recipients of English teaching from the more advanced civilization, and as equally passive recipients of English middle-class morality: Johnson, lamenting the 'female lack of chastity' described in detail by Anglican clergymen, feels it important that the Welsh in 'his' area 'are taught to regard their present customs with a sense of shame and decency'.[60] The *Report* also uses abstract nouns (that is, those referring to abstract qualities rather than concrete things) to talk about the Welsh, another means of putting a linguistic distance between them and the Commissioners writing about them: for example, 'the poverty of information possessed by the children is surprising ... Utter ignorance generally prevails as to the size of the world ... Strange notions prevail as to Her Majesty, who is generally believed to sit in London "making money"'.[61] The fact that notions so much at variance with patriotic English beliefs can be held by some of Her Majesty's subjects within Britain is clearly a cause of considerable official English disquiet, and is matched by their lack of identification with the glorious achievements of the British Empire – Symons, for example, laments that 'I have seldom obtained any account of our great victories',[62] while Lingen declares 'I have no hesitation in saying that a child might pass through the generality of these schools without learning either the limits, capabilities, general history or language of that empire of which he is born a citizen' and demands rhetorically 'What share in those notions which constitute our national existence can a lad have who calls the capital of England, Tredegar ...?'[63] His comment reveals a difference in perspectives which the *Report* acknowledges in order to demand its removal.

Also highly revealing of the Commissioners' view of the Welsh is their choice of lexical items possessing particularly strong connotations and associations when discussing the Welsh 'labouring classes'. These key-words fall clearly into sets of opposing pairs – one positive and one negative – which are linked with and frequently based on clearly-defined value-judgements; the criteria for these judgements are not made explicit but can be retrieved from context.

One of these contrasting pairs is formed by *reason* and *emotion*; neither is defined, but the contexts make it clear that the former has entirely positive associations and that the latter is negative. The *Report* not only states that the Welsh have 'an utter lack of method in thinking',[64] but makes comparisons in terms of so-called national characteristics: 'the reasoning powers [of the Welsh] are less developed than those of the English'.[65] This judgement by the colonizer that he can reason while the colonized cannot, was a major component of nineteenth-century European stereotypes (as Edward Said has demonstrated), since it provided both an important justification for colonial control and reassurance of the colonizers' intellectual superiority.[66] It follows, in the view of the Commissioners, that the Welsh must be taught to reason by the English, otherwise their 'peculiar excitability', which goes hand in hand with 'the most unreasoning prejudices' will lead to the 'wild fanaticism' and 'aroused passion' of the sort responsible in the

Commissioners' eyes for the Rebecca Riots and the 'Chartist outbreaks'.[67] Thus a lack of rationality is constructed not merely as a defect in the 'national character' but as a potentially dangerous weakness which could lead (again) to civil insurrection.

When a community has been thus represented as possessing inadequate powers of reasoning coupled with 'peculiar excitability' and 'unreasoning prejudices', it is a short step on the part of those who so characterize them to regard them as easily led into other varieties of erroneous thinking. Symons, particularly, regards the prevalence of superstition in the area he surveyed as a necessary consequence of ignorance, credulity, and a culture which encouraged religious speculation untempered by reason:

> Superstition prevails. Belief in charms, supernatural appearances, and even in witchcraft, sturdily survive all the civilisation and light which has long ago banished these remnants of the dark ages elsewhere. Little or none of such light has as yet penetrated the dense darkness which, harboured by their language, and undisturbed by availing efforts of enlightenment, enshrouds the minds of the people.[68]

Superstition is constructed here not merely as erroneous belief, but as carrying the connotations of evil which darkness has always possessed in Christian metaphor, as well as being a relic of an earlier and more primitive historical period: 'dark ages', in context, carries both a historical and theological charge. As often happens in the *Report*, significant (in this context, one hesitates to say 'illuminating') assumptions are so completely internalized that they can be referred to in a subordinate phrase, as 'truths' apparently so self-evident to the writer that proof is unnecessary. The 'dense' metaphorical 'darkness' of superstition is 'harboured by their language', where 'harbour', with its sense of 'giving shelter or protection to a criminal' presents the language as actively conniving at wrong-doing. The text here charges a set of rural working-class attitudes with the significance of a Manichean battle between the forces of good and evil: the 'dark' evil of superstition 'prevails', 'surviving' here in spite of having been 'banished' elsewhere, against the 'light' of 'civilisation' which is unable to 'penetrate' the evil superstition because it is 'harboured' by Welsh. Lexis with strong connotations and associations is used here to construct an implicit justification for the 'extirpation' of the language which makes possible the survival of this evil and which, by 'enshrouding' the minds of the people, acts not merely as a barrier to the forces of civilization but as a carrier of metaphorical death.

Another set of semantic networks falls within the antonymic fields of *good* and *evil*. Those within the *good* field tend to be few and relative: references to 'the best' usually make it clear that schools or practices are thus described only in comparison with the highly inadequate remainder, and frequently involve an explicit criticism as well: 'even in the best schools in North Wales, the true method of teaching geography is inverted';[69] 'an insufficiency being here measured, not by what is required by a proper system of education, but with reference to the limited subjects of instruction'.[70] The Commissioners clearly assumed that there were 'true' and 'proper' methods of doing things and that those in a position of knowledge and authority were equipped to recognize these absolutes when they met them.

Evil appears far more frequently than antonymic vocabulary items and forms part of a description of 'facts' and events which range from untrained teachers to illegitimacy to the use of Welsh in courts of law to workers reading 'low and unprincipled publications of a profane and seditious tendency' [by Tom Paine and Robert Owen].[71] For all of these perceived ills, education through the medium of English was presented as an instrument of civilization and a route to material prosperity: in one of the most famous passages of the *Report*, Symons declared that:

> The Welsh language is a vast drawback to Wales, and a manifold barrier to the moral progress and commercial prosperity of the people. It is not easy to over-estimate its evil effects. It is the language of the Cymri, and anterior to that of the ancient Britons. It dissevers the people from intercourse which would greatly advance their civilization, and bars the access of improving knowledge to their minds ... good schools would remove ... this disastrous barrier to all moral improvement and popular progress in Wales.[72]

Here Symons is endeavouring to dissociate the Welsh language – which is the subject of so much opprobrium and must be eradicated – from the 'ancient Britons' who are constituted as important elements in the invented notion of the English. The representation of Welsh as a 'barrier' that 'bars' and 'dissevers' from good is used repeatedly throughout the *Report*, but the ground on the two sides of the barrier is not seen as being in any way level; references to the effects of a morally effective programme of teaching English work through terms such as 'to rise', 'to improve', 'above', 'over' and 'superiors', while references to the contemporary condition of the Welsh work through terms in the semantic field of 'inferiority'; crucially, class and linguistic divisions are presented as coinciding. Lack of knowledge of English is conceived as a barrier which prevents those it affects from leaping from the lower to the higher side: 'My district,' comments Lingen, 'exhibits the phenomenon of a peculiar language isolating the mass from the upper portion of society'.[73] The proprietory note of 'my' district strengthens the implication in 'exhibits' and 'phenomenon' of an anthropologist analysing an alien community where he did fieldwork (and, given the respective numbers involved in 'the mass' and 'the upper portion of society', Lingen's attitude here is remniscient of the apochryphal headline in a London newspaper when bad weather prevented sea-crossings between southern England and northern France: 'Fog in Channel – Continent isolated'). The Welsh language is thus presented as necessarily imprisoning the Welsh people at the bottom of the social hierarchy:

> The Welsh element is never found at the top of the social scale
> ... his [sic] language keeps him under the hatches ... His superiors
> are content, for the most part, to ignore his existence in all its moral
> relations. He is left to live in an under-world of his own, and the
> march of society goes so completely over his head, that he is never
> heard of, except when the strange and abnormal features of a
> Revival, or a Rebecca or Chartist outbreak, call attention to a phase
> of society which could produce anything so contrary to all that we
> elsewhere experience.[74]

This paragraph makes very clear the extent to which the *Report* is written from the perspective of the 'higher' (English) culture and language, in which 'all that we elsewhere experience' is taken as the norm and 'we', as authoritative English observers, are empowered by our position to view any deviation from that norm as precisely that – deviant. The position of the Welsh speaker is constructed as entirely passive, and considered not as it is but as it 'is found' by, and in relation to, the 'higher' English culture. 'He' is 'ignored' by his social superiors, and 'left' by them 'to live in an under-world of his own', 'never' to be 'heard of' (by them, but also by 'us' – the Commissioners) except when involved in activities which are not only potentially dangerous but alien ('strange') and which threaten the 'natural' order of things ('abnormal'). 'He' is also presented as the victim of 'his' own language, which acts to keep him passively imprisoned in a linguistic dungeon while 'the march of society' goes on 'over his head'. From this perspective, the Welsh are separated by their language from 'society', which is seen by the Commissioners as composed of English-speaking social 'superiors' who have not given the Welsh the help they need to 'raise' themselves sufficiently to become part of it. This structure of perception acknowledges the existence of a different ('non-English') social and cultural system, of which language is the most obvious marker, and simultaneously assumes that it is in the interests of all that this difference should be removed and that the culture and language of the English should be universalized. Welsh is seen here as keeping its speakers 'below decks' ('under the hatches'), and the language is identified again as a barrier impeding upward progress to the higher social status of the English. From the Commissioners' viewpoint, the removal of the barrier of language is in the best interests of the Welsh themselves, since its existence condemns them to the 'barbarous' and the 'primitive', in contrast to English 'civilization'.

In most of its uses in the *Report*, `civilization' carries the sense of 'an advanced stage of human social development', and is mainly used to point up the Welsh deficiency, in the judgement of the Commissioners, particularly in relation to their language: one of Johnson's margin-headings – 'Imperfect civilization as seen in the Welsh language'[75] – is echoed in evidence quoted approvingly by Symons: 'from the little intercourse they have with strangers, and the prevalence of the Welsh language, they are but slightly acquainted with the common observances of civilized life'.[76] The Welsh are thus constructed as possessing a set of properties which is the antithesis of this civilization, and which extends from undesirable behaviour frequently found in the lower social orders (particularly the exercise of bodily functions in a manner unconstrained by Victorian bourgeois codes of behaviour and classified sternly as 'immoral') to those found in other (by definition, inferior) societies (they are 'rude and primitive',[77] have 'barbarous practices',[78] and their ignorance is 'almost heathen').[79] Perceptions of animality are never far away – 'the sexes ... herd together like the beasts',[80] and the result is 'bestial indelicacy'.[81] Indeed, this extends to their speech, which is also accorded subhuman characteristics: children in class, for example, recite material in English learned by heart, 'in a Welsh screech which seems expressly devised to annihilate all chance of expression or modulation of tone'.[82]

This notion of the relative evolutionary levels of Welsh and English underlies the whole *Report*. Lingen, for example, declares that the typical Welshman 'possesses a mastery over his own language far beyond that which the Englishman of the same degree possesses over his', but that this serves only to create a sense of linguistic insecurity in the Welshman when speaking the more highly-developed English language: 'Hence, in speaking English, he has at once to forego the conscious power of displaying certain talents whereon he piques himself, and to exhibit himself under that peculiar form of inability which most offends his self-esteem'.[83] Here the use of 'piques' is crucial, since it undermines the previously-mentioned 'certain talents' and, abetted by 'peculiar' with its connotations of 'strange, abnormal' as well as its denotational meaning in the context of 'particular', prepares the reader in advance to regard the 'self-esteem' which ends the sentence as closer to easily-hurt vanity than modest self-respect. Lingen continues by arguing that the two languages cannot operate in the same arena and that the influence exerted by Welsh is another powerful reason for its dispossession:

> The Welsh language thus maintained in its ground, and the peculiar
> moral atmosphere which, under the shadow of it, surrounds the

population, appear to be so far correlative conditions, that all attempts to employ the former as the vehicle of other conceptions than those which accord with the latter seem doomed to failure ... Through no other medium than a common language can ideas become common. It is impossible to open formal sluice-gates for them from one language to another.[84]

Lingen's final comments here suggest a view of the relationship between language and thought close to that of Sapir and Whorf in the early twentieth century; the image of the sluice-gates, however, also carries the implication that, as the water on either side of sluice-gates is at different levels so also, metaphorically, are the two separated languages and the ideas that they respectively carry. Lingen comments that the Welsh language casts a dark 'shadow' which influences the 'peculiar moral atmosphere' which 'surrounds the population'. Since Lingen has in previous pages of his report analysed the most important elements in 'the popular character of the Welsh' as 'an utter want of method in thinking and acting' which can easily lead to 'wild fanaticism', and 'a widespread disregard of temperance, chastity, veracity and fair dealing', the reader is not led to put any favourable interpretation on 'peculiar moral atmosphere'. The dark and sinister connotations of 'shadow' and the implication (in 'surrounds') that it imprisons 'the population' conveys an image of the Welsh people as too tightly held in the clutches of an oppressive language to realize that they need to be rescued by the English language, like a knight on a white charger. The language and the attitudes of the people who speak it are seen as so closely intertwined that any attempts to disentangle the language from the conceptions connected with the 'peculiar moral atmosphere' are 'doomed to failure': the only solution is for the English language to slay the Welsh Dragon for ever.

THE COMMISSIONERS' GENERAL CONCLUSIONS

Hardly surprisingly, given the perspectives of the Commissioners, the conclusions of the *Report* fulfilled the expectations of Williams's speech and Kay-Shuttleworth's instructions: with a few shining exceptions, teachers in Welsh schools were represented as ill-equipped for their job in terms of training, educational attainment, interest and temperament; the school buildings were found to be inadequate, impractical and often damp and dirty; the children, though taught through the medium of English, were not taught the language itself, and in many cases had been drilled to recite by heart English answers to English questions with little or no idea of the meaning of what they were saying. The Welsh 'labouring classes' were represented as sunk in ignorance, dirt, dishonesty and immorality, open to potentially disruptive influences (as the civil unrest earlier in the century seemed to demonstrate). The remedy suggested for all these ills was the efficient teaching of English, presented as an instrument of civilization in contrast to Welsh, 'the language of slavery'.[85]

In sum, the Commissioners believed that, as things were, the Welsh working classes remained dangerously separate from England, and that their cultural values were distressingly different. (Johnson, in his report on 'North Wales', calculated that of 405 books then in print in Welsh, 309 related to religion or poetry and only 50 concerned scientific subjects; a working-class community which regarded religion and poetry as so much more important than scientific knowledge was clearly out of step with Victorian England.) Their values were also represented as clearly non-English in respect of religion, placing importance on detailed knowledge of 'abstruse points of doctrine',[86] and having a different concept of personal religion: one child, asked 'Where is Jesus Christ now?', responded not with the expected 'in heaven/sitting at the right hand of God the Father' but 'In every parish in Wales', which the Commissioner described stiffly as 'a very singular answer'.[87] The Welsh were also presented as having a non-English code of sexual morality: the custom known as 'courting in bed'[88] was described by one of the witnesses (chaplain to the Bishop of Bangor) and quoted with full agreement by Johnson as proof that 'the principles of the Welsh people are totally corrupt and abandoned in this respect' and his language becomes increasingly hysterical, finally arriving at the conclusion that 'the minds of our common people are become thoroughly and universally depraved and brutalized'.[89] Even more importantly, the education of the working-class Welsh had also, claimed the *Report*, left them feeling (dangerously) alienated from the construction of Englishness; some of them knew nothing of 'the reign of Elizabeth or our Indian empire', or that Magna Carta was 'the bulwark of English liberties'.[90] The potential for disaffection was clear.

WELSH REACTIONS TO THE REPORT

Many Welsh readers of the *Report* were prepared to agree with its central argument that the English language would be more useful than Welsh to Welsh school-children in educational and economic terms (indeed, many of them had given evidence to the Commissioners to this effect, and English-medium schools were already very popular, as indicated earlier). The presentation of Welshwomen as sexually immoral, however, provoked outrage,[91] and the *Report*'s attacks on non-conformity were seen as an even greater betrayal.[92] Reactions in Wales to the *Report* were immediate and bitter, especially because the Commissioners' inquiries had raised great expectations. Welsh people were well aware that schools, teachers and children's attainments were in many cases in-adequate; this had been why so many had responded enthusiastically to Hugh Owen's initiative, and many had been prepared to co-operate with the Commissioners' inquiry in the hope that the government would improve educational provision. Instead they felt themselves to have been insulted and stigmatized unfairly, their goodwill thrown back in their faces. The Assistants – not only Welsh, but Welsh-speaking – who as well as acting as interpreters had made comments on their own visits to schools which were just as damning as those of the Commissioners themselves, were the objects of great public fury: one of them, John James, who had worked with Johnson in the north and whose comments were regarded as especially severe, was particularly disliked, and there is a story that at his funeral in 1851 one of the assembled crowd called out in Welsh 'Here is buried a traitor to his country' and spat on the coffin,[93] the depth of the insult showing the depth of the outrage. There were more formal objections from many quarters, including the Dean of Bangor, who had given evidence to the Commission, and Sir Thomas Philips, who had defended Newport against the Chartists in 1839. Some queried the Commissioners' technique of asking the children leading or misleading questions, and all doubted their understanding of and goodwill towards a society that functioned differently from theirs.

The *Report* rapidly acquired the name by which it is popularly known in Welsh: as a publication of H.M. Stationery Office it was bound in blue, and the nickname Brad y Llyfrau Gleision (the Treachery of the Blue Books) deliberately recalled the story of the Saxon lord in the sixth century who treacherously murdered British chieftains at a banquet held to celebrate a truce. This had entered Welsh popular mythology as Brad y Cyllyll Hirion (the Treachery of the Long Knives), and had frequently been used (for example, by the Daughters of Rebecca) as an example of Anglo-Saxon betrayal of Celtic trust and goodwill.[94] The *Report* rapidly assumed a similar place in the popular mythology; it was influential in shaping not only English attitudes to Wales but in showing the Welsh a picture of themselves that they had to respond to. It helped to crystal-lize, and to give official backing to, attitudes which already existed about the 'superiority' of English and the people who spoke it, and the innate 'inferiority' of Welsh and Welsh-speakers. The Welsh language, under this attack from English officialdom, became even more clearly marked as the property of the Welsh common people, and its use the clear asser-tion of deeply-felt national and class differences in defiance of the official English attitudes which the *Report* so clearly exhibited;[95] the 1847 *Report* has been described as the major catalyst in the radicalization of the Welsh people in the latter part of the nineteenth century.[96] In succeeding generations, many writers in Wales seemed to be preoccupied with defending themselves against the slurs of the 1847 *Report* and in proving to themselves as well as to England that the Commissioners had misjudged the country: the image of itself which much of Welsh-speaking Wales tried to project was expressed in tags such as 'Cymru lan, Cymru lonydd'[97] ('pure Wales, peaceful Wales') and 'Gwlad y Menyg Gwynion',[98] (literally, 'Land of White Gloves', deriving from the custom of presenting white gloves to judges on circuit when there were no cases for them to try; by the end of the century it had developed into a symbol of a Welsh nation where no crime or immorality existed).[99] The 1847 *Report* cast a long shadow.

CONCLUSION

The question raised by the *Report* is as relevant today, in communities throughout the world, as it was in the middle of the nineteenth century: should a minority linguistic community within a larger state with a world language keep to its own language – uniquely adapted to and intermeshed with its own way of being – and run the risk of being isolated from intellectual advances communicated in the dominant national language, or should it reject its own language for that of the greater state, and run the risk of cutting itself off from its own history and culture by changing to a language unsuited to the particular forms of expression it needs?

The two sides of the argument are effectively laid out by Gramsci when writing about the roles of Sard and of standard Italian; in a letter to his sister which discusses the upbringing of their niece, he argues strongly for the value of using the minority language: 'I thought it was a big mistake not to let Edmea speak Sardinian when she was a little girl. It damaged her intellectual development and put a strait-jacket on her imagination . . .'[100]

Equally, he stresses the intellectually-limiting results of having a minority language as one's sole form of expression:

Someone who only speaks dialect, or understands the standard language incompletely, necessarily has an intuition of the world which is more or less limited and provincial, which is fossilized and anachronistic in relation to the major currents of thought which dominate world history . . . While it is not always possible to learn a number of foreign languages in order to put oneself in contact with other cultural lives, it is at the least necessary to learn the national language properly.[101]

The crux of this position resides in the *only*: the implication of the two passages taken together is that being brought up to speak the language of one's parents and community allows one access to the culture in which one is rooted, and that denial of this will stunt emotional and intellectual growth; if that language is a minority language within a larger state, however, to know *only* that language will restrict growth at a later stage of development, and in order not to be marginalized within the broader national culture, one must acquire an effective knowledge of the standard national language.

The 1847 *Report*, as has been demonstrated, allows for no such composition of competing claims: it presents the situation in mid-nineteenth-century Wales entirely from the perspective of the dominant English culture, and denies any role to Welsh except as an instrument for learning English. The *Report*, and the official English attitudes it demonstrates, can be seen as a part of the colonial process which Ngugi wa Thiong'o has called a 'cultural bomb', whose effect is:

> to annihilate a people's beliefs in their names, in their languages, in their environment, in their heritage of struggle, in their unity, in their capacities and ultimately in themselves. It makes them see their past as one wasteland of non-achievement and makes them want to distance themselves from that wasteland. It makes them want to identify with that which is furthest removed from themselves: for instance, with other people's languages rather than their own.[102]

Although, as has been suggested, a complex and intermeshing range of elements was involved in the representation of the working-class Welsh in the 1847 *Report*, the crucial determinant, it could be argued, was language; and since 'the existence of the Welsh language presented a potentially powerful revolutionary force, in that it served to keep the majority of the population of Wales aloof from the influence of the ideological forces of the dominant class, which were almost exclusively expressed in English', it had 'either to be appropriated or eliminated'.[103] For many Welsh-speaking members of what has been described as 'a small bereft nation frantic with longing for a commendable place in the English imperial sun',[104] the wholesale adoption of English and consequent rejection of Welsh was the way to demonstrate that they were progressive members of a forward-looking society which subscribed to the standard English Victorian values as well as standard Victorian English (that is, they had been blasted into submission by Ngugi wa Thiong'o's cultural bomb). Others, including the influential Thomas Gee, owner of one of the major Welsh periodicals (*Y Faner*) and one of the most prominent Welshmen of his time, were prepared, as he said in 1866, for English to have the outside world as long as Welsh could have the inner sanctum;[105] but in these circumstances the inner sanctum itself soon comes under attack.[106] The song which became the Welsh national anthem was composed in the aftermath of the *Report* (1856), and the last line of its chorus expresses feelings of insecurity as well as hope for the language which a community with greater power over its own future would not have needed to make explicit: 'O bydded i'r hen iaith barhau'. (May the ancient language endure.)

In the words of the Bishop of Avila to Isabella of Spain in 1492, 'Language is the perfect instrument of empire'.[107] The 1847 *Report* demonstrates the force of the Bishop's dictum in two ways: its argument illustrates some of the techniques by which a dominant culture attempted to establish the primacy of its language over that of a minority culture, and its own use of language operates as an 'instrument' to establish the 'empire' of Englishness over the Welsh.

NOTES

1 C.A. Bayly, *Imperial Meridian The British Empire and the World 1780–1830*, Longman, Harlow, 1989, p.6.
2 Gwyn A. Williams, *When was Wales?*, Penguin, London, 1985, pp.202, 221.
3 Michael Hechter, *Internal Colonialism*, Routledge & Kegan Paul, London, 1975, pp.185–6, etc.
4 John Berger, *Pig Earth*, Writer and Readers Publishing Cooperative, London, 1979, pp.203–5.
5 Bayly, *Imperial Meridian*, p.109.
6 Hugh Trevor-Roper, 'The invention of tradition: the Highland tradition of Scotland', in Eric Hobsbawm and Terence Ranger (eds), *The Invention of Tradition*, Cambridge University Press, Cambridge, 1983.
7 Saunders Lewis, 'The fate of the language' ('Tynged yr iaith', trans. G. Aled Williams), Alun R. Jones and Gwyn Thomas (eds), *Presenting Saunders Lewis*, University of Wales Press, Cardiff, 1983, p.130.
8 Norman Fairclough has effectively discussed the way in which power relationships determine discourses in *Language and Power*, Longman, London, 1989.
9 George Owen of Henllys, *The Dialogue of the Goverment of Wales*, 1594, *Owen – Description of Pembrokeshire III*, Cymmrodorion Record Series No.1, Society of Cymmrodorion, London, 1906, p.37.
10 27 Henry 8, c.26; quoted in D.M. and E.M. Lloyd (eds), *A Book of Wales*, Collins, London, 1953, p.139, as are the other quotations from this Act.
11 Peter R. Roberts, 'The Welsh language, English law and Tudor legislation', *Transactions of the Honourable Society of Cymmrodorion*, 1989, p.21.
12 Glanmor Williams, 'The Act of Incorporation and the Welsh language', *Planet* 72, December/January 1988–9, pp.48–53.
13 A.M. Johnson, 'Wales during the Commonwealth and Protectorate' in Donald Pennington and Keith Thomas (eds), *Puritans and Revolutionaries*, Clarendon Press, Oxford, 1978, pp.233–56.
14 Meic Stephens (ed.), *The Oxford Companion to the Literature of Wales*, Oxford University Press, Oxford, 1986, p.592.
15 Prys Morgan, 'From a death to a view: the hunt for the Welsh past in the Romantic period', Hobsbawm and Ranger, *The Invention of Tradition*, p.88.
16 Catherine Sinclair, *Hill and Valley: or, Wales and the Welsh*, J.M. Burton and Co., Ipswich, 1850 (3rd edn.), p.140. Sinclair says that the journals which compose the book were written June–August, 1833. I am grateful to J.K. Roberts for drawing my attention to the quoted comment.

17 Prys Morgan, Hobsbawm and Ranger, *The Invention of Tradition*.
18 Gwyn A. Williams, *When was Wales?*, pp.191, 192, 194, 195.
19 D. Gareth Evans, *A History of Wales 1814–1906*, University of Wales Press, Cardiff, 1989, pp.133–6.
20 Ibid., pp. 139–44.
21 Gwyn A. Williams, *The Merthyr Rising*, University of Wales Press, Cardiff, 1988 edn., esp. chs. 3, 4.
22 *The Times*, 6 November 1839, quoted in Ivor Wilks, *South Wales and the Rising of 1839*, Croom Helm, London, 1984, p.145.
23 Gwyn A. Williams, *When was Wales?*, p.196.
24 Quoted in Wilks, *South Wales and the Rising of 1839*, p.26.
25 Tudor Powell Jones, 'The contribution of the Established Church to Welsh education (1811–46)' in Jac L. Williams and Gwilym Rees Hughes (eds), *The History of Education in Wales*, vol. 1, Christopher Davies, Swansea, 1978, passim.
26 D. Gareth Evans, *A History of Wales*, pp.56, 143.
27 Frank Price Jones, 'The Blue Books of 1847', in Williams and Hughes, *The History of Education in Wales*, p.127.
28 T.M. Bassett, 'The Sunday School', in Williams and Hughes, *The History of Education in Wales*, p.74.
29 Ibid., p.79. See also Sian Rhiannon Williams, 'Y Brad yn yr Tir Du: ardal ddiwydiannol sir Fynwy a'r Llyfrau Gleision', in Prys Morgan (gol.), *Brad y Llyfrau Gleision*, Gwasg Gomer, Llandysul, 1991, tt.125–45.
30 A.L. Trott, 'The British School Movement in Wales 1806–46', in Williams and Hughes, *The History of Education in Wales*, p.95.
31 Goronva Camlan, from 'Education in Wales', 1846, in Raymond Garlick and Roland Mathias (eds), *Anglo-Welsh Poetry 1480–1980*, Poetry Wales Press, Bridgend, 1984, pp.120–1.
32 D. Gareth Evans, *A History of Wales*, p.102.
33 B.L. Davies, *Hugh Owen 1804–1881*, Gwasg Prifysgol Cymru, Caerdydd, 1977, p.16.
34 John Davies, *Hanes Cymru*, Allen Lane/Penguin, London, 1990, t.375.
35 D. Gareth Evans, *A History of Wales*, p.96.
36 Glanmor Williams, *Religion, Language and Nationality in Wales*, University of Wales Press, Cardiff, 1979, p.25.
37 G.J. Williams, *Agweddau ar Hanes Dysg Gymraeg*, Aneirin Lewis (ed.), Gwasg Prifysgol Cymru, Caerdydd, 1969, pp.115–20.
38 Mab Dewi Du, Tredegar, *Y Gwyliedydd*, 1825, tt.47–8, quoted in Ieuan Gwynedd Jones, *Communities: Essays in the Social History of Victorian Wales*, Gomer Press, Llandysul, 1987, p.235.
39 E.T. Davies, *Religion and Society in the Nineteenth Century* (in the series *A New History of Wales*), Christopher Davies, Llandybie, 1981, ch. 1.
40 Emyr Humphreys, *The Taliesin Tradition*, Black Raven Press, London, 1983, p.134.
41 See Hans Aarsleff, *The Study of Language in England 1780–1860*, Athlone Press, London, 1983, esp. chs 4 and 5.
42 The debates are discussed in outline in Geoffrey Sampson, *Schools of Linguistics*, Hutchinson, London, 1980, ch. 1.
43 Welsh views in the early part of the century often took diametrically opposite views: in 1834 the Rev. Thomas Price (Carnhuanawc), Celtic antiquary and advocate of education through the medium of Welsh, declared with impressive optimism that English was likely to go the way of Latin and 'be known only in musty parchments and records, and that the ancient language of this island will again be the universal language of its inhabitants'.

(Ieuan Gwynedd Jones, 'Language and community in nineteenth century Wales', in David Smith (ed.), *A People and a Proletariat: Essays in the History of Wales 1780–1980*, Pluto, London, 1980, p.61).

44 Quotations from *Parliamentary Debates*, House of Commons Papers LXXIV (1846), p.848.

45 W.J. Gruffydd, in his biography *Owen Morgan Edwards* (1937), commented caustically that for Williams, who had made his money in the wholesale cotton trade in London, the prime function of education in Wales was to give Welsh children the chance to become successful London drapers too (cited in B.L. Davies, 'Sir Hugh Owen and the Cambrian Educational Society', *Transactions of Anglesey Antiquarian Society and Field Club*, 1973, pp.137–51).

46 *Parliamentary Reports* (870), vol. xxvii (Part I), p.iii–iv. Further references will be to the Part of the Report followed by the page number, e.g. Part II, p.23.

47 D. Gareth Evans, *A History of Wales*, p.125.

48 Identified and discussed by Frank Burton and Pat Carlen in *Official Discourse*, Routledge & Kegan Paul, London, 1979.

49 Part II, p.4.

50 Part III, p.8.

51 Part III, p.25.

52 Part II, p.28.

53 Part I, p.16.

54 Part II, p.62.

55 Part I, p.28.

56 Part I, p.2.

57 Part II, p.26.

58 Part III, p.47.

59 Part II, p.66.

60 Part III, p.68.

61 Part II, p.43.

62 Part II, 43.

63 Part I, p.28.

64 Part I, pp.5–6.

65 Part II, p.60.

66 Edward W. Said, *Orientalism*, Routledge & Kegan Paul, London, 1978, ch. 1.

67 All from Part I, pp.5–6

68 Part II, p.64.

69 Part III, p.22.

70 Part III, p.10.

71 Part II, p.67.

72 Part II, p.66.

73 Part I, p.12.

74 Part I, p.3.

75 Part III, p.59.

76 Part II, p.65.

77 Part II, p.2.

78 Part II, p.67.

79 Part II, p.35.

80 Part III, p.68.

81 Part I, p.21.

82 Part II, p.25.

83 Part I, p.7.

84 Part I, p.7.

85 Part I, p.61.

86 Part I, p.5.

87 Part I, Appendix, p.270.

88 'A custom among the Welsh peasantry' by which 'maidservants, denied the use of the parlours, were sometimes allowed to receive their sweethearts in their own rooms', Meic Stephens, *The Oxford Companion to the Literature of Wales*, p.99.

89 Part II, p.68.

90 Part I, Appendix, p.306.

91 W. Gareth Evans, 'Y ferch, addysg a moesoldeb: portread y Llyfrau Gleision 1847', in Prys Morgan (gol.), *Brad y Llyfrau Gleision*, tt.74–100.

92 Prys Morgan, 'R.J. Derfel a'r ddrama *Brad y Llyfrau Gleision* 1847', in Prys Morgan (gol.), *Brad y Llyfrau Gleision*.

93 Frank Price Jones, 'The Blue Books of 1847', p.135.

94 Prys Morgan, 'From long knives to Blue Books', in R.R. Davies *et al.*, *Welsh Society and Nationhood*, University of Wales Press, Cardiff, 1984, pp.199–215.

95 Ieuan Gwynedd Jones, 'Language and community in nineteenth century Wales', pp.67–8.

96 Frank Price Jones, 'Effaith Brad y Llyfrau Gleision', in Alun Llywelyn-Williams ac Elfed ap Nefydd Roberts (gol.), *Radicaliaeth a'r Werin Gymreig yn y Bedwaredd Ganrif ar Bymtheg*, Gwasg Prifysgol Cymru, Caerdydd, 1977, pp.48–64.

97 Hywel Teifi Edwards, *Codi'r Hen Wlad in ei Hol*, Gwasg Gomer, Llandysul, 1989, p.3.

98 Hywel Teifi Edwards, *The Eisteddfod*, University of Wales Press, Cardiff, 1990, p.26.

99 Russell Davies, '"Hen Wlad y Menig Gwynion": profiad Sir Gaerfyrddin', in Geraint H. Jenkins (gol), *Cof Cenedl VI: Ysgrifau ar Hanes Cymru*, Gwasg Gomer, Llandysul, 1991, t.137.

100 *Gramsci's Prison Letters – Lettere dal Carcare. A selection*, translated and introduced by Hamish Henderson, Zwan Publications, London, 1988, p.47.

101 Antonio Gramsci, *Selections from the Prison Notebooks*, Quintin Hoare and Geoffrey Nowell Smith (eds and trans), Lawrence and Wishart, London, 1971, p.325.

102 Ngugi wa Thiong'o, *Decolonising the Mind*, Heinneman/Zimbabwe Publishing House, London, 1986, p.3. The process of making people ashamed of their own language and culture so that they want to identify with another is, of course, frequently supported by sanctions: in the same way that nineteenth-century children caught speaking Welsh at school, and often outside it, were punished by having to wear a heavy piece of wood suspended around their necks – the 'Welsh Stick' or 'Welsh Not' (E.G. Millward, 'Yr Hen Gyfundrefn Felltigedig', *Barn* 207/208, Ebrill/Mai 1980, tt.93–95, dates the earliest reference to this practice as 1799) – Ngugi wa Thiong'o describes how children in his home area of Kenya caught speaking Gikuyu were punished by having to wear around their necks a metal plate with inscriptions such as I AM STUPID, or I AM A DONKEY. There are, unfortunately, parallels from many other language communities: for example, see Eileen Holt, 'The Provençal Not', *Planet* 8, Oct/Nov 1971, pp.33–5.

103 Glyn Williams, 'The ideological basis of nineteenth-century Wales: the discourse of Michael D. Jones', in Glyn Williams (ed.), *Crisis of Economy and Ideology: Essays on Welsh Society 1840–1940*, Glyn Williams (ed.), British Sociological Association – Sociology of Wales Study Group, 1983, p.181.

104 Hywel Teifi Edwards, *The Eisteddfod*, p.21.

105 Ibid., p.25.
106 This process is outlined in Jean Aitchison, *Language Change: Progress or Decay?*, Fontana, London, 1981, ch. 4.
107 Lewis Hanke, *Aristotle and the American Indians*, Hollis and Carter, London, 1959, p.8. Antonio de Nebrija had just presented his Spanish *Gramatica*, the first grammar of a modern European language, to Isabella, who asked 'What is it for?'; the Bishop's answer preempted the grammarian's. Hanke points out that Nebrija's own view (in the introduction to his book) was 'siempre la lengua ha sido companera del imperio' (roughly, 'language has always gone hand in hand with empire'); the Bishop's rewording makes its own point.

8

FERTILE LAND, ROMANTIC SPACES, UNCIVILIZED PEOPLES

English Travel-Writing about the Cape of Good Hope, 1800–50

Kenneth Parker

INTRODUCTION

Supplanting the Dutch East India Company administration that had inaugurated permanent white settlement in 1652, Britain invaded and occupied the Cape in June 1795. Cession of the territory in February 1803, to the Batavian Republic that had been imposed upon the Dutch nation by Napoleon, was short-lived: in January 1806 the British invaded again, this time to stay, administering it, largely by direct rule, until the granting of representative government to the Colony in 1853. A study of British policy at the Cape in this period therefore becomes, ineluctably, not only one concerned with the impact of imperial rule abroad, but also one of transformations at home: notably about discursive strategies deployed in the annexation of the metropolitan population to dispossession of those at the periphery.

Occupation of the Cape had a threefold impetus: the first, strategic, stemmed directly out of the wars with France because of the perceived importance of the sea route via the Cape – on the part of the French about their possessions in Mauritius and the Ile de Bourbon and on the part of the British about their interests in India; the second, economic, as the Cape became an increasingly significant contributor of materials for manufacturing industry at home as well as supplier of goods to India; the third, cultural, as a space for emigration and implantation of varieties of British identities upon indigenous peoples who are dispossessed not only of their lands but also of their ways of living in the world.[1]

To highlight the events at the Cape is, in the first instance, to recognize the same combination of military-economic-cultural dispossession that characterizes a period marked by events such as the Treaty of Waitangi

(1840), the transfer of the administration of India to the British Crown in the aftermath of the Indian 'Mutiny' (1857), but (by contrast) the conferment of Dominion status on the white settlers in Canada (1867). What will be stressed in this chapter, however, is not similarity, but singularity: of the Cape as a space in which British imperialism takes on a unique inflection as consequence of the encounter with white settlers who had preceded them as invaders of lands occupied by blacks.[2]

It is essential to stress, from the outset, that British imperial policy and practice should be seen in the context of transformations in the construction of national identities begun in the 1740s which had reached their maturity in the 1830s and 1840s. It is a period characterized by Philip Corrigan and Derek Sayer as that in which the 'great arch' – a phrase first used by E.P. Thompson in his essay 'The Peculiarities of the English' (1965) – is finally erected in England. Concentrating upon English history from medieval times to the nineteenth century, Corrigan and Sayer's initial premise is that the repertoire of activities and institutions which can eventually be identified as 'the State', are cultural forms; indeed, are cultural forms which have a particular centrality for bourgeois civilization, and that the 'great arch' might be seen as an appropriate metaphor whereby to characterize not only the period of embourgeoisement of the dominant classses, but also of the proletarianization of the ruled.

For Corrigan and Sayer, whose text lays especial stress upon mutuality between consensus and coercion as means whereby the great arch is topped out in England, there occurs:

> a triple making, which taken together cements a distinctively new kind of civilization. First, 'Society' – comprising men of property – is extended, reformed, kept flexibly 'open'; it enlarges itself, shifts and inflects its voice, founds and celebrates a 'middle class'. Second, the working class is resistingly involved in its own being made. Third, forms of rule – features of state formation – are equally made and making ... In these years, the Great Arch is finally finished, many of the bricks marked by the graffiti of the vanquished, and much blood – most of it foreign – mixed with the cement.[3]

While conceding that the Corrigan and Sayer argument is not uncontested, the application of that argument to the story of English conquest of the Cape is, nevertheless, a prime illustration of the operation of mentalities, as well as practices, that connects the erection of the great arch at home to implantations abroad. Thus, while policy at home foregrounded class by seeking to guarantee the dominance of the propertied English male possessive individual in a common society into which 'domestic foreigners' (Scots; Welsh; to a lesser degree, Irish) are incorporated at the periphery, policy at the Cape stressed, instead, an overarching shared identity of 'Britishness', itself in the process of being made.

What the traveller's tale reveals is that policy was marked by, firstly, a congeries of differential actions to cope with resistances by different groups of the dispossessed – in the Cape, by blacks as well as Boers, at different historic moments;[4] secondly, the constant awareness that dispossession of far-flung lands and peoples was being undertaken in the face of competition from other European states bent upon a similar task. Here the continuing contest with France was especially important; the British state deployed a range of discourses that were anti-cosmopolitan, anti-aristocratic, pro-nativist, and which have been described as 'essentially ethnic in its central concerns', antiquarian in content and educational in contemporary impact.[5] Notwithstanding its self-projection as an empire that denounced all that was French, not only did private emulation of French ways thrive, but, as C.A. Bayly asserts:

> Taken as a whole, the British empire had as much in common with the continental neo-absolutisms which emerged out of the Napoleonic Wars as it did with the liberal nation state of the 1850s into which it did, very slowly and unevenly, transform itself.[6]

In the context of the attempt, in this chapter, to decode the discourses of key officials who had penetrated the interior as travellers, it is essential to recognize the nature of English absolutism at the Cape. The government there was an absolute despotism – the governor was responsible only to the Secretary of State for War and the Colonies (a telling conjuncture!); proclamations about either the enactment of new laws, or revision of existing laws, were issued in his name alone. Not only was the possibility, under the Dutch, of appeal to the High Court in Batavia, now transferred to the governor, but in the bestowal of patronage or policy, he was increasingly assisted by a class of stiff-necked officers and officials who felt no need for contact with blacks, and whose contacts with Boers was often only through the (temporary) mediation of their unmarried women.

TRAVELLERS' TALES

It is in terms of some of these connections between class, ethnicity, history, and education that the stories told by travellers take on an especial resonance, and it is here that texts published in England by travellers who penetrated the interior of the Cape Colony have a particular importance. What did English readers know about these specific colonial others, when did they know it, and what was the contribution to that knowledge by the tales told by travellers?

The traveller's tale presents a particular problem for cultural theory.

A hybrid form, it belongs neither exclusively to the inventions of fiction nor the 'facts' of science, neither to the public world of 'official discourse' nor the private one of diary or autobiography, but contains and displays elements of all of these. What is important for our purpose is to note, as Michael McKeon has convincingly shown, the pivotal position of the traveller's tale in the long march of the destabilization of generic categories that culminates in the hegemonic triumph of the novel.[7]

Several generalizing observations are in order at this point. The first is of the role of the traveller's tale constructing a model that posits harmonious social relations at 'home' and of the absence of such social relations as characteristic of foreign spaces. That difference will be developed as justification for intervention in those foreign spaces in order to institute 'harmony'. The second is that the tales emphasize differences, especially between peoples, who inhabit these foreign spaces. It is, arguably, the dominant precedent interest in the Orient and in the New World that leads to the discursive emplotment of 'the Cape' as different from both of these, notably on the part of voyagers to the Orient and the East, who stop very briefly at the Cape, but who do not penetrate the interior.

If the tales about different foreign spaces seek to inscribe the alterity of those spaces not only from that of Europe, but also between them, it is important to note a third aspect, that of historic specificity. If the moment of McKeon's story of the origins of the novel more or less coincides with the moment of first white competition in dispossession at the Cape, then the moment of English conquest more or less coincides with, and corroborates, the general thesis by Philip Curtin that, by the 1780s, a new view of Africa had begun to emerge which

> drew some of its novelty from a new attitude on the part of Europeans, but even more from the flood of new data that began to pour in – first from coastal travellers, then from explorers into the interior ... finally from the refinement and synthesis of these data in the hands of stay-at-home scholars and publicists ...[8]

While I have argued elsewhere[9] that the date of this 'new view of Africa' is rather earlier than that suggested by Curtin, it is, nevertheless, essential to stress that his choice of the moment of codification and synthesization of the image of Africa coincides, more or less, with that of the erection of the great arch that Corrigan and Sayer argue is being topped out at home, recall also that this new view had impeccable philosophical underpinnings. If John Locke's well-known assertion that '... subduing or cultivating the earth, and having dominion, we see are joined together. The one gave title to the other, so that God, by commanding to subdue, gave authority so far to appropriate ... '[10] is a general thesis for dispossession, David Hume adds a specifically black-and-white complexion to that thesis, with his equally famous observation that: 'There never was a civilized nation of any other complexion than white, nor even any individual eminent either in action or speculation. No ingenious manufactures among them, no arts, no sciences ... Such a uniform and constant difference could not happen, in so many countries and ages, if nature had not made an original distinction betwixt these breeds of men.[11]

In this context, the celebrated instance in which Locke makes use of the 'facts' of English travellers to validate his case for the dislodgement of doctrines of innate ideas[12] leads to a number of key assertions to be demonstrated. The first of these is that of the utility of the traveller's tale as the appropriate form for the promulgation of colonial discourse, by which is meant '... an ensemble of linguistically-based practices of colonial relationships, an ensemble that could combine the most formulaic and bureaucratic of official documents ... with the most non-functional and unprepossessing of romantic novels ...'.[13] One feature that marks traveller's tales is, therefore, how they are conform to what has been described by Michel Foucault, as '... not ... an ideal, continuous, smooth text that runs beneath the multiplicity of contradictions, and resolves them in the calm unity of coherent thought ... ', but rather '... a space of multiple dissensions; a set of different oppositions ...'.[14]

One of the key hypotheses of this chapter is that there developed, in the period here dealt with, a 'discourse of the Cape' that marks it off from discourses about other spaces – notably those of the Orient and of the New World – because of two overwhelming singularities: (i) the presence, at the Cape, of white settlers – Boers – who refuse to act out the racial roles required of them as people with white skins, of subduing and cultivating the earth to the glory of God; their indolence, as well as other social practices, affronts the British traveller; (ii) the presence of not one undifferentiated, but at least three definably different groups of blacks: San ('Bushmen'); Khoikhoi ('Hottentots'); Xhosa ('Kaffirs'). Representation of these peoples will depend, dominantly, upon perceptions of the nature and extent of their resistance to dispossession and incorporation. As the travellers penetrate the interior, as the nature of the British presence transforms itself from mere occupation to permanent settlement, the texts reveal an increasing urgency to make sense of perceived contradictions between the categories of fertile land, romantic spaces, savage peoples.

A second hypothesis is that while the different categories of traveller all share the common objectives of the colonial project, the tales are marked, as well, by differential strategies for the achievement of those objectives. Five different groups may be distinguished: (i) officials in the employ of the colonial government, or other agencies (notably the military), who seek to map the landscapes, as well as the peoples – John Barrow; Robert Percival; James Alexander; (ii) scientists and/or artists – John Semple; Samuel Daniell; William Burchell; George French Angas; (iii) missionaries – John Campbell; Christian Latrobe; John Philip; Barnabas Shaw; Robert Moffatt; James Backhouse; Nathaniel Merriman; J.J. Freeman; (iv) the 1820 settlers, or travellers who write specifically about that event – C.G. Curtis; William Burchell; George Thompson; Cowper Rose; Stephen Kay; Henry Methuen; J.C. Chase; Harriet Ward; (v) – outside the chronological scope of this chapter, hunters (Roualeyn Cumming; Alfred Drayson; William Cornwallis Harris; John Moodie).

One of the consequences of demarcation and categorization according to rôle is to offer some contribution in support of the assertion that the image of the imperial project as a coherent and monolithic process will no longer do. Events at the Cape during the period covered in this chapter are evidence not only of differential strategies between competing white colonists, but evidence especially of competition between different kinds of traveller about strategies for the maintenance of domination. The origin of many of these perceptions, as well as proposed strategies, often seen as contradictions, might be traced back to contradictions rooted in European Enlightenment theory.[15]

Based upon an analysis of these texts is a third hypothesis: that with the coming of the British 'settlers' in 1820 there occurs a marked fracture in the travellers' tales of the way in which the different groups of original inhabitants were represented. The overwhelming reason for that fracture lies not only in the popular perception, in Britain, of rebellious Boers trekking into the interior to seek freedom to continue to enslave blacks, in defiance of benign British protocols, that government having abolished slavery in 1834. We also need to see how the 1820 settlers themselves were responsible for the cementation of a modernized white racism. In contrast to the naked version practised by the Boers, that of the British constructed the different groups of blacks (to different degrees) as 'unutterably Other', whilst finally annexing the Boers as junior partners, as 'negotiated Other', in the imperial enterprise.

One of the key discursive strategies deployed is the travellers' consistent endeavour to map the peoples in such a way as to dispossess them of their terrain, and to annex that terrain to British interests. Three exemplary figures here are Sir John Barrow, particularly for his deployment of the discourse of race as gendered; Robert Percival, for his application of the discourse of anti-slavery to the situation at the Cape; and Sir James Alexander, whose texts celebrate the moment of British victory over blacks, as well as Boer.

MAP-MAKING: ROMANTIC SPACES,
FERTILE LANDS, SAVAGE PEOPLES

The foundation tale of English penetration of the interior starts with John Barrow (1764–1848). Born in a small Lancashire village, Barrow left school at thirteen to work as a clerk/timekeeper in an iron foundry. Later, participation in an expedition to Spitzbergen enabled him to develop his interest in mathematics and in navigation sufficiently for him to be recommended to be appointed a teacher of mathematics at Greenwich school. It was here that he met, and taught, the sons of men of influence, one consequence of which was that – because of his scientific knowledge – he was invited to accompany Lord McCartney's embassy to the Emperor of China (1792–5).

With McCartney's appointment as Governor of the Cape Colony (1797), Barrow accompanied him as private secretary; later he was appointed Auditor-General. Having married a Boer woman, Anna Maria Truter, the daughter of a judge at the Cape, Barrow returned to England in 1803 where, for the next forty years he worked in the Admiralty. Not only was he elected to fellowships of the Linnaean and Royal Societies, and had a baronetcy conferred upon him, but he was also a founder member of the Royal Geographical Society, of which he became the third president (1835–7).[16]

Barrow's celebrated *An Account of Travels in the Interior of Southern Africa*[17] became, for European readers, the exemplary model of the tale that acquired the status of comprehensive authority for descriptions of peoples and societies, mainly because of its claim that these were 'actual observations made in the course of travels'. Subsequently, especially in the years preceding the arrival of the 1820 Settlers in the eastern Cape, extensively re-written and edited versions tended to overshadow the original.[18] Even more important, from the point of view of policy-making, Barrow had become an influential figure: for instance, in a speech in support of the motion that culminated in the establishment of the Select Committee on Aborigines, Buxton reminded the House of Commons that 'In reference to South Africa ... I will refer to an authority which few Gentlemen in this House will be disposed to question – I mean Mr Barrow of the Admiralty'.[19]

Perhaps the most telling example was Barrow's publication, at the express wish of Pitt the Younger, of his second volume of *An Account* ... (1804). Barrow was pleased to inform his readers that his objective in publishing was to show the importance of the Cape '. . .to the different European powers. . .'; his actual project was to defend the retention of the Cape for English interests – the economic case for which he later presented in a separate article in the *Monthly Magazine* of New Year's Day, 1805. The overwhelming reason for annexation, he argued, was as

'. . . part of security to our [English] Indian ocean trade and settlements during a war, and as a territorial acquisition and commercial emporium in time of peace'.

If the evidence for the utility of travellers' tales for readers in the metropolis in defining and legitimating the colonizing project could not be clearer, those tales also reveal the existence of a problem for officialdom not encountered elsewhere: how to order into a hierarchy and annex to the British interest the apparent chaos of ethnic and racial groups encountered at the Cape. The presence there of three groups of original inhabitants (in the parlance of Europe, respectively 'Bushmen'; 'Hottentots'; 'Cafres') as well as an earlier group of white settlers ('Boers') made the need for such ordering an urgent task.[20] What framed these encounters was the physical terrain and what it yielded:

> The natural productions of the Cape Peninsula, in the vegetable kindgom, are perhaps more numerous, varied, and elegant than on any other spot of equal extent in the whole world. . . Of these, by the indefatigable labours of Mr. Masson, His Majesty's botanic garden at Kew exhibits a choice collection; but many are still wanting to complete it.[21]

Hitherto there had been no problem: characterization of the local peoples encountered by coastal travellers had been brief and of incidental ethnographic interest; for these transients (mostly on official embassies to the Orient or the East) the local peoples were unutterably Other. What was distinctive of Barrow was not simply that his was an especially influential intervention in the act of mapping as well as establishing these ethnic hierarchies; much more importantly, his discourse lays bare Michel Foucault's identification of 'multiple dissensions' referred to earlier on, best illustrated by reference to the portrayal of the peoples encountered.

For metropolitan readers, Barrow's description of 'Bushmen' or 'Bosjeman' would not have been unfamiliar: his assertion that they are 'known in the colony [that is, by the Dutch colonists] by the name of Bosjemans, or men of the bushes, from the concealed manner in which they make their approaches to kill and to plunder' occurred in similar vein in works by travellers who had visited the Cape in the years immediately prior, as well as subsequent to, British annexation: Masson, Kolben, Sparrman, Thunberg, Le Vaillant and Patterson.[22] More importantly, however, the tale elides the real relations between the San and the colonists.[23] What Barrow brought to the discourse of the Cape was the application of Locke's dictum on dispossession, cited earlier: these people '. . .neither cultivate the ground nor breed cattle, but subsist, in part, on the natural produce of their country, and make up the rest by depredations on the colonists on the one side, and the neighbouring

tribes of people that are more civilised than themselves, on the other';
later on, while he will confirm the antecedent view that though the San
are 'justly' characterized as 'savage' he will also concede that they have
been 'rendered more worthy by the conduct of the European settlers'.[24]
How, he does not say.

If the Khoi are the lowest in the hierarchy at the Cape, they are
also portrayed as, aesthetically, the least attractive of beings; from an
enumeration of their 'flat noses, high cheek-bones, prominent chin,
and concave visage'. Barrow not only borrows from the voyagers the
accusation that they 'partake much of an apish character'; he also
registers their alterity by re-asserting another observation, culled from
the texts of the voyagers, to the effect that 'as a means of increasing their
speed in the chase, or when pursued by an enemy, the men have adopted
the custom, which was sufficiently remarkable, of pushing the testicles
to the upper part of the root of the penis, where they seemed to remain
as firmly and conveniently as if placed there by nature'.[25]

And yet, the problem for the traveller is that simple and unequivocal
rejection of the San was not possible. For instance, while Barrow
can dismiss some examples of San cave paintings as 'caricatures', he
cannot help acknowledging that 'others were too well executed not to
arrest attention. So well discriminated, that the originals, from whence
the representations had been made, *could, without any difficulty, be
ascertained* [my emphasis]'. The reluctant recognition of the skills of
the inferior other can be conceded only in the context of signalling the
discriminating gaze of the observer, as art critic, to the reader. Not only
do the '. . .bold touches, judiciously applied. . .' indicate to Barrow that
these drawings could not have been executed by 'savages', but the
inevitable comparison is made with European practice – 'for accuracy
of outline and correctness of the different parts, worse drawings than
that have passed through the engraver's hands'.[26] Whether intentionally
or not, confrontation with San art brings into question the sense of a
stable white masculine self.

By contrast, description of the Khoi is tied to a different post of white
racist discourse, that of 'liberal' English values confronting Boer genocide
in the common and contested Cape terrain. Because of Boer expansion
there is now not 'a single horde of independent Hottentot to be found'
on the eastern frontier. 'These weak people', Barrow asserts, 'the most
helpless, and in their present condition perhaps the most wretched,
of the human race, duped out of their possessions, their country,
and finally out of their liberty, have entailed upon their offspring a state
of existence to which that of slavery might bear the comparison of
happiness'. Later still, he will concede that, 'Low as they are in the scale
of humanity, their character seems to have been very much traduced
and misrepresented'; the Khoi are 'a mild, quiet and timid people;

perfectly harmless, honest, faithful; and though extremely phlegmatic, they are kind and affectionate to each other, and not incapable of strong attachments'.[27] The language shows remarkable affinities with that used when writing about the rural poor in England of the time.[28]

If Barrow the moralist and aesthetician finds the San irredeemable; if Barrow the cultural historian finds the Khoi capable of 'improvement' (into a rural proletariat and, to a lesser extent, part of the military machine) then encounter with the 'Kaffer' both relies upon, yet calls into question the teachings of contemporary science. If the comments on San and Khoi betray elements of residual doubt about a stable European self, those on the Xhosa reveal unintentional awareness of the fragility of its philosophical foundations. For Barrow the scientist:

> The comparative anatomist might be a little perplexed in placing the skull of a kaffer in the chain, so ingeniously put together by him, comprehending all the links with the most perfect European to the ourang-outang, and then through all the monkey-tribe. The head of a kaffir is not elongated: the frontal and the occipital bones form nearly a semi-circle; and a line from the forehead to the chin drawn over the nose is convex like that of most Europeans. In short, had not Nature bestowed upon him the dark-colouring principle that anatomists have discovered to be owing to certain gelatinous fluid lying between the epidermis and the cuticle, he might have ranked among the first of Europeans. . . A young man about twenty. . . was one of the finest figures that perhaps was ever created. He was a perfect Hercules; and a cast from his body would not have disgraced the pedestal of that deity in the Farnese palace.[29]

Seeming even-handedness should not obscure real relations. By his own admission, Barrow was in the eastern Cape on behalf of the government of the Colony 'to bring about a conversation with some of the chiefs . . . to try if, by presents and a lenient conduct, they could be prevailed upon to quit their present wild and marauding ways of life. . .'.[30] And what were these 'wild and maurauding ways of life'? What Barrow's record suppresses – one that is, moreover, common to virtually every text of the period – is that of marauding on the part of white settlers, and of resistance, on the part of the Xhosa, to dispossession of their land in a series of wars of liberation characteristically reduced in the white historical record as 'Kaffir Wars'.[31] Barrow is unequivocal about the nature of his task: in a 'conversation' with one of the Xhosa chiefs who complained to him about Boer depredations, he tells the chief that the Boers had not only established a right to hunt, but also to sow and plant their crops and graze their cattle.

If the dominant sense here is that of official denial of the Xhosa not only to the right to their land, but also of resistance in its defence, Barrow is seemingly unaware that his encounter with the chiefs affords him information about a wholly alternative social ethos and structure. Barrow recounts that, according to the story told by the chiefs, every Xhosa male:

> . . .is a soldier and a tradesman. The first is not a profession, but taken up occasionally as the state, of which he is a member, may demand his services. War is not made for the extension of territory or for individual aggrandizement, but for some direct insult or act of injustice against the whole, or some member, of the community.[32]

Even if the portrait of the Xhosa polity of the time might be questioned as somewhat gilded, what the encounter with the Xhosa brings into sharp relief is the position of the Boers: not simply as a matter of race and colour, but fundamentally as a matter of their place in the scheme of the managing of dispossession. While their initial European ancestry and their skin colour made the Boers obvious potential allies, British perceptions of the extent to which that European ancestry had been contaminated by settlement at the Cape, made such an alliance neither self-evident nor even uncontested. Indeed, Barrow was arguably the most influential source for English popular perceptions of Boers.

According to Barrow, the Boer male is '. . . ill made, loosely put together, awkward, and inactive. Very few have those open ingenious countenances that among the peasantry of many parts of Europe speak their simpleness and innocence . . . many a peasant whose stock consists of several thousand sheep and as many hundred heads of cattle . . .' lives in hovels with '. . . low mud-walls, with a couple of square holes to admit the light, and a door of wicker-work, a few crooked poles to support a thatch of rushes, slovenly spread over them. . .'; he '. . . bestows no kind of labour on the ground but that of throwing in the seed; the rest is left to chance and the effects of an excellent climate. . .'. Any suggestion that these people might be prevailed upon to change would '. . . require more labor and activity, and more attention, than the body and mind of a Dutch farmer seem capable of supplying: his avarice, though great, is yet overcome by the habits of indolence to which he has been educated'.[33]

Barrow locates Boer indolence to one single cause, that of the presence of slavery at the Cape, concerning which he observes there was '. . . perhaps, no part of the world, out of Europe, where the introduction of slavery was less necessary than at the Cape'. That his explanation for the existence of slavery relies on what he calls a 'fall away', on the part of the Boer settlers, from 'the spirit of Batavian industry' flies in the face of the evidence of the nature and extent of Dutch slaveholding[34] is perhaps less noteworthy than the emphasis he places upon the morally corrosive nature of the practice. Even if there is neither easy nor obvious explanation for either the origin, or the content, of the anti-slavery discourse (especially in the context of one that is supportive of dispossession), what is noteworthy is how the animadversion is tied to a sense of Boer ethnicity. Barrow provides a vivid example of Boer cruelty: the habit of punishment by organized flogging, 'not by any given number of lashes, but by time; and as they have no clocks nor substitutes for them capable of marking the smaller divisions of time, he has invented an excuse for the indulgence of one of his most favorite sensualities, by flogging them till he has smoked as many pipes of tobacco as he may judge the magnitude of the case to deserve'.[35]

In the context of British animus against Boer in this early stage, I cannot help citing one of my favourite examples, taken from the much-reprinted tales of that influential Scots missionary, John Campbell. Passing a Boer farm, his party was:

Saluted with the barking of many dogs, which seem to abound in Africa more than men. These animals are only useful as watchers. A shepherd's dog from Britain would have assisted us more in driving our spare cattle than a thousand African ones. It would be well if some of these were sent over to instruct African dogs to be more useful to their masters. Perhaps were the people here to witness their sagacity, they would suspect they were rational beings.[36]

If the discourse of the British male commentator is sometimes either ambivalent or perhaps even contradictory when seeking to represent other males encountered at the Cape, there is manifestly no uncertainty when that gaze is trained upon the women. Barrow, uniquely in my reading, informs his readers that what had become known as the 'Hottentot apron'[37] was present also among San women he encountered. He not only assures his readers that 'there was no difficulty in satisfying his curiosity' about this 'unusual appendage to those parts that are seldom exposed to view'; he thereupon proceeds to offer a 'tolerable good idea of the whole appearance both as to color, shape, and size'.[38] As with San males, so with San females: for the English traveller there would appear to be an obsessive British interest in black sexual organs!

Khoi women, whose breasts, hands, and gait are described in some detail, 'when young, and previous to child-bearing, might serve as models of perfection of the human figure'. Such 'charms, however, are fleeting', because of physical changes, described in detail, which set in after childbirth.[39]

Xhosa women, on the other hand, are praised for their 'good temper, animation, and cheerfulness of mind'; their attributes of being 'modest without reserve; extremely curious without being troublesome; lively but not impudent; and sportive without the least shadow of being lascivious' reads like a catalogue of the ideal requirements of the British male. Where Khoikhoi women fall short is the colour of their skin: 'getting over the prejudice of color, which was that of a dark and glossy brown verging on black, several of them might have been accounted handsome'.[40] Evidently, skin colour is *the* insurmountable prejudice for the British traveller.

Blackness is not, however, the only obstacle. Where Barrow excels is in his classic description of Boer women. While the sentiments expressed are not new,[41] and while some later travellers and artists will repeat the sentiments,[42] it is Barrow's description that has stood out, especially for the interweaving of categories of class, gender, and race in the rhetoric of animus. For Barrow:

> The women of the African peasantry pass a life of the most listless activity. The mistress of the family, with her coffee-pot constantly boiling before her on a small table, seems fixed to her chair like a piece of furniture. This good lady, born in the wilds of Africa, and educated among slaves and Hottentots, has little idea of what, in a state of society, constitutes female delicacy. She makes no scruple of having her legs and feet washed in warm water by a slave before strangers; an operation that is regularly performed every evening. If the motive for such a custom were that of cleanliness, the practice of it would deserve praise; but to see the tub with the same water passed round through all the branches of the family, according to seniority, is apt to create a very different nature. Most of them go constantly without stockings and shoes, even when the thermometer is down to freezing point. They generally make use of small stoves to place the feet on. The young girls sit with their hands before them as listless as their mothers. Most of them, in the distant districts, can neither read nor write, so that they have no mental resources whatsoever. Luckily, perhaps for them, the paucity of their ideas prevents time from hanging heavy on their hands. The history of a day is that of their whole lives.[43]

Given that Barrow had married a Boer woman, with whom he lived in apparently happy union at the Cape as well as in England, and taking into account as well the earlier dismissive remarks about San and Khoi women, but the (precisely qualified) neutrality about Xhosa women, it is pertinent to register the extent to which racial and colonial discourse at the Cape is gendered discourse, and to note that one of the chief features for future analysis might be how that discourse located in the representation of female, rural, peasant characteristics paradoxically reveal uncertainty about self in the English, metropolitan, male.

While one of Barrow's constellation of tasks was to persuade the leaders of the Xhosa not to cross the border imposed upon them by the colonial government,[44] the administration, under Governor Cradock, at the same time, proceeded to clear the area known as the Zuurveld by sweeping out the Xhosa and replacing them with Europeans.[45] One of the military officers whose record of the early period of occu- pation is highly revelatory of the real relations on the frontier is Robert Percival. Not only from the content of the title-page ('With a view of the political and commercial advantages which might be derived from its possession by Great Britain'), but also from the outset of the tale, Percival can state that he was

> enabled to observe, with patriotic pride, the improvements which took place in the civil and military establishments; and the economy and useful regulations introduced as soon as it came into the possession of the British nation, which never fails to carry civilization, opulence, and industry, into every quarter of the globe which is reached by her arms or her commerce.[46]

One important detail to register here was the arrival of a large number of British citizens on the Eastern Frontier, in 1803; that is, some seventeen years before the much-celebrated moment of 1820. A double line of block-houses, garrisoned by troops (British, as well as Khoi) was anathema, not only to the Xhosa, but especially to the Boer frontiers- men, whose resistance to British occupation culminated in the Slagtersnek Rebellion of 1815, one consequence of which was that five Boers were hanged in public by the colonial administration under distressingly bungled conditions.

For Percival, 'the white society at the Cape requires to be described as a people differing extremely from the natives of any part of Europe', for reasons which include their inhumanity towards their cattle, their enslavement of the Khoi, their indolence and their ignorance. In this catalogue, the influence – indeed, the unacknowledged lifting – from Barrow's text is often quite obvious. Not only are Boer males described as 'clumsy, stout made, morose, illiterate, and truly ignorant; few have any ideas what ever of education', but 'Little of female delicacy can be expected ' of Boer women. 'No amusement varies the scene with them, but one day is like all the rest of the year'.[47]

As with Barrow, so for Percival: the reasons for this state of affairs is located in the Locke dictum, cited earlier. In Percival's estimation, neither the original inhabitants, nor the Boer settlers, are appropriate custodians of this romantic and fertile African space: 'A person, indeed, on observing the innumerable local advantages which the colony possesses, and the infinite means of becoming opulent and comfortable, which nature holds out to the inhabitants, cannot but express a degree of regret that so fruitful a portion of the globe should be assigned to those who are so little capable of estimating its value'.[48]

As was the case with Barrow, Percival's qualified support of the Khoi had more to do with what British intervention had made possible than any qualities these people may have had in themselves. Thus, while he repeats a by that time well-known tale to British readers concerning the Khoi that 'Some of them have their testicles cut out, whilst they are young, to increase their speed; and all have a method of pushing them up into the abdomen, where from habit they remain, and exhibit the same appearance as if they were wholly deprived of them', he was even more keen to celebrate Khoi skill as an army corps commanded by a British officer: they were 'dressed in red jackets, canvas waistcoats and trousers, leathern caps and shoes; and armed with muskets and bayonets... and were excellent marksmen'.[49]

From that story, Percival has no doubt that 'should ever the Cape fall permanently into the hands of Great Britain' the Khoi, 'with proper management, may speedily arrive at a great degree of civilization', which course of action he commends to his readers, suggesting that, to begin with, by granting the Khoi '... those rights which ought to be common to the whole human race, although barbarously withheld from them by the Dutch'. His conclusion is that, 'Averse as we are, by our education and habits, to slavery, perhaps more so than any other people upon the earth, it should be totally and immediately abolished by us in this colony, if it ever came into our possession.'

Interestingly, however, it should be noted that on the next page he asserts that while 'many arguments might be adduced to show the necesssity for employing slaves' in the East and West Indies, at the Cape that system might be dispensed with.[50]

At the simplest level, the contradictions in Percival's text might be explained as an example of public liberal discourse generated against the 'uncivilized' Boers at the Cape, while at the same time (at best) remaining silent about slavery by 'civilizing' British in the Caribbean.

But that is to speculate: Percival's text offers no explanation for the distinction he makes, and therefore for the ordering of racial hierarchies – not now between the inhabitants of the Cape, but between blacks at the Cape and in the West Indies. Both Barrow and Percival's texts (as well as those by others)[51] reveal that in these early years of British rule, there is as yet no clear-cut decision about which of the various groups of inhabitants will be chosen to assist as junior partners in the management of colonial relations. It was not simply a problem at the Cape; C.A. Bayly has argued that it was world-wide crisis that manifested itself in quite specific ways in different parts of what he calls the 'imperial meridian in the years between 1790 and 1820'.[52]

The moment of major break in the discursive construction of the Cape dates from the moment of the implantation of a large body of British settlers on the eastern frontier in 1820, and the simultaneous further expropriation and dispossession of the Xhosa. It is at this moment, and on this terrain, that the equation fertile land/romantic spaces/savage peoples undergoes rapid transformation: the emphasis, from now on, is to seek to justify the active disciplining process by which not only physical space, but especially peoples, are shaped into conformity in the aftermath of British victory in the shared colonial space.

The travel writer who most vividly presents this story – indeed, is an active participant in the disciplining processes he describes – is the Scot, James Edward Alexander (1803–85). Prior to his arrival at the Cape, Alexander had already made his career in the colonial wars as a soldier in Burma (1824) and in the Russo-Turkish War of 1829 in the Balkans. His participation in the eastern Cape for part of the Sixth War of Dispossession (1834–5), during which period he was aide-de-camp to the governor, was followed by further service in the Crimea (1855) and against the Maori (1860); he also played an important role in the 1877 transfer of Cleopatra's Needle to Britain. For our purposes it is his writings about his journey to Namaqualand, under the joint auspices of the government and the Royal Geographical Society, and of his campaigns in 'Kaffir-land', that are of interest.[53]

Unlike Barrow and Percival, whose texts are produced, in part, in support of British possession, Alexander writes in the knowledge that the government he serves has established hegemony over all the inhabitants in what is an emergent common society. Alexander's text is, therefore, from the outset, much more confident than those of his predecessors, not only about the national but also about the personal project. For him, the sojourn at the Cape is liberation from the constraints of home:

> I now felt all 'the glorious liberty of the bush and of the road.'
> I could dress as I liked, could rise and lie down when it suited my pleasure, went fast or slow, sang aloud or kept silent, ate my food with an appetite of the keenest Savigny edge, and was gratified with the appearance of picturesque hills and verdant plains.[54]

That the freedom he celebrates is acquired in the context of policing and disciplining others is not mentioned, except with reference for the need to be eternally vigilant, for the need for self-control:

> Among barbarians a stranger ought to have the greatest command over himself, and be under strict self control, or there is a chance that we will not travel far, or long sojourn in safety among them. If his moral principle is not strong enough to control him, and to cause him to refrain from committing a great sin, then common prudence ought to dictate to him not to covet what is his neighbour's, when he places himself in that neighbour's power. Savages have affections and feelings like other men.[55]

Kipling will, of course, restate those sentiments much more succinctly later on in *Beyond the Pale*, where the opening injunction is that 'A man should, whatever happens, keep to his own caste, race, and breed. Let the White go to the White and the Black to the Black. Then, whatever trouble falls is in the ordinary course of things – neither sudden, alien, nor unexpected.' What is significant about Alexander's narrative is how the stiff-upper-lip masculinity at one and the same time is fearful of the unmentionable threat yet manages to deflect that fear by describing an act of dispossession as an act of 'sojourn' amongst those so dispossessed. Even though they have 'affections' and 'feelings', the reason for imperial intervention is to save the dispossessed from their characteristic shortcomings.

A typical instance is one in which Alexander situates Boer indolence and English 'victory', not now in some ideal English landscape, but (for the first time) in the (albeit still idealized) landscape of the Cape: the Englishman, Kennedy, he tells his readers, with the help of a single hired black man, had constructed a dam in two days. While that work was going on, two of the Englishman's '. . . Dutch connections stood about with their hands in their pockets, and never offered to take their jackets off to assist him'.[56]

Alexander is especially keen to drive home the point that, whereas the Englishman had *hired* his black worker, it was the '. . . taint of slavery' that accounted for Boer indolence. What is important to observe here is not simply that Alexander echoes and reinforces the sentiments encountered earlier in Barrow, as well as in Percival, but for the conclusion which he draws for his readers: the qualification, 'Had we been born and brought up among the boors, we would doubtless have thought and acted as they do', is immediately submerged by the somewhat ambivalent patriotic recognition that 'thank Heaven! slavery is now at an end in the British dominions; though, as far as regards the Cape, emancipation may not have been so judiciously carried into effect as it might have been, and with justice to the slave owners'.[57]

If one aspect of Alexander's tale is sympathy for the view that Boer slave-owners were victims of rough economic justice on the part of the British state, his views on the San and the Khoi reveal a return to constructions of alterity first encountered in the tales told by voyagers, of these peoples as unutterably other. What is noteworthy about the representation, in Alexander, however, is the frequency with which there is a comparison of the inhabitants of the Cape with 'domestic foreigners' (Scots, Irish, Welsh). One particularly arresting example is the concluding observation of his description of the hunting technique of the San:

with his small weapon bent, and holding the slight arrow in the middle between the first and middle fingers of his left hand, and

214

the notched end fitting on the string between the thumb and closed fore finger, *and this in different manner from that of our Queen's Body Guard, the Royal Archers of Scotland, and other British toxopholites*' [my emphasis].[58]

Alexander's interest in Khoi women is shaped by the impact upon British and French sensibilities of the exhibition between 1810 and 1814, in London and Paris, in the most degrading circumstances, of Saartje Baartman, a woman who reputedly possessed a particularly large posterior. Named 'the Hottentot Venus' (though she may have been San, rather than Khoi), she was made the butt of popular Regency ballads in England, and after her death the object of dissection and experimentation by Cuvier. It is the popular memory of that woman and events around her that was the context for Alexander's observation, that:

> Talking to a Hottentot woman reminds me that there is in this district a rival to the Hottentot Venus, if she does not excel her in the quantity of 'cebaceous deposit'. Rewarded by a trifle of money or tobacco, she will goodnaturedly allow a cloth to be spread behind, and on which four plates will be laid, thus forming a peripatetic table![59]

If 'goodnaturedly' is a revealing choice of word that tells much about the attitude of the traveller to the Khoi, no such linguistic qualifications mark the text when it comes to Boer males and the way in which (as previously emphasized by Barrow) these have fallen from the ways of European social habits:

> It is not to be wondered at that the Dutch are occasionally annoyed with bowel complaints, from the gross manner in which they swallow grease of all kinds, pouring spoonsful of melted sheep's tail fat over their food, and heaping butter in lumps over their bread. A supply of butter I had bought at a farm house to last us for a week, disappeared in one sitting, before two young boors invited to partake an evening meal.[60]

The apposite choice of 'partake', with its sense of sharing, in the context of the description of the meal, draws attention to British perceptions of awareness of Boer deficiencies, as well as of British objectives. Recall that the place to which Alexander is sent to assist with the act of dispossession of the original inhabitants is that place referred to by the British as 'Kaffirland'. That region, soon to be the site for implantation of British settlers, Alexander describes as being 'highly favoured by Nature. The air is so pure, the sky generally so serene and the whole face of the country so park-like and inviting, that it realises all that we have read of Arcadia'.[61]

So why intervene in Arcadia? Because Arcadia should have an English stamp. As justification, Alexander cites the transformation of the village of Wynberg, near Cape Town, which is

> a paradise, and ought to reconcile even English people – most difficult to reconcile – to perpetual absence from home. Among its shady avenues of oak and pine, the fruits and flowers in the gardens, the abundant vegetables, the sublime mountain rising behind with its varying canopies of clouds, the running streams, and the air ever fresh and light, I felt that I could live with exceeding pleasure in company with some suitable Eve, and that I should die here with great regret.[62]

Leaving aside what the traveller might mean by 'some suitable Eve', as well as the manner in which 'British', at key moments, becomes 'English' (a feature that characterizes all the texts), what is excised from this account is that the development of Wynberg was not only designed as some part of the Cape that is forever Home Counties, but even more importantly, that it was built by skilled slave labour brought from the East Indies. In other words, in the same ways that 'improvement of the estate' in England was dependent upon the combination of class exploitation at home and slavery in the Caribbean, so 'improvement' at the Cape was dependent upon the combination of dispossession of the indigenous peoples and the dependence upon East Indian slaves.

ET IN ARCADIA? SHAPING THE CONTOURS OF HEGEMONY

While Alexander's texts record the moment of the consolidation of British hegemony, they are remarkably silent on the processes by which that was accomplished, both at home and abroad. At the Cape, one of the first acts of the Irish-born Governor, the Earl of Caledon, was to seek to implement a recommendation by one of his officers, in 1809, that the Xhosa be expelled from the Zuurveld (lit. sour field – pasture of indifferent quality) and that it be settled with immigrants from Britain. In the next few years, under the administrations of Caledon, Cradock, and the ill-fated patrician Lord Charles Somerset, some 20,000 Xhosa were driven across the Fish River by British soldiers assisted by Boer militia. In parallel with this act of 'ethnic cleansing' of the Xhosa, by the infamous Hottentot Proclamation of 1 November 1809, the Khoi within the colonial territory became subject to colonial law. By the further requirement that all Khoi have a fixed abode, and carry a pass, the administration ensured that white settlers – Boer, as well as British – had a regular supply of cheap labour. The eminent scholar, Monica Wilson, records that Khoi were not only cooks and herders, labourers, wagon-drivers, and interpreters; they also hunted for their masters, and were sent as soldiers on commando against the San and Xhosa. By 1808, Professor Wilson writes, nearly a hundred men out of a population of about eight hundred from the mission station at Genadendal (Vale of Grace) were serving as recruits in the Cape Regiment. Not only did they sometimes outnumber whites on commando against the Xhosa, they were also part of the contingent sent to protect the Scots settlers on the frontier against the Xhosa.[63]

If economic and military needs on the eastern frontier required that the Khoi be not set free, the situation in Britain at the end of the wars with France was a place from which many sought to emigrate, especially to North America, to escape the consequences of the topping-out of the great arch. While the government encouraged emigration as a means to mitigate social and economic unrest, it preferred the settlers be dispersed in other spaces governed by the Union flag. The eastern Cape, where the size of the garrison had been reduced from 4,000 to 2,400 in the interests of reducing the military budget, and where Boers were leaving because of Xhosa resistance and objections to British policy, was believed to be an ideal place for settlement and a comparatively dense implantation of British settlers was seen as being next best to a garrison.[64] In other words, the arrival of the 1820 settlers had as much to do with economic and social unrest at home as it had with the need to defend a frontier which the Xhosa simply refused to recognize.

The debate on emigration had both general and specific aspects: general, in that the period under discussion is marked by the publication of many texts debating Britain's rôle as an imperial power; specific, in that the Cape is invariably one of the spaces adduced as evidence for the theories expounded. What should be emphasized about many of the texts in this category is that they are written by people who had no direct personal knowledge of the place and/or its peoples.[65]

My argument here is not that absence of direct knowledge is a disqualification; rather, it is to signal the heavy reliance, on the part of the authors of these texts, upon the texts of their predecessors – most notably Barrow: his originals, as well as the various re-writings. One consequence is that, by the time the British arrived in the eastern Cape, they brought with them an extensive array of carefully orchestrated views of Boers and blacks.[66]

One of the most influential views is that by George Thompson, a traveller who, in 1827, could boast that he was neither missionary, nor scientist, but that 'out of motives of business' could observe, twenty years after Barrow's texts that 'the boundaries of the settlement have been greatly extended, the circumstances of the old inhabitants, both white and coloured, have been much altered'. Also, almost for the first time, there begins a serious and sustained defence of the Boer as the junior partner in the imperial enterprise. What is noteworthy is that it is a defence specifically against the representations by Barrow. For Thompson, while the earlier traveller's facts may have been 'correct', the delineation of the Boer was, nevertheless, an unfair representation of the predecessor settlers. Where Barrow was especially remiss, according to Thompson, was in not recognizing the redeeming features of the Boers and in not taking into account sufficiently the hostility between Boer victors and black vanquished.[67]

One reason why the pro-Boer case was still to be argued is that, in the first three decades of British settlement, one dominant strain of the travel tale continued to be about the effects of slavery and dispossession. Thus, for Cowper Rose, slavery at the Cape had some advantages over class exploitation in Britain: the careful attention to gradation based upon national and spatial difference in the assertion that the slave '. . . never knows the extreme of want felt frequently by the labouring classes of Ireland, and sometimes by that of England . . .' leads Rose to the conclusion that the slave is, ultimately, better off because in old age, 'he [sic] is supported by the family with whom he has lived from childhood, compared with the system operating in Britain, where old age leads either to beggary, or the workhouse'.

With reference to the dispossession of the Xhosa, Rose does not find it 'strange that the savages should be unable to see the justice of all this; that they should be troublesome neighbours to the settlers in a country of which they had been dispossessed'. Indeed, the only serious dissent he records with policy at the Cape is that it 'turns the English soldier into the cold-blooded butcher of the unresisting native'. Finally, for Rose, the consequence of British relations with the Xhosa is that 'if we find them trusting, we leave them treacherous; if we find them temperate, we leave them drunkards; and in after-years, a plea for their destruction is founded on the very vices they have learnt from us'.[68]

This theme of the effects of Prospero's relations on the eastern Cape frontier was echoed by the the likes of Henry Methuen and Stephen Kay.[69] Especially noticeable is the tortured discourse seeking to account for the real relations between settlers and indigenous peoples, whilst exculpating the British: 'though no immediate act of injustice on the part of the settlers can be alleged as the cause, the white man has been the aggressor'.

By the 1840s, marked by events such as continuing wars of resistance by the Xhosa, the freeing of the slaves and the subsequent trek out of the colony on the part of the Boers, in order to be free to enslave the blacks in those spaces outside the writ of British law, the nature of the discourse had changed again. British settler discourse against the colonial government and of the policy of the missionaries, hitherto a relatively minor aspect, now becomes massive. The theme is simple: it is government and missionaries who are seen as the cause of black unrest. Two influential texts are those by John George Nicholson and John Centlivres Chase.

Nicholson's text is marked especially by the animus displayed against the missionaries. Right at the outset, whilst assuring his readers that he 'advanced no speculative opinions under the guise of facts', and that his intention is to 'portray the real truth', he speedily proceeds to echo faithfully, and uncritically, the common settler sentiment about 'the injury so often inflicted upon the white population by the establishment of ... [mission] stations in the neighbourhood', where, 'no sooner is a Hottentot, or other coloured servant, discontented or hopelessly lazy, then off he flies to the nearest station'. Such palpable lack of generosity towards their employers on the part of the servant classes leads Nicholson to the conclusion that he infinitely prefers the 'unsophisticated nature, of any of the various races in the colony, to the converted heathens'.

It is Nicholson who expresses yet another popularly-held sentiment on the part of the settlers: the 'hasty, fanatical, and oppressive manner in which emancipation of the slaves was conducted in the colony ... converting ... previously loyal subjects [the Boers] into bitter enemies'. For that action he blames the 'sleek humanity-mongers' and a 'well-meaning John Bull'.[70]

Chase, who had come to the eastern Cape as a member of Bailie's party of settlers, had set up as a merchant and farmer. When those ventures failed, he worked in various capacities in the civilian administration, later becoming involved in local settler politics, one key plank of which was the demand for an administration free of the control of the remote metropolis of Cape Town. Chase was particularly influential because many of his texts were first printed, and sold, in South Africa, one aspect of the agitation being the demand, on the part of the settlers, for freedom of the press against a colonial administration that sought to curb settler protest against a 'despotic' administration.

Ultimately, for Chase, '... whatever other reasons may have been the cause [of the disappearance of some of the original inhabitants – to which Barrow had made reference some forty years earlier, and which process of decimation had continued unabated] disease and not oppression, and feuds amongst themselves, not the aggression of the colonists, must chiefly account for their gradual and still progressive extinction'. As for the Boers, 'All their orders relative to the aborigines, whether Hottentot, Bushman, or Kafir, breathe the spirit of kindness and conciliation'. Perhaps most interesting is how Chase quotes with approbation the assertion by Wilberforce that 'Christian nations must be colonizing nations' as the foundation for what he hopes for: that 'as soon as the Boers are firmly seated under the British ... their presence will repress the murderous inroads of the savage tribes upon each other'.[71]

If the dominant strain of British settler discourse in the first two decades after implantation is increasingly anti-black and pro-Boer, few writers did more to advance that than Harriet Ward, one of the few women to be published in the period covered by this chapter.[72] A prolific writer, who not only produced an abridged version of *Clarissa Harlowe*, Ward wrote extensively, in different genres, about her experiences at the eastern Cape, where she had accompanied her husband who had been sent as an officer to the military headquarters at Grahamstown during the period of the seventh (1846–7) of the Xhosa wars of liberation – events which settlers and white historians have tended to refer to, dismissively, as 'Kaffir Wars'.[73]

As with Nicholson, immediately evident is the venom of the utterance against the indigenous peoples. Nowhere in the earliest accounts of travel literature do we find comments to match the following, from the 'Not a Preface, but a few words to the Reader' of Mrs Ward's many-times-reprinted adventure novel for British boys: 'The late accounts from the Cape of Good Hope show that these Savages [the Xhosa] have been reduced to a pitiable condition through their own folly and superstition; and that the colonists, forgetting all old grievances, have come forward nobly to their assistance'.

Furthermore, addressing arguably Nicholson's 'sleek humanity-mongers', Mrs Ward's discourse, more than most, reveals not only how speedily and hermetically the racial and national issues had been resolved in the three decades since British settlement; it also locates, and targets, the enemy within:

> Ye philanthropists – fallacious reasoners on subjects of which ye know nothing certain who romanticise about savages and slavery till ye be entangled in a web of metaphysics of your own weaving, from which ye have neither the power nor the courage to extricate yourselves – who would leave the savage in undisturbed posses-sion of a vast tract of country as much in need of population as England is of the reverse; who would take the yoke from the slave's neck. . .[74]

As to revolting blacks, Harriet Ward's suggested solution again is in line with popular sentiment, as well as instances of practice: 'hanging one chief, (shooting him in a kloof, like Hintza, would not go half as far) and there will be a sudden stop to cattle-stealing'[75] is a reference to one of the most traumatic events in the history of frontier relations – the murder, and subsequent mutilation, of the dead body of the Xhosa paramount chief Hintza (c. 1790–1853) by British soldiers.[76]

Mrs Ward's overall prescriptions deserve quotation, in full, as index of the trajectory travelled in the half-century of debate about the management of colonial relations:

Establish a Vagrant Act, and carry it into execution. Have a treadmill in Graham's Town; nothing will so effectively punish the indolent coloured population in the Colony. . . . Make the Keiskamma [river] the boundary between Kaffirland and the Colony. Enforce an edict forbidding any kaffir, armed or unarmed, from crossing it, at least without proper authority from the colonial government, send the first who disobeys the law to the treadmill; the second to hard labour in Robben Island. Even more summary measures than these may be found necessary for the preservation of many British lives.[77]

With the sole exception of the treadmill, every one of these recommendations was eventually put into operation by the colonial government.

Finally, in order to show the continuing force of the travel tale as ideological instrument, and indeed to show how deeply the texts of the likes of Barrow and others concerning romantic spaces, fertile land, savage peoples had become embedded as colonial commonsense, in a very short space of time, the remarks by Harriet Ashmore, who had stopped briefly at the Cape whilst travelling to and and from India, are perhaps instructive:

We saw a few Hottentots – miserable looking creatures, who were crouching near their still more wretched looking huts: their faces bore the stamp of idiotism; and these savage inhabitants of the southern extremity of Africa resembled in countenance and grimace the lowest order of the baboon race: degraded in moral and physical inclinations to a level with the brute creation, the unfortunate wretches who crossed our path were to be seen almost devoid of clothing and mumbling and grinning in pitiable imbecility. . . . The most delicious fruits were daily brought or sent on board, as grapes, figs, etc. were just in perfection; but great complaints were made that all kinds of ship's stores, meat, vegetables, and eggs, were intolerably dear; the farmers in the interior were withholding their supplies; and Dingan [Dingane: 1795–1840, Zulu king] and his followers were keeping Southern Africa in a state of disquietude.[78]

CONCLUSION

One outstanding feature is that in the tales they tell the travellers are remarkably reticent about their selves. With the exception of missionaries, who from time to time reiterate belief in their faith, we know virtually nothing about these travellers, except in their public roles. About their lives when not engaged in their assigned activities, the tales are virtually mute. While such reticence about the self might be expected about these travellers, it marks an interesting shift: one feature of the

221

texts by English Renaissance travellers was the manner in which their texts contributed to the fashioning and re-fashioning of their selves.[79] Furthermore, in contrast to British male self-reticence, one of the features that marks out the tales is the confidence with which the travellers can assert their 'right' to be invasive of the lives – and very often the physical bodies – of those others they encounter; chiefly those of black women, whom they submit to their 'scientific' scrutiny.

A second feature is that the majority of the male travellers who visit the Cape come from within the ranks of a British society that is being radically transformed by the erection of the great arch. John Barrow's transit from son of a Lancashire journeyman-tanner to presidency of the Royal Geographical Society is exceptional only in the extent of the trajectory. While other travellers and settlers may not have risen to the same level of prestige at the Cape, they nevertheless soon occupy positions of dominance by virtue of their role as agents of the metropolitan ruling class. Thus, whatever differences there might have existed between civilian and military, between missionary and scientist, between artist and hunter, they all share in an unshakeable belief in the rightness of British imperial objectives.

Arguably, the most obvious proof here is that of the transformation in ethnicity: origins as Scots, Welsh, Irish, or English, transform and become subsumed under the overarching category of British (except in instances of especial prestige, in which case it is, once again, English!).

It is a transformation that takes place in apparent denial of the otherwise pervasive emphasis on class. Recall that the term '1820 Settlers' has obscured the reality that the participants were not only constituted out of parties with different class and regional backgrounds, but that some were quite explicitly constituted on the basis of ethnicity: Synnot's party of mostly labourers, from Armagh; Thomas Butler's, from Wicklow; William Russell's party, of Scottish artisans and tradespeople.[80]

The arguments in connection with class and ethnicity are important because of the ideological affinities in the construction of the notion of 'Great Britain' and that of 'South Africa', the term that, increasingly, becomes used. In both instances, as well as in both spaces, the real relations of 'internal colonialism' are obscured: 'South Africa is at once motherland and colony. No seas separate the governed from the governors, and the latter are unable to contemplate the former with detachment... The European South African is in daily contact with his colonial African subjects'.[81]

One central conclusion that might, therefore, be drawn from the reading of these tales about the Cape is not only the well-known one that there are different models of colonialism that are geographically, spatially and historically specific, but that each of these has a distinctive discursive strategy. To argue along these lines is to register (but not enter into) a dialogue of dissent with the influential work of recent critics.

Mary Louise Pratt,[82] for instance, concludes that the encounters in what she calls the 'contact zone' – why the sanitizing euphemism for what was, in reality, the 'dispossession zone'? – centres landscape, separates people from place, and effaces the speaking self. What I have tried to show is that at the core of the discourse of the Cape there is a constant emphasis upon the materiality of property relations; that setting up differences between physical landscape and indigenous peoples is the dominant mode for the justification of the imperial project. Furthermore, as I hope to have shown, Pratt's claim that 'the goal of expanding the capitalist world-system is, as a rule acknowledged in prefaces, but only there', is too conservative a reading: from the moment of first occupation, but especially in the tales centred around the 1820 settlers, one of the features that characterizes these texts is the extent to which they rehearse the arguments in support of British hegemony as the preferred agency for capitalist expansion.

If my rather perfunctory dismissal of 'contact zone' – Pratt's 'attempt to invoke the spatial and historical copresence of subjects previously separated by geographical and historical disjunctures, and whose trajectories now intersect' (as if by accident) – is well taken, it is potentially so for her other main categories as well. From my citations, it is clear that the notion of 'anti-conquest', used to describe how 'European bourgeois subjects seek to secure their innocence in the same moment as they assert European hegemony' will not do: at the Cape they proudly proclaim, not innocence, but active engagement. What follows is that the discourse of the Cape in this half-century would appear to deny her two other categories as well: there is evidence, neither of 'autoethnography' by which colonized subjects apparently 'undertake to present themselves in ways that *engage with* [her emphasis] the colonizer's own terms', which process 'involves partial collaboration with and appropriation of the idioms of the conqueror', nor of 'transculturation', that particular phenomenon of the 'contact zone', whereby 'subjugated peoples' which, not readily capable of being able to 'control what emanates from the dominant culture...do determine to various extents what they absorb into their own, and what they use it for'.

What I have, furthermore, endeavoured to show is that, by praising the land and by dispraising the peoples, the travellers construct a discourse of dispossession that is identifiably attachable to the theories and policies of one European nation, and a particular class. A test of that hypothesis might be to look at German travel literature in what is now Namibia at a later period, as John Noyes has recenly done, to brilliant effect.[83] His enormously elegant readings on spatiality reinforce and contribute to recent influential interrogations of the topic, especially on the part of Michel Foucault, whose contentions overturn the conception of space as fixed, as well as of Edward Said's valuable analysis of the purposeful construction of geographies in imperialist texts.[84]

That eminent historian, V.G. Kiernan, had earlier argued that the situation in the colony was one of race, rather than class. Part of the reason is that Kiernan continues the long line of British radical historians who cannot divest himself of a residual belief in the 'civilizing mission' of the British empire. For Kiernan, it is the British settlers who are to blame, because, 'Any enlightenment they received from abolition of slavery ... they failed to pass on to the Boers', because 'whatever successes it may have had with native races, Britain made a poor job of the two European stocks it became responsible for, Boers and French Canadian'. Not only is there a great temptation to ask which 'successes' the historian had in mind, but to enquire why conquest and dispossession is transformed into 'became responsible for'. Tellingly – and oddly – there is the surprising unwillingness on the part of a Marxist historian, to recognize that, in South Africa, class and gender relations manifest themselves as race relations.

Finally, Kiernan repeats the double canard that 'The southern tip of the continent held a medley of the *most primitive races*' [my emphasis] and that these '... had been pushed down into it...', thus giving credence to the popular justification by European settlers that the Cape was uninhabited space into which, by sheer chance, competing groups penetrated.[85]

Since this chapter has been written in response to that most influential of Victorian imperial historians Sir John Seeley, it is important to draw attention to the attractiveness of the theory of imperial enterprise he had advanced. When emigrants leave the (presumably natal) state, he argued, they should not be regarded as going out of it, but as carrying it with them: 'where Englishmen are there is England, where Frenchmen are there is France', from which he posits the general theory that 'the organization of the modern state admits of unbounded territorial extension'. For Seeley, what happened at the Cape (as well as in other spaces), was that Britain simply had 'occupied parts of the globe which were empty', that these empty spaces had offered not only unbounded scope for emigrants, but that 'the natives were not in a condition sufficiently advanced to withstand *even the peaceful competition* [my emphasis], much less the power of the immigrants', and that what distinguished the British empire from predecessor empires was that it was not 'in the main, founded on conquest, and because in the main the inhabitants of the distant provinces are of the same nation as those of the dominant country'.

While Seeley admits that, in the case of the Cape there is the 'double difficulty' of the Dutch, followed by the English (his term), the story he proceeds to tell wholly suppresses recognition of the existence of the other: the only 'inhabitants' are the settlers from the dominant countries.[86]

The fit between the philosophy of history that Sir John Seeley advocates, and the tales told by the travellers about the first fifty years of British rule at the southern tip of the African continent could not be more symmetrical.

NOTES

1 See *i.a.* William Freund, 'The Cape under the transitional governments' in Richard Elphick and Hermann Giliomee, (eds), *The Shaping of South African Society 1652–1820*, Longman, Paarden Island, 1979; Monica Wilson and Leonard Thompson, *A History of South Africa to 1870*, Croom Helm, London and Canberra, 1982, esp. chs v–vii.; T.R.H. Davenport, *South Africa, A Modern History,* Macmillan, Basingstoke, 4th edn, 1991, esp. ch.2.

2 See Michael Streak, *The Afrikaner as Viewed by the English 1795–1854*, Struik, Cape Town, 1974.

3 Philip Corrigan and Derek Sayer, *The Great Arch. English State Formation as Cultural Revolution*, Oxford University Press, Oxford, OUP, p.119.

4 Two instances: during the first British occupation, between 1799 and 1802 the frontier Khoi and the Xhosa joined together in rebellion against British rule; more famously, in England the hanging and banishment of Boer rebels by the patrician Lord Charles Somerset following the events of the Slagtersnek 'rebellion' of 1815 was, in later years, placed on a par with events such as Boston and Peterloo.

5 Gerald Newman, *The Rise of English Nationalism. A Cultural History 1740–1830*, Weidenfeld and Nicolson, London, 1987, pp.111–12.

6 C.A. Bayly, *Imperial Meridian: The British Empire and the World 1780–1830*, Longman, London and New York, 1989, p.162.

7 Michael McKeon, *The Origins of the English Novel 1600–1740*, Johns Hopkins Press, Baltimore and London, 1987, esp. pp.100ff; pp.159–66.

8 Philip Curtin, *The Image of Africa. British Ideas and Action 1780–1850*, University of Wisconsin Press, Madison, Wisconsin, 1964, p.41.

9 'Telling tales. Early modern English travellers and the Khoikhoi at the Cape of Good Hope', *The Seventeenth Century*, vol. 10, no. 1 (Autumn) 1995, pp.121–49.

10 'Of Property', chap. v; sect. 35 in *Two Treatises of Government. In the former, the false principles and foundations of Sir Robert Filmer and his followers are detected and overthrown. The latter is an essay concerning the true origins, extent, and end of civil government*, 6th edn, London, 1764; see also editions by Peter Laslett (Cambridge University Press, Cambridge, 1988) and Mark Goldie (Everyman, London, 1994).

11 'Of National Characters', in *Essays and Treatises on Several Subjects. In two volumes. By David Hume, Esq.* vol. 1. *Containing essays moral, political and literary*, London, A. Millar; Edinburgh, A. Kincaid & A. Donaldson, 1767, pp.223–41. See also K. Haakonssen (ed.), *Hume: Political Essays*, Cambridge University Press, Cambridge, 1994, pp.78–92.

12 Responding to a challenge to his *Essay Concerning Human Understanding* (1690) on the part of Edward Stillingfleet, Bishop of Worcester (1697), Locke cited the 'evidence' of two English voyagers: Sir Thomas Roe, *Journal of a*

Voyage to the East Indies (1644), and John Ovington, *A Journey to Suratt, in the Year 1689*, 1696.

13 Peter Hulme, *Colonial Encounters: Europe and the Native Caribbean 1492–1797*, Methuen, London, 1986, p.2.

14 Michel Foucault, *The Archaeology of Knowledge and the Discourse on Language*, trans. by A.M. Sheridan Smith, Pantheon, New York, 1972, esp. introduction, part II, ch.2, part IV, ch.3, ch.6.

15 See *i.a.* Peter Hulme and Ludmilla Jordanova (eds), *The Enlightenment and its Shadows*, Routledge, London, 1990.

16 Charles C. Lloyd, *Mr. Barrow of the Admiralty. A Life of Sir John Barrow, 1764–1848*, Collins, London, 1970.

17 John Barrow, *An Account of Travels in the Interior of Southern Africa, in the Years 1797 and 1798. Including cursory observations on the geology and geography of the southern part of the continent; the natural history of such objects as occurred in the animal, vegetable, and mineral kingdoms, and sketches of the physical and moral characters of the various tribes of inhabitants surrounding the settlement of the Cape of Good Hope. To which is annexed a description of the present state, population, and produce of that extensive colony: with a map constructed entirely from actual observations made in the course of the travels*. T. Cadell and W. Davies, London, 1801; vol.2, 1804.

18 See, for example, *Travels in the interior of Africa, by Mungo Park, and in South Africa, by John Barrow. Interspersed with notes and observations, geographical, commercial and philosophical*. By the Author of the New System of Georgaphy, A. Napier, Glasgow, 1812. In 1822, an identical edition to the above (although it is called a 'shortened version') is published in Glasgow by Khull, Blackie & Co.

The 'author' of the 'New System of Geography' (assisted by Edward Warren Blake and Alexander Cook) was the Revd Thomas Bankes, vicar of Dixton in Monmouthshire. Selective quotation from the comprehensive title-page will reveal not only the extensive reliance upon the tales the travellers told, but the official nature of the whole enterprise: *'A New Royal Authentic and Complete System of Universal Geography Antient and Modern. Including all the important discoveries made by the English, and other celebrated navigators of various nations, in the different hemispheres; and containing a complete genuine history and description of empires, kingdoms, states, republics, provinces, continents, islands, oceans, etc. with the various countries, cities, towns, promontories, capes, bays, peninsulas, isthmusses, gulphs, rivers, harbours, lakes, aqueducts, mountains, volcanoes, caverns, deserts, etc., etc. througout Europe, Asia, Africa and America . . . with an account of the religion, laws, customs, manners, genius, tempers, habits, amusements, and singular ceremonies of the respective inhabitants . . . including every thing curious as related by the most eminent travellers and navigators, from the earliest accounts to the present time. Likewise the essence of the voyages of the most enterprising navigators of different nations and countries . . .* Published by the Royal licence and authority of His Britannic Majesty King George III. . . London: printed for J. Cooke, No. 17 Paternoster-Row, 1790 (2nd edn 1792).

The text explicatory of the frontispiece shows 'Neptune raising Captain Cook up to immortality, a genius surrounding him, and with a wreath of oak and Fame introducing him to History. In the front ground are the four quarters of the world, presenting to Britannia their various stores'.

19 Hansard, Part XXIV, I July 1934, cols 1601–3.

20 My practice, throughout, shall be as follows: where quoting or citing the

travellers, to use the terminology they employ; where commenting or inter-
preting, to use the word 'settler' for those who came from Europe, and San,
Khoi, Xhosa respectively for 'Bushman', 'Hottentot', 'Cafre' or 'Kaffir'. While
I am aware that there has recently been a controversy about continuing to
retain a San/Khoi dichotomy (see for example Richard Elphick, *Khoikhoi and
the Founding of White South Africa*, Ravan, Johannesburg, 1985, chs 1 and 2)
it is important to retain the distinction between San and Khoi, inaugurated
in travellers' tales, for the purposes of this chapter.

21 Barrow, *An Account*, 1801, p.24. The reference is to Francis Masson, *An Account
of Three Journeys from Cape Town into the Southern Parts of Africa undertaken
for the discovery of new plants, towards the improvement of the royal botanical
gardens at Kew*, London, 1776. Kew was, at that time, the private property of
George III, where Masson was employed as an under-gardener.

22 For Masson, see note 21, supra. Anders Sparrman, *A Voyage to the Cape of
Good Hope, towards the Antarctic polar circle, and round the world, but chiefly into
the country of the Hottentots and Caffres, from the year 1772 to 1776*. Translated
from Swedish. 2 vols, Perth, Morison, Mudie and Lackington, London, 1782;
White, Cash and Byrne, Dublin, 1785; Robinson, London, 1785, 2nd rev. edn
1786; François le Vaillant, *Anecdotes of Travel from the Cape of Good Hope into
the Interior Parts of Africa*. Translated from French, 2 vols, William Lowe,
London, 1790; further versions 1790, 1796; Carl Per Thunberg, *Travels in
Europe, Africa, and Asia, performed between 1770 and 1779*, London 1793, 1795;
also 'An account of the Cape of Good Hope, and some parts of the interior
of Southern Africa (extracted from his travels)', in John Pinkerton, *A General
Collection of the Best and Most Interesting Voyages and Travels in All Parts of the
World*, London, vol.16, 1808; William Patterson, *A Narrative of Four Journeys
into the Country of the Hottentots*, J. Johnson, London, 1789; 2nd edn, corrected,
1790.

23 See for example Donald Moodie, *The Record of a Series of Official Papers Relative
to the Condition and Treatment of the Native Tribes of South Africa*, compiled, translated and edited by Donald Moodie, A.S. Robertson, Cape Town, 1838–(1841);
A photostatic reprint, A.A. Balkema, Amsterdam and Cape Town, 1960.

24 Barrow, *An Account*, pp.234, 239.

25 Ibid., pp.277–8.

26 Ibid., p.239.

27 Ibid., p.251.

28 John Barrell, *The Dark Side of Landscape: The Rural Poor in English Paintings,
1730–1840*, Cambridge University Press, Cambridge, 1980.

29 Barrow, *An Account*, pp.205–6.

30 Ibid., p.202.

31 In the period framed by this chapter, there were Xhosa Wars of Liberation
in the eastern Cape in 1789–93, 1799–1803, 1811–12, 1818–19, 1834–5, 1846–7,
1850–3.

32 Barrow, *An Account*, pp.172–3.

33 Ibid., pp.81, 135–6, 88–9.

34 See for example Neil Worden, *Slavery in Dutch South Africa*, Cambridge
University Press, Cambridge, 1985; R.H. Elphick and H. Giliomee (eds), *The
Shaping of South African Society*, Longman, Paarden Island, South Africa, 2nd
edn, 1989.

35 Barrow, *An Account*, pp.45–6.

36 John Campbell, *Travels in South Africa, Undertaken at the Request of the
Missionary Society*, London, 1815, pp.77–8; reprinted 1822; abridged version
1834.

37 For the 'Hottentot apron' (*sic*), as well as for further analysis of European scientific/aesthetic constructions of Khoi female sexuality, see *i.a.* Paula Weideger, *History's Mistress*, Penguin, Harmondsworth, 1986, especially ch.viii; Sander Gilman, 'Black bodies, white bodies: towards an iconography of female sexuality in late nineteenth-century art, medicine, and literature', *Critical Inquiry* 12, Autumn 1985, pp.204–42; Sander Gilman, *Difference and Pathology. Stereotypes of Sexuality, Race, and Madness*, Cornell, Ithaca NY, and London, 1985, esp. chs 3–6; J. Edward Chamberlain and Sander L. Gilman, *Degeneration: The Dark Side of Progress*, Columbia, New York, 1985; Stephen Jay Gould, 'The Hottentot Venus', *Natural History* 91, 1982, pp.20–7; Bernth Lindfors, 'The Hottentot Venus and other African attractions in nineteenth century England', *Australian Drama Studies* 1, 1983, pp.83–104. See also note 59 for the so-called 'Hottentot Venus'.

38 Barrow, *An Account*, pp.278–9.

39 Ibid., p.159. The 1812 version (see note 18, supra.) adds the following, not present in Barrow, and written in a style intended to give the impression that the information is based in direct observation; it is also a fascinating instance of obliteration of race and colour difference by the foregrounding of reputed gendered affinity: 'The Hottentot females are no less fond of finery than their more civilized sisters in Europe. Their desire of trinkets, indeed such as buttons and beads, was equally advantageous to the Dutch colonists, and pernicious to the independent Hottentot. Many of these gaudy females could never think that they had had a sufficient number of ornaments, while their husbands had any cattle remaining', p.344.

40 Barrow, *An Account*, p.168.

41 See, for instance, *Voyages to the East Indies; by the late John Splinter Stavorinus, Esq., Rear Admiral in the Service of the States General*. Translated from the original Dutch, by Samuel Hull Wilcocke, with notes and additions by the translator, 3 vols, G.G. and J. Robinson, London, 1798, vol.1, pp.565–6; vol.3, pp.438–9; *A Voyage Round the World in the Gorgon Man of War: Captain John Parker. Performed and written by his widow; for the advantages of his numerous family. Dedicated, by permission, to Her Royal Highness the Princess of Wales*, London, 1795, pp.40, 47.

42 For example J.H. Tuckey, *An Account of a Voyage to Establish a Colony at Port Philip in Bass's Strait, on the south coast of New South Wales, in His Majesty's ship Calcutta in the years 1802–3*, Longman, Hurst, Rees and Orme, London, and J.C. Mottley, Porstmouth, 1805, pp.135–6; George Barrington, *An account of a voyage to New South Wales. . .*, M. Jones, London, 1803, pp.96–8; *Travels of Mirza Abu Taleb Khan, in Asia, Africa, and Europe, during the years 1799, 1800, 1801, 1802, and 1803. Written by himself in the Persian language*. Translated by Charles Stewart, Esq., M.A.S., Professor of Oriental Languages in the Hon. East India Company's College, Hertford, Longman, Hurst, Rees and Orme, London, 1810, ch.iv.

One example from the visual arts in which a Boer woman is portrayed in terms closely modelled on Barrow's description was the enormously popular pen, ink and watercolour print by Rowlandson, *circa* 1792, entitled 'A Dutch Academy'.

43 Barrow, *An Account*, p.80. Compare, again, the extended rewriting of the 1812 version, pp. 313–14. That Barrow's description of the Boers was used as part of European imperial rivalry might be deduced by citing one example, that of W. von Meyer, *Reizen in sud-Afrika wahrend der Jahre 1840 und 1841. Beschreibung des jetzigen Zustandes der Colonie des Vorgebirges der Guten-Hoffnung*, Verlag von J.B. Grie, Hamburg, 1843. Meyer writes: 'Est ist wahrlich

night ehrenvoll, ein kleines Voelkche, wie die holland-Afrikaner, an den Drangen zu stellen, wenn man worher wiss, das sie weder die Zeit noch die Mittel haben, sich selbst mit gleichen Waffen zu vertheitigen'. Alternatively stated, Barrow stands accused by the German of not abiding by the vaunted rules of English 'fair play'!

44 To cite but one example of how dispossession of peopled space is elided by foregrounding landscape: 'The following day we passed the Great Fish River, though not without some difficulty, the banks being high and steep, the stream strong, the bottom rocky, and the water deep. Some fine trees of the willow of Babylon, or a variety of that species, skirted the river at this place. The opposite side presented a very beautiful country, well wooded and watered, and plentifully covered with grass, among which grew in great abundance, a species of indigo.../ The first night we encamped in the Kaffir country was near a stream called Kowsha, which falls into the Great Fish river...and the next day we came to a river of very considerable magnitude called the Keiskamma'. What is omitted here is that the Great Fish River was designated as the colonial frontier by 1798, and that in subsequent years that frontier was inexorably extended by the government, first to the Keiskamma, later to the Kei rivers.

45 *Records of the Cape Colony*, compiled by G.M. Theal, vol. vii, pp.101–3, 136.

46 Robert Percival (Captain of Her Majesty's Eighteenth Royal Irish Regiment ...), *An Account of the Cape of Good Hope, containing an historical view of its original settlement by the Dutch, its capture by the British in 1795, and the different policy pursued there by the Dutch and British governments. Also a sketch of its geography, productions, the manners and customs of the inhabitants, etc. With a view to the political and commercial advantages which might be derived from its possession by Great Britain*, London, 1804, p.3.

47 Percival, *An Account*, pp.205–6.

48 Ibid., pp.4, 58, 82, 205–6, 211.

49 Ibid., p.84.

50 Ibid., pp.80, 90, 246–7.

51 See, for example, John Semple, *Walks and Sketches at the Cape of Good Hope* ..., London, 1803 and 1805; and Samuel Daniell, *A Collection of Plates Illustrative of African Scenery and Animals, with descriptive letterpress*, London, 1804.

52 C.A. Bayly, *Imperial Meridian*, chs 3–6.

53 Sir James Edward Alexander, *An Expedition of Discovery into the Interior of Africa... performed under the auspices of Her Majesty's Government and the Royal Geographical Society*, 2 vols, Henry Colburn, London, 1838; Sir James Edward Alexander, *Narrative of a Voyage of Observation Among the Colonies of Western Africa, in the flagship Thalia, and a campaign in Kaffir-land, on the staff of the Commander-in-Chief, in 1835*, 2 vols, Henry Colburn, London, 1837.

54 Alexander, *An Expedition*, pp.47–8.

55 Ibid., p.81.

56 Ibid., pp.69–70

57 Ibid., pp.70–1.

58 Ibid., pp.283–4.

59 Ibid., p.45. For the 'Hottentot Venus' see Peter Fryer, *Staying Power. The History of Black People in Britain*, Humanities Press, Atlantic Heights, NJ, 1984, pp.229–30, and the associated note on contemporary commentary on the event; for the so-called 'Hottentot apron', see note 37.

60 Alexander, *An Expedition*, p.47.

61 Alexander, *Narrative*, p.383.

62 Ibid., p.325.

63 'Co-operation and conflict: the Eastern Cape Frontier' in Monica Wilson and Leonard Thompson (eds) *A History of South Africa to 1870*, Croom Helm, London and Canberra, 1982, pp.246–7.

64 'Despatch fom Lord Charles Somerset to Earl Bathurst, recommending emigration to South Africa, 18 December 1817', in Theal, *Records*, vol.xi, pp.425–31. (Bathurst was the Secretary of State for War and the Colonies).

65 Some of the key texts include: Patrick Colquhoun, *A Treatise on the Wealth, Power and Resources of the British Empire, in every corner of the World. . .*, Joseph Mawman, London, 1814; Richard Barnard Fisher, *The Importance of the Cape of Good Hope as a Colony to Great-Britain, independently of the advantages it possesses as a military and naval station, and the key to our territorial possessions in India*, T. Cadell and W. Danes, London, 1816, 3rd edn, with additions; E.A. Kendall, *A Proposal for Establishing in London, a New Philanthropical and Patriotic Institution, to be called, The Patriotic Metropolitan Colonial Institution for the assistance of new settlers in his Majesty's Colonies, and for the encouragement of new branches of colonial trade*, Davidson, London, 1817. (Kendall was a prolific author of books for children, notably the highly popular *Keeper's Travels in Search of his Master*. He also wrote what is arguably the first novel with a South African setting, *The English Boy at the Cape: An Anglo-African Story*, London, 1835; C.G. Curtis, *An Account of the Colony of the Cape of Good Hope, with a view to the information of emigrants, with an appendix, containing the offers of government to persons disposed to settle there*, Rest, Fenner, London, 1819; James Griffin, *A Correct Statement of the Advantages and Disadvantages attendant on emigration to the new colony forming near the Cape of Good Hope*, Duncombe, London, 1819. (This is one of the few texts that sought to challenge the orchestrated official propaganda in support of the Cape); G.A. Robertson, *Notes on Africa: particularly those parts which are situated between Cape Verde and the River Congo . . . to which is added, an appendix, containing a compendious account of the Cape of Good Hope, its production and resources; with a variety of important information, very necessary to be known by persons about to emigrate to that colony*, Sherwood, Neeley and Jones, London, 1819.

66 Selected texts which rely on travellers' tales for their commentaries about the Cape include: Thomas Hope, *Origins and Prospects of Man*, 3 vols, John Murray, London, 1831; John C. Colquhoun, *The Moral Character of Britain the cause of its political eminence. Introductory lecture delivered in the Mechanics' Institution of Glasgow*, William Collins, Glasgow, Edinburgh, Dublin and London, 1832; William Adams, *The Modern Voyager and Traveller, through Europe, Asia, Africa, and America*, vol.1, Fisher and Son, London, 1839.

67 George Thompson, *Travels and Adventures in Southern Africa. . . comprising a view of the present state of the colony, with observations on the progress and prospects of the British emigrants*, dedicated to the Earl of Bathurst, Colonial Secretary, London, 1827, Preface p.vi, pp.313–14.

68 Cowper Rose, *Four Years in Southern Africa*, London, 1828, pp.29–34, 75, 76.

69 Henry H. Methuen, *Life in the Wilderness; or, wanderings in South Africa*, London, 1846; Stephen Kay, *Travels and Researches in Caffraria: Describing the character, customs, and moral condition of the tribes inhabiting that portion of Southern Africa: with historical and topographical remarks illustrative of the state and prospects of the British settlement in its borders, the introduction of Christianity, and the progress of civilization*, John Mason, London, 1833.

70 George Nicholson, *The Cape and its Colonists, with hints to settlers*, London, 1848, pp.3–4, 33, 100–2.

71 John Centlivres Chase, *The Cape of Good Hope, and the Eastern Province of Algoa Bay, with statistics of the Colony*, Pelham Robertson, London, 1843, pp.8, 9, 11.

72 The writings of Lady Anne Barnard (1750–1825) are excluded; some of these were not published until 1849, and then only as part of a book of family history: Alexander Lindsay, *Lives of the Lindsays; or, a memoir of the houses of Crawford and Balcarres. . ..* Privately printed, 4 vols, Wigan, 1840; 3 vols, 1849; 3 vols, 1858.

73 Harriet Ward, *The Cape and the Kaffirs; a diary of five years' residence in Kaffirland; with a chapter of advice to immigrants*, Henry G. Bohn, London, 1848; *Five Years in Kaffirland; with sketches of the late war in that country, to the conclusion of the peace*, 2 vols, London, 1848; *Past and Future Emigration; or, the Book of the Cape*, London, 1849; *Jasper Lyle, a Tale of Kaffirland*, George Routledge & Co., London, 1851; *Hardy and Hunter. A Boy's Own Story*, George Routledge & Co., London, 1858. (For the 'Kaffir Wars', see note 31.)

74 Harriet Ward, *Five Years in Kaffirland*, pp.27–8.

75 Ibid., pp.27–8, 135.

76 See Jay Naidoo, *Tracking Down Historical Myths*, Ad Donker, Johannesburg, 1989, ch.4, for a review of the documentation, as well as an appraisal, of the event.

77 Harriet Ward, *The Cape and the Kaffirs*, p.45.

78 Harriet Ashmore, *Narrative of a Three Months' March in India; and a residence in the Dooab, by the wife of an officer of the 16th Foot*. With plates, from drawings on the spot, R. Hastings, London, pp.22–3, 336.

79 See Andrew Mousley, 'The making of the self. Life writing in the English Renaissance', unpublished PhD thesis, University of Kent, 1991.

80 The most thorough and detailed work on the 1820 Settlers has been done by M.D. Nash; especially her *The Settler Handbook, a New List of the 1820 Settlers*, Chameleon, Diep River, Cape, 1987. I am indebted to Dee Nash for her generous time, as well as access to unpublished material. Two important recent studies are Clifton C. Crais, *White Supremacy and Black Resistance in Pre-Industrial South Africa. The Making of the Colonial Order in the Eastern Cape, 1770–1865*, Cambridge University Press, Cambridge, 1992, and Cecille Swaisland, *Servants and Gentlewomen in the Golden Land. The Emigration of Single Women to South Africa, 1820–1839*, Berg, Oxford, 1993.

81 Leo Marquard, *The Peoples and Policies of South Africa*, Oxford University Press, Oxford, 1952, pp.238–9.

82 Mary Louise Pratt, 'Scratches on the face of the country; or, What Mr Barrow saw in the land of the Bushmen', *Critical Enquiry* vol.12, no.1, 1985, p.143; *Imperial Eyes. Travel Writing and Transculturation*, Routledge, London and New York, 1992, chs 1 and 3.

83 John Noyes, *Colonial Space. Spatiality in the Discourse of German South West Africa 1884–1915*, Harwood, Reading, Berkshire, 1992.

84 Michel Foucault, 'Questions of geography' in *Power/Knowledge. Selected Interviews and Other Writings 1972–1977*, edited by Colin Gordon, Pantheon, New York, 1980, pp.63–76; Edward Said, 'Narrative and geography', *New Left Review* 180, March/April 1990. I am also deeply indebted to Benita Parry for her insights and advice.

85 V.G. Kiernan, *The Lords of Human Kind*, Cresset, London, 1988, p.220.

86 J.R. Seeley, *The Expansion of England: Two Courses of Lectures*, Macmillan, London, 1883, pp.41, 43, 46.

9

FOREIGN DEVILS AND MORAL PANICS

Britain, Asia and the Opium Trade

Andrew Blake

DREAMS OF CATHAY

Dreams and fantasies about China have figured in Western discourse since the travels of Marco Polo; until the nineteenth century most were dreams of a better place. Missionaries arriving in China from the anarchy of sixteenth-century Europe depicted an empire of splendour and civility. Jesuits, active in Peking from the 1650s until the 1770s, consistently portrayed Chinese civilization in positive and respectful terms; even during the eighteenth century, China could be seen under Western eyes as admirable in its bureaucratic government, in its production of tea and silks, and in its artistic production. Indeed in many ways eighteenth-century Europe, enthralled by its dream of China, tried to realize it. Key elements in the European culture of the time – the paintings of Watteau and George Cozens; Chippendale's furniture; the penchant for the 'Chinese Garden', full of wandering paths and pagodas, realizing the Willow Pattern; the lighthearted grace of rococo architecture and decoration – all bespeak a fascination with China.[1] It was common for Enlightenment intellectuals to compare favourably the apparent meritocracy of the Chinese political system against the corrupt *ancien régime*, Voltaire claiming that the Chinese had 'perfected moral science', while François Quesnay's *Le Despotisme du Chine* proposed a political economy on the Chinese model.[2]

China was also the site of more disturbing images. As John Barrell's study of Thomas De Quincey has shown, China was one of the imaginary centres of a notional 'Orient' massively populated, inhumane, terrifying.[3] Barrell's reading of De Quincey's work associates it with a set of childhood memories: a mix of guilt and desire on the death of a sister, and his learning of the success of Tipu Sultan against the British in the seventeen years before Tipu's death in battle in 1799, became locked together as he obsessively renarrated his memories as oriental dangers.

232

De Quincey feared tigers and crocodiles; he feared sultans, Turks, Asians – dangers which threatened him and other British men and women – and he felt impelled to call on the whole British imperial project in his, and their, defence. De Quincey, anticipating the boys' stories of succeeding generations, narrated the British empire as the masculine rescue of an effeminized colonial subject from an evil oppressor, as exemplified by the replacement of Mogul rule over the Hindu in India.

Barrell's exploration of this 'psychopathology of imperialism' is in many ways an exemplary demonstration of the application of psycho-analysis to history; yet, curiously, it ignores the material base on which De Quincey's dreams were built. Like those other fantasists of empire, Coleridge and Wilkie Collins, De Quincey was an opium user. Through-out his life, opium produced in British India was sold to China, against the wishes of the Chinese government. Dreams and fantasies clarified by the effects of opium no doubt increased De Quincey's fear of his own orientalization and effeminization. Above all, the text in which he discussed his addiction, *Confessions of an English Opium Eater*, provided a foundation on which many of the later arguments in Britain about the morality of opium use were based.

Dreams, fantasies and other fictions help to drive the reading of reality in any culture. Stories are told in order to explain and justify any set of duties, responsibilities, rights, rites and actions. The economics and politics of empire have always been imbued with rich fantasies which – far from standing at one remove from reality in the merely discursive worlds patronized by deconstructionist theory – have themselves been productive of economic and political change. This chapter explores fictions erected in Britain and India about the opium trade with China, and their effects, telling in its turn the story of an ideology whose eventual victory over mercantile and political opposition has set a continuing moral limitation on capitalism, by proscribing the trade in drugs for personal, pleasurable use. The eventual triumph of this ideology was due to its successful articulation with the wider, prevailing ideologies of race, empire, gender and class in the Edwardian years. The case proclaimed by the non-conformist critics of opiates fared better than the mixture of free-trade imperialism and individual liberalism offered by both mercantile interests and the governments of Britain and India in defence of the opium trade. At issue here is a discussion of the formation of a particular set of subjectivities, which through the course of the nineteenth century reconstructs the central trope of the rectilinear, rational English man, contrasting this figure to the hopelessly degenerate 'orientalized' Chinese, the victim of a debauched addiction.

THE OPIUM TRADE

Trade between Europe and China was difficult in the eighteenth and early nineteenth century. The rulers of the Middle Kingdom, established by Heavenly mandate, considered their empire to be self-sufficient in all produce: they had no need of contact with people from outside its boundaries, who were routinely referred to as 'barbarians' or 'foreign devils'. Portuguese, Dutch, British and American trade was officially tolerated only at Macao and Canton; foreign merchants were not allowed to live, or to travel, in the interior. By 1715, however, the East India Company had established itself at Canton, and soon built up a large trade in tea and silks, for which either Indian calicoes or silver were exchanged.[4] Demand by the British consumer for tea increased faster than that of the Chinese for calicoes; and the American and French Wars seriously reduced both the amount of silver available to pay the Chinese, and the willingness to pay it.[5] The East India Company, which needed the tea trade in order to pay dividends to its London investors, was impelled to find a substitute for silver.

Luckily for the English tea-drinking public a substitute was found which the Chinese would accept, and which was produced in India: opium. As early as the seventeenth century, Portuguese traders had serviced Chinese desires for opium from their base at Macao. The East India Company, having established a monopoly of opium-growing in Bengal in 1773, began to supply it to China – but not, officially, in Company vessels. The Ch'ing government at Peking forbade the import of opium, and the Company did not import it as such. Instead, the opium was sold at Calcutta, and smuggled into China by British and Indian merchants, trading under licence from the Company but not in its name.[6] A complex smuggling system evolved. Opium clippers would put in at the island of Lintin, downriver from Canton. Chinese officials would register routine protests, and then stand by while the opium was loaded into smuggling vessels crewed by pirates, which plied the coasts and rivers.[7] When there was a glut at Lintin, the merchants from Britain and India would smuggle the drug themselves, taking their clippers along the coast.[8] Fortunes founded by these activities included those of Jardine, Matheson and Co.; David Jardine, himself a smuggler, was convinced by 1830 that opium was 'the safest and most gentlemanlike speculation I am aware of'.[9] Yet the objective among the British mercantile community remained the official opening of China to the free market, and the merchants lobbied both British and Chinese officials to that end, attempting to explain the benefits of the market to the latter: in May 1831 the *Canton Register* offered a prize of £50 for a work on political economy, in Chinese, 'applicable to all the errors and abuses which may exist in China'.[10]

Before such enlightened discourse could reach Peking the Tao-Kuang Emperor heard of the abuses of trade at Lintin, and a debate started at court on the best means of halting it. The Chinese officials were disturbed on three counts. Firstly, they considered the use of opium (especially by the mass of the people) to bring moral degradation. Secondly, they were concerned at the increased power and influence which trading in the drug had given to smugglers and secret societies. Thirdly, convinced that a nation's wealth consists principally in its stock of precious metals, they were upset at the fact that opium was usually paid for in silver. The increasing export of silver bullion was accompanied by inflation in the domestic currency, copper cash. Several of the memorials presented to the Emperor stressed this: one of these, by Heu Nai-tsi, put forward a classic mercantilist argument: the trade must be legalized, and an import duty charged on opium; and it must be bartered for, and not paid for in silver. The Chinese authorities eventually adopted this view, but more immediately influential was the view of Lin Hse-tsu. He believed that all trade with the foreign barbarians was vile and degrading to the people of the celestial empire, and that as opium was destroying the people, the trade should be banned at once. The Emperor, impressed with Lin's forcefulness, commissioned him to end the trade.[11]

Lin's efforts led to war with Britain in 1839. Since the end of the Napoleonic wars, the merchants and manufacturers of Great Britain had been looking for new markets for their mass-produced textiles.[12] The merchants' agitation had brought about the end, in 1833, of the East India Company's monopoly of trade with China. But the restrictions imposed by the Chinese remained.[13] The merchants began to put pressure on the British government to open the door to trade for them, dreaming of an El Dorado of free trade with 400 million Chinese. Both merchants and government realized that this would only be achieved by force – especially after Peking's contemptuous treatment of special envoy Lord Napier in 1834.[14] When Commissioner Lin confiscated and destroyed all the opium at Canton and Lintin, on 18 March 1839, the merchant community and British government took his action as the perfect *casus belli*; this war, fought on behalf of the Lancashire manufacturers and traders, has become known as the First Opium War.

In fact the treaty of Nanking, 1844, did not mention opium. Hong Kong was obtained by Britain, and four more ports were opened to British trade, but British merchants were still not permitted to live or travel in inland China. The smuggling of opium, now based at Hong Kong, continued.[15] Merchants, dissatisfied with the new provisions, pressed the government for further action against the Chinese; Sir Henry Pottinger, the first Governor of Hong Kong, agreed with them, telling a Manchester audience in 1846 that he foresaw a new market so vast that 'all the mills of Lancashire could not make stocking-stuff sufficient for one of its provinces'.[16] However, a House of Commons Select Committee appointed in 1847 to inquire into the state of trade between Britain and China reported that China was economically self-sufficient, and that if China wanted Manchester goods, she certainly by now had enough money to pay for them: by the 1850s China was once again a net importer of silver.[17] But there was no such demand for British goods: the value of British exports to China in 1850 was only a little higher than in 1843.

Yet the merchants continued to dream. In an adventure extraordinary even by the standards of nineteenth-century exploration, Robert Fortune was commissioned by the East India Company in 1848 to enter China and search for tea plants. Travelling in disguise (complete with false pigtail), and at some personal danger, he visited all the principal tea-growing districts and obtained some 20,000 plants which were taken to India via Hong Kong, effectively establishing the tea industry in Assam. This particular traveller's tales are very different from those describing Africa or the Orient. Time and again Fortune describes with admiration the gardens of the Chinese: China is seen as a cornucopia, a highly organized, well-cultivated, green and pleasant land, its people ready both for the commerce of the West, and for conversion to Christianity – a link common in the discourse of visitors to China in the mid-nineteenth century. The problem as Fortune saw it was that both the Chinese people, and their government, seemed fundamentally untrustworthy. Having acknowledged the deceitful nature of his own project, he then transferred this unpleasant trait to the Chinese he was dealing with: in general, 'no dependence may be made upon the veracity of the Chinese'; in particular, discussing an Imperial edict, Fortune claimed that 'those who have had some experience of the Chinese, treated it as so much waste paper – as a collection of high-sounding words without meaning'. Yet the potential for a share in this cornucopia remained. All that was needed for the mercantile dream to be realized, believed Fortune, was the defeat of the Peking government; and the transformation of Chinese culture could then proceed apace with the arrival of Christian missionaries:

> It may be that another war and all its horrors is inevitable, and whenever that takes place this vast country will be opened up to foreigners of every nation. Then the Christian missionary will be able to extend his labours to those far-distant stations among the Bohea hills ... with the blessing of God those temples may yet be the spots from which the sun of righteousness shall shine. The 'glad news of the gospel' may yet be proclaimed in them, and spread from hill to valley ... until the whole of this vast country shall be glad to hear the glad and joyful tidings.[18]

Fortune was prescient. Missionaries were waiting with increasing impatience to 'enter the gates of China'.[19] The London Missionary Society had welcomed the First Opium War, anticipating that 'a way is gradually opening, by means of these events, for the unfettered diffusion of Gospel light through the length and breadth of that vast Empire'.[20] The treaty of Nanking did nothing to fulfil these desires, and consequently missionaries backed merchants in pressure for further British intervention to open China to free trade both in goods and church services. Palmerston, the British Prime Minister, was convinced of the merchants' case at least, and found his excuse for war in the 'Arrow' incident, when the Canton authorities imprisoned the (Chinese) crew of the *Arrow*, a vessel trading under licence from Hong Kong and therefore technically British. The 'Second Opium War' of 1856 to 1860 attempted to satisfy the demand for free access to the Chinese interior. It was fought by France, and a British regime already stretched by the Indian 'mutiny' – troops and warships originally despatched to China had to be rerouted to Calcutta, before returning in the following summer. Partly due to this, the war took longer than planned; the ferocity of the indemnity provisions of the eventual treaty of Tientsin, between Britain, China and France, and the sacking of the Peking Summer Palace, are arguably signals of the British humiliation suffered during the Indian revolt. As a result of the revolt, the East India Company was disbanded, and direct British State control over all aspects of Indian life, including the growing, preparation and sale of opium, increased immeasurably.[21]

The treaty of Tientsin legalized the trade in opium, which from this point became an important part of the Chinese economy, providing revenue for the Peking government and increasingly serving as a cash-substitute in many parts of inland China.[22] Lord Elgin, who negotiated the terms of the treaty, tried to disabuse the merchants of their visions; like the 1847 Committee, he assured them that the Chinese simply did not need British goods; his official, W.H. Mitchell, stressed to the Hong Kong merchants that Chinese civilization was ancient and respectable, and that Christian civilization would have to prove itself against the most hard-working people on earth; above all, he insisted, 'We bring the Chinese nothing that is really popular among them ... opium is the only "open sesame" to their stony hearts'.[23] It was Foreign Office policy hereafter to quieten the merchants' continuing demands for interference against the Chinese authorities, and to ensure stable conditions for trade by upholding the Ch'ing regime. The Foreign Office did not wish to acquire a second India; successive British governments for example contributed to political stability in China by helping in the suppression of the Taiping rebellion (*c.* 1850–64). But the treaty of Tientsin had in fact provided much of what the merchants wanted: as well as legalizing the opium trade, it opened, for the first time, direct diplomatic relations between China and Britain. The existing Chinese customs service was disbanded, replaced by an institution run on Western lines and staffed by Western officials, notably Sir Robert Hart.[24] More ports were opened and, in an ambiguously worded clause, rights of inland residence and travel were granted to merchants and missionaries; toleration was granted to Chinese converts to Christianity.

THE MISSION TO CHINA

The churches and missionary societies had seen the second war as a heaven-sent opportunity – the *Baptist Magazine* in 1859 writing that it would not

> look upon the iniquitous cupidity of our opium traffic otherwise than as a great crime, and the war to which we resorted to enforce it, as at once a national calamity and a disgrace. But it is the prerogative of God, out of evils which nations inflict upon [one] another, to bring forth their greater good, and even to make the very sins of man subserve the designs of this mercy to the world.[25]

At once there was a considerable expansion of missionary activity among British and American Protestants. In 1851 there were eighty-one Protestant missionaries in China, representing twenty different societies. By 1864 there were 189, from twenty-four societies; by 1874, the year of the foundation of the Society for the Suppression of the Opium Trade, there were 436 from twenty-nine societies.[26] The increase in missionary activity brought a very strong reaction from the Chinese. Where Catholic missionaries often followed the example of the Jesuits in Peking, who had learnt to read and write in Chinese, had worn Chinese costume, and had evolved a syncretically adapted Christianity suitable to Chinese custom, Protestant missionaries were awesomely convinced of their own superiority, and remained culturally separate. Anglican missionary Arthur Moule for example announced that

> There is much to admire ... in the teachings of Confucianism, Buddhism and Taoism in China ... But they in no sense meet Christianity half way. Every knee shall bow to Christ alone: not one to idol, or hero, or philosopher, or sage.[27]

The inevitable clash resulting from these robust beliefs is well summed up by the comparatively liberal China missionary Griffith John's critical statement, 'Are we not more manly and intelligent, more skillful, more humane, more civilised? ... Yes, according to our way of thinking. No, a thousand times no, according to theirs'.[28]

This cultural collision produced predictable results. Converts to Christianity, who were required to renounce ancestor worship, the sale and consumption of opium, concubinage, and Sunday work, were in consequence isolated from their native culture. Converts thus tended to be those already on the fringes of Chinese society, those with least to lose from its renunciation. This put a further barrier in the way of recruitment from the respectable parts of Chinese society: criminals and landless labourers, despised anyway by Chinese society, tended to transfer the odium in which they were held to the institution to which they belonged.[29]

Converts were most numerous in the treaty ports, where their professed beliefs affected their chances of employment – 'rice Christians' in the eyes of their fellow Chinese.[30] The clause in the treaty of Tientsin stating that Christians should not be punished for their faith was abused: converts often instituted legal proceedings against non-Christian Chinese knowing that they had the backing of missionaries, and therefore indirectly of foreign governments. Few such cases were lost. Small wonder that, as Bishop Faurie naïvely (or cynically) remarked, 'Every one of the individuals who has been punished for reviling our faith have embraced with ardour the true faith after leaving prison'.[31] So as well as irritating a very deep tradition of Chinese anti-foreignism and prejudice against extraneous religions, missionaries aroused specific hostility by their attempts to protect their converts, confronting in the process the two main pillars of China's ruling elite, the gentry and the bureaucracy. This caused a severe reaction: as early as 1861, anti-missionary propaganda had appeared in Hunan; the Tientsin massacre of 1870, the largest outbreak of anti-missionary activity before the Boxer Rebellion of the 1890s, marked the climax of an anti-foreign campaign led by the gentry and directed specifically against the missionaries.[32]

Missionaries reacted by seeking stronger support from Western governments. Just as the merchants dreamed of a vast market of some 400 million ready to buy their wares, so the missionaries could dream of the same number of souls flocking to their churches. They hoped that government aid in crushing the local officials who led the anti-missionary campaign would leave the way clear for the creation of the China of their dreams. In reality, however, their progress in winning converts was agonizingly slow: the 1896 missionary census claimed that there had been 6,753 Protestant Chinese in 1869, and 30,000 in 1885.[33] Finding that they were reviled, often physically attacked, for trying to teach what they considered to be a message of truth and love, the missionaries contemplated the possible reasons. One, they believed, was that the Chinese associated them, as foreigners, with the opium trade. Leading China missionary Griffith John observed in a report sent in 1884 to the London Missionary Society:

The opium trade has ... retarded the progress of Christianity by creating against us, the preachers of it, a strong prejudice. ... As a people, the Chinese cannot distinguish between England and Christianity, and consequently the acts of the British government are supposed to be the expression of Christian morality.[34]

Far from being identified with the trade in opium, however, the missionaries took upon themselves the task of eradicating what they perceived as an unmitigated evil. Missionary prejudice against opium smokers was so strong that they were excluded from most churches. William Muirhead claimed that 'opium smoking utterly unfits its victims for the appreciation of the pure and spiritual teachings of Christianity'.[35] Griffith John's report complained that many smokers of the drug, once converted, lapsed back into the opium habit, and were therefore lost to the church (though in fact they were usually excommunicated first).[36] Opium became the missionaries' symbol of Chinese resistance to Christianity, an icon in whose power most missionaries believed absolutely:

> Dr. Legge had a long conversation with the schoolmaster resident at the Temple of Confucius [in Pok-Lo]. He seemed open to conviction enough, but happening, through mistaking a doorway, to go into his bedroom, Dr. Legge saw there the opium pipe and lamp, and felt that there was little hope for him.[37]

THE ANTI-OPIUM SOCIETY

By the early 1870s the Foreign Office had arrived at the view that the best way to increase trading prospects in the long term would be to give the Ch'ing regime as much help as possible to modernize itself. Those committed to this view considered the missionaries as an obstacle to the improvement of Anglo-Chinese trade and diplomatic relations, and that if they wished to meddle in Chinese affairs by raising awkward ethical controversy, they must do so at their own risk. The Foreign Office wrote to Sir Thomas Wade in June 1870: 'We shall certainly not be disposed to fight the Chinese on the missionary ground'.[38] In the hope of speeding the modernization of China, Sir Rutherford Alcock, British plenipotentiary at Peking, renegotiated the terms of the treaty of Tientsin. Alcock conceded that the duty on opium, still the largest single item imported into China, should be raised. However, after opposition from the Chinese and English mercantile communities, and especially from the Indian government (some 14 per cent of whose revenue in the 1870s came from the sale of opium), the British government in London refused to ratify the revised treaty.[39]

The Anglo-Oriental Society for the Suppression of the Opium Trade with China (hereinafter called the Society) was formed in response to this situation. Protestant missionaries in China and their friends in

Britain felt isolated and angry at the conniving of the Foreign Office with a trade they were convinced was harmful to their cause. The Society's foundation belongs to the high moment of mid-Victorian Liberalism, when several other voluntary moral-reform pressure groups were active in carrying their 'civilizing mission' into public life: the Contagious Diseases Acts had been repealed; the United Kingdom Alliance was a powerful movement pressing for temperance; the Society for the Prevention of Cruelty to Animals had just launched a test case in the courts which led to anti-vivisection legislation in 1876.[40] In early 1874 a group of Quaker and other non-conformist businessmen offered prizes of £200 and £100 for essays on the government's opium policy and its consequences. The winner of the competition, the Rev. Frederick Storrs Turner, determined to set up a society to oppose the opium trade, and on 13 November 1874 a meeting attended by prominent business-men and missionaries was held in London. 'Nothing which is morally wrong can be politically right ... we can put down the opium traffic as we put down slavery', announced Alderman McArthur, MP, who chaired the meeting.[41] Four wealthy Quakers set the Society on a firm financial footing. Edward Pease provided a first £1,000 and promised a further £200 per year; Arthur Pease promised £100 per year; Thomas Hansbury and Arthur Albright gave £250 each. These four men – all deeply involved in other moral reform movements – found and set up the Society's first offices and paid the Secretary, Storrs Turner, who also became editor of the Society's monthly magazine *Friend of China*. It was agreed that the Society should be non-denominational; other anti-opium societies associated with various churches were soon organized and running in parallel, with the agreed strategy being to disseminate information in order to build public support, and then press for favourable legislation.[42]

The Society did not merely call for the complete cessation of the trade. Remembering a principal objection to the abolition of slavery – the question of compensation for slave owners – it recognized that a substitute for the Indian government's opium revenue would have to be found, and tried hard to find it.[43] But before it could do this, it proposed firstly that the government should end its monopoly, and should charge a high duty on opium exported; secondly that the British Government should allow China to impose its own duties on imported opium.[44] Furthermore, the Society's case was founded on the belief of the inseparability of morality and economics, its literature insistent that trade with China would improve if the stigma of the opium trade were removed: 'Intelligent Chinese ascribe the stagnation of foreign trade to the alarming progress which opium cultivation is making through the country ... We are killing the goose that laid the golden eggs'.[45] The Society wished to see trade with China flourish; but even so, this was essentially a moral crusade. *Friend of China* continually rehearsed the basic ethical argument: Britain has forced opium on China for purposes of gain; opium, necessarily destroying all its users, is an unmitigated evil; all non-medical use of the drug must therefore be prohibited completely, and the trade should be made illegal – or in the words of the Society's motto: 'Righteousness before Revenue'.

While the final section of this chapter will deal more closely with the ideological ramifications of the Society's position, it is worth pausing here to examine the way in which notions about the evils of opium use fit with the rest of the 'Non-conformist Conscience'. Protestantism in all its forms encouraged the power of prayer, the personal, rational relationship with the divine, and the manly independence of the believer. The emphasis on the 'calling', the need for continual justification of the self to itself before God, required continuous hard work and rational self-discipline. Drugs like alcohol and opium were evil because they could undermine this rationality, and thereby expose the heart of darkness contained within most forms of Protestantism – the *uncertainty* of salvation that most Protestants felt. Given the division of the world between good and evil, then anything not calculated to glorify God must be the work of the Devil. The user of drugs, losing his rationality, thereby displays to himself and to the rest of the world his unmanliness, his degradation, his Fall. Those with the discipline to avoid temptation were convinced of the superiority of their moralized vision of world politics (if continuously uncertain over their own positions as individuals), and of their duty to carry their convictions from their churches into public debate. Congregationalist leader R.W. Dale claimed in 1862 that 'those who decline to use their political power are guilty of treachery both to God and to man'.[46] The campaign against the opium trade was part of a series of interventions in both domestic and foreign policy in which non-conformists conscientiously opposed aspects of British foreign policy they considered to be evil (examples are the campaign against the Crimean War in the 1850s, and the opposition to British support for Turkey over the 'Bulgarian Atrocities' question in the 1880s).

The Society's view was refracted by the political as well as the ethical and ascetic ideologies of religious non-conformity. Fellow non-conformists were inherently trustworthy. The Society's investigation of the social and moral effects of opium use consisted in accepting the views of those sharing its moral credentials: it relied on the evidence of missionaries of its own religious persuasion, and accepted their views without question; missionaries observed the effects of opium without trying it for themselves, as they did with the rest of Chinese culture.[47] In the second issue of *Friend of China*, for instance, a lurid description of an opium den, by an anonymous missionary, is followed by a description of a typical opium refuge, staffed by missionaries, in which details are given of the number of religious services held and of inmates catechized, rather than of attempts to cure addicts. No success rate, either for cure or conversion, is claimed: both were typically very low.[48]

The missionaries' faith, their world-view, are seen here as a fiction, created within the culture and constantly reinforced discursively within both written texts and the mutual exhortations of public meetings. The Society disseminated its views through the sale and distribution of its own literature; through correspondence with the press; and through Parliamentary debate.[49] With an active middle-class leadership,[50] and membership based on various non-conformist churches, the Society had a wide base for the distribution of its literature. As several speakers at the 1874 meeting had noted, the primary need was for the Society to publish its views as widely, and as quickly, as possible. Parliamentary debates, or reports of public meetings, were reprinted in pamphlet form, as were a series of essays. The literature addressed specific sub-groups within the population. Titles included *Reasons why every voter should protest against the opium trade*; *A Plea for the Oppressed* was offered to 'ladies', while for the 'juvenile' there was: *Poppies: A talk with English boys and girls about opium. By a lady. 12 pages. 3 full-page illustrations.* The monthly *Friend of China* itself was at the heart of the Society's literary campaign. From its first appearance in March 1875 it contained evidence from China, India and elsewhere, with reports of Parliamentary activity and public meetings. Always present were exhortations to prayer and to action, and incitements to raise or simply to give more money.

The increasingly public profile of the Society was eventually matched by a less well organized opposition, drawn in the main from traders working in the Far East. Public meetings and publications set out to produce a coherent counter-fiction about the opium trade. Provoked by the missionary crusade, the trading company Jardine Matheson claimed that

> since 1860 it has been rendered abundantly clear that the use of opium is not a curse but a comfort to the hard-working Chinese. As well say that malt is a curse to the English labourer, or tobacco one to the world at large ... we feel justified in claiming that those who deal in opium shall be permitted to supply the inland Chinese with the drug as freely as they who are the dwellers at the ports.[51]

Many China Hands simply inverted the economic argument of the Society: 'the missionaries and their ways are really the great trouble and drawback to the liking of Europeans all over China'.[52] Others emphasized the weakness of the missionaries' economic case; that trade in China was expanding (partly as a result of the opium trade), and that the Chinese themselves were despite the opium habit 'the most active, industrious and enterprising race in the Eastern world'[53] who, in time, would become equal partners of the Western merchants.[54]

It should be emphasized, however, that the missionary and anti-opium view was never simply opposed to that of all merchants and manufacturers. The Lancashire cottonocracy was still waiting for El Dorado, and was quite prepared to believe that the opium trade was delaying its arrival. In October 1878 a deputation from the Society visited Liverpool and Manchester, urging the respective chambers of commerce to press the government for the ratification of the revised treaty of Tientsin, arguing that the disappearance of the opium trade would free Chinese silver and would anyway make the Chinese more kindly disposed to trade with the West. This visit was successful: in June 1880 Sir Joseph Pease presented to the House of Commons petitions from the chambers of commerce of Manchester, Liverpool and Glasgow, praying that the opium trade might cease.[55] Much use was also made of the more conventional petitions from interested groups up and down the country – especially religious bodies.[56] Local anti-opium committees were asked to interview prospective parliamentary candidates, and support those willing to vote for the Society's objectives in Parliament – another well-tried procedure for all pressure groups, and one which imbricated the Society with the larger formation of political Liberalism.[57]

In the early 1880s, the Society's parliamentary spokesmen concentrated on the ratification of the revised treaty of Tientsin, thinking that as soon as she was able, China would raise the import duty on opium to a prohibitive level and in effect tax the trade out of existence.[58] In 1885 the Indian government withdrew its opposition to the ratification of the treaty, at least partly because of increasing parliamentary support for the Society.[59] The revised treaty was duly signed on 18 July 1885, ten years after it had first been negotiated. This was the first agreement between Great Britain and China to treat China as an equal, allowing her to have a genuine opium policy of her own.

Having realized this aim, the Society considered dissolution; but in 1886 it was decided to continue to press the governments of Britain and India to cease their patronization of the trade. It became apparent that the key assumption of the movement, that the Chinese government wished to stop the growth and consumption of opium, had been mistaken.[60] The role of opium in the Chinese economy, the growth of native Chinese opium in the inland provinces, and the increasing importation of Persian opium into China, meant that pro-opiumists could now argue convincingly that both the Chinese government and people had accepted the drug, and that cessation of the Indian trade would merely mean that the growth of opium in China would increase.[61] The Society accepted that the Chinese government was as little interested in giving up its opium revenue as was the Indian. *Friend of China* reported in October 1889:

The recent interview of our friend, Mr. William Jones, with the great Chinese statesman, Li Hung Chang, confirms the suspicion, which we already had but too much reason for entertaining, that the days are past when we might rely on the Chinese Government to use all its influence in helping to put a stop to the import of Indian opium for the poisoning of its own subjects. The share in the opium revenue which China now receives . . . is a very large sum.[62]

(The magazine did not point out that Li Hung Chang himself grew opium.) Tactics had to change: the attention of the Society came to be firmly fixed on the supply side, the growth and sale of Indian opium.

In 1889 Storrs Turner was replaced as secretary by F.G. Alexander, a Quaker barrister who encouraged a renewal of activity at all levels, raising £2,000 and using it to issue 40,000 tracts in 1890 and to hold over one hundred public meetings in 1891; advertisements called on church people of all denominations to produce a 'holy fire of indignation' against the trade.[63] This renewed campaigning paid off: on 10 April 1891, in a vote on a motion to adjourn the House, the Commons in effect voted that India should cease to collect its opium revenue or to grow opium.[64] *Friend of China* carolled with joy: 'The Lord hath done great things for us, whereof we are glad [Psalms cxxvi. 3] . . . an object lesson in the power of prayer'.[65]

In 1892 the Society campaigned, with the various churches and missionary groups, and with the smaller, denominational anti-opium societies, for a Liberal victory.[66] But when the Liberals gained their expected victory, Kimberley, a pro-opiumist, was appointed Secretary of State for India. The Society, convinced that it could prove that the opium revenue could be replaced, pressed for a Royal Commission to decide how best to do this. Kimberley threatened to resign if such a Commission were set up, and Gladstone, fighting to keep his Cabinet together in order to pass the Irish Home Rule Bill, and prepared therefore to appease Kimberley, placed on the order paper an amendment to the Society's request for a Royal Commission proposing the investigation not of *how* but of *whether* the Indian opium revenue should be replaced. Gladstone's amendment was carried with a majority of 79; Kimberley, convinced that the Indian Government could prove its case and hold onto the opium revenue, remained in the Cabinet.[67]

The Society was undismayed at the amendment of its proposal, and enthusiasm remained high when the composition of the Commission was announced:

The Constitution of the Opium Commission has strengthened our conviction that it will be an instrument in God's hand for accelerating the movement that aims at freeing our beloved land from the shame of participation in the opium traffic.[68]

The first session of Commission hearings was held in London in September 1893. The anti-opium case was presented firstly by missionaries such as James Legge and Hudson Taylor, arguing that the use of opium for pleasure was immoral, degrading, and a hindrance to the spread of Christianity in China.[69] They were supported by a representative of the Edinburgh Chamber of Commerce, who argued that Japan (which did not import opium) was becoming a good trading partner, and that China would only become so if the opium trade ceased.[70] Sir Joseph Pease and J.G. Alexander also made statements to the Commission, Alexander presenting several of its publications, including an address whose peroration represents the Society's dream of Cathay – a dream the obverse to that of Robert Fortune in 1848. Should the trade cease,

A powerful stimulus will be given to the desire for friendly intercourse with Western Nations; prejudice against European civilisation and inventions will be removed; the construction of railways will be encouraged; a free interchange will be established of the products of British and Chinese industry; and two mighty and peaceful empires, linked together in commerce and amity, will bestow on each of them an effectual barrier against northern aggression. The message of salvation will once again resume its westward course . . . thousands of ardent evangelists from the British Isles, from the United States, from the Canadian Dominion, with the Gospel in their hearts, and on their lips, will speed forward with the sun, to the abodes of this ancient but still vigorous nation, will supply the lamentable defects of the noble but mournful teachings of Confucius, and will sow the seeds of Divine truth that may grow up in a soil still strange to it, and yield at length some new proof of its transforming power, to the Glory of Him who is Truth and who is Love.[71]

Assured in this confident self-belief, the Society professed itself pleased with the first session: 'So far all that we have seen . . . leads us to believe that the Commission is as fair-minded and impartial a tribunal as we could have desired to hear our case'.[72] This optimism was naïve. The Society's argument that the use of opium was degrading, immoral, and personally destructive to all users was itself a fiction, which it had carefully constructed. Medical missionary Dr Dudgeon summarized this fundamental belief, stating baldly to the Commission, 'Many drink, but few abuse; many smoke opium, but all abuse'.[73] People who disagreed with this position also appeared before the Commission; through their evidence the counter-fiction which had already been constructed was presented.[74] Opium could, they claimed, be taken in moderation; its use did not inevitably lead to painful death; it was important to many Indian cultures, whose practices should be respected. Surgeon General Sir

William Moore, for example, claimed that 'A moderate use would brighten the intellect and strengthen the system, render the people more able to go through fatigue'; he admitted to having tried the drug for himself, in a Bombay opium den.[75] Several witnesses noted that the two Indian groups to use opium most extensively, the Sikhs and Rajputs, were in the words of Sir John Strachey the 'finest physical specimens' of all the Indian ethnic and religious groups.[76] They stressed that the social use of opium, far from being considered degrading and shameful, was on occasion obligatory among those groups, at such ceremonies as weddings. Others, with experience of China, also denied the Society's claims. H.N. Lay noted that 'During the whole time of my official connexion with China I never heard any Chinese official or otherwise complain of our action in regard to opium'.[77] Henry Lazarus, a former Shanghai trader, claimed that the missionary description of the effects of opium use was 'a terrible perversion of the truth', and that Chinese from all classes smoked it, often without ill-effects; he too had tried the drug.[78] The Society's moral case was revealed as precisely that: the assertions of missionaries apart, it was ludicrously lacking in empirical evidence. None of the Society's officers would admit to having taken opium themselves. None had visited China or India. Their ability to speak for the effects of opium use was challenged by merchants, Indian medical officers and British diplomats with such first-hand experience. Sir Thomas Wade, who had served in China for forty years, said that while he agreed that opium taken in excess was physically destructive, 'the treatment of the question by the anti-opiumists engages me on the other side'.[79]

The hearings moved on to India. The Commission was now on the territory of the Society's main opponent, the Indian Government; it stayed at Government residences, was entertained by the Government, and heard Government witnesses – all of whom took the view that opium could be taken in moderation without the user automatically becoming addicted; that it was not harmful taken in moderation; that other drugs (both alcohol and ganja, the dried leaves of cannabis) had if anything a worse effect on their users; and that the opium revenue was irreplaceable to the Indian economy. Henry Wilson, one of two Commissioners chosen to represent the anti-opium viewpoint, and Alexander, who had travelled to India as his secretary, had to find their own witnesses. This they found difficult; the Government's evidence, notably that from medical civil servants, they found disturbing, as it upset all their preconceptions about both the metabolic and the moral effects of opium use; they were shocked when the Anglican Bishop and clergy of Calcutta, supported by the Catholic hierarchy of that city, sent a letter to the Commission approving the use of opium.[80] Perhaps most shocking of all, they failed to find in the Indian opium dens the wan, emaciated drug addicts their own propaganda had described: by and large, they saw instead healthy people puffing away quite happily. Wilson and Alexander's confusion on this point is tragicomic, and demonstrated distinct racism: evidence given by Chinese and Indians is described as 'stupid and contradictory'.[81] Arthur Pease, the other anti-opiumist on the Commission, became increasingly persuaded by the evidence before him, and began to suggest that the question was not after all, as he had once believed, a simple moral issue. Back in London, the Society's confidence in the impartiality of the Commission evaporated as they read Alexander's reports. Belatedly and in retreat, it wrote to the Commission stressing that China, not India, should be the centre of the debate.[82]

The *Final Report of the Royal Commission on Opium*, published on 25 April 1895, concluded with the libertarian position that

> whilst there are evils in the abuse of opium, they are not sufficiently great to justify us in restricting the liberty which all men should be permitted to exercise in such matters, medical testimony seeming to show that opium used in moderation is in this country [India] harmless, and, under certain conditions of life, extremely beneficial.[83]

It was, therefore, morally acceptable for the Indian Government to continue to export opium to China. Wilson wrote a minority Report advocating the Society's position, but Arthur Pease signed the majority Report and resigned from the Society. The Report temporarily discredited the Society in the eyes of many of its former supporters in Parliament, and an anti-opium motion proposed in the Commons on 24 May 1895 was defeated by a majority of 117.[84]

And yet in the medium term the Society's work paid off. In the General Election of June 1895, Lord Salisbury, a former Secretary of State for India and a pro-opiumist, returned as Prime Minister. The Conservatives ruled for the next ten years, during which time there was no parliamentary debate on the opium question. The Society's activities continued, if at a lower level: *Friend of China*, reduced in size, became biannual. With the return of Liberal Government in 1905, the Society's parliamentary activity revived, this time successfully: the opium trade was gradually reduced from 1906 after negotiations with the Chinese, and was ended officially in 1917. There are several reasons for this, not all the direct consequence of the Society's moral pressure. The Society did, however, play its part: it succeeded in discrediting the Royal Commission's report by exposing the way in which witnesses had been prepared (often to the extent of coaching) by the Indian government, and showing that anti-opium evidence given to the Commission had been suppressed or ignored. It became the accepted view that the

Commission had produced a whitewash – a position accepted by many historians.[85] By this time opposition from the India Office to the Society's case was muted: the Indian opium revenue was decreasingly important – less than 5 per cent of total revenue in the early 1900s.[86]

Furthermore, international moral pressure to end the trade was growing, from the USA in particular. The imperial project was by no means dominated by Britain at the turn of the century, as it had been at the time of the First Opium War: the idea of free trade came under attack as other European countries and the United States joined the scramble for overseas markets, and an evolving legal framework to supervise international trade was increasingly dominated by the largest single economy. American public opinion, convinced by the anti-opium argument, forced the United States government to lead an international campaign to proscribe the opium trade. The large-scale use of morphine as a painkiller in the Civil War had alerted American opinion to the possibilities of addiction, and the arrival in California of large numbers of Chinese workers, many of whom smoked opium, gave this fear of addiction an urgent, racialized dimension which also emerged in Britain by the end of the century. Fears of the opium-smoking habit passing to whites, of their 'degeneration', and of its use in the seduction of white girls by Chinese men, led to a California law against opium use in 1891.[87] Anti-opium consciousness in America had also been raised through missionaries' experience of opium use in both China and the Philippines, which had been seized from Spain's control in 1898. An official American report published in 1906, heavily influenced by Protestant churchmen, announced that the use of opium in the Philippines had such degrading consequences that its import should be ended forthwith, whatever the economic cost.[88] In 1909 all importation of opium into the USA was controlled.[89] A series of international conferences, beginning in Shanghai in 1909 (a conference chaired by American missionaries) proclaimed the evil of drug trafficking – a moral position which has controlled international law on the matter ever since.[90] Britain was put under severe diplomatic pressure to attend these conferences, almost to stand trial, though she had already taken steps to cease involvement in the trade: after a series of bilateral meetings with the Chinese authorities in 1906, collection of revenue from the opium trade ended in 1907, as the first step in an agreed run-down of the trade. All official importation of Indian opium into China ceased in 1917, when J.G. Alexander was able to sign off the final edition of *Friend of China* with the triumphant exclamation, 'A Victory for Righteousness'.[91]

NIGHTMARES OF CATHAY

The eventual success of this particular campaign to limit the operations of the free market may seem paradoxical. Certainly the tactical defeat by the Royal Commission was unsurprising. By the 1890s, when the Society was at the height of its influence, the 'non-conformist conscience' associated with the politics of the pressure group was itself coming under pressure. *The Times* wrote on the eve of the debate on the proposal to set up the Royal Commission that Gladstone's proposed amendment was 'As strong as can reasonably be expected from a government which is obliged to angle for the votes of all the doctrinaires and amateur philanthropists in the country',[92] while of the anti-opiumists themselves it wrote: 'The British Pharisee has already won for himself the hearty aversion of many races, white, black, and brown, upon this earth for his unsolicited anxiety for their moral welfare'.[93] The decade of revived Conservatism and concomitant celebration of imperialism was perhaps the least likely period in recent British history for the success of a Society calling for restraint in any aspect of imperial policy.

And yet the Society at the height of its influence was not an anachronism. In many ways its views fitted rather better the evolving narrative of empire which was being undertaken in late nineteenth-century Britain than the views of its opponents. And as the influence of that narrative remained strong, in its representation both of the evils of opium use, and of the nature of the Chinese (the two being strongly connected), the Society's influence also remained strong. At the beginning of the nineteenth century, the taking of opium in the form of tablets or of the alcohol-based drink laudanum, had been socially acceptable – tolerated if not welcomed as a personal habit. This tolerance disappeared. Partly due to changing medical opinion, and partly to an extension of non-conformist attitudes to alcohol, the taking of drugs for pleasure came increasingly to be seen as an anti-social activity and, increasingly controlled by isolation, treatment for addiction, or imprisonment, as an 'abuse' – as both a disease and a crime. The medicalized and criminalized category of 'the addict' thus joined other emergent discursive categories – such as the unemployed man; the common prostitute; the incorrigible loafer; the hooligan – as a subject of surveillance and professional control. Like the prostitute, the addict was seen as particularly dangerous because of the possibility of contagion; the danger posed by the addict was further emphasized, at a time of concern over the future of the 'race', by the category being itself racialized.[94]

The Society played an important part in these categorical changes in the position of the drug user. The moral argument which supported this revaluation is a complex of ideas, drawing in part from the romantics and other writers who had used opium – the first edition of *Friend of*

China calls on De Quincey's *Confessions of an English Opium Eater*, and others consistently cited in discussion of the dangers of opiate use included Coleridge and Wilkie Collins. Medicine was arguably the crucial field of discourse used by the anti-opiumists. Though some medical opinion remained unconvinced by theories of addiction – and many doctors gave pro-opiumist evidence to the Royal Commission – in general the arguments used to justify the increasing power over the body's diseases and desires exercised by the medical profession supported the Society's case. While opium was still taken in Britain (especially in the fens, where chemists successfully prevented the inclusion of opium in Schedule A, of restricted poisons, in the Pharmacy Act of 1868),[95] by the 1890s medical opinion had refined the concept of drug addiction. The experiences of Americans in the Civil War, followed by the realization after 1870 that the subcutaneous injection of morphia, via the new hypodermic syringe, carried with it the risk of addiction, finally turned the British medical profession against the free use, the 'self administration', of opiates, even as pain-killers. The further realization that cocaine, proposed as a substitute for morphia in Vienna in the 1880s by Sigmund Freud among others, was also potentially addictive, underlined the concept of addiction, and reinforced the arguments for professional medical control of drugs.[96]

At stake in the anti-opium campaign was the shape of the grand narrative of British expansion, a narrative which sought to reconcile the conflicting views of government, merchants and missionaries into one sublime whole, a moral, political and economic *apologia* for the entire imperial project which placed the English man as its centre, the hero of the story. And the villain? The Other. There is in these discourses of empire a strong tendency for moral transposition, in which evil or degradation are ascribed to the victim rather than the perpetrator of imperial aggression. This happens in much of the fiction – in Haggard, Henty, Buchan and indeed Conrad. The evil lies in the 'heart of darkness', and not in the hearts of the Europeans, unless (and this is a perpetual danger) they came to be corrupted by it – as, in these fictions as in the earlier dreams of De Quincey, they can be all too easily. The Protestant, succumbing to temptation, can lose rationality and all chance of salvation; by analogy the white man can become, through contact with the other or the other's cultural products and practices, non-white. Thus while empire is morally justified, the assertion of cultural and racial superiority over the inferior 'Other', these discourses of empire are also constructed in response to a set of anxieties about the possibilities of failure which threaten the very existence of an English imperial heroism.[97]

Many writings about opium and users of opium, from De Quincey onwards, promote this narrative of race and infection. James F. Johnston's *The Chemistry of Common Life*, published in 1855, in its discussion of the uses and effects of opium, notes 'this power of seduction even over the less delicate and susceptible organisation of our North European races',[98] ranking Malays, Javanese and Africans as 'Orientals', claiming that 'upon all of them [opium] produces those marked and striking effects which, among ourselves, we only see in rare instances, and in persons of uncommonly nervous disposition'.[99] The Society's descriptions of opium dens simply reproduced this perspective; a set of slides showing 'the downward progress of an opium smoker', depicting a Burmese, was the only set of visual images it ever produced. Similarly, a missionary biography claimed that the Chinese smoked opium because they lacked 'moral courage',[100] and that by the very act of opium smoking the users became 'low, lying, irredeemable wretches'.[101]

The Society had always approached China from a viewpoint of convinced cultural superiority. It did not invent this position. The view that Chinese civilization, however admirable, was at best static, at worst decaying, as opposed to the progressive, history-driven Europe, is a cliché of 'Orientalism' expressed at its most banal in Tennyson's *Locksley Hall* (1848): 'Better fifty years of Europe than a cycle of Cathay'. The Abbé Huc, a Catholic missionary writing from Peking in 1853, while seeking to confute the prejudices of the most pessimistic European views of China, pictured

a civilised nation almost wholly removed from religious influence ... and falling rapidly to decay, from no other cause than that of internal moral corruption ... Christianity alone ... can heal this inward corruption, and arrest the downward progress of this mighty nation.[102]

Such views became the very commonsense of the Society. Storrs Turner wrote in 1876, in a passage suffused with Darwinian racial imagery, 'We are summoned to pour the new life-blood of our religion, our science, our education, into the stagnant veins of the dying East',[103] while *Friend of China* proposed in the same year that 'To communicate what we have gained of liberty, science, religion, to the vast Asiatic Empire under our control, is England's chief function in world history'.[104] While this attitude was often contradicted by the Society's insistent condemnation of Britain's part in the shameful trade, the terms of comparison always reinforced the missionaries' belief in their project of absolute and universal enlightenment – 'Whilst they, the pagans, the semi-civilised barbarians, have [justice] on their side, we, the enlightened and civilised Christians, are pursuing objects at variance both with justice and with religion'.[105]

A crucial transformation in the discourses emerging around opium occurred when attention turned from China to England. Here the panic over contagion was reinforced by growing fear of an enemy within, the first post-Darwinian generation's displaying all too dramatically anxieties about racial degeneration 'at home'. The implication, already present in De Quincey's fears of Orientalized subjectivity, is drawn out and emphasized to make opium use of itself a signal of irredeemable Otherness. The opening of China to missionaries in 1860, and the debates over the Pharmacy Bill later in the decade, were crucial in constructing opium-as-problem within the public imaginary. Where in *Hard Times* (1854) Dickens might merely mention the use of opium in passing, as an alcohol substitute,[106] by the time of *Edwin Drood* (1870) a new rhetoric of disapproval is in play. Here Cathedral choirmaster Jasper leaves the cloisters for an East End opium den, dreams of murder while under the influence of opium, and then indeed commits a murder.[107] The East End of London, where the native British can meet foreign purveyors and users of opium, and thereby lose their innocence, their respectability, even their humanity, is perhaps the most potent symbol of internal Otherness; indeed, the East End was itself *already* a racialized Other, its creation as 'Darkest England' signalled by Jerrold and Dore's *A London Pilgrimage* (1872), from which this description of an East End opium den characterizes the new structure of feeling: '... upon a mattress heaped with indescribable clothes, lay, sprawling, a lascar, dead-drunk with opium ... It was difficult to see any humanity in that face, as the enormous grey lips lapped about the rough pipe and drew in the poison'.[108]

The image of the opium den involves a very specific transposition, for now it is the Chinese owners of opium dens who are the importers of opium: *they* are the foreign devils, the corruptors of the native British. Consider the opening of the Sherlock Holmes story 'The Man with the Twisted Lip': Watson's friend Whitney is found in an East End opium den. 'I can see him now', the good Doctor recalls, 'with yellow, pasty face, drooping lids, and pin-point pupils ... the wreck and ruin of a noble man'.[109] Racial 'degeneration' is evident: Whitney's use of opium has made him, yellow-faced and drooping-lidded, into a *para-Chinese*, corrupted by the evil foreigners who supply the drug. The fictional archetype of this construction of the Chinese – of this transposition of imperial guilt – is Sax Rohmer's character Fu Manchu, who first appeared in 1913, just after the official ending of the opium trade had effectively criminalized it worldwide.[110] Such works as Rohmer's *Yellow Claw* (1925) emphasize the drug's 'evil' nature, associating it with the seduction of innocent white women; fictionally driven fear of miscegenation was one reason for constant harassment of the East End Chinese community by the police.[111] Fu Manchu is the epitome of many other characteristics ascribed to the Chinese: intelligence, sophistication and cruelty; his followers, while they are slaves to his will, are at least dedicated workers. The final picture of China and the Chinese, virtually unchallenged by the 1890s, is of corruption, cruelty, hypocrisy and degradation, of people virtually enslaved by their rulers and unable to help themselves: a far cry from the respectful view of Chinese civilization to be found in eighteenth-century writers such as Voltaire and François Quesnay.[112]

There is another trope at work here, even in the Holmes story, which should be noted: another sustaining fiction of non-conformist ideology in fact, and one which continues to colour notions of Englishness, and especially English masculinity, heroism, and enterprise. This is the condemnation of aristocratic hedonism. Even in the late nineteenth century this was still a powerful moving influence. A popular version is Stevenson's *Dr Jekyll and Mr Hyde*, in which a professional 'gentle-man' takes a drug and is transformed. The author's disapproval marries Darwinist and Christian concerns: 'Mr Hyde was pale and dwarfish; he gave an impression of deformity', which impresses one of his observers thus: 'God bless me, the man seems hardly human! ... my poor old Harry Jekyll, if ever I read Satan's signature on a face, it is on that of your new friend'.[113] Similarly, Oscar Wilde's *The Picture of Dorian Gray* uses the image of the East End opium den in a way almost identical to Conan Doyle's, and is suffused with images of luxury and drug-induced ecstasy whose tendency, again, is degradation rather than mere decadence: Lord Harry remarks 'Our limbs fail, our senses rot. We degenerate into senseless puppets'.[114] All these years after 1832 the culture of the leisured is under attack. In the case of personal drug use this ascetic ideology remains hegemonic. Far from being a simple pleasure-seeker, the drug user is seen as the devil within: whatever her or his ostensible social position, however innocent before using drugs, she or he became – by the 1890s – an outsider, an internal Other beyond the boundaries of respectable Englishness. Conan Doyle, wishing to emphasize his hero Sherlock Holmes's separation from the accepted, respectable world of late Victorian England, portrayed him as a bachelor, a violinist, and most importantly as an occasional user of both morphia and cocaine – to the hearty disapproval of the quintessentially respectable English Dr Watson.[115] The legacy of moral censure, due in no small part to the efforts of the Society for the Suppression of the Opium Trade, is still an almost unquestioned part of contemporary ideology. Thousands die and billions of dollars are wasted each year because the international legal system attempts to control the illicit trade in drugs for personal use. We still inhabit the Society's dreams.

NOTES

Much of the research for this essay was undertaken while studying for the degree of MA in Victorian Studies, University of Keele. I am grateful to all the staff and students on this course; to my colleagues at the University of East London; and to the librarians of the University of Keele, the University of East London, the Horniman Museum, and the India Office Library.

The Wade-Giles system has been used for the transliteration of all Chinese names.

Abbreviations

RC: *The Royal Commission on Opium*. This was ostensibly published in seven volumes; these are in fact hidden within *Parliamentary Papers*, London, HMSO:
RC, vol. 1: *PP 1894* vol. LX, pp.593–760;
RC, vol. 2: *PP 1894* vol. LXI, pp.1–666;
RC, vol. 3: *PP 1894* vol. LXI, pp.673–972;
RC, vol. 4: *PP 1894* vol. LXII, pp.1–524;
RC, vol. 5: *PP 1894* vol. LXII, pp.531–906;
RC, vol. 6: *PP 1895* vol. XLII, pp.31–220;
RC, vol. 7: *PP 1895* vol. XLII, pp.221–544.
PP: *Parliamentary Papers*
FOC: *Friend of China*
SSOT: The Society for the Suppression of the Opium Trade with China.

1 J. Needham, *Within the Four Seas. The Dialogue of East and West*, Allen and Unwin, London, 1969, pp.11–30.; G.F. Hudson, *Europe and China*, Edward Arnold, London, 1931.
2 Hudson, *Europe and China*, p.318.
3 J. Barrell, *The Infection of Thomas De Quincey. A Psychopathology of Imperialism*, Yale University Press, New Haven and London, 1991.
4 H.B. Morse, *The Chronicles of the East India Company Trading to China*, Oxford University Press, Oxford, 1926, vol.VII, pp.68–131; M. Collis, *Foreign Mud. Opium at Canton and the First Opium War*, Faber, London, 1946, pp.14–15.
5 D.E. Owen, *British Opium Policy in China and India*, Yale University Press, New Haven, 1934, p.61; F. Wakeman Jr, 'The Canton trade and the Opium War', in J.K. Fairbank (ed.), *The Cambridge History of China*, Cambridge University Press, Cambridge, vol.10, 1978, pp.168–71.
6 J. Rowntree, *The Imperial Drug Trade*, SSOT, London, 1905, pp.12–13, 19–20; Owen, *British Opium Policy*, p. 25.
7 Morse, *The Chronicles of the East India Company*, p. 93.
8 W.E. Cheong, *Mandarins and Merchants. Jardine Matheson and Co., A China Agency of the Early Nineteenth Century*, Curzon Press for Scandinavian Institute of Asian Studies, London and Malmo, 1979, pp.100–34.
9 M. Greenberg, *British Trade and the Opening of China 1800–1842*, Cambridge University Press, Cambridge, 1951, p.105.
10 D.R. Sardesai, *British Trade and Expansion in South-East Asia*, Allied Publishers, New Delhi, 1977, p.55.
11 Owen, *British Opium Policy*, pp.127–9; Wakeman Jr, 'The Canton trade and the Opium War', pp.174–85.
12 M. Greenberg, *British Trade and the Opening of China*, pp. 179–91.
13 Wakeman Jr, 'The Canton trade and the Opium War', p.173.
14 Collis, *Foreign Mud*, p.185; but see N.A. Pelcovits, *Old China Hands and the Foreign Office*, American Council for Honolulu Institute of Race Relations, New York, 1948, p.4; and in general Hoh-cheung Mui and L.H. Mui, *The Management of Monopoly. A Study of the East India Company's Conduct of its Tea Trade 1784–1833*, University of Vancouver Press, Vancouver, 1984.
15 Greenberg, *British Trade and the Opening of China*, p.206.
16 Sardesai, *British Trade and Expansion in South-East Asia*, p.58.

17 Pelcovits, *Old China Hands and the Foreign Office*, pp.4–5; Owen, *British Opium Policy*, pp.210–13.
18 R. Fortune, *A Journey to the Tea Countries*, John Murray, London, 1852, reprinted Mildmay, London, 1987, pp.21, 104, 311. See also Fortune, *A Residence among the Chinese*, John Murray, London, 1857.
19 B. Harrison, *Waiting for China. The Anglo-Chinese College at Malacca, 1818–1843*, Hong Kong University Press, Hong Kong, 1979, p.103.
20 Ibid., p.109.
21 G.S. Graham, *The China Station. War and Diplomacy 1830–60*, Oxford University Press, London, 1978, pp.352–417; J.Y. Wong, 'The building of an informal British Empire in China in the middle of the nineteenth century', *Bulletin of the John Rylands Library of Manchester* 59, 1976, pp.472–85.
22 J. Spence, 'Opium smoking in Ch'ing China', in F. Wakeman Jr and C. Grant (eds), *Conflict and Control in Late Imperial China*, Cambridge University Press, Cambridge, 1978, pp.143–73; Yen-p'ing Hao, *The Commercial Revolution in Nineteenth-Century China*, University of California Press, Berkeley, 1986.
23 Pelcovits, *Old China Hands and the Foreign Office*, p.18.
24 K.F. Bruner, J.K. Fairbank, and R.J. Smith (eds), *Entering China's Service. The Journals of Robert Hart*, Harvard University Press, Cambridge, Mass., 1986.
25 H.R. Williamson, *British Baptists in China*, Kingsgate Press, London, 1957, p.21.
26 K.S. Latourette, *A History of Christian Missions in China*, SPCK, London, 1926, p.406.
27 A.E. Moule, *Half a Century in China*, Hodder and Stoughton, London, 1911, p.240.
28 P.A. Cohen, *China and Christianity: the Missionary Movement and the Growth of Chinese Antiforeignism*, Harvard University Press, Cambridge, Mass., 1963. The quotation is the book's epigraph.
29 P.A. Cohen, 'Christian missions and their impact to 1900', in J.K. Fairbank (ed.), *Cambridge History of China*, vol.10, p.553; E.S. Wherle, *Britain, China and the Antimissionary Riots 1891–1900*, University of Minneapolis Press, Minneapolis, 1966, p.14.
30 J. Chesneaux, M. Bastid and M. Bergere, trans. by A. Destenay, *China from the Opium Wars to the 1911 Revolution*, Harvester Press, Hassocks, 1977, p.182.
31 Cohen, *China and Christianity*, p.151; also *RC*, vol.1, pp.641–2 (evidence of Rev. F. Brown).
32 Cohen, 'Christian missions', pp.560–9; also Cohen, *China and Christianity*, pp.269–73. For the missionaries' attitudes, *RC*, vol.1, pp.638–40 (Marcus Wood), and 693–5 (Rev. A. Langman); and for the merchants', 701–2 (H. Lazarus).
33 Chesneaux *et al*, *China from the Opium Wars to the 1911 Revolution*, p.182.
34 R.W. Thompson, *Griffith John*, SPCK, London, 1908, p.405; see also H. Beattie, 'Protestant missions and opium in China, 1858–1895', *Harvard Papers On China* vol.22A, 1969, pp.104–33.
35 *FOC*, vol.XII, no.12, December 1891, p.355.
36 Hospitals are available where they can be 'cured', John says, but goes on to admit that post-hospitalization lapses are the rule rather than the exception. This is hardly surprising, since the 'cure' at this time often consisted of the administration of tablets of morphia, an alkaloid refined from opium, which quickly became known as 'Jesus opium': many missionaries freely sold it as a cure, until the medical and addictive effects were explained to them at the Shanghai missionary conference of 1890, when its use was banned. Thompson, *Griffith John*, pp.405–6. Beattie, 'Protestant missions', p.121.

37 H.E. Legge, *James Legge, Missionary and Scholar*, Constable, London, 1905, p.108.
38 Pelcovits, *Old China Hands and the Foreign Office*, p.83.
39 Owen, *British Opium Policy*, pp.245–51; *PP China no.1 and China no.4*, HMSO, London, 1870, vol.LXIX, pp.667–99 and 749–65.
40 P. Hollis (ed.), *Pressure from Without*, London, Edward Arnold, 1974; B.D. Johnson, 'Righteousness before revenue: the forgotten moral crusade against the Indo-Chinese opium trade', *Journal of Drug Issues* vol.5 no.4, 1975, pp.304–26; compare B. Harrison, *Drink and the Victorians*, Faber, London, 1971, pp.260–80; R.D. French, *Antivivisection and Medical Science in Victorian Society*, Yale University Press, London, 1975, pp.75–142.
41 *The Opium Trade*, SSOT, London, 1875, p.3.
42 Ibid, pp.1, 12, 14–15.
43 J.G. Alexander, *India's Opium Revenue. What It Is and What should be Done with it*, and Alexander, *Substitutes for the Opium Revenue*, both SSOT, London, 1890.
44 *FOC*, vol.I, no.1, March 1875, pp.16–19. Johnson, 'Righteousness before revenue', pp.307–8.
45 *FOC*, vol.I, no.3, June 1875, pp.86–7.
46 I. Bradley, *The Optimists. Themes and Personalities in Victorian Liberalism*, Faber, London, 1980, p.100.
47 Beattie, 'Protestant missions', 112–13. Again, compare Harrison, *Drink and the Victorians*, p.123, and French, *Antivivisection and Medical Science in Victorian Society*, p.250.
48 Beattie, 'Protestant missions', p.110.
49 P. Hollis, introduction to Hollis (ed.), *Pressure from Without*, pp.1–6.
50 All non-conformist reform groups used these strategies; they also shared a common leadership. Lord Shaftesbury, president of the Society until his death in 1886, and one of the first people to oppose the opium trade in the House of Commons (as Lord Ashley, in 1843) is the obvious example; his successor as president, Sir Joseph Whitwell Pease, was, like most members of this Quaker family, active in other reform movements: at one time president of the Peace Society, on 22 June 1881 he moved the second reading of a Bill to abolish capital punishment: *Dictionary of National Biography*, compact edn, Supplement 1901–60, Oxford University Press, London, 1978, p.2830. Other leading members with informative *DNB* or *Who Was Who* entries include Edward, Joseph and Arthur Pease, Joseph Grundy, Sir R.N. Fowler, Bart., Donald Matheson, Henry Broadhurst, Henry Gurney, Edmund Sturge, Sir Mark Stewart, Bart., Dr T.J. Barnardo.
51 Owen, *British Opium Policy*, p. 244. Pro-opium publications include W.H. Brereton, *The Truth About Opium*, Smith, Elder, London, 1882; H.H. Sultzberger (ed.), *All About Opium*, Sultzberger, London, 1884.
52 *RC*, vol.1 p.563, evidence of former Shanghai merchant Henry Lazarus.
53 L. Oliphant, *Narrative of Lord Elgin's Mission to China and Japan in the Years 1857–59*, Harper and Brothers, New York, 1860, vol.1, p.29; see also pp.40, 66–7.
54 Pelcovits, *Old China Hands and the Foreign Office*, pp.126–31.
55 *The Times*, 5 June 1880, pp.8f–9f.
56 *RC*, vol.1, p.594, evidence of Sir Joseph Pease; also *FOC*, January 1891, vol.XII, no.2, pp.12–13.
57 *FOC* vol.XII, no.4, July 1891, p.178; Hollis, introduction to *Pressure from Without*, p.12.

58 Sir Joseph Pease to House of Commons, *The Times*, 4 April 1883, pp.9c–9e.
59 Owen, *British Opium Policy*, p.273.
60 Ibid., pp.264–70; Spence, 'Opium smoking in Ch'ing China'.
61 E.G. Sir R. Temple to the Commons: *The Times*, 4 May 1889, p.9c–9d.
62 *FOC*, vol.XI, no.4, October 1889, pp.192–3.
63 *FOC*, vol.XII, no.1, January 1891, p.5.
64 *RC*, vol.6, p.204; *The Times*, 11 April 1891, pp.9b–10a.
65 *FOC*, vol.XII, no.3, May 1889, p.81.
66 The smaller societies included the Christian Union for the Severance of the Connection of the British Empire with the Opium Traffic, publisher of the magazine *National Righteousness* (3 vols, 1888–1917); and The Anti-Opium Urgency and Women's Anti-Opium Urgency Committee, which published *Anti-Opium News*, an occasional supplement to the temperance journal *The Sentinel*.
67 *The Times*, 1 July 1893, pp.9f–10c.
68 *FOC*, vol.XIV, no.5, October 1893, pp.145–6.
69 *RC*, vol.1, pp.603–7, 619–23.
70 *RC*, vol.1, pp.647–9.
71 *RC*, vol.1, p.755.
72 *FOC*, vol.XIV, no.5, October 1893, p.146.
73 *RC*, vol.1, p.596.
74 *RC*, vol.1, pp.642–75 (evidence of Brigade Surgeon R. Pringle); pp.651–60 (Sir John Strachey); pp.661–5 (Surgeon General Sir William Moore) – all Indian officials – and pp.676–89 (Sir Thomas Wade); pp.671–6 (H.N. Lay), both British civil servants who had spent years in China. Compare the liberalism of this counter-fiction with the liberalism of the contemporary Royal Commission on Indian Hemp and Foreign Hemp (*PP* 1893–4, HMSO, London, vol.LXVI, pp.79–256), which argued for the toleration (in India) of the social use of cannabis-derived drugs.
75 *RC*, vol.1, p.661.
76 *RC*, vol.1, p.672.
77 *RC*, vol.1, p.673. Lay worked in China for seventeen years.
78 *RC*, vol.1, p.699.
79 *RC*, vol.1, p.676.
80 *FOC*, vol.XIV, no.6, January 1894, pp.184, 190–2.
81 *FOC*, vol.XIV, no.6, January 1894, p.179.
82 *FOC*, vol.XIV, no.6, January 1894, p.180.
83 *RC*, vol.7, p.438.
84 *The Times*, 25 May 1895, pp.11d–12c.
85 Owen, *British Opium Policy*; Wen-tsao Wu, *The Chinese Question in British Opinion and Action*, Academy Press, New York, 1928.
86 Rowntree, *The Imperial Drug Trade*, p.119; see also Rev. E. Lewis, *Black Opium*, Blackwood, Edinburgh, 1910; and in general B.R. Tomlinson, 'India and the British Empire 1880–1935', *Indian Economic and Social History Review* 12, 1975, pp.337–80.
87 B. Whitaker, *The Global Fix. The Crisis of Drug Addiction*, Methuen, London, 1987, pp.1–36.
88 Ibid., p.27.
89 T. Parsinnen, *Secret Passions, Secret Remedies. Narcotic Drugs in British Society 1820–1930*, Manchester University Press, Manchester, 1983, p.214.
90 Whitaker, *The Global Fix*, p.28.
91 Johnson, 'Righteousness before revenue', pp.322–3.
92 *The Times*, 30 June 1893, p.10b–10c.

93 *The Times*, 4 September 1893, p.7b–7c.
94 In general see V. Berridge and G. Edwards, *Opium and the People*, Allen Lane, London, 1981, reprinted Yale University Press, 1987; Parsinnen, *Secret Passions, Secret Remedies*; B. Schwarz (ed.), *Crises in The British State*, Hutchinson, London, 1985; F. Mort, *Dangerous Sexualities*, Routledge, London, 1987.
95 Berridge and Edwards, *Opium and the People*, pp.38–48, 123–38.
96 Ibid., pp.135–72, 278–81; Parsinnen, *Secret Passions, Secret Remedies*, pp.68–114.
97 See for example J. Needham, *Within the Four Seas*; V. Kiernan, *The Lords of Human Kind*, Weidenfeld and Nicolson, London, 1969; E. Said, *Orientalism*, Penguin, Harmondsworth, 1984.
98 J.F. Johnston, *The Chemistry of Common Life*, Blackwood, Edinburgh, 1885, vol.2, p.76 – thanks to Glyn Perrin for the loan of this book; also in general H.H. Sultzberger, *All About Opium*.
99 Johnston, *The Chemistry of Common Life*, vol.2, p.93.
100 W. Thompson, *Griffith John*, p.99.
101 Ibid., p.406.
102 M. Huc, trans. Mrs P. Sinnett, *The Chinese Empire*, Longman, London, 1855; translator's introduction.
103 Storrs Turner, p.175.
104 *FOC*, vol.1, no.3, June 1875, p.78.
105 Alexander, *India's Opium Revenue*, p.17, quoting Gladstone in an unidentified (presumably 1842) House of Commons debate.
106 C. Dickens, *Hard Times*, Chapman and Hall, London, 1854, book 1, ch.5.
107 Dickens, *Edwin Drood*, Chapman and Hall, London, 1870.
108 Berridge and Edwards, *Opium and the People*, p.197, quoting G. Dore and W. Jerrold, *A London Pilgrimage*, Grant, London, 1872, pp.147–8.
109 A. Conan Doyle, 'The man with the twisted lip', *The Adventures of Sherlock Holmes, The Strand Magazine*, London, 1891–3; here, *The Penguin Complete Sherlock Holmes*, Penguin, London, 1981, p.229.
110 Parsinnen, *Secret Passions, Secret Remedies*, pp.119–21.
111 Ibid., pp.123–33.
112 This disrespectful view has been continually reproduced in the West, in novels, and film versions of the Holmes and Fu Manchu stories among others, throughout the twentieth century: Ian Fleming's massively popular *Doctor No* (novel 1958; film, 1962, shown annually on British television since 1968) reproduces the Sax Rohmer picture of the polite but fiendish Chinese leader supported by mindless servants more or less verbatim.
113 R.L. Stevenson, *Doctor Jekyll and Mr. Hyde*, London, 1889, ch.3; here Collins, n.d., p.66.
114 O. Wilde, *The Picture of Dorian Gray*, Ward Lock, London, 1891; here The Modern Library, New York, n.d., pp.246–7.
115 Holmes's hypodermic first appears in *The Sign of Four*, Spencer Blackett, London, 1890.

INDEX